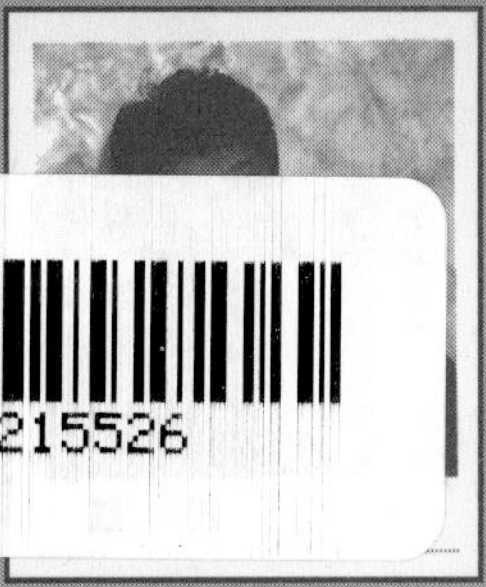

Diet fiend!!

That's the honorable title I was recently awarded.

One December day, after *Knights of the Zodiac* had finished running in *Weekly Shonen Jump* magazine, I went in for my first-ever comprehensive medical checkup. The shocking result: I was 128 percent overweight! From that day on I began a fierce battle regimen of daily jogging and a mostly vegetarian diet.

Now I can pen my next manga in a trimmer, fitter body! Or so I hope...

Masami Kurumada—1990

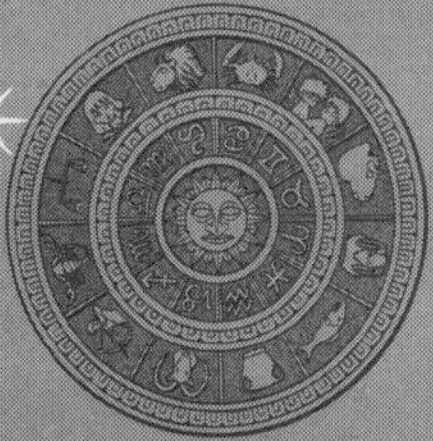

Masami Kurumada made his manga debut in 1974 with **Sukeban Arashi** (Delinquent Storm), the story of the life of a teenage girl. His first big hit came in 1977 with the popular series **Ring ni Kakero** (Put It All in the Ring). In 1986, he truly hit it big when he created **Saint Seiya** (Knights of the Zodiac), which was first serialized in **Weekly Shonen Jump** magazine, then went on to span 28 volumes, 114 TV episodes, four movies and a video game!

KNIGHTS OF THE ZODIAC (SAINT SEIYA) Volume 27
The SHONEN JUMP Manga Edition

STORY AND ART BY
MASAMI KURUMADA

Translation/Mari Morimoto
Touch-up Art & Lettering/Vanessa Satone
Design/Ronnie Casson
Editor/Shaenon K. Garrity

VP, Production/Alvin Lu
VP, Publishing Licensing/Rika Inouye
VP, Sales & Product Marketing/Gonzalo Ferreyra
VP, Creative/Linda Espinosa
Publisher/Hyoe Narita

Printed in Canada

Published by VIZ Media, LLC
P.O. Box 77010
San Francisco, CA 94107

SHONEN JUMP Manga Edition
10 9 8 7 6 5 4 3 2 1
First printing, October 2009

www.viz.com

PARENTAL ADVISORY
KNIGHTS OF THE ZODIAC is rated T for Teen and is recommended for ages 13 and up. This volume contains graphic fantasy violence.
ratings.viz.com

SHONEN JUMP MANGA

SAINT SEIYA KNIGHTS OF THE ZODIAC

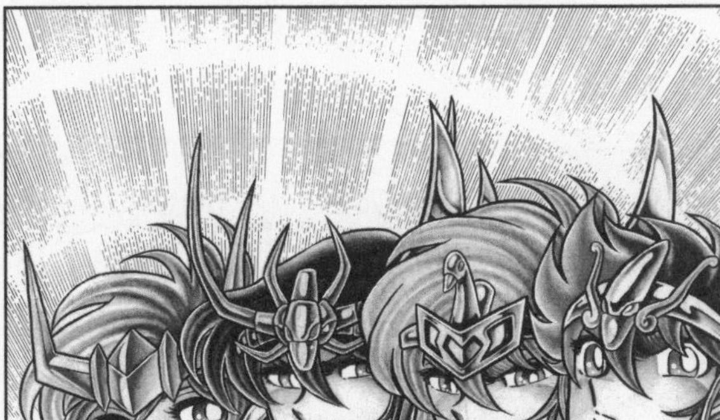
SAINT SEIYA
KNIGHTS
OF THE
ZODIAC

Vol. 27

Death and Sleep

Story & Art by **Masami Kurumada**

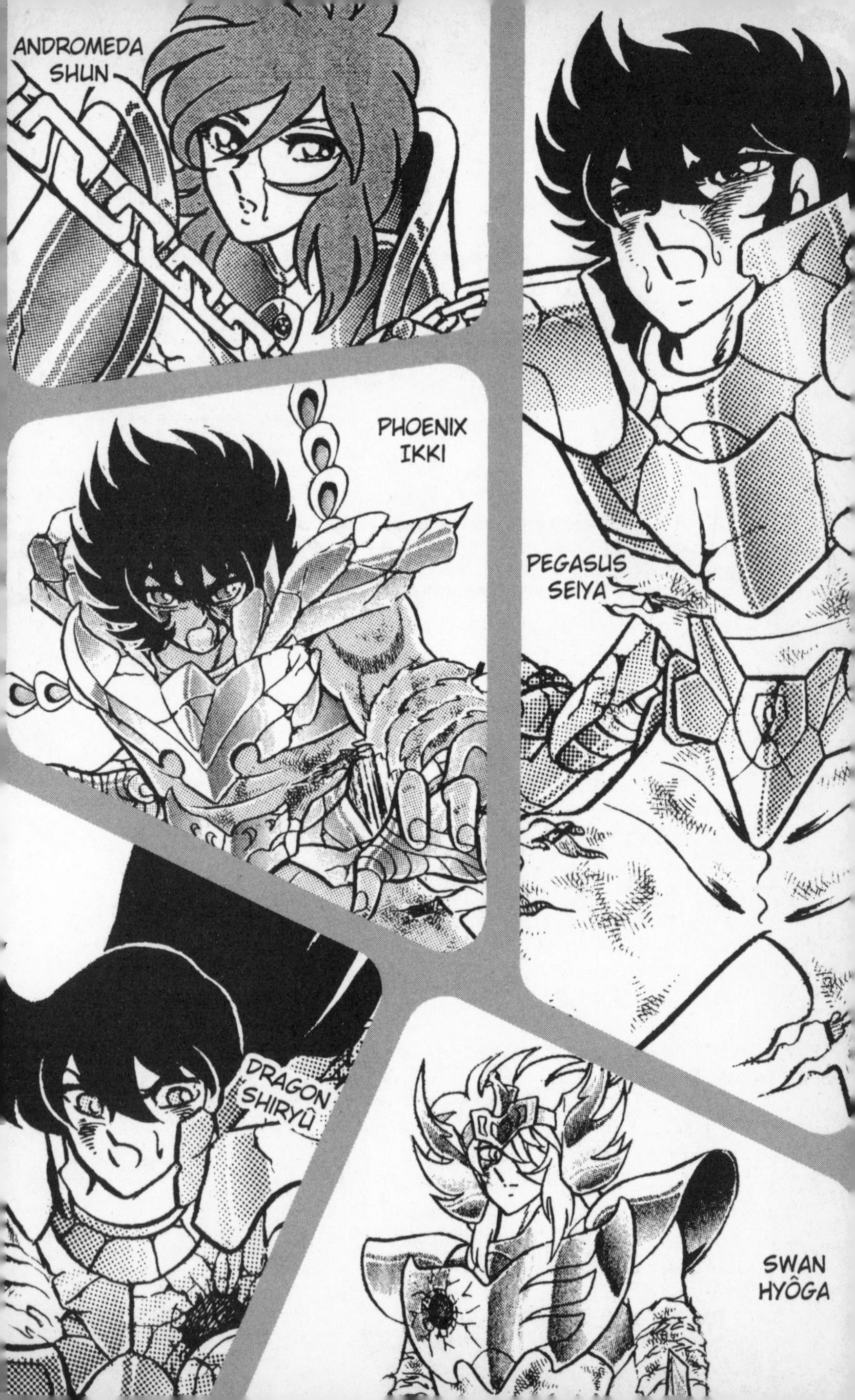
PEGASUS SEIYA
ANDROMEDA SHUN
PHOENIX IKKI
SWAN HYÔGA
DRAGON SHIRYÛ

MARIN
SHINA
PANDORA
THANATOS,
HYPNOS
HADES
ATHENA/ PRINCESS SIENNA

THE STORY THUS FAR ...

LEGENDS SPEAK OF YOUNG MEN WHO PROTECTED THE GREEK GODDESS ATHENA. KNOWN AS ATHENA'S KNIGHTS, THEY WERE SAID TO WIELD PUNCHES THAT CRACKED THE SKY AND KICKS THAT SPLIT THE EARTH. TO RAISE WARRIORS WITH THE STRENGTH TO FIGHT FOR PRINCESS SIENNA, THE INCARNATION OF ATHENA, LORD NOBU OF THE GRANDE FOUNDATION SENT 100 BOYS OUT INTO THE WORLD TO TRAIN AS KNIGHTS. FOUR BRONZE KNIGHTS--SEIYA, HYÔGA, SHIRYÛ AND SHUN--SUCCEEDED BRILLIANTLY IN THEIR TRAINING. IN BATTLES AGAINST THE CORRUPT MASTER OF SANCTUARY AND THE SEA GOD POSEIDON, THE LOVE AND JUSTICE OF ATHENA AND HER KNIGHTS TRIUMPHED.

BUT THIS PEACE HAS BEEN FLEETING, AS HADES, THE GOD OF THE UNDERWORLD, HAS ARISEN TO INVADE THE EARTH WITH HIS ARMY OF SPECTERS. ATHENA PIERCES HER OWN THROAT AND DESCENDS TO THE UNDERWORLD TO BATTLE HADES. THE BATTLE BETWEEN ATHENA AND HADES MOVES TO ELYSIUM, BEYOND THE UNDERWORLD AND THE IMPASSABLE WALL OF LAMENTATION. THE 12 GOLD KNIGHTS ASSEMBLE AND OPEN A PASSAGE IN THE WALL FOR THE BRONZE KNIGHTS, BUT DARKNESS STILL THREATENS THE EARTH...

Contents

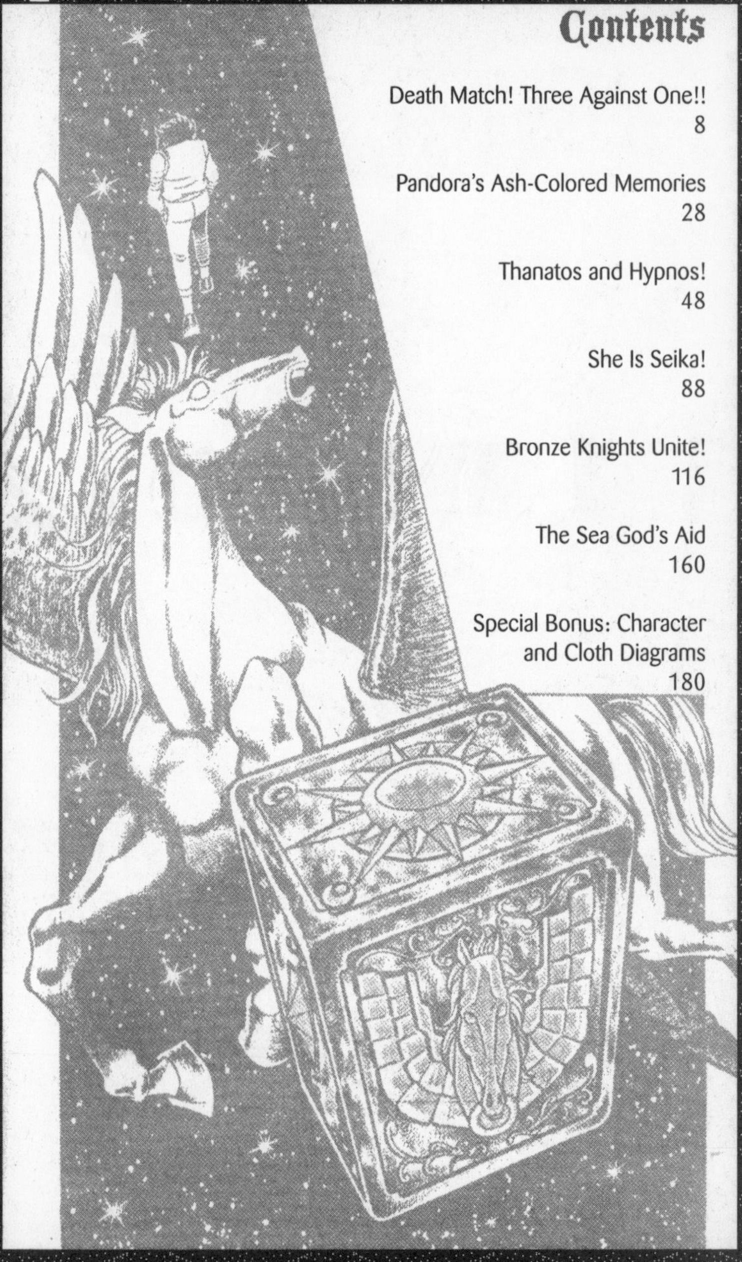

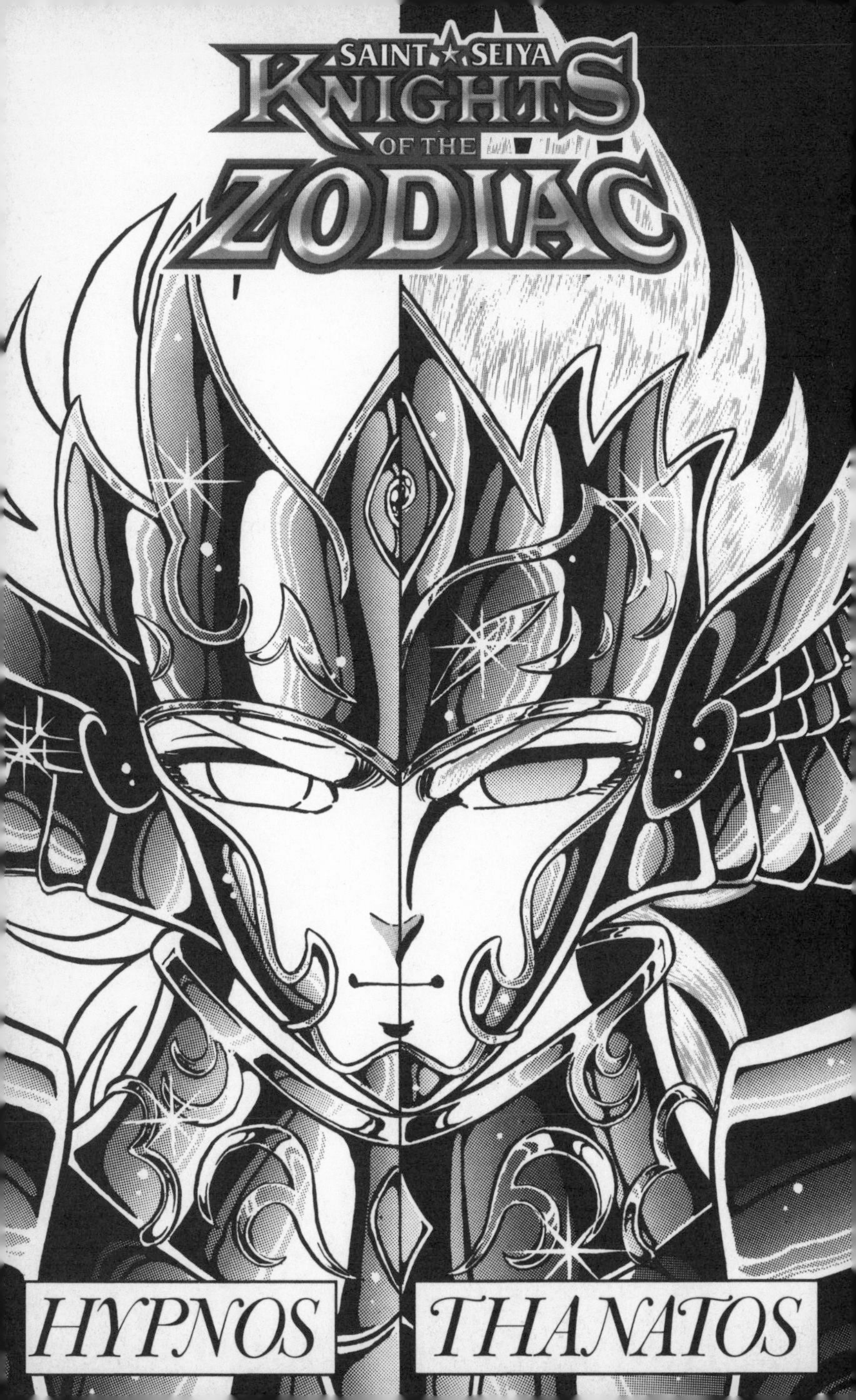
SAINT SEIYA
KNIGHTS OF THE ZODIAC
HYPNOS
THANATOS

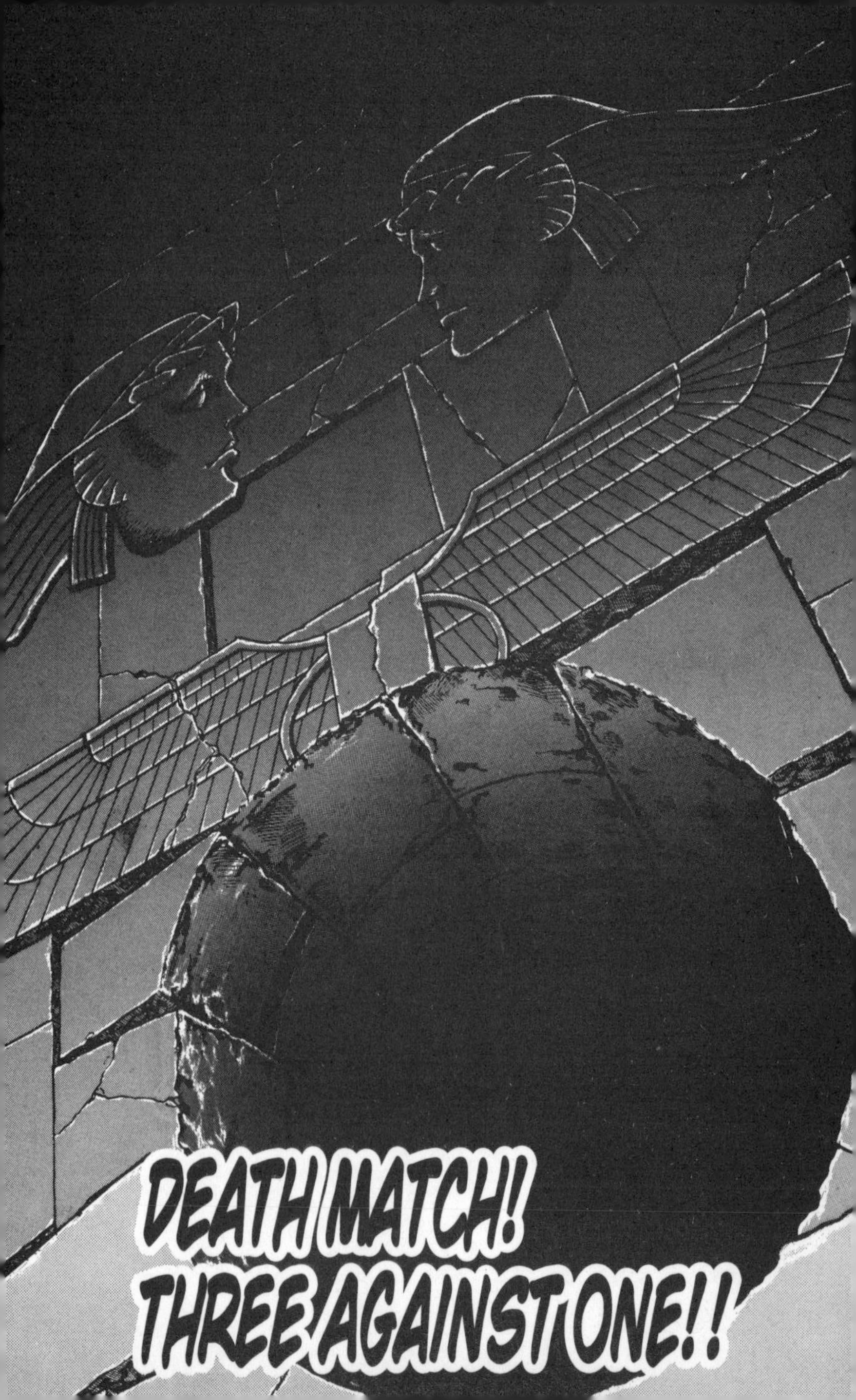
DEATH MATCH!
THREE AGAINST ONE!!

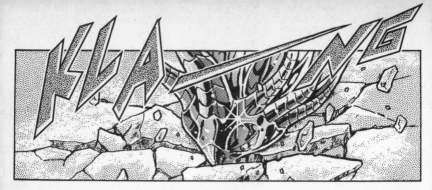

SYLPHIDE!!

UNH...
UGH...

IF YOU WANT IT SO BADLY, DRAGON, WE'LL GLADLY END YOUR LIFE FOR YOU!

VERY WELL...

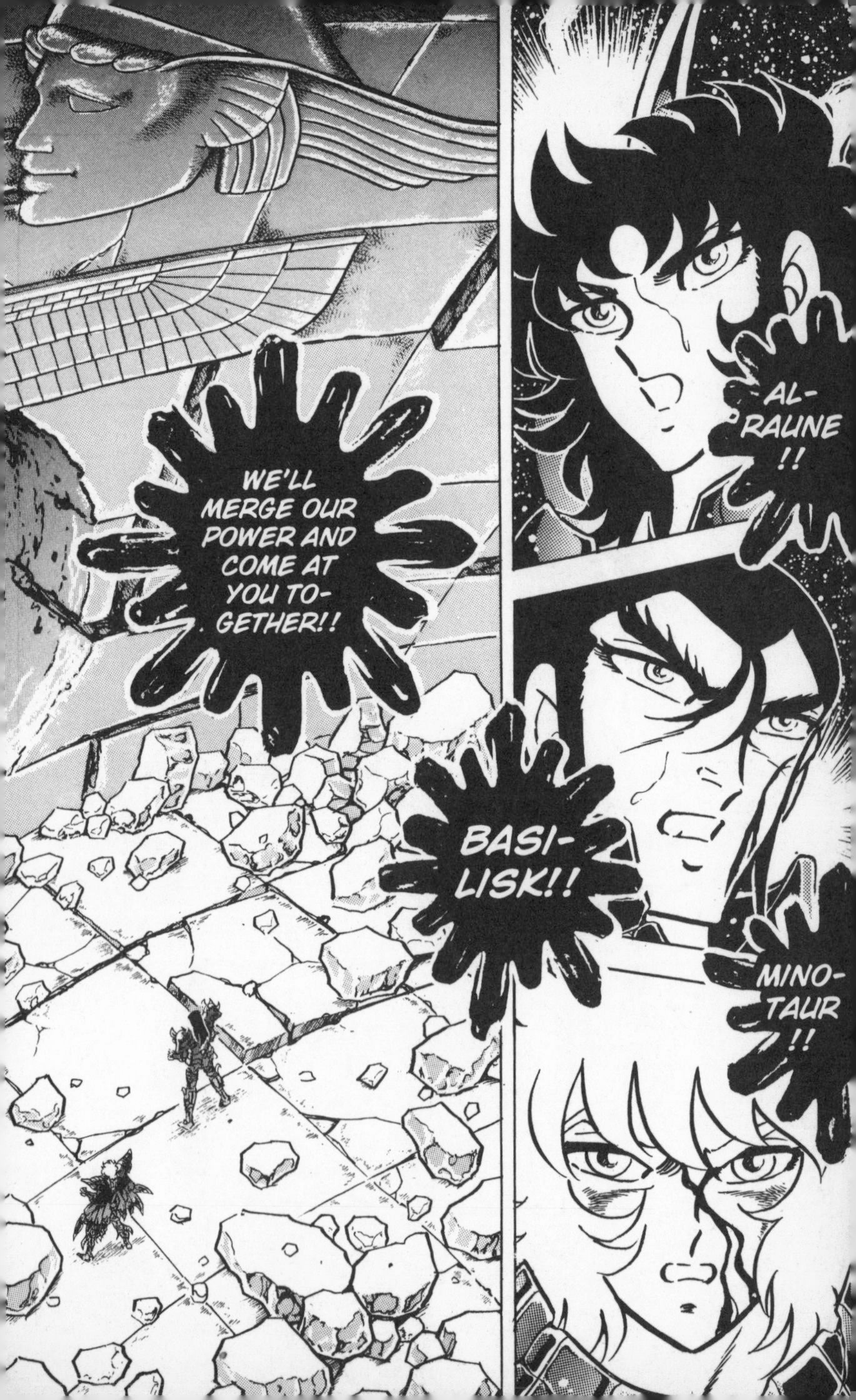
AL-RAUNE!!
BASI-LISK!!
MINO-TAUR!!
WE'LL MERGE OUR POWER AND COME AT YOU TO-GETHER!!

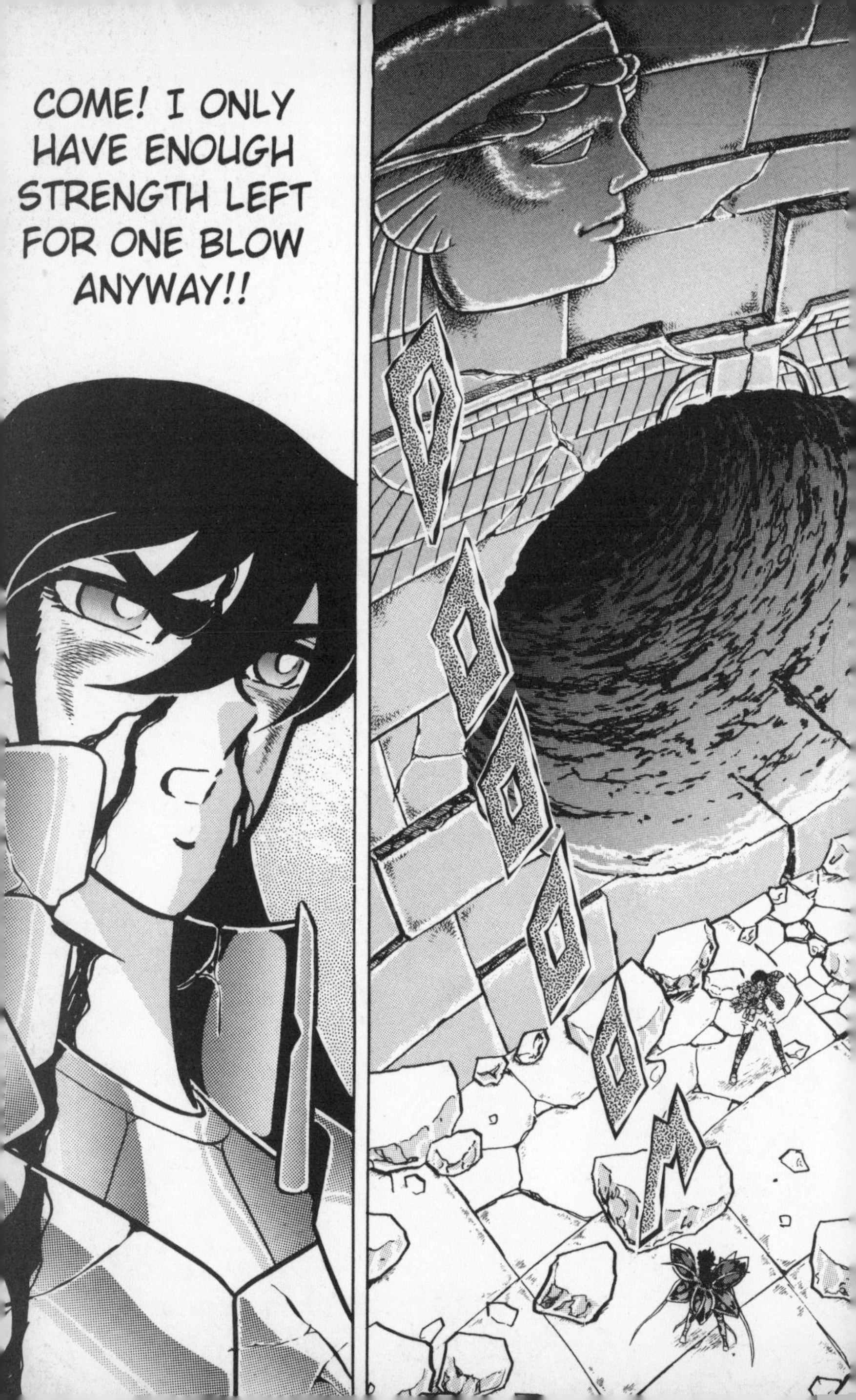
COME! I ONLY HAVE ENOUGH STRENGTH LEFT FOR ONE BLOW ANYWAY!!

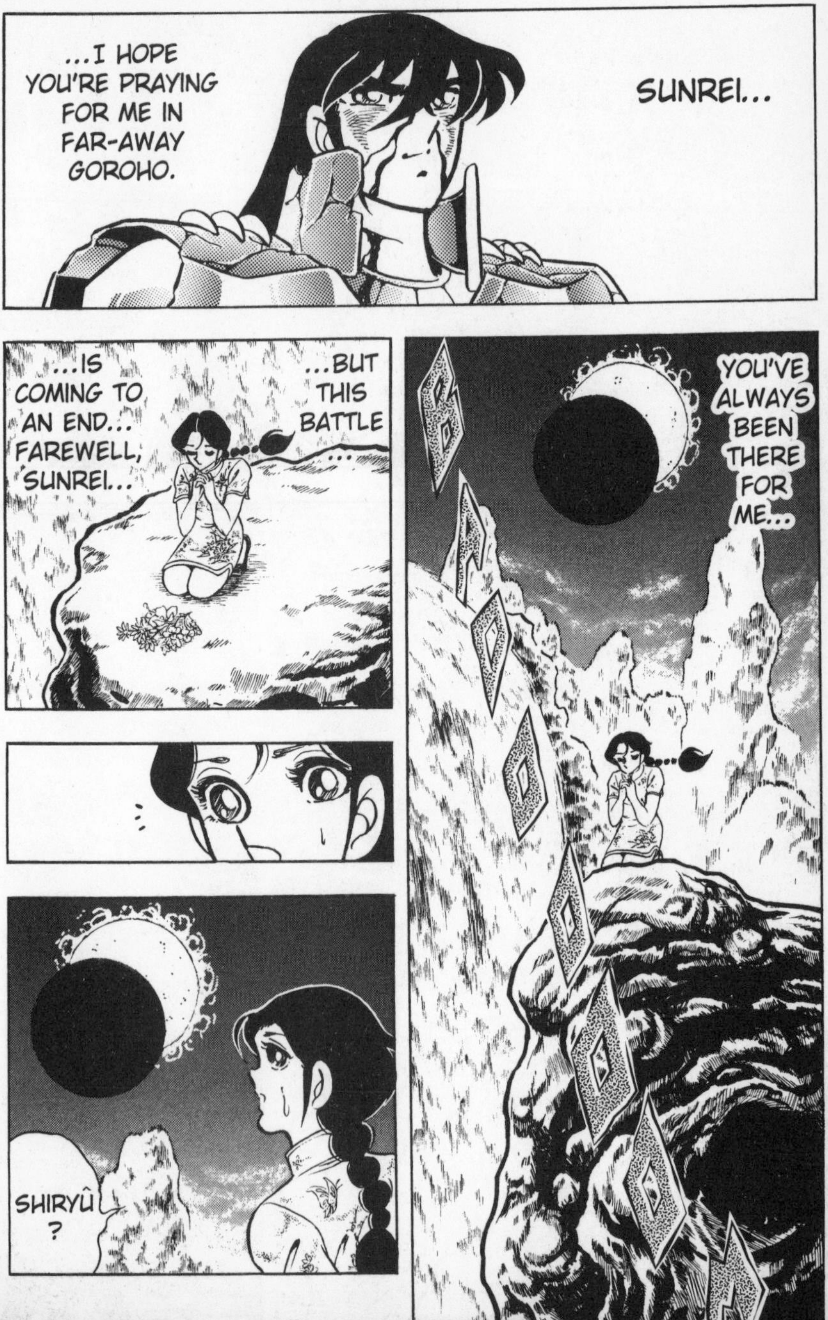
SUNREI...
...I HOPE YOU'RE PRAYING FOR ME IN FAR-AWAY GOROHO.
YOU'VE ALWAYS BEEN THERE FOR ME...
...BUT THIS BATTLE ...
...IS COMING TO AN END... FAREWELL, SUNREI...
SHIRYÛ ?

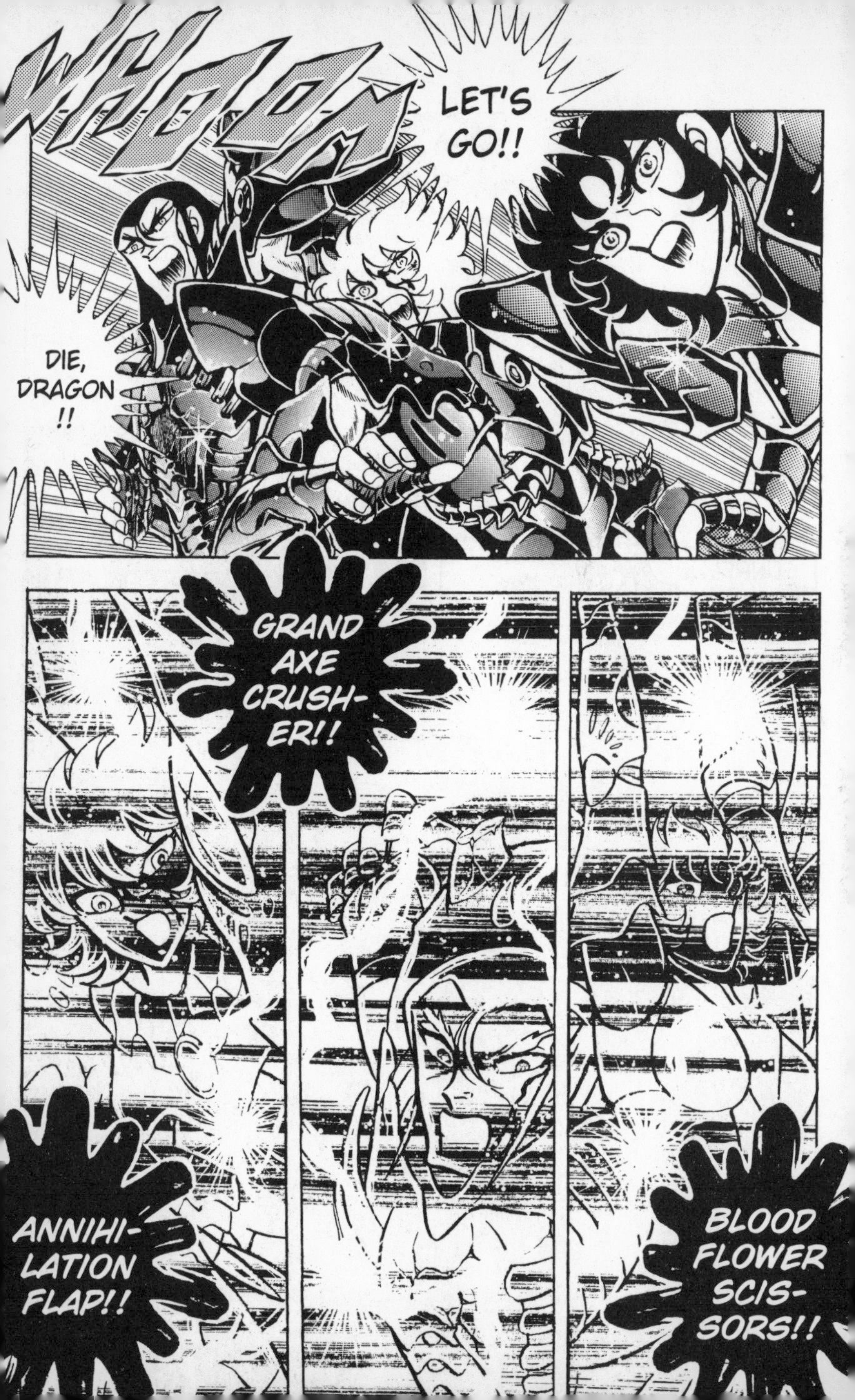
LET'S GO!!
DIE, DRAGON!!
BLOOD FLOWER SCIS-SORS!!
GRAND AXE CRUSH-ER!!
ANNIHI-LATION FLAP!!

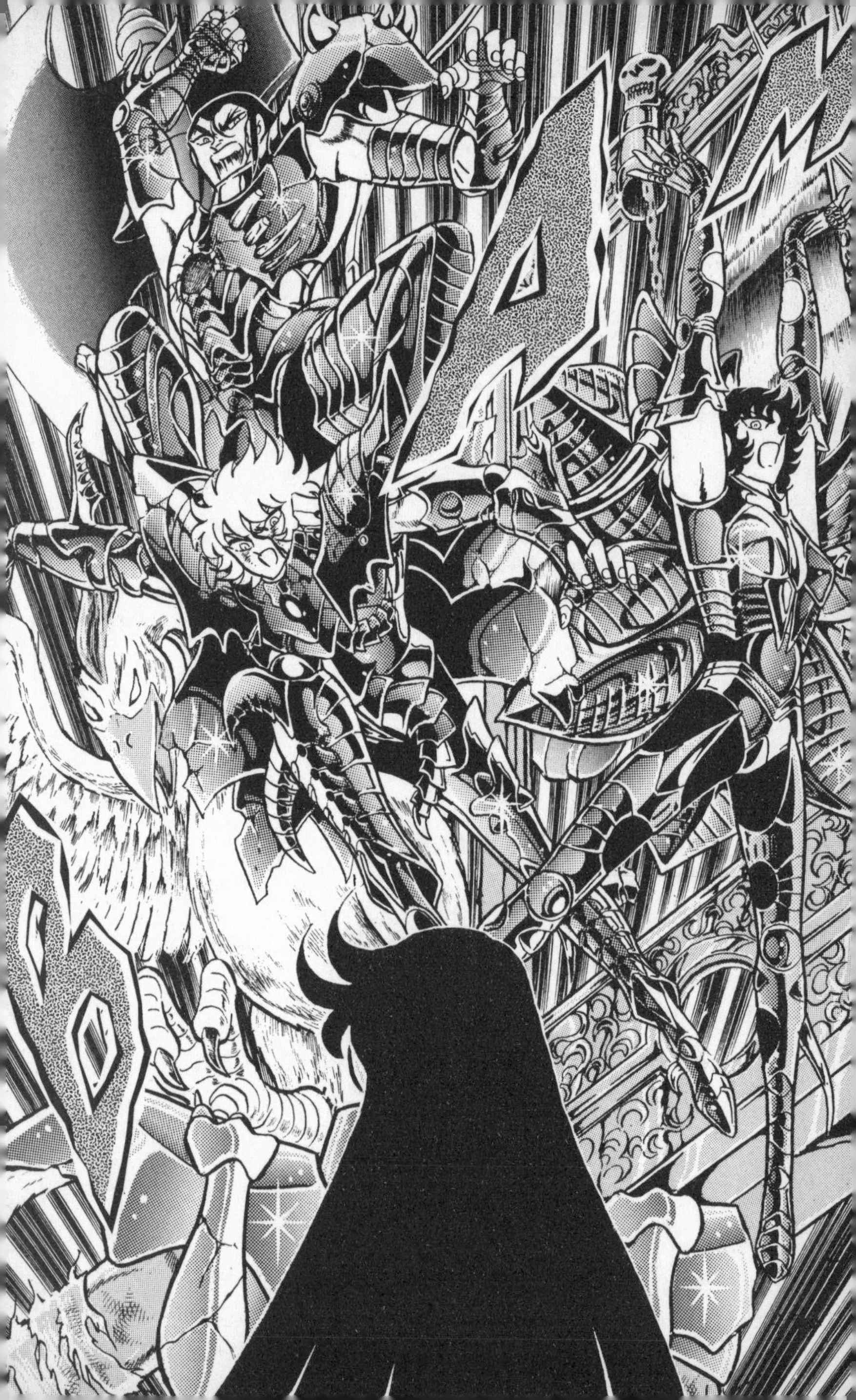

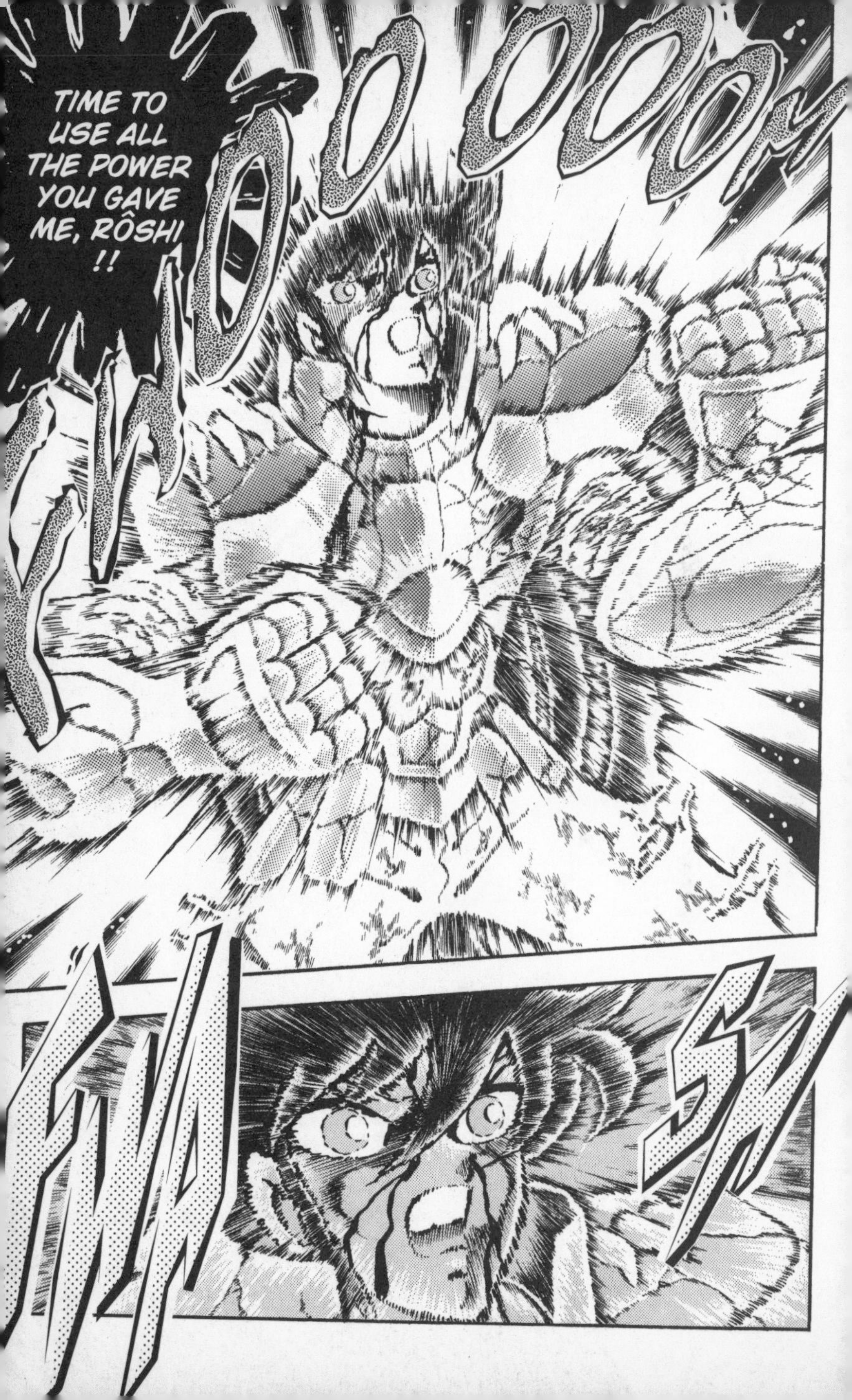
TIME TO USE ALL THE POWER YOU GAVE ME, RÔSHI !!

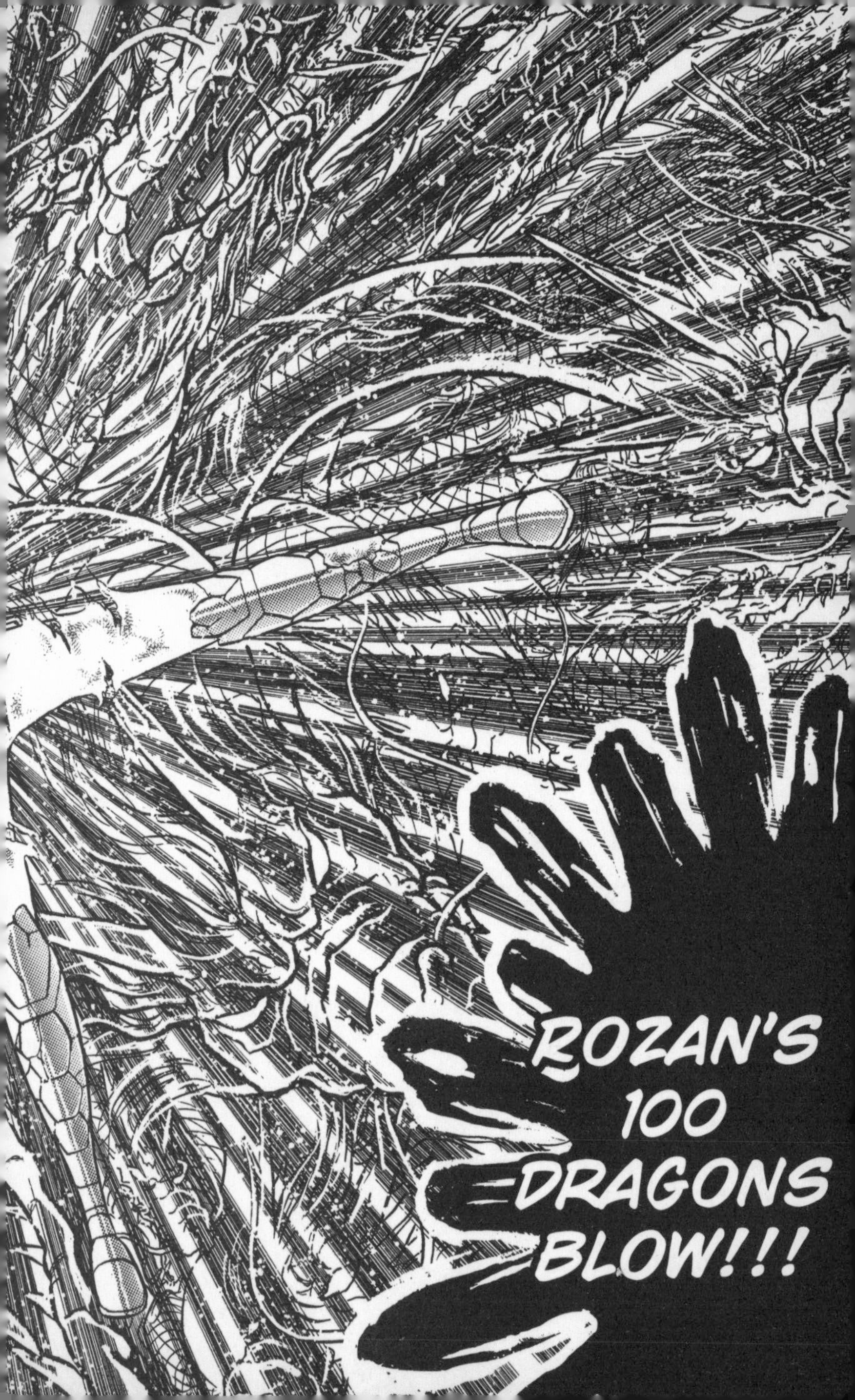
ROZAN'S 100 DRAGONS BLOW!!!

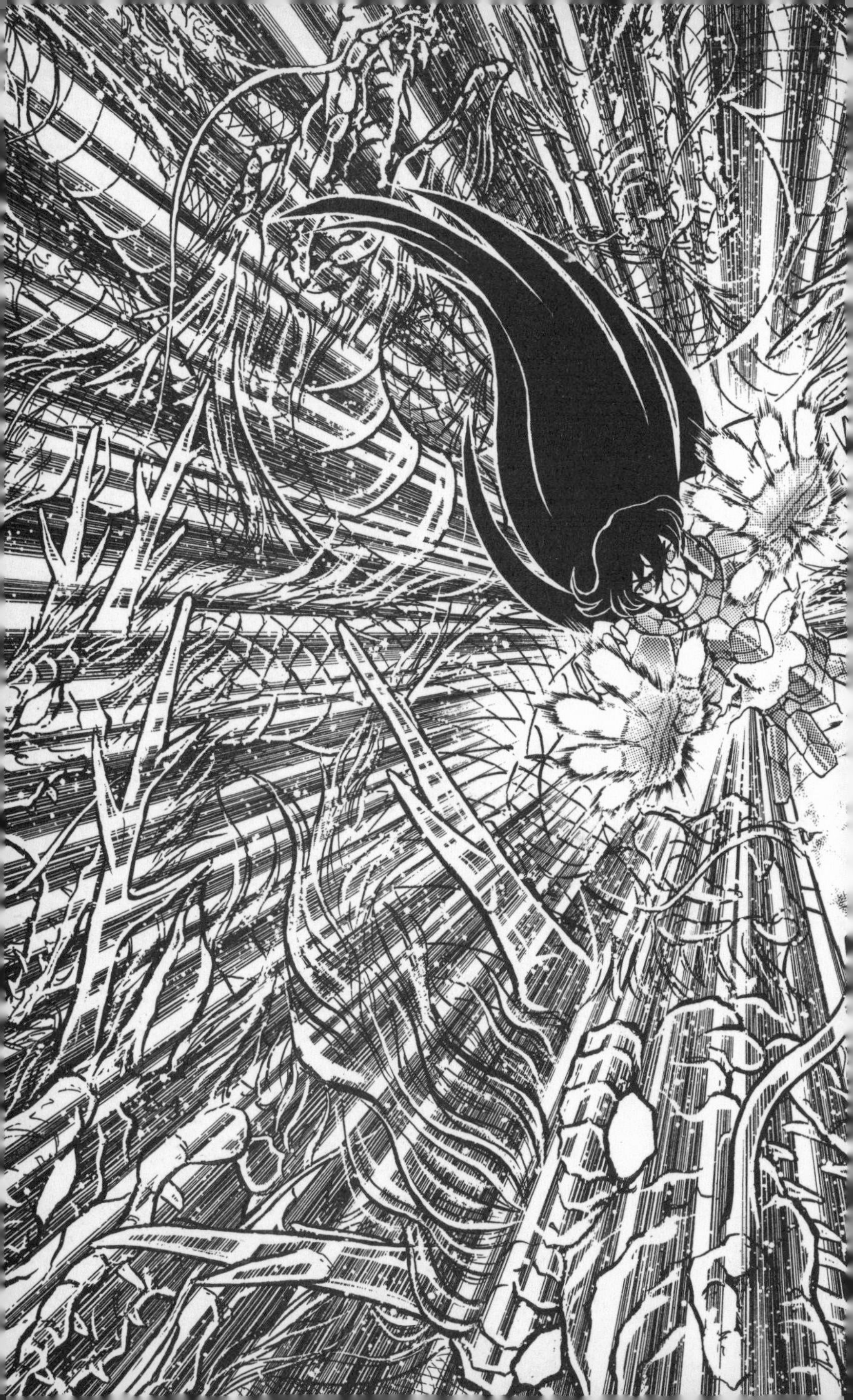

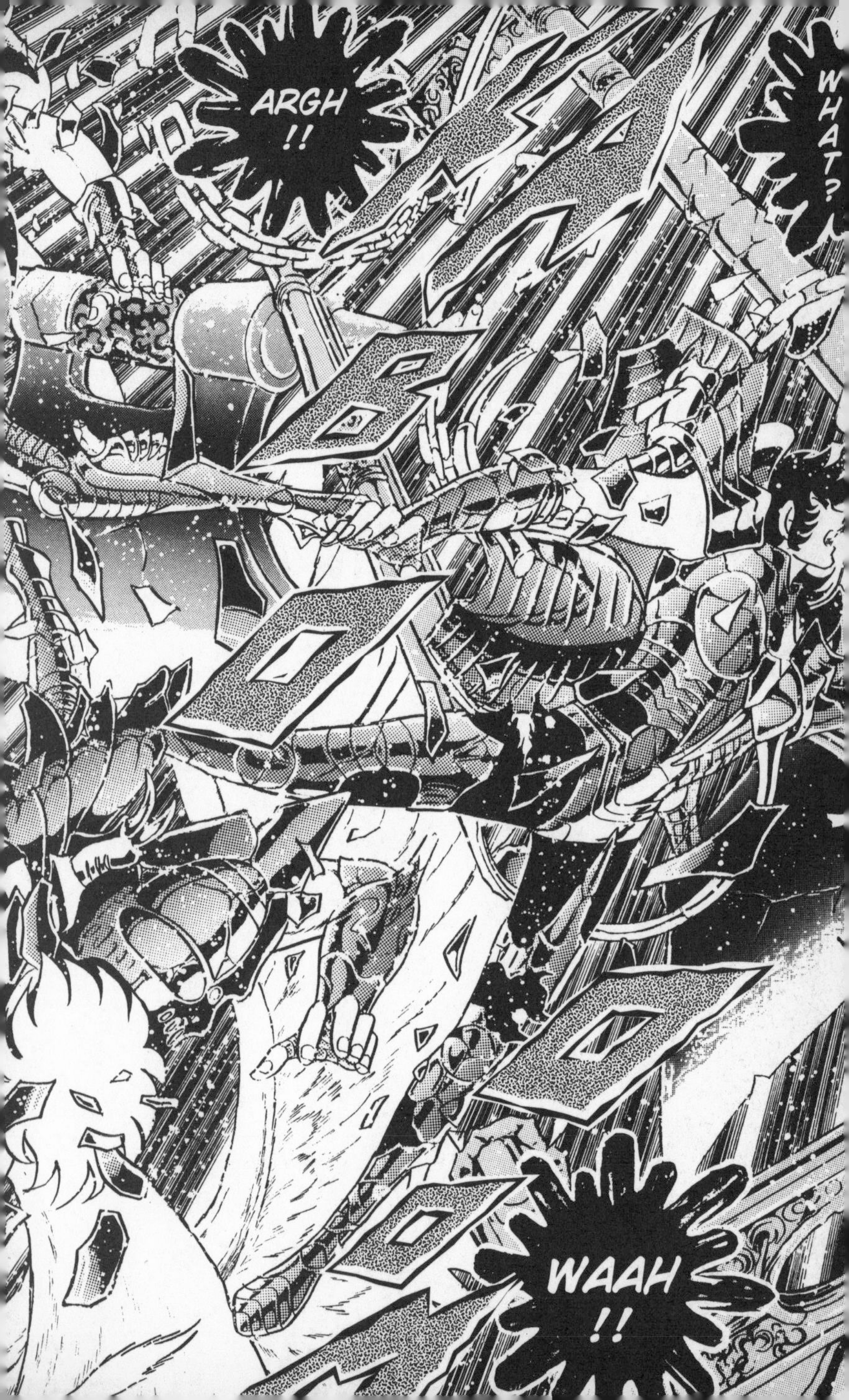
WHAT?
ARGH !!
WAAH !!

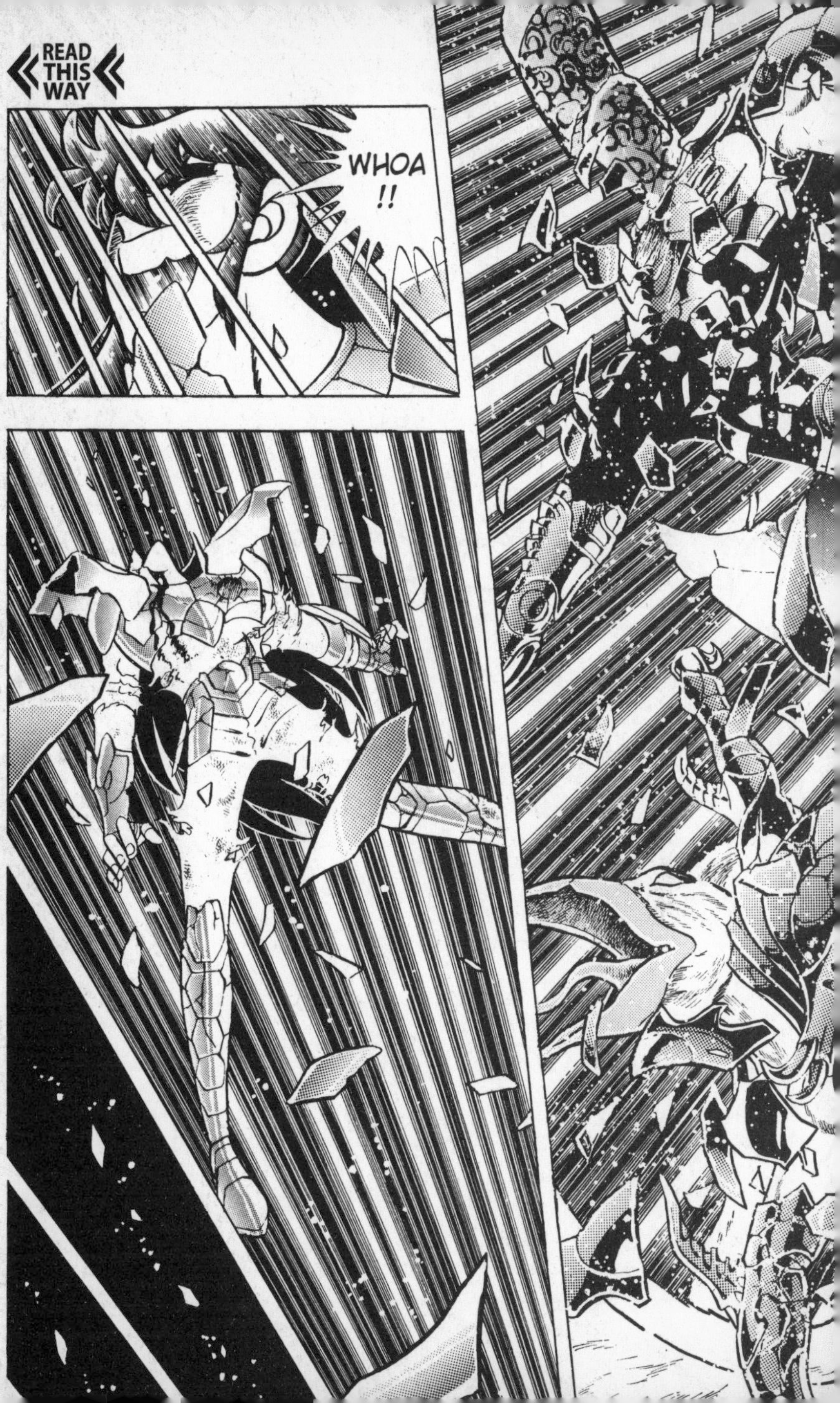
READ THIS WAY
WHOA !!

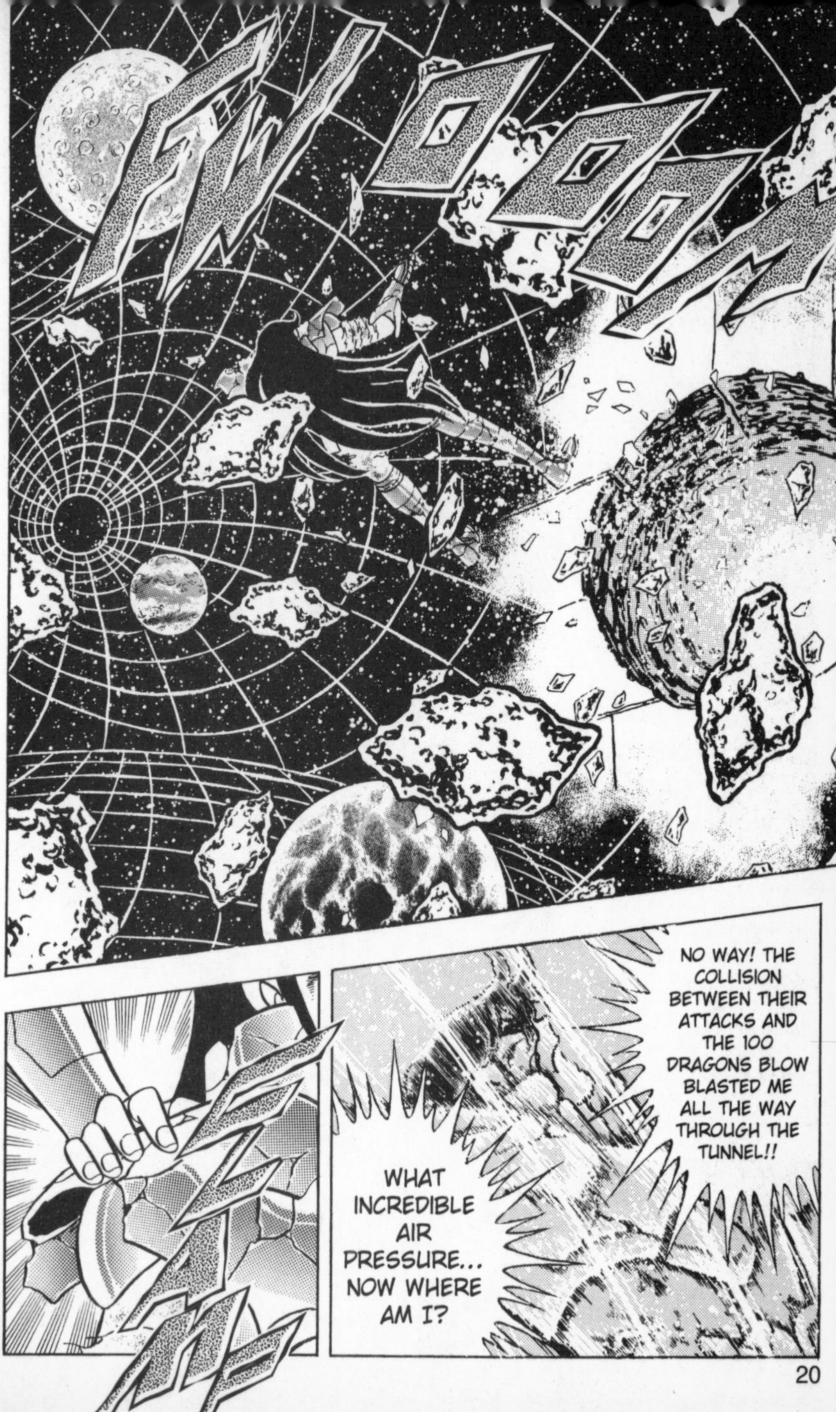
NO WAY! THE COLLISION BETWEEN THEIR ATTACKS AND THE 100 DRAGONS BLOW BLASTED ME ALL THE WAY THROUGH THE TUNNEL!!
WHAT INCREDIBLE AIR PRESSURE... NOW WHERE AM I?

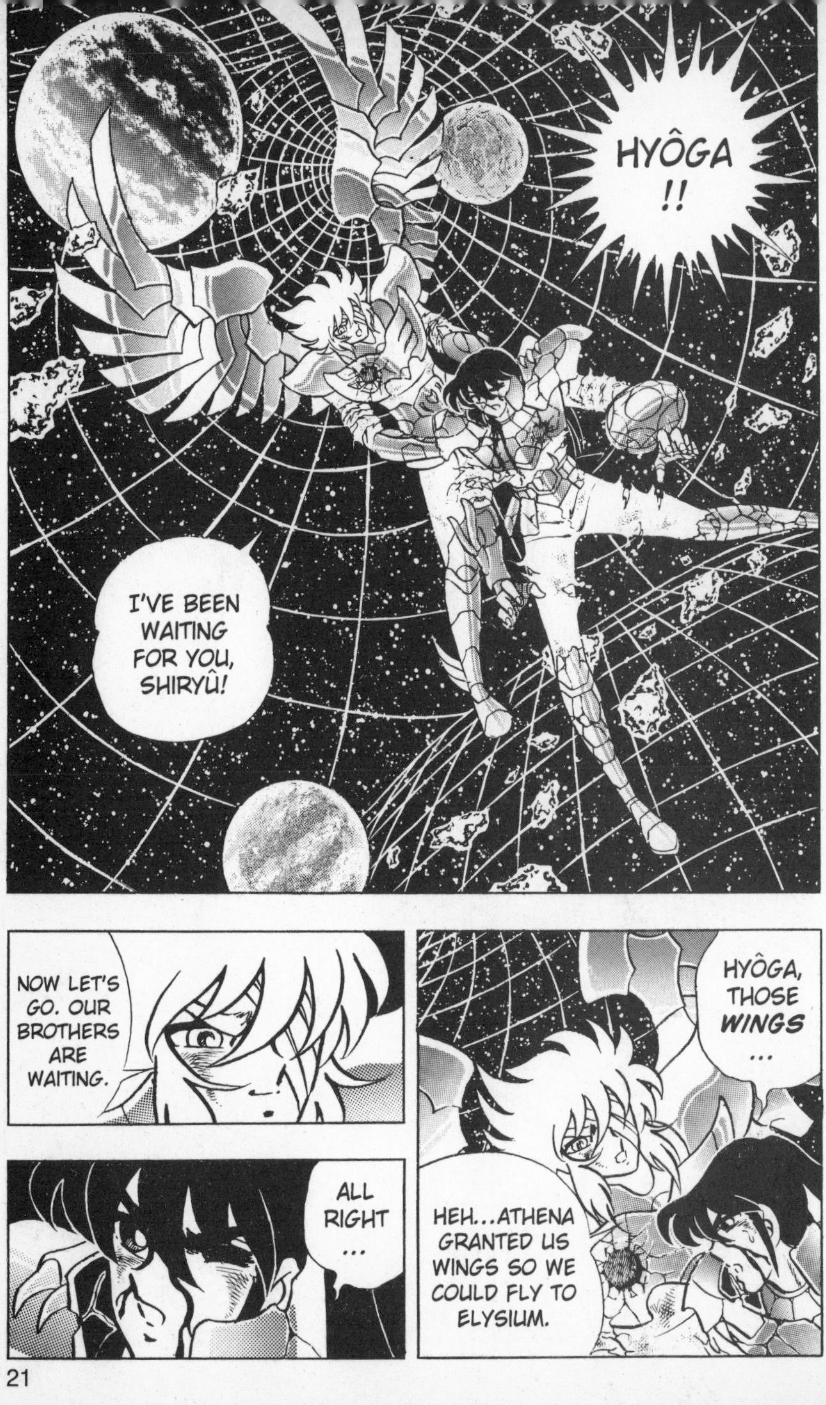
HYÔGA !!
I'VE BEEN WAITING FOR YOU, SHIRYÛ!
HYÔGA, THOSE *WINGS* ...
HEH...ATHENA GRANTED US WINGS SO WE COULD FLY TO ELYSIUM.
NOW LET'S GO. OUR BROTHERS ARE WAITING.
ALL RIGHT ...

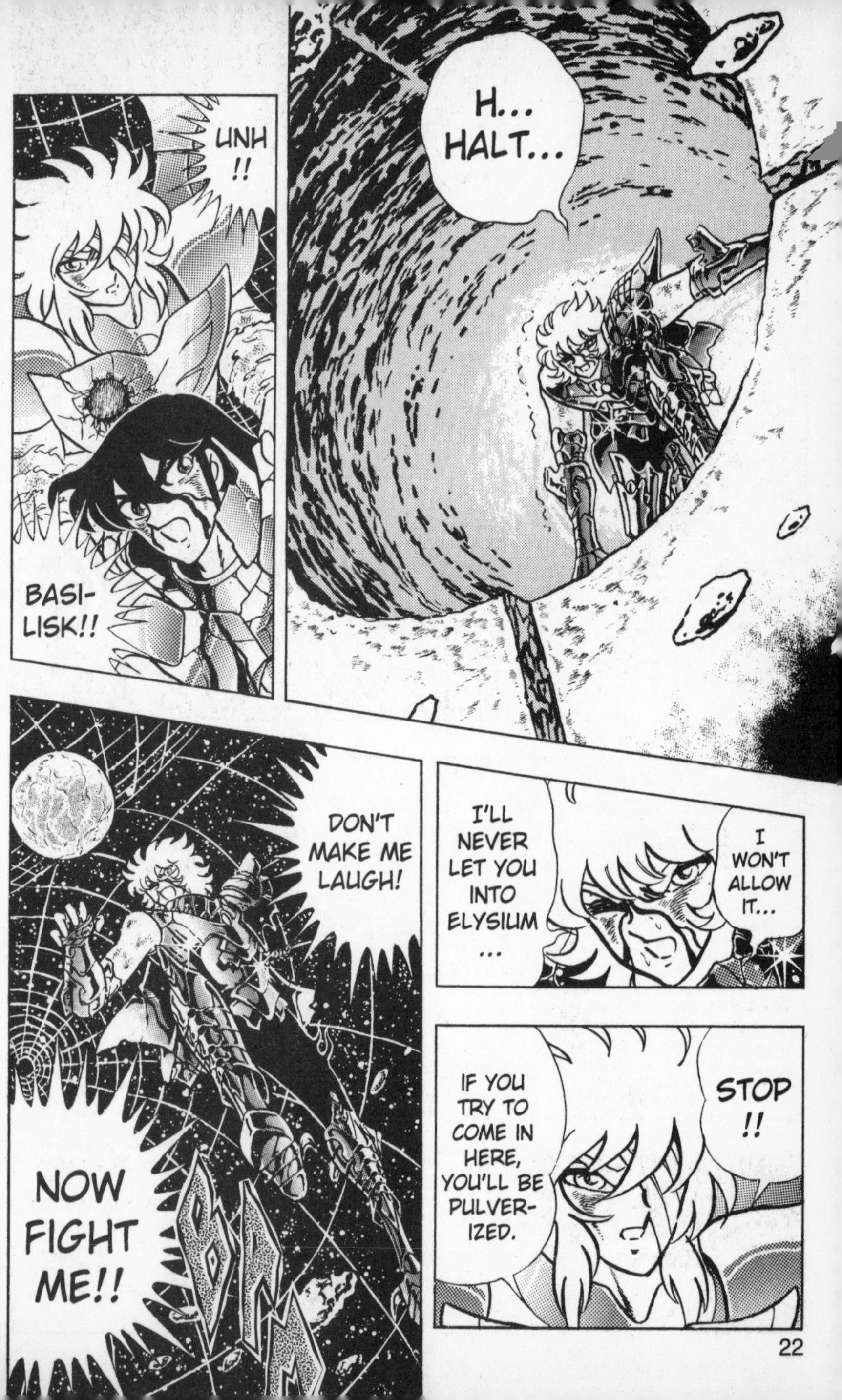
H... HALT...
UNH !!
BASI-LISK!!
I WON'T ALLOW IT...
I'LL NEVER LET YOU INTO ELYSIUM ...
STOP !!
IF YOU TRY TO COME IN HERE, YOU'LL BE PULVER-IZED.
DON'T MAKE ME LAUGH!
NOW FIGHT ME!!

READ THIS WAY

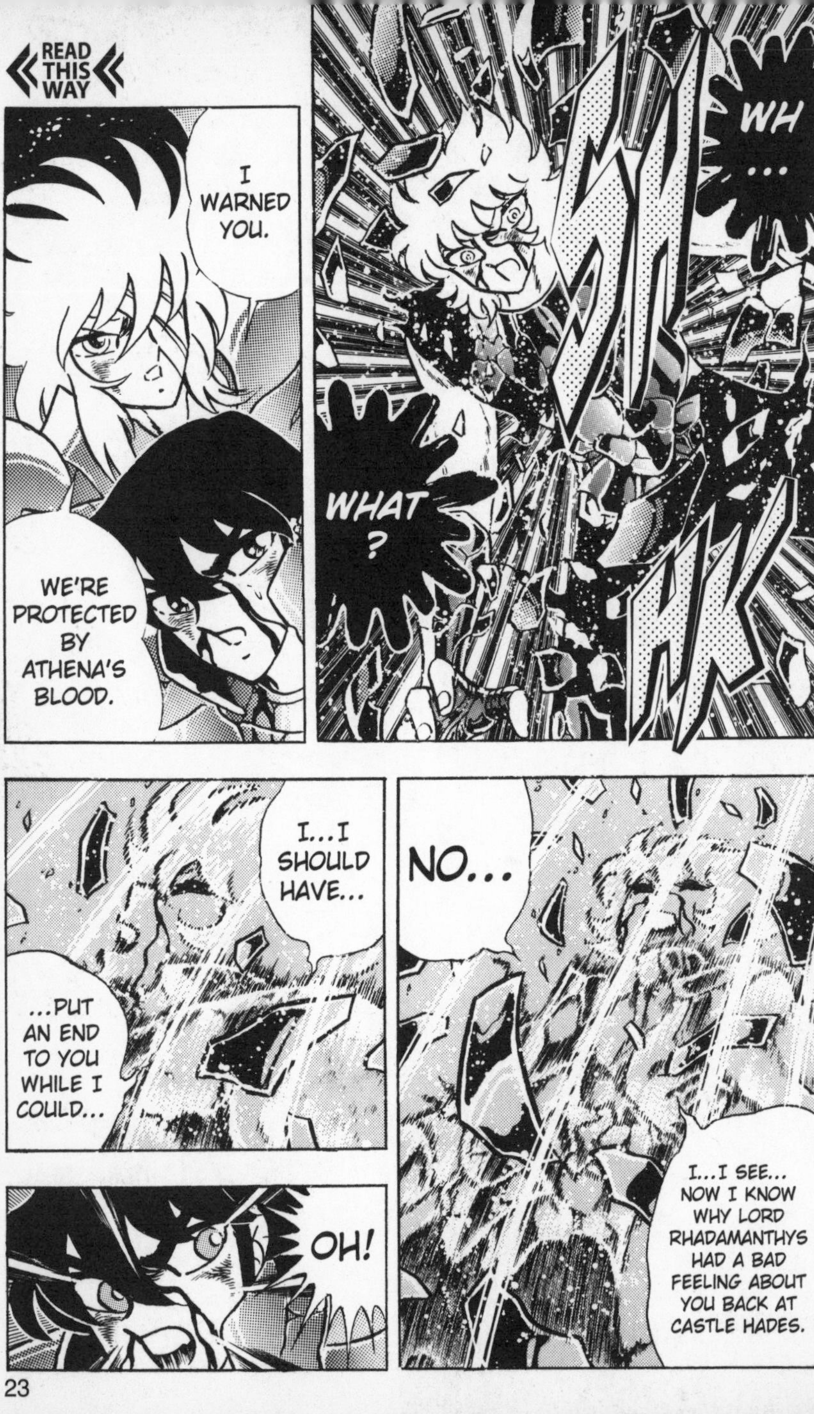

WH...
WHAT?
I WARNED YOU.
WE'RE PROTECTED BY ATHENA'S BLOOD.
NO...
I...I SEE... NOW I KNOW WHY LORD RHADAMANTHYS HAD A BAD FEELING ABOUT YOU BACK AT CASTLE HADES.
I...I SHOULD HAVE...
...PUT AN END TO YOU WHILE I COULD...
OH!

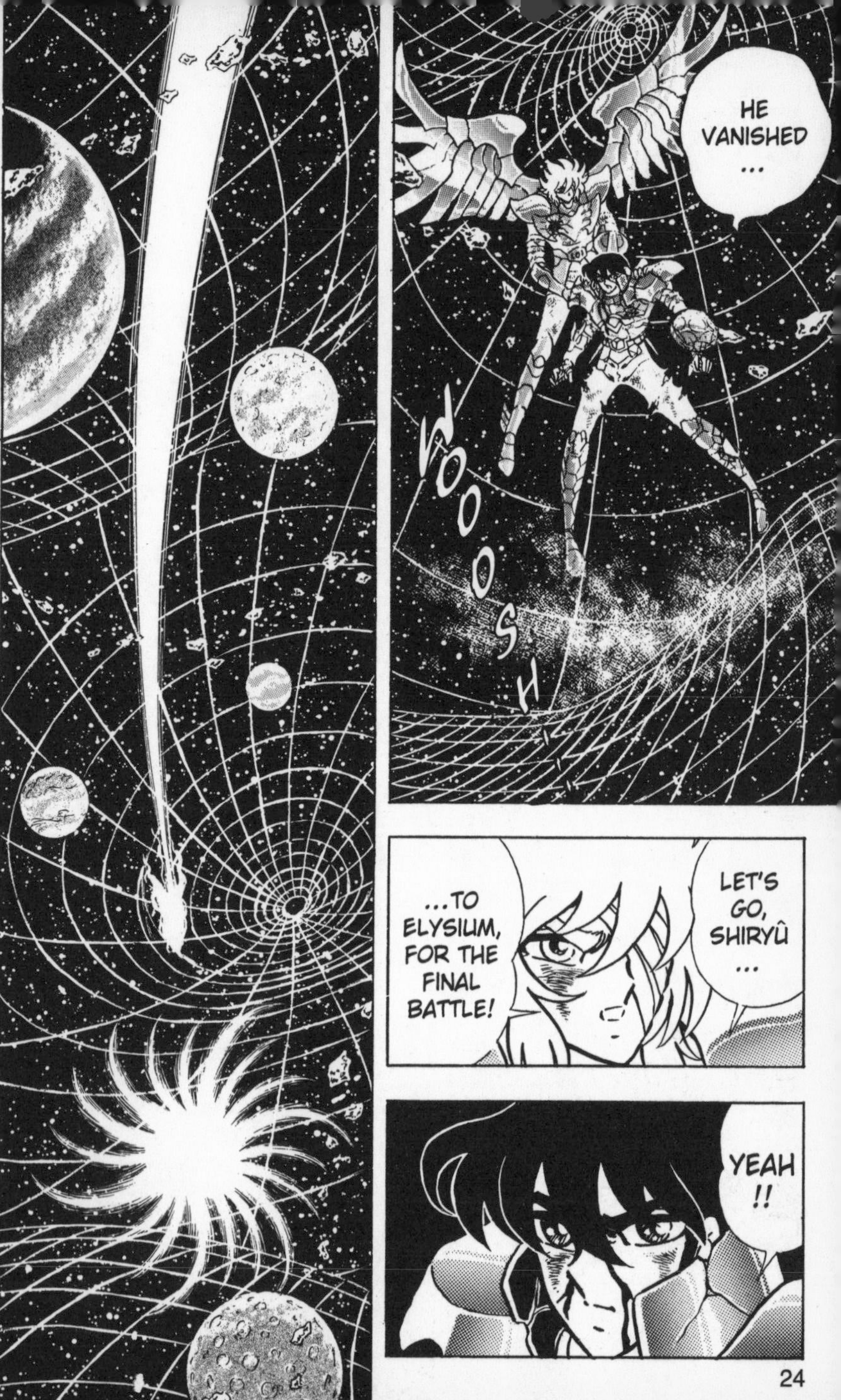
HE VANISHED ...
WOOOOSH
LET'S GO, SHIRYÛ ...
...TO ELYSIUM, FOR THE FINAL BATTLE!
YEAH !!

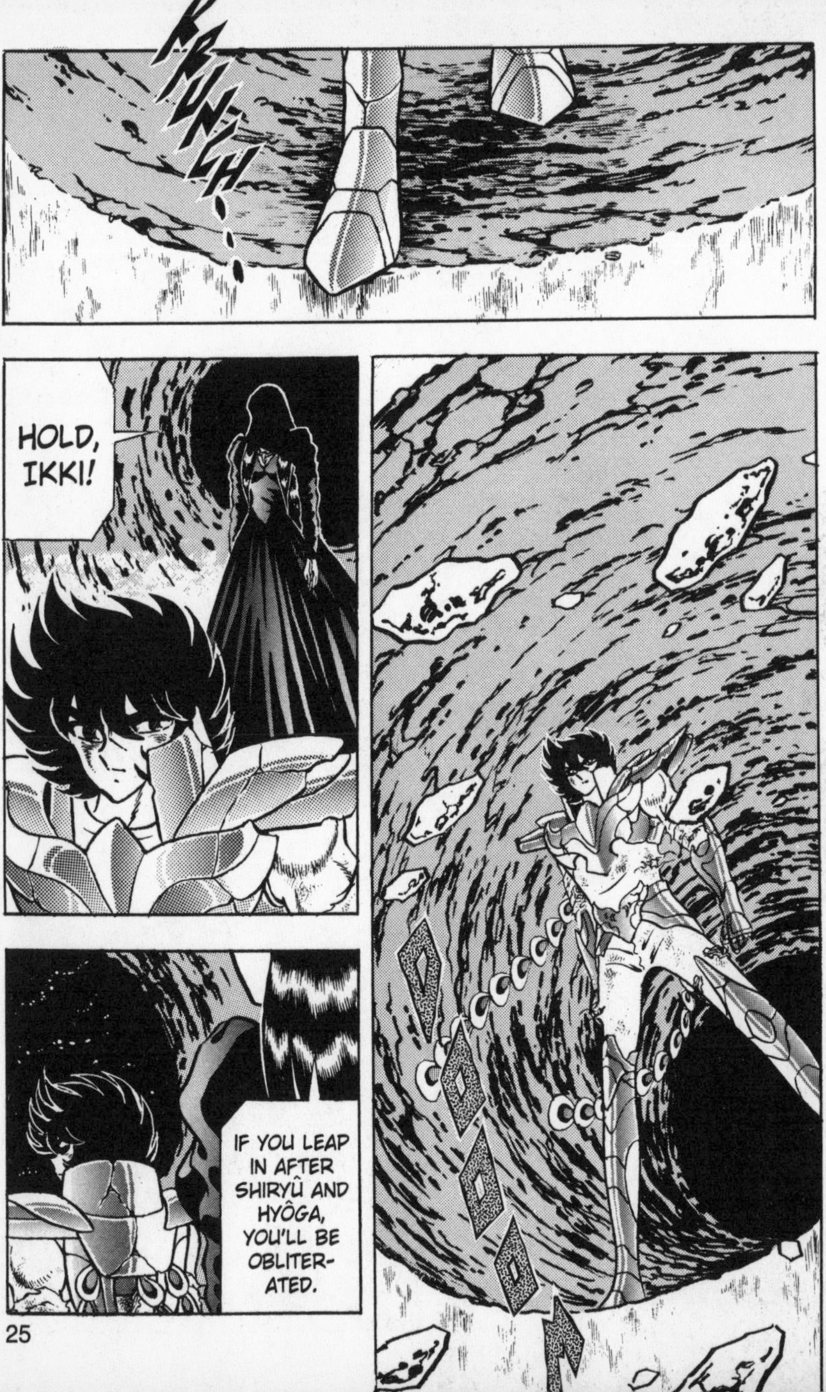
KRUNCH...
HOLD, IKKI!
IF YOU LEAP IN AFTER SHIRYÛ AND HYÔGA, YOU'LL BE OBLITERATED.

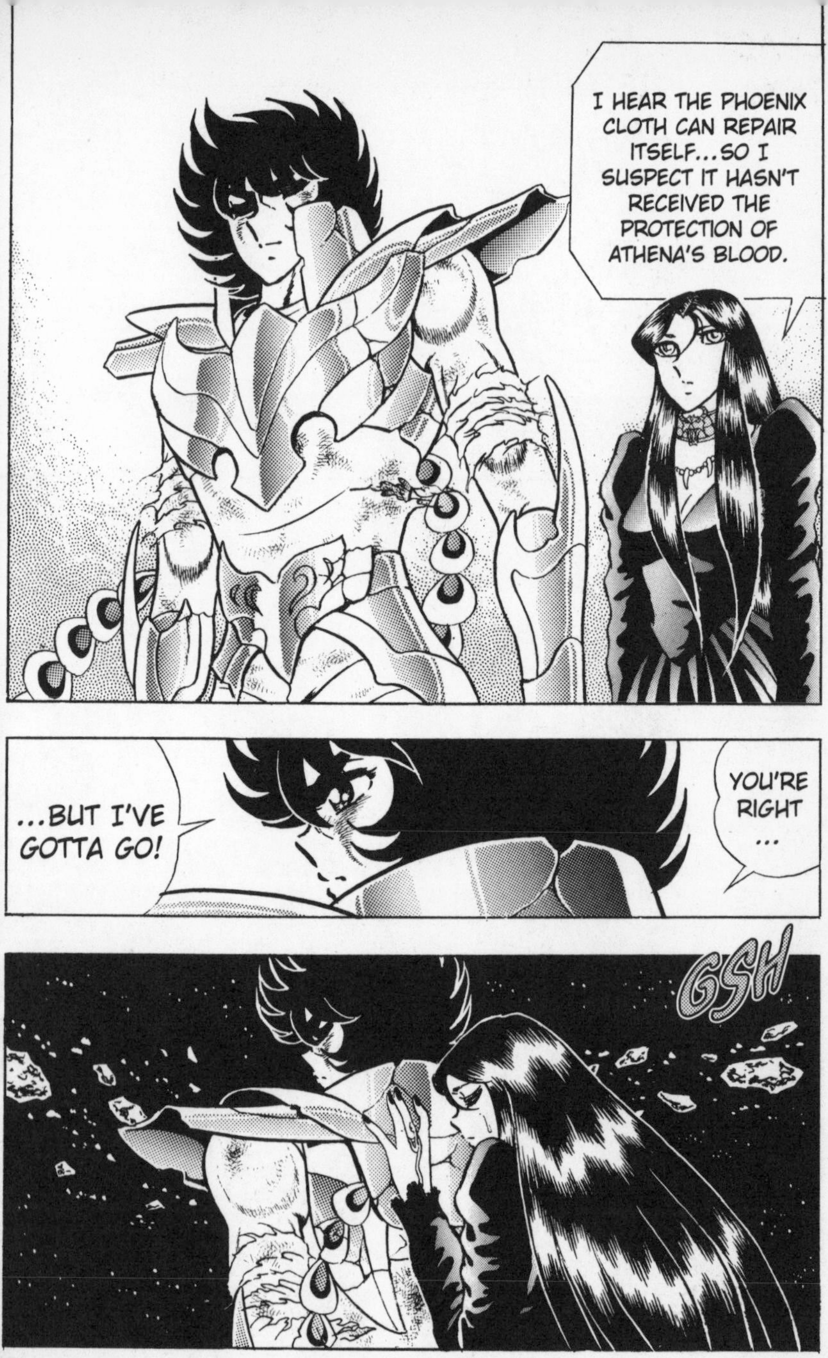
I HEAR THE PHOENIX CLOTH CAN REPAIR ITSELF...SO I SUSPECT IT HASN'T RECEIVED THE PROTECTION OF ATHENA'S BLOOD.
YOU'RE RIGHT ...
...BUT I'VE GOTTA GO!
GSH

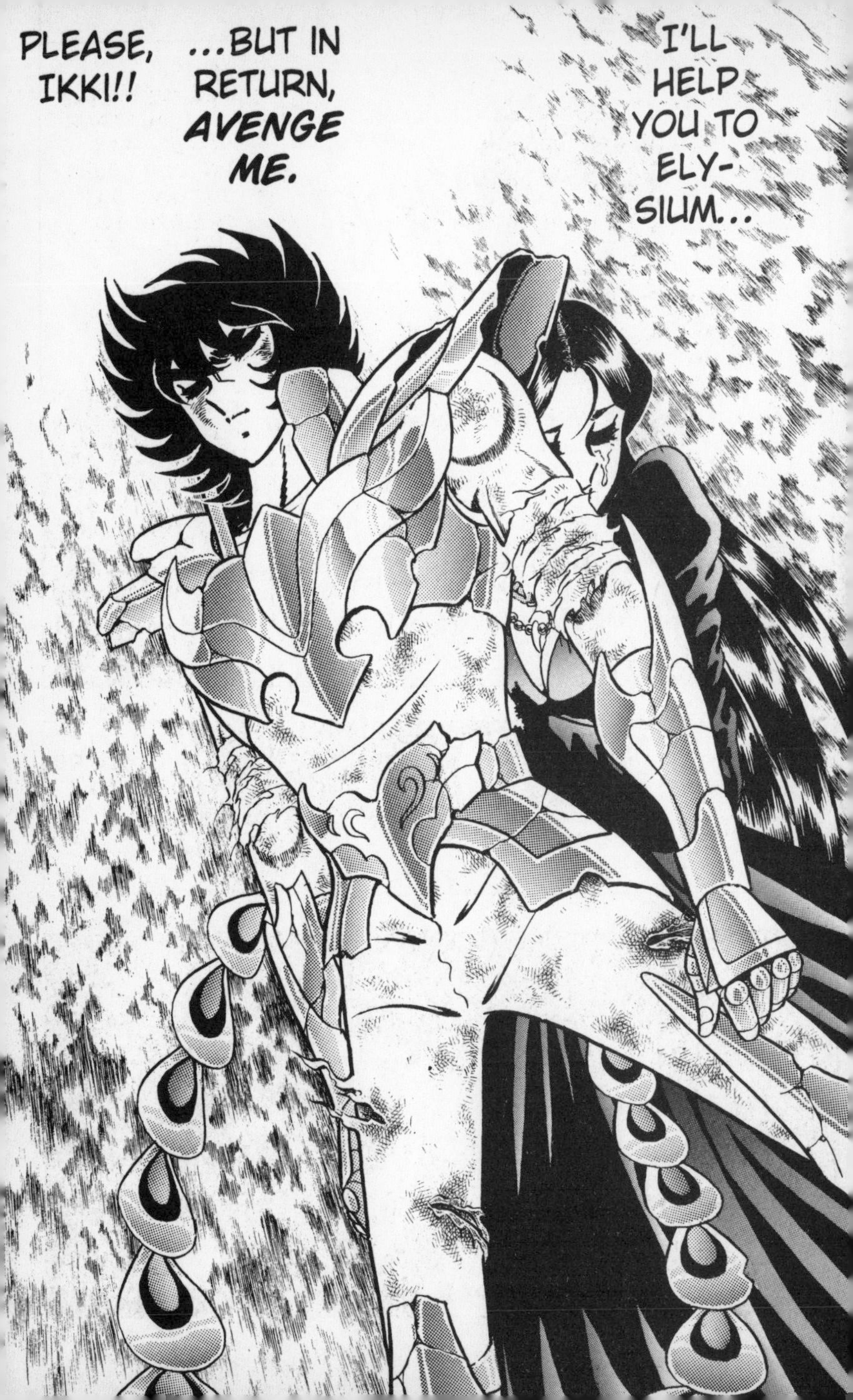
I'LL HELP YOU TO ELY-SIUM...
...BUT IN RETURN, **AVENGE ME.**
PLEASE, IKKI!!

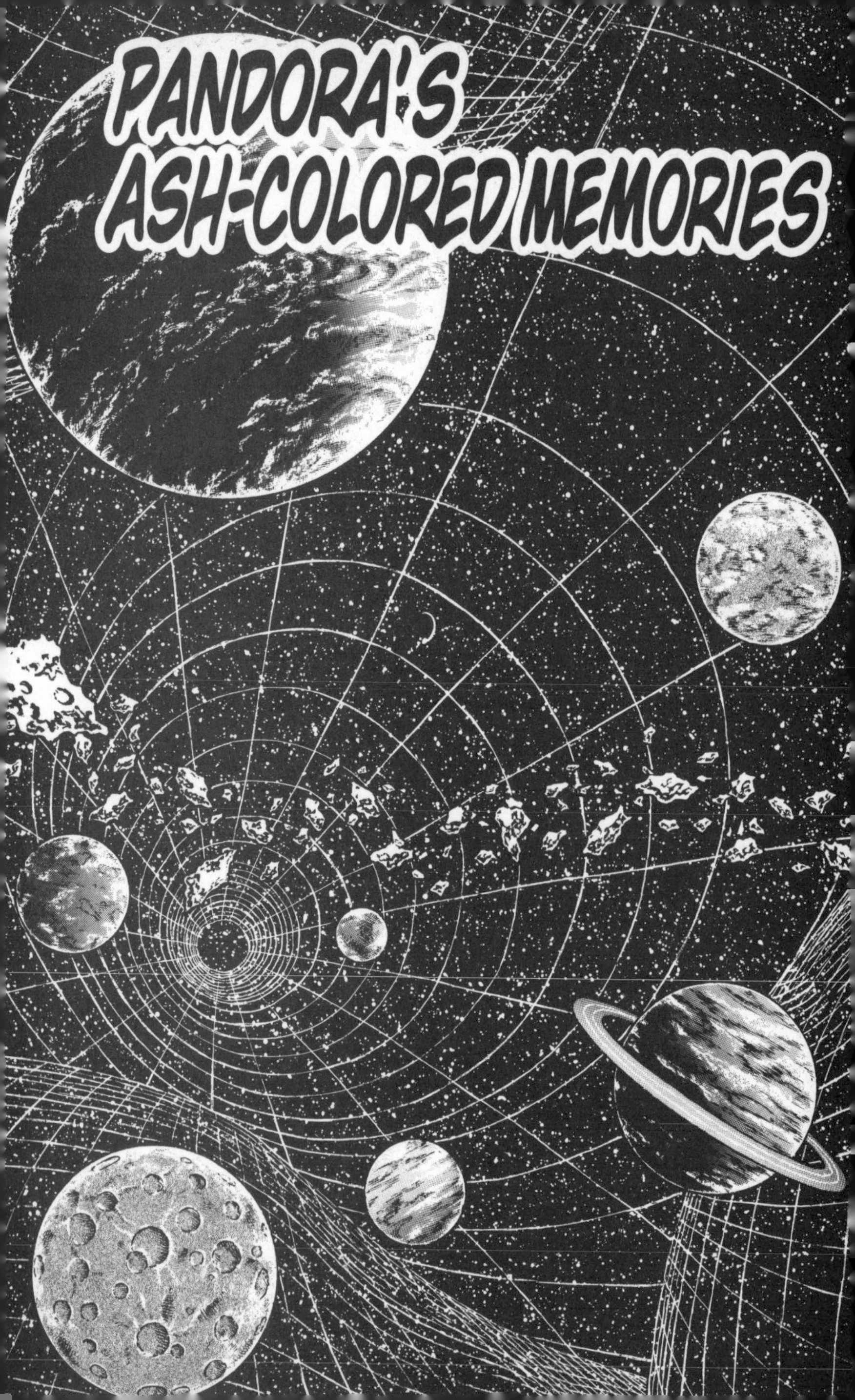
PANDORA'S
ASH-COLORED MEMORIES

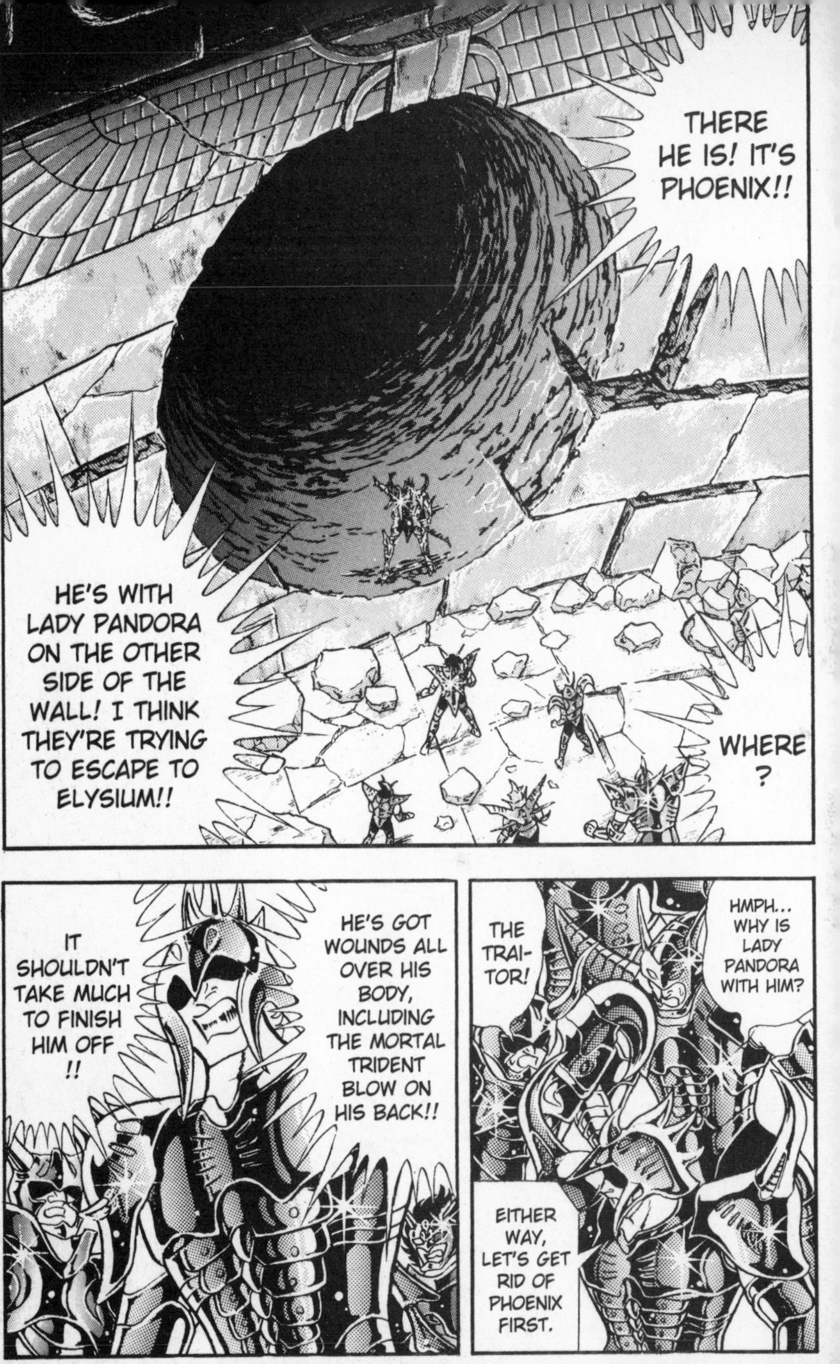
THERE HE IS! IT'S PHOENIX!!
WHERE?
HE'S WITH LADY PANDORA ON THE OTHER SIDE OF THE WALL! I THINK THEY'RE TRYING TO ESCAPE TO ELYSIUM!!
HMPH... WHY IS LADY PANDORA WITH HIM?
THE TRAITOR!
EITHER WAY, LET'S GET RID OF PHOENIX FIRST.
HE'S GOT WOUNDS ALL OVER HIS BODY, INCLUDING THE MORTAL TRIDENT BLOW ON HIS BACK!!
IT SHOULDN'T TAKE MUCH TO FINISH HIM OFF!!

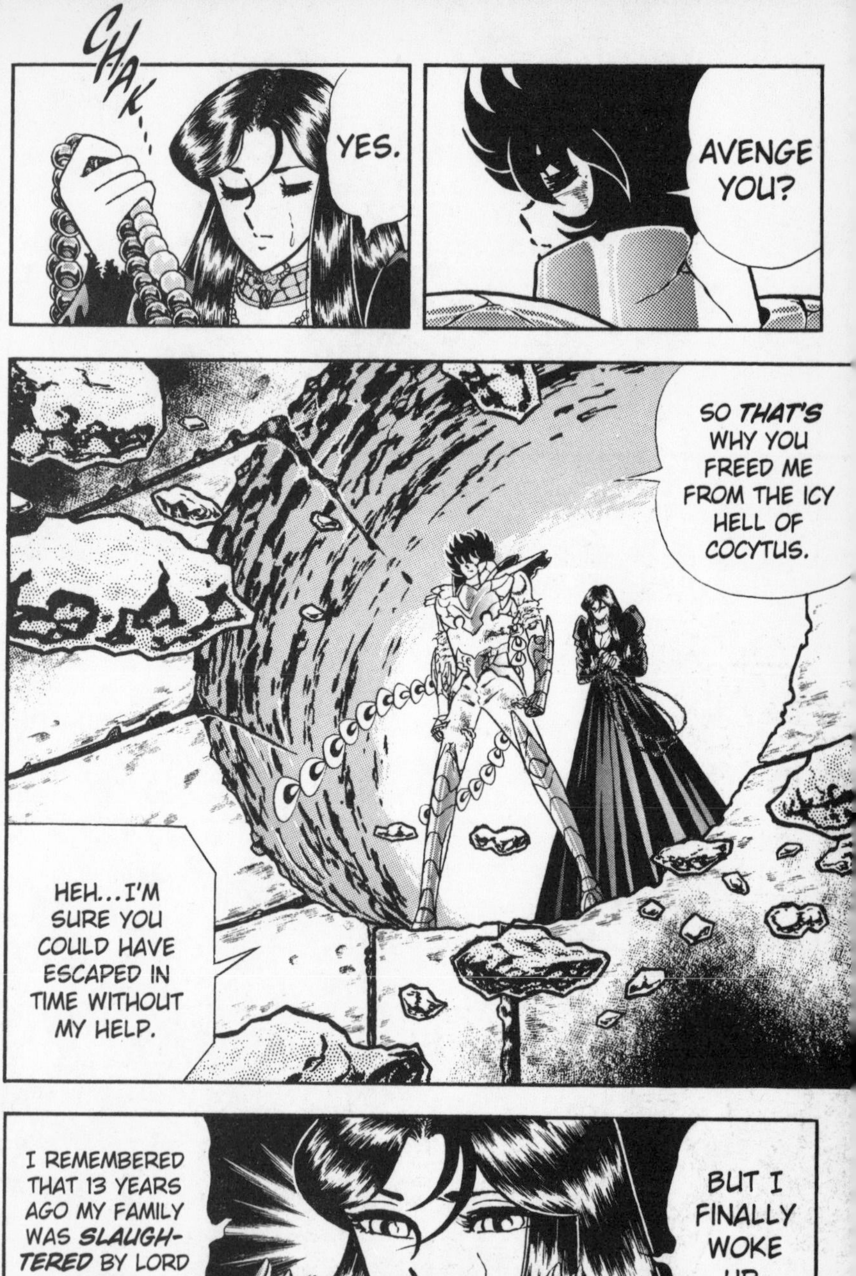
AVENGE YOU?
CHAK...
YES.
SO THAT'S WHY YOU FREED ME FROM THE ICY HELL OF COCYTUS.
HEH...I'M SURE YOU COULD HAVE ESCAPED IN TIME WITHOUT MY HELP.
BUT I FINALLY WOKE UP.
I REMEMBERED THAT 13 YEARS AGO MY FAMILY WAS SLAUGHTERED BY LORD HADES.

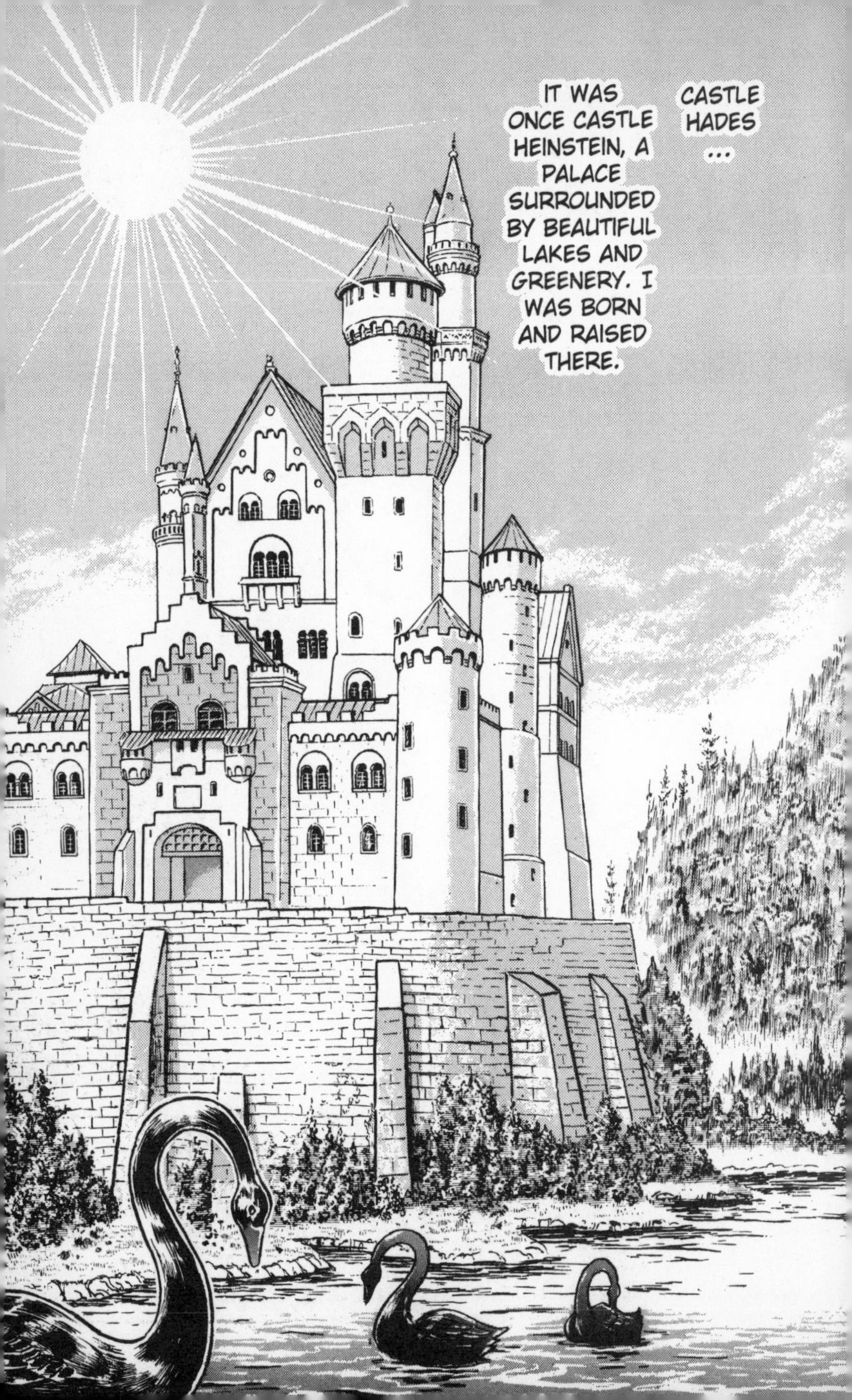
CASTLE HADES ...
IT WAS ONCE CASTLE HEINSTEIN, A PALACE SURROUNDED BY BEAUTIFUL LAKES AND GREENERY. I WAS BORN AND RAISED THERE.

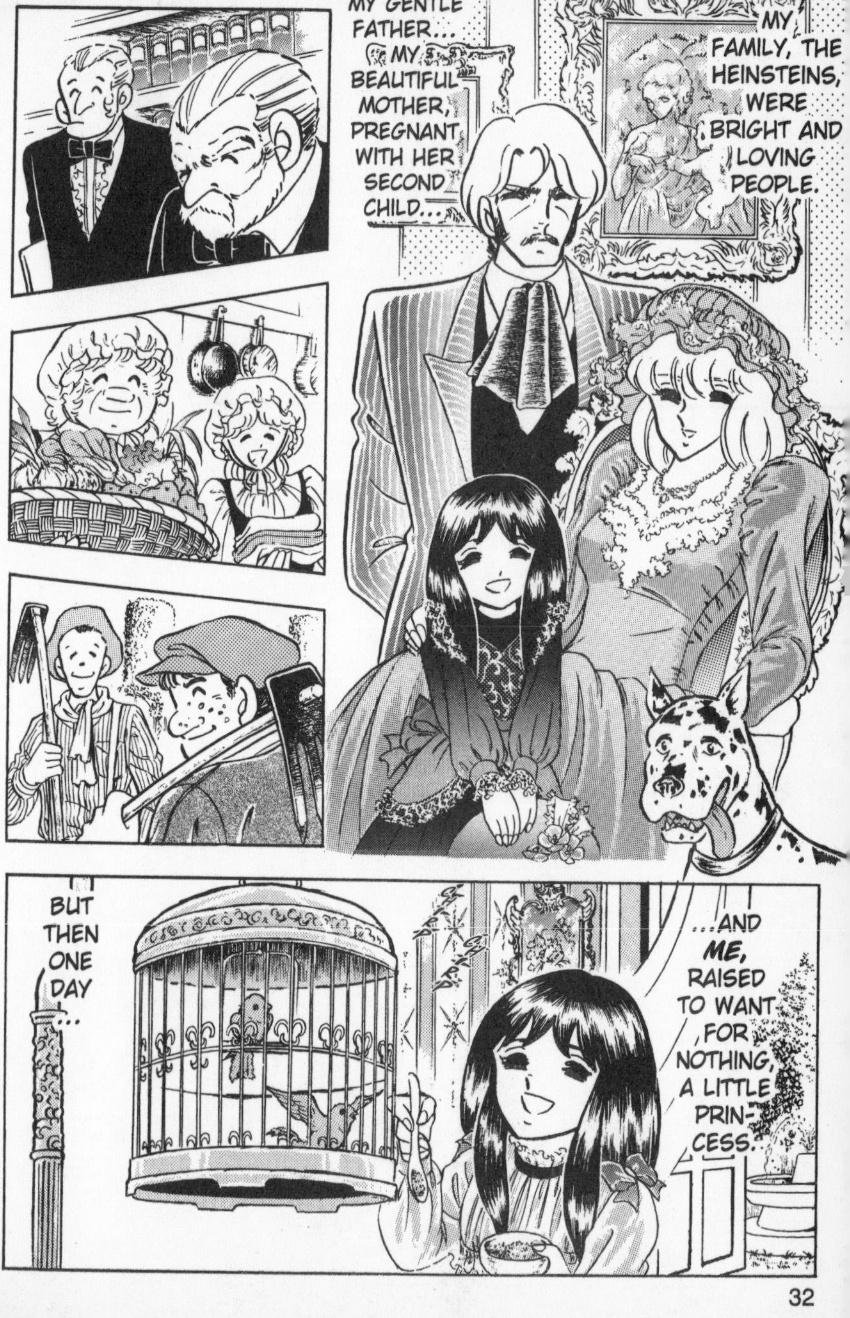
MY FAMILY, THE HEINSTEINS, WERE BRIGHT AND LOVING PEOPLE.
MY GENTLE FATHER... MY BEAUTIFUL MOTHER, PREGNANT WITH HER SECOND CHILD...
...AND *ME*, RAISED TO WANT FOR NOTHING, A LITTLE PRIN-CESS.
BUT THEN ONE DAY...

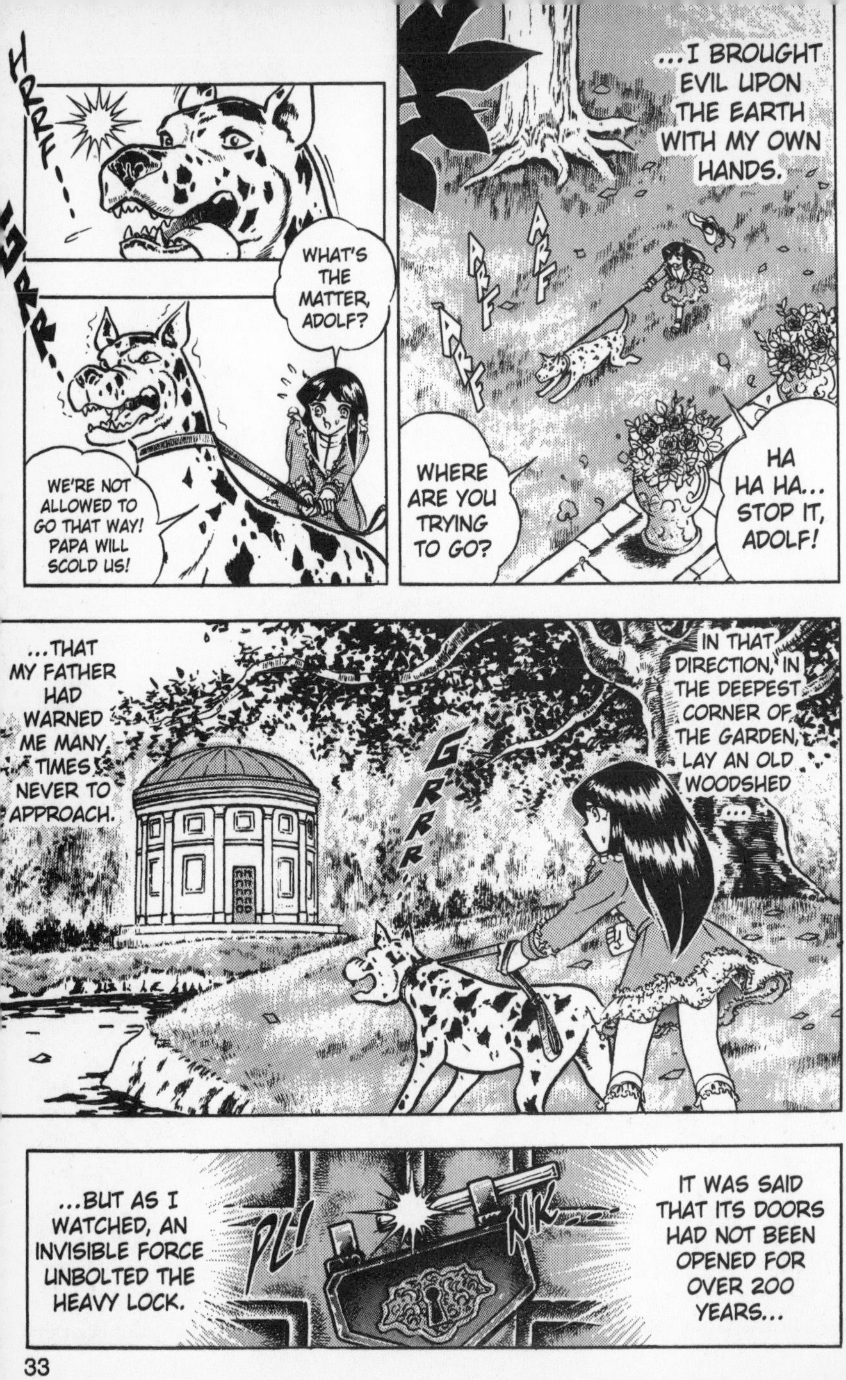
...I BROUGHT EVIL UPON THE EARTH WITH MY OWN HANDS.
ARF ARF ARF
HA HA HA... STOP IT, ADOLF!
WHERE ARE YOU TRYING TO GO?
HRRF
GRRR
WHAT'S THE MATTER, ADOLF?
WE'RE NOT ALLOWED TO GO THAT WAY! PAPA WILL SCOLD US!
IN THAT DIRECTION, IN THE DEEPEST CORNER OF THE GARDEN, LAY AN OLD WOODSHED...
GRRR
...THAT MY FATHER HAD WARNED ME MANY TIMES NEVER TO APPROACH.
IT WAS SAID THAT ITS DOORS HAD NOT BEEN OPENED FOR OVER 200 YEARS...
PLINK
...BUT AS I WATCHED, AN INVISIBLE FORCE UNBOLTED THE HEAVY LOCK.

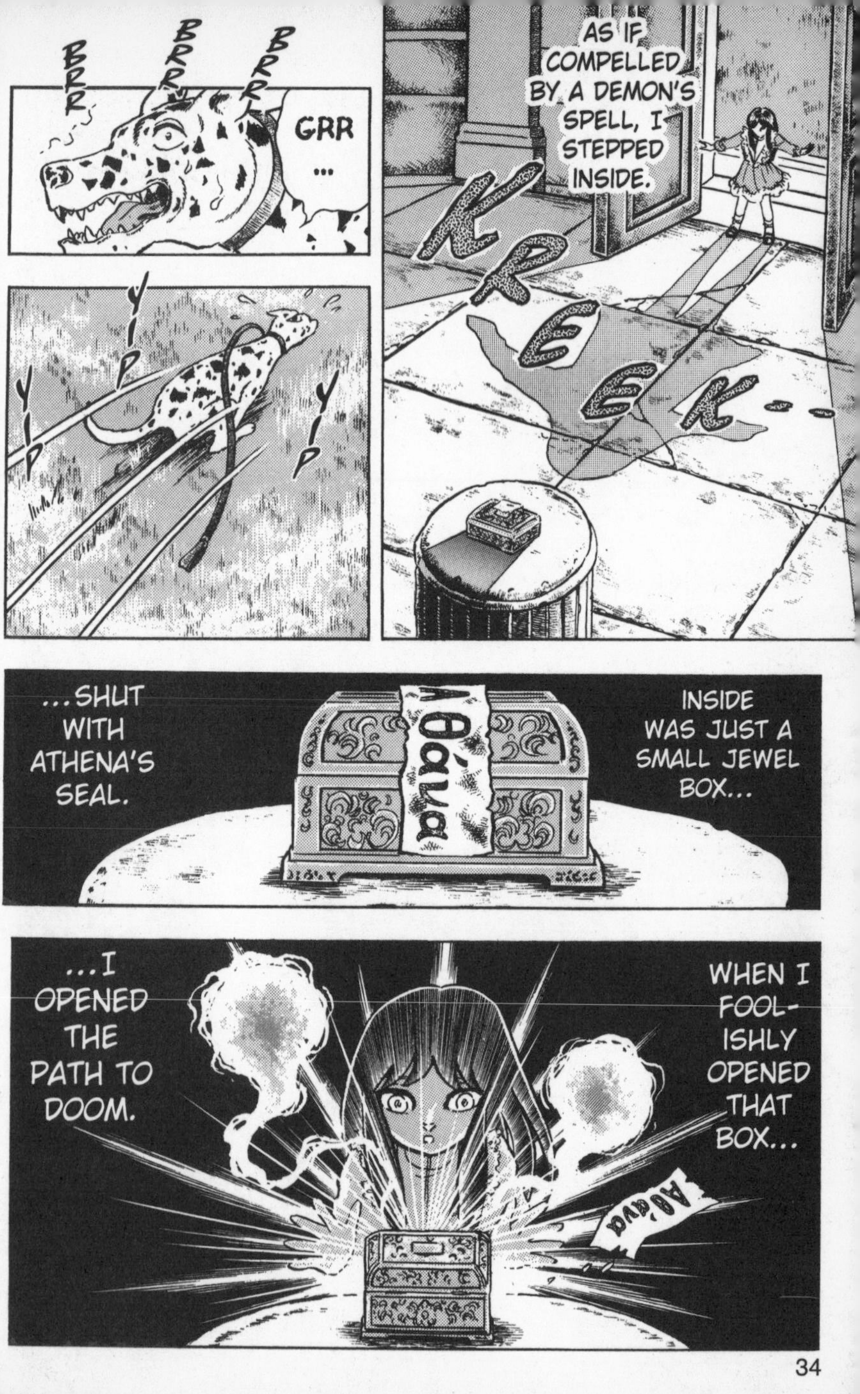
AS IF COMPELLED BY A DEMON'S SPELL, I STEPPED INSIDE.
KREEK...
BRRR
BRRR
BRRR
GRR...
YIP
YIP
YIP
INSIDE WAS JUST A SMALL JEWEL BOX...
...SHUT WITH ATHENA'S SEAL.
Αθάνα
WHEN I FOOL-ISHLY OPENED THAT BOX...
...I OPENED THE PATH TO DOOM.
Αθάνα

READ THIS WAY

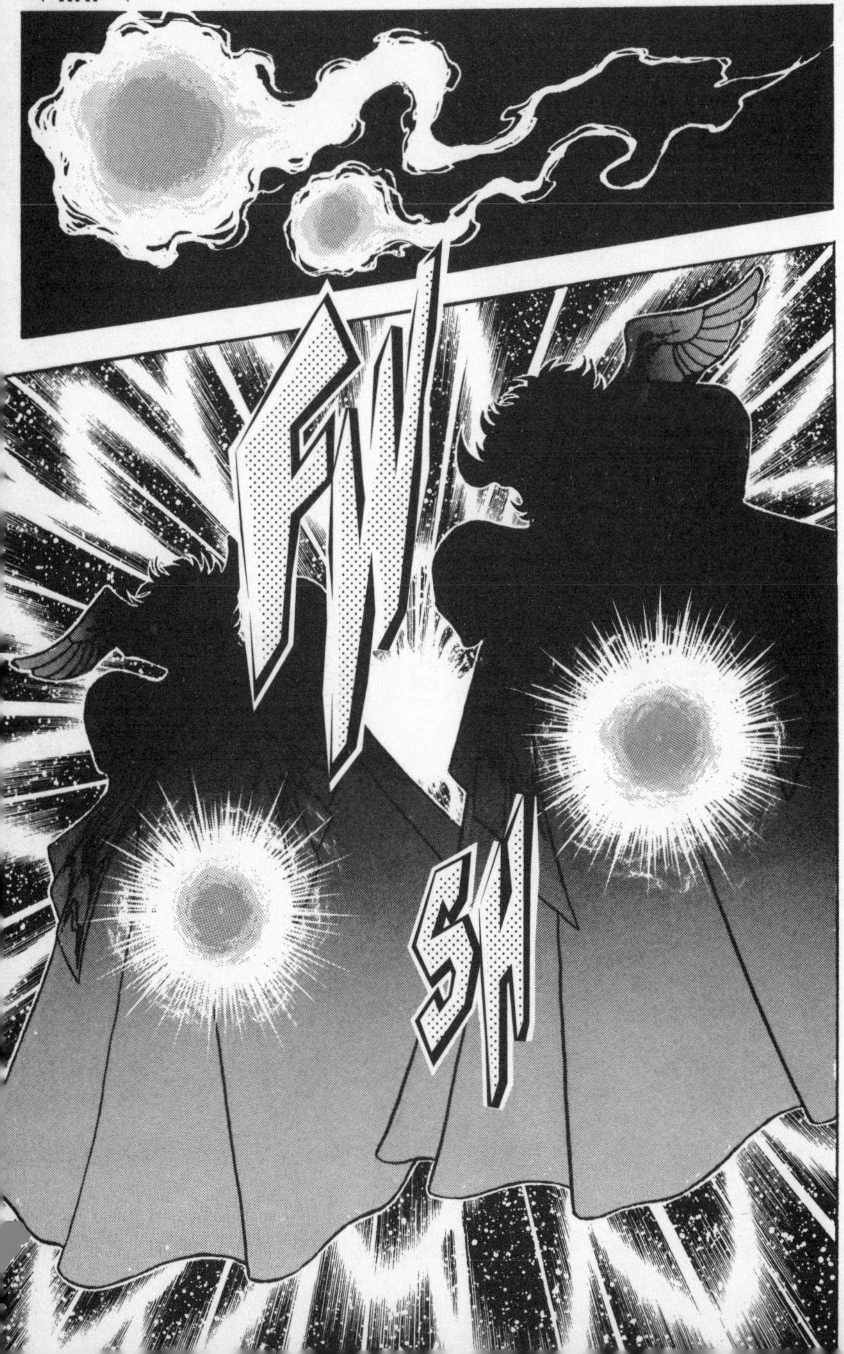
FWI
SH

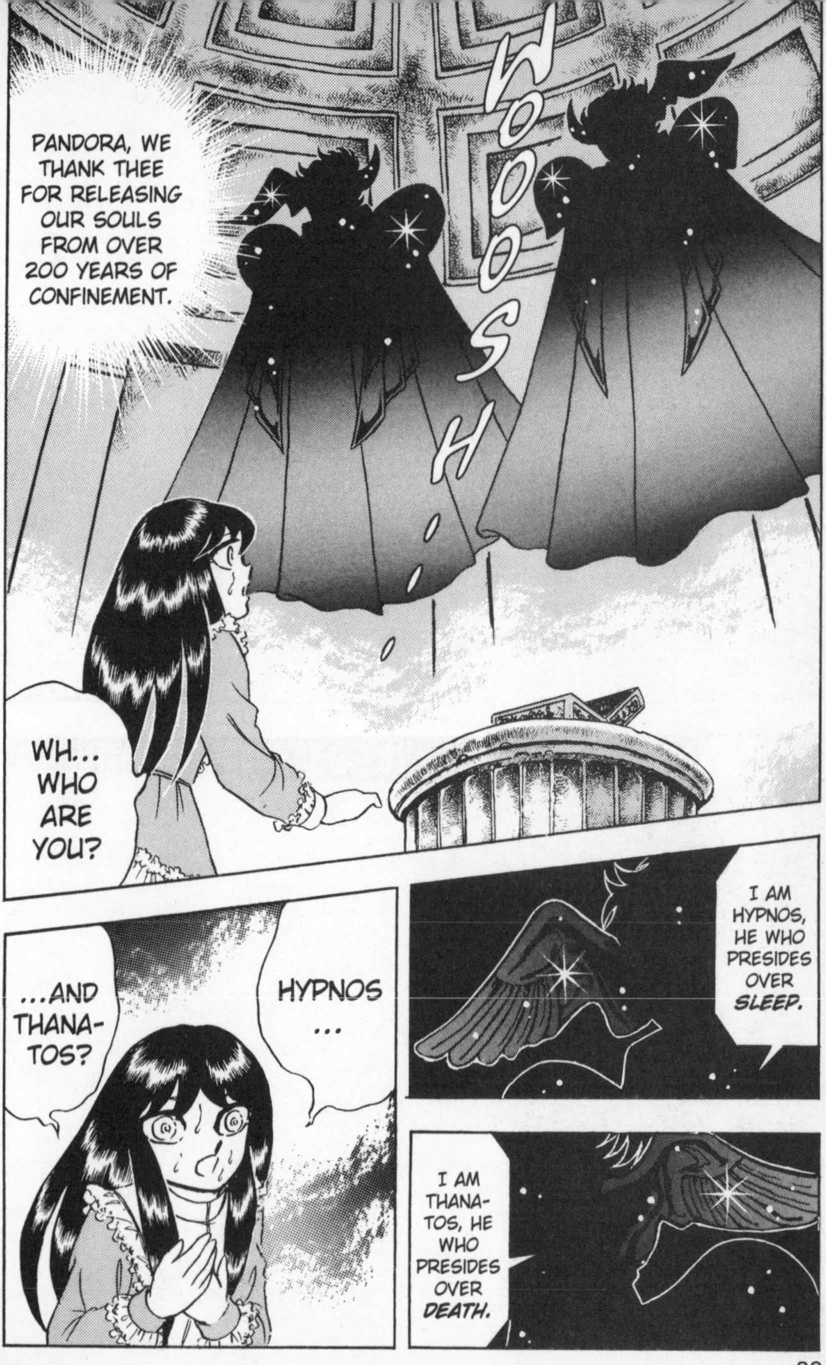
WOOOOSH
PANDORA, WE THANK THEE FOR RELEASING OUR SOULS FROM OVER 200 YEARS OF CONFINEMENT.
WH... WHO ARE YOU?
I AM HYPNOS, HE WHO PRESIDES OVER *SLEEP.*
I AM THANATOS, HE WHO PRESIDES OVER *DEATH.*
HYPNOS ...
...AND THANATOS?

READ THIS WAY

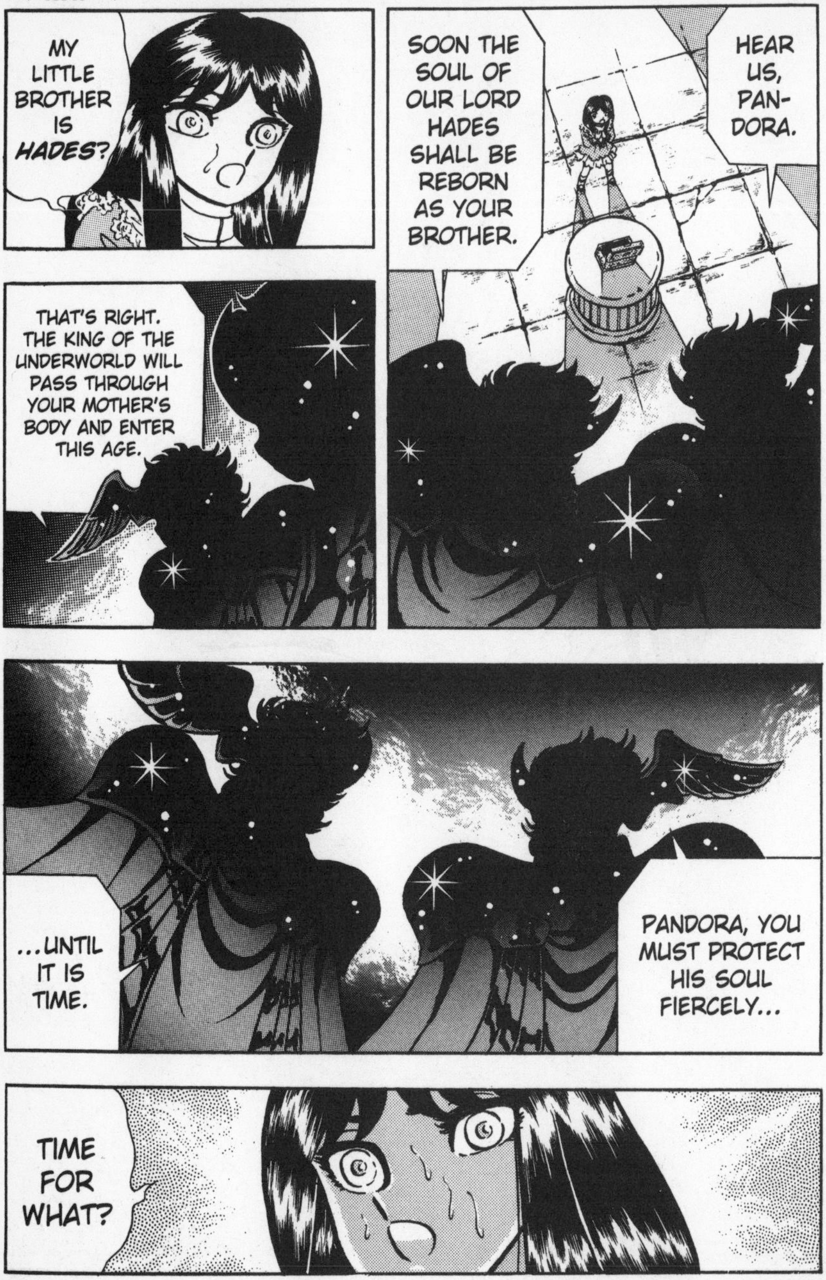
HEAR US, PAN-DORA.
SOON THE SOUL OF OUR LORD HADES SHALL BE REBORN AS YOUR BROTHER.
MY LITTLE BROTHER IS *HADES*?
THAT'S RIGHT. THE KING OF THE UNDERWORLD WILL PASS THROUGH YOUR MOTHER'S BODY AND ENTER THIS AGE.
PANDORA, YOU MUST PROTECT HIS SOUL FIERCELY...
...UNTIL IT IS TIME.
TIME FOR WHAT?

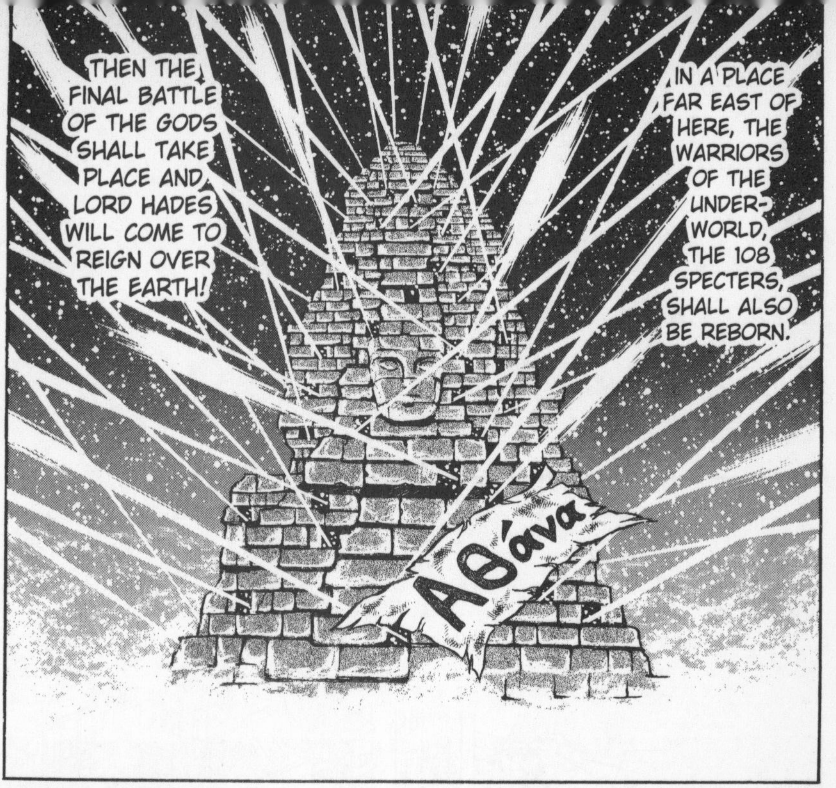
IN A PLACE FAR EAST OF HERE, THE WARRIORS OF THE UNDER-WORLD, THE 108 SPECTERS, SHALL ALSO BE REBORN.
THEN THE FINAL BATTLE OF THE GODS SHALL TAKE PLACE AND LORD HADES WILL COME TO REIGN OVER THE EARTH!
Αθάνα

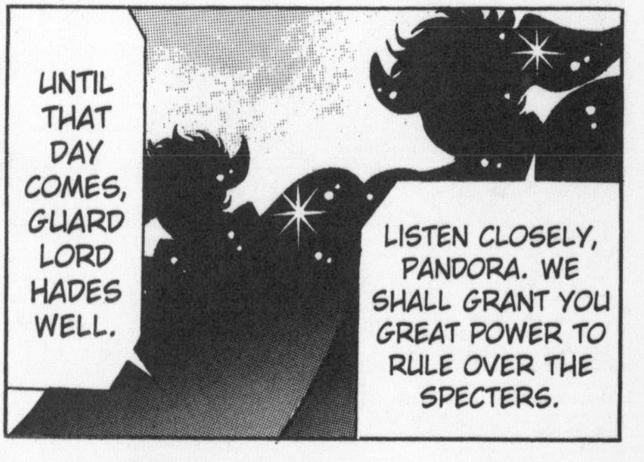
LISTEN CLOSELY, PANDORA. WE SHALL GRANT YOU GREAT POWER TO RULE OVER THE SPECTERS.
UNTIL THAT DAY COMES, GUARD LORD HADES WELL.

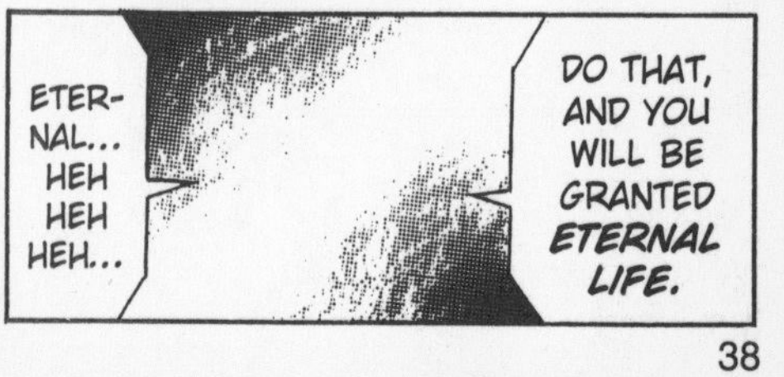
DO THAT, AND YOU WILL BE GRANTED *ETERNAL LIFE.*
ETER-NAL... HEH HEH HEH...

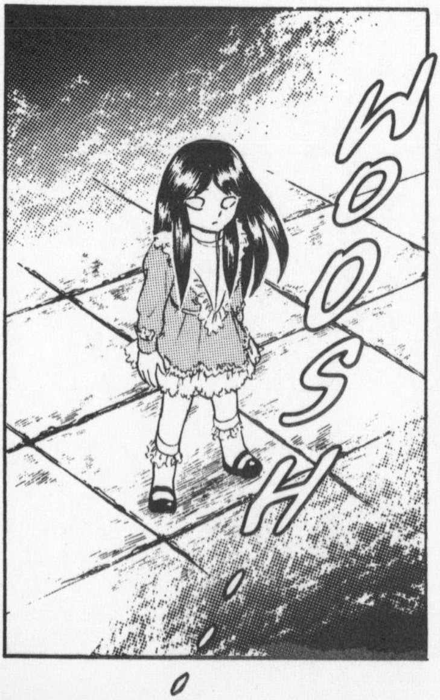
WHOOOSH

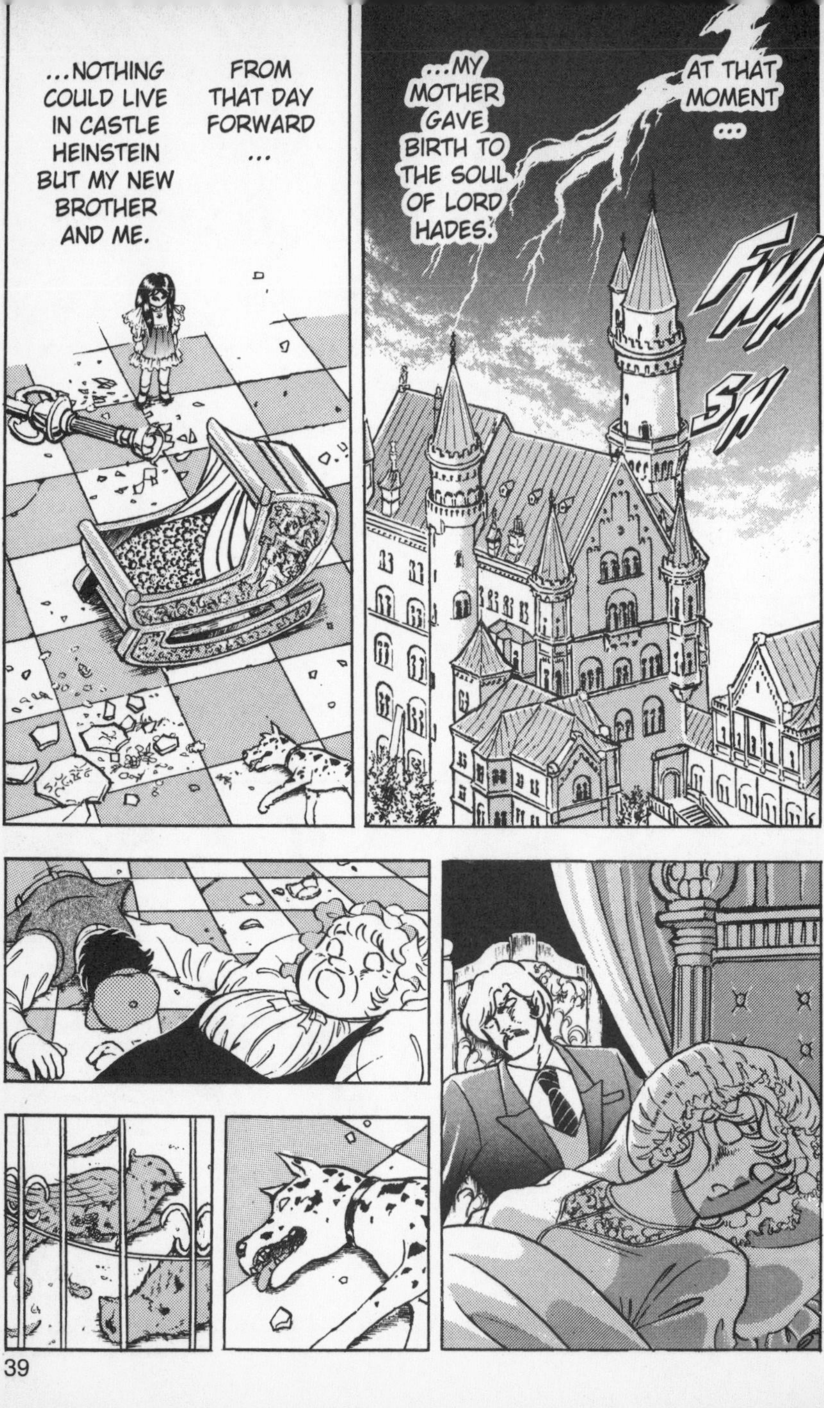
AT THAT MOMENT ...
...MY MOTHER GAVE BIRTH TO THE SOUL OF LORD HADES.
FWA
SH
FROM THAT DAY FORWARD ...
...NOTHING COULD LIVE IN CASTLE HEINSTEIN BUT MY NEW BROTHER AND ME.

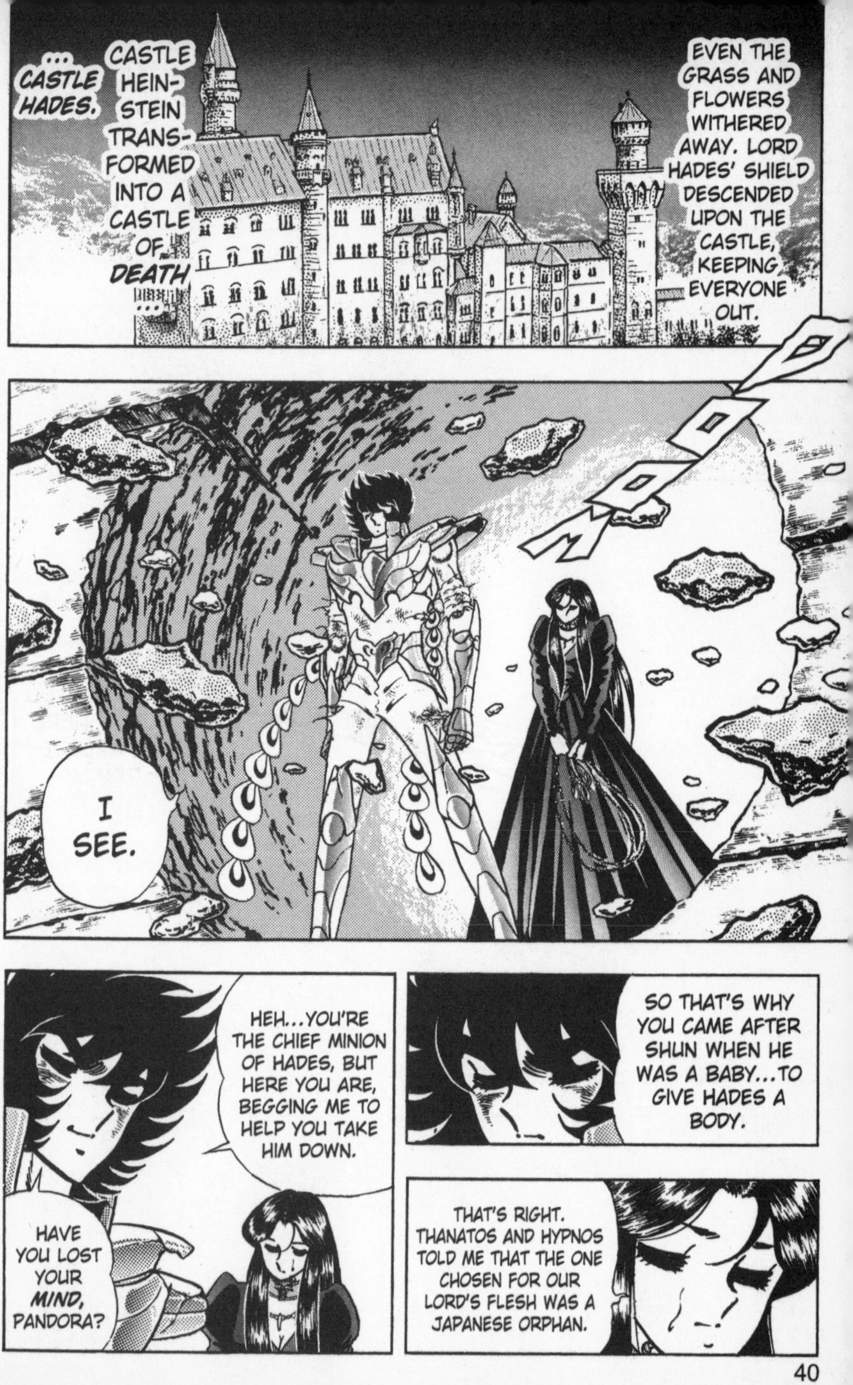
EVEN THE GRASS AND FLOWERS WITHERED AWAY. LORD HADES' SHIELD DESCENDED UPON THE CASTLE, KEEPING EVERYONE OUT.
CASTLE HEIN-STEIN TRANS-FORMED INTO A CASTLE OF *DEATH*...
...CASTLE HADES.
I SEE.
SO THAT'S WHY YOU CAME AFTER SHUN WHEN HE WAS A BABY...TO GIVE HADES A BODY.
THAT'S RIGHT. THANATOS AND HYPNOS TOLD ME THAT THE ONE CHOSEN FOR OUR LORD'S FLESH WAS A JAPANESE ORPHAN.
HEH...YOU'RE THE CHIEF MINION OF HADES, BUT HERE YOU ARE, BEGGING ME TO HELP YOU TAKE HIM DOWN.
HAVE YOU LOST YOUR *MIND*, PANDORA?

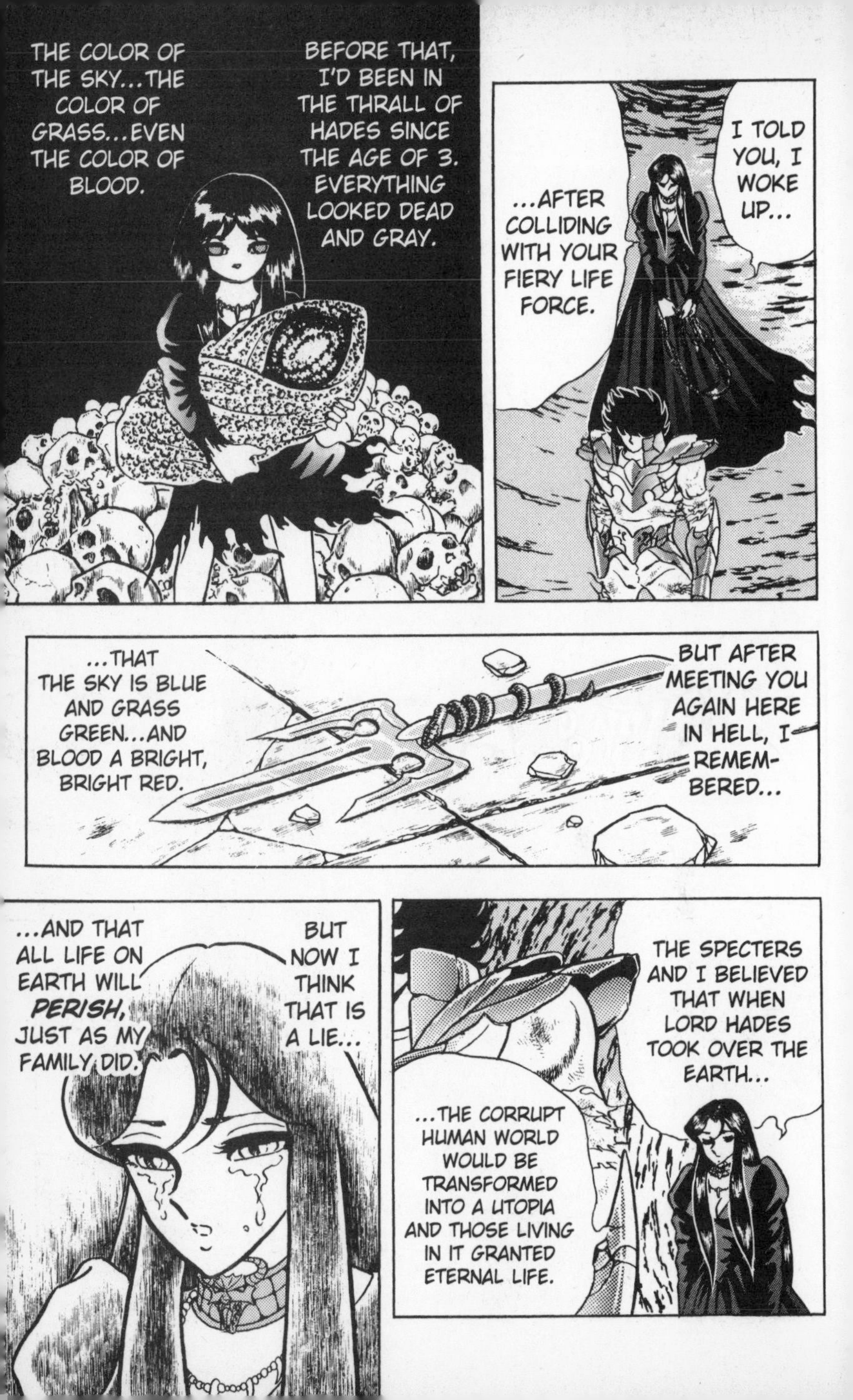
I TOLD YOU, I WOKE UP...
...AFTER COLLIDING WITH YOUR FIERY LIFE FORCE.
BEFORE THAT, I'D BEEN IN THE THRALL OF HADES SINCE THE AGE OF 3. EVERYTHING LOOKED DEAD AND GRAY.
THE COLOR OF THE SKY...THE COLOR OF GRASS...EVEN THE COLOR OF BLOOD.
BUT AFTER MEETING YOU AGAIN HERE IN HELL, I REMEMBERED...
...THAT THE SKY IS BLUE AND GRASS GREEN...AND BLOOD A BRIGHT, BRIGHT RED.
THE SPECTERS AND I BELIEVED THAT WHEN LORD HADES TOOK OVER THE EARTH...
...THE CORRUPT HUMAN WORLD WOULD BE TRANSFORMED INTO A UTOPIA AND THOSE LIVING IN IT GRANTED ETERNAL LIFE.
...AND THAT ALL LIFE ON EARTH WILL *PERISH*, JUST AS MY FAMILY DID.
BUT NOW I THINK THAT IS A LIE...

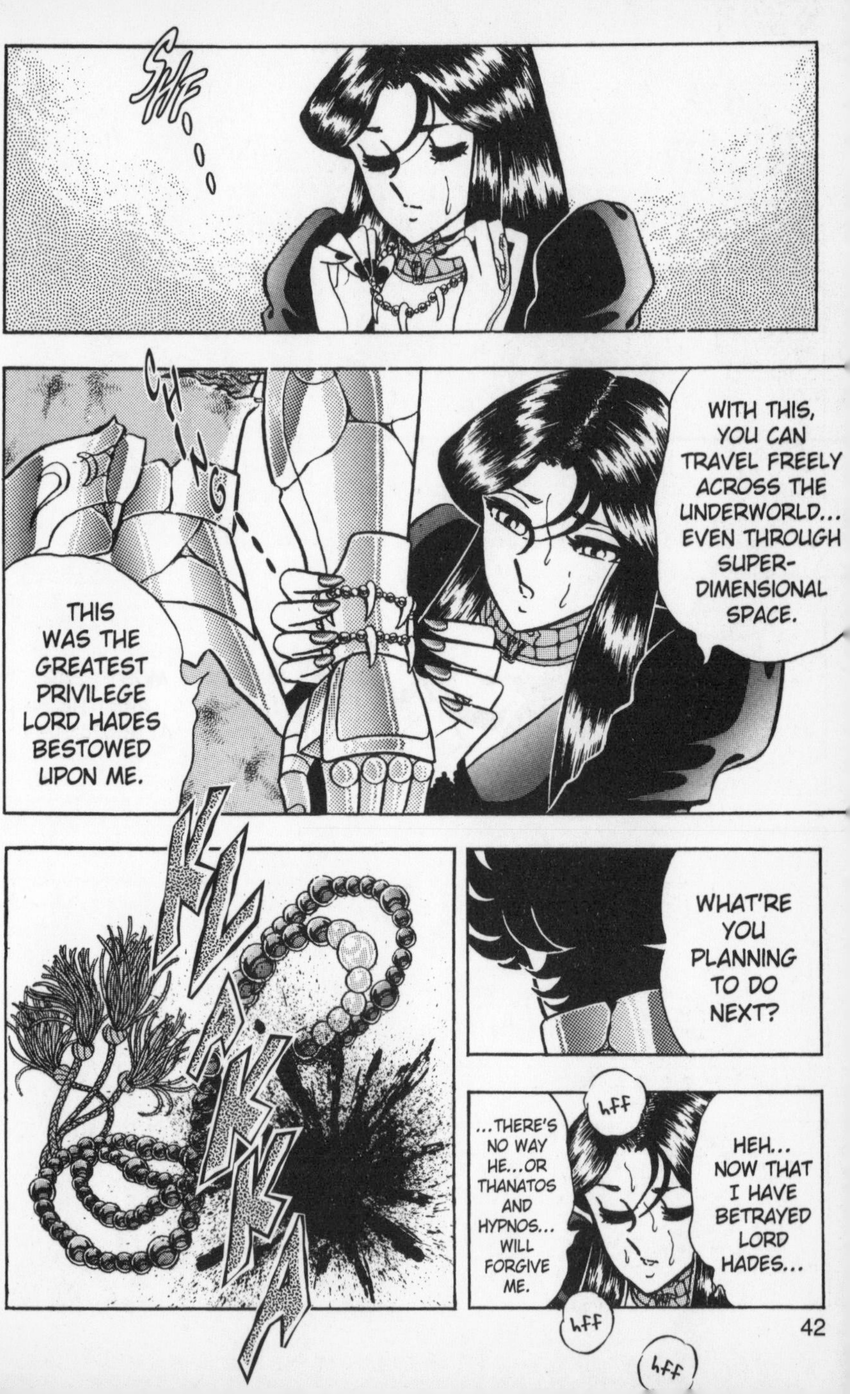
WITH THIS, YOU CAN TRAVEL FREELY ACROSS THE UNDERWORLD... EVEN THROUGH SUPER-DIMENSIONAL SPACE.
CHING
THIS WAS THE GREATEST PRIVILEGE LORD HADES BESTOWED UPON ME.
WHAT'RE YOU PLANNING TO DO NEXT?
hff
HEH... NOW THAT I HAVE BETRAYED LORD HADES...
...THERE'S NO WAY HE...OR THANATOS AND HYPNOS... WILL FORGIVE ME.
hff
hff

READ THIS WAY

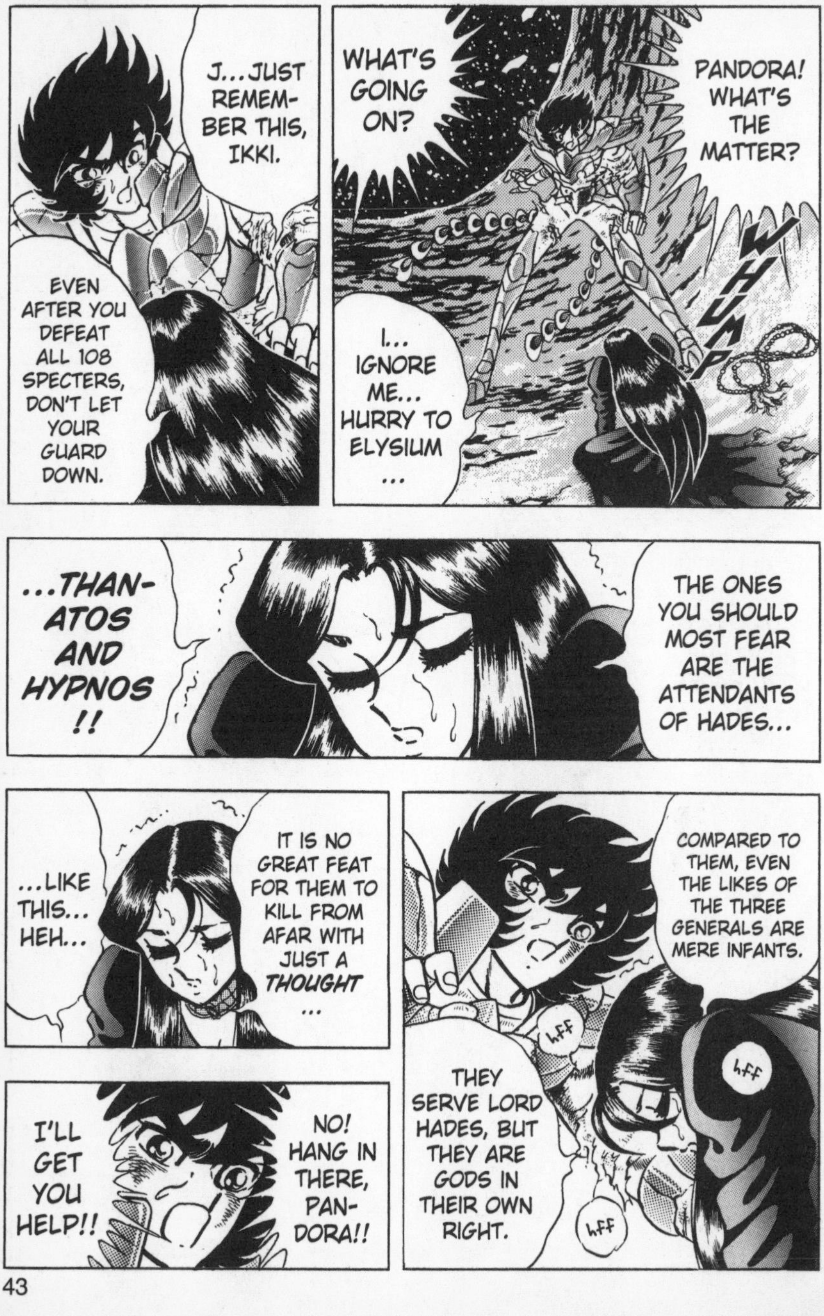
PANDORA! WHAT'S THE MATTER?
WHAT'S GOING ON?
WHUMP
I... IGNORE ME... HURRY TO ELYSIUM ...
J...JUST REMEMBER THIS, IKKI.
EVEN AFTER YOU DEFEAT ALL 108 SPECTERS, DON'T LET YOUR GUARD DOWN.
THE ONES YOU SHOULD MOST FEAR ARE THE ATTENDANTS OF HADES...
...THANATOS AND HYPNOS!!
COMPARED TO THEM, EVEN THE LIKES OF THE THREE GENERALS ARE MERE INFANTS.
hff
hff
THEY SERVE LORD HADES, BUT THEY ARE GODS IN THEIR OWN RIGHT.
hff
IT IS NO GREAT FEAT FOR THEM TO KILL FROM AFAR WITH JUST A THOUGHT ...
...LIKE THIS... HEH...
NO! HANG IN THERE, PANDORA!!
I'LL GET YOU HELP!!

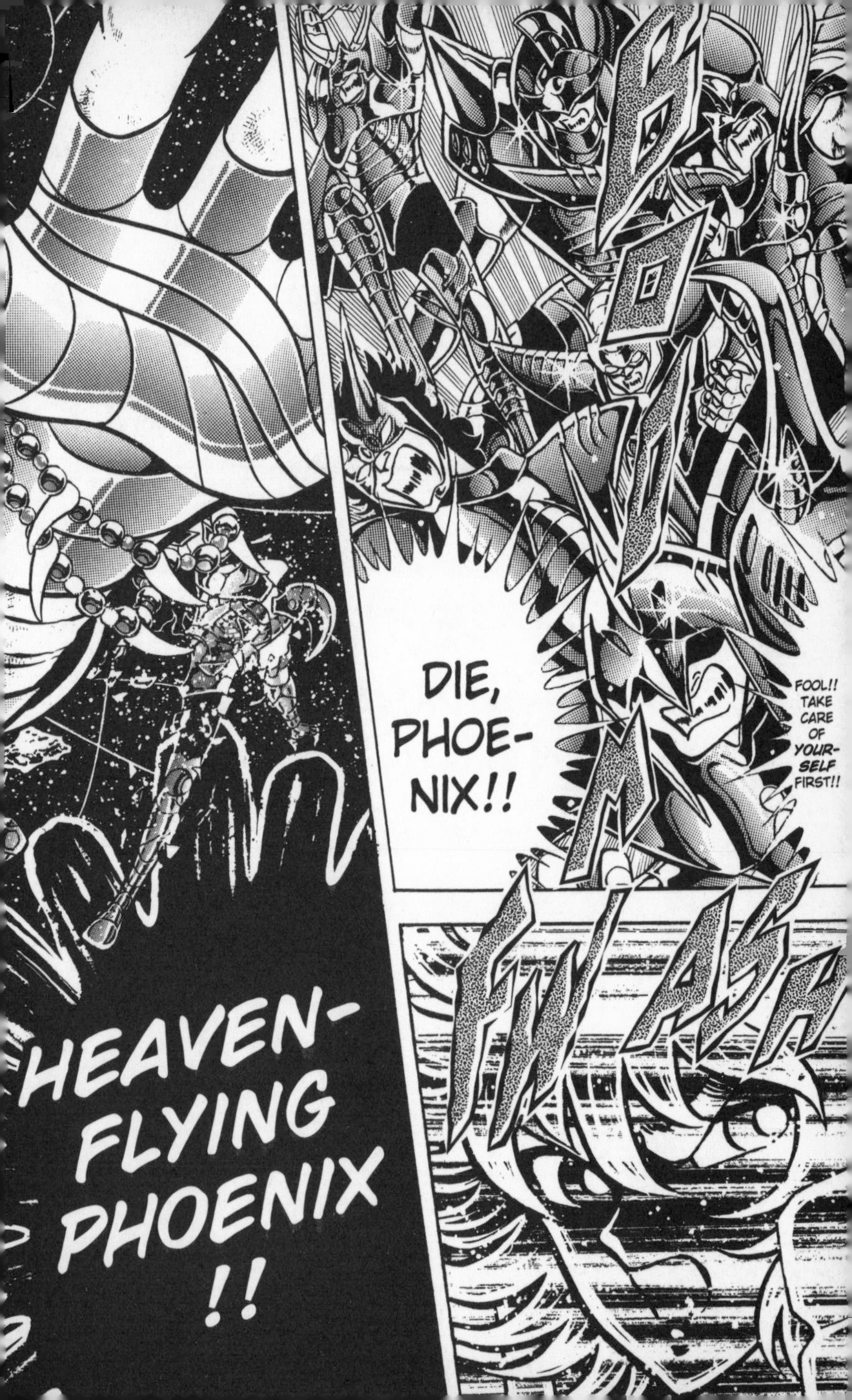
DIE, PHOE-NIX!!
FOOL!! TAKE CARE OF YOURSELF FIRST!!
FWASH
HEAVEN-FLYING PHOENIX!!

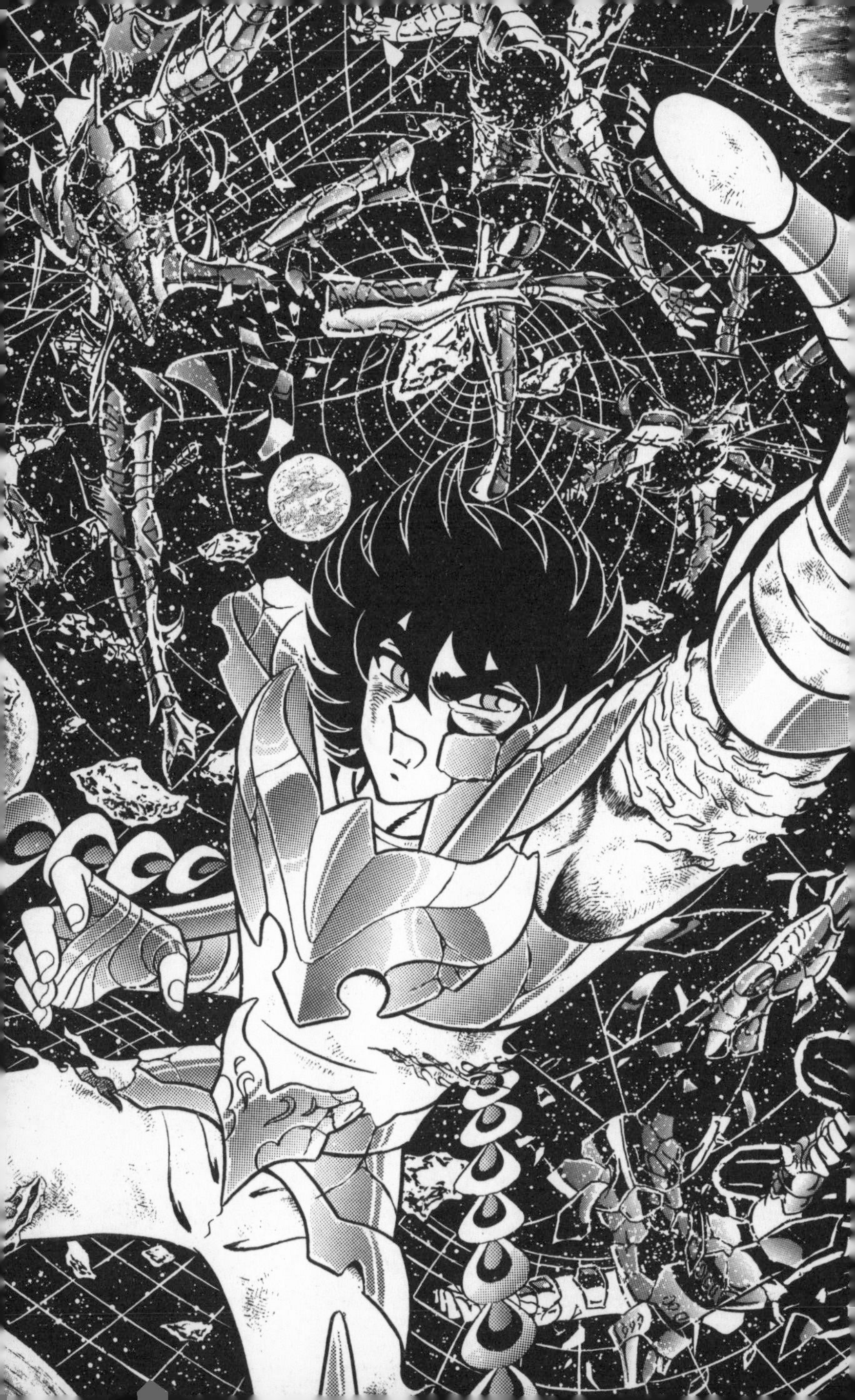

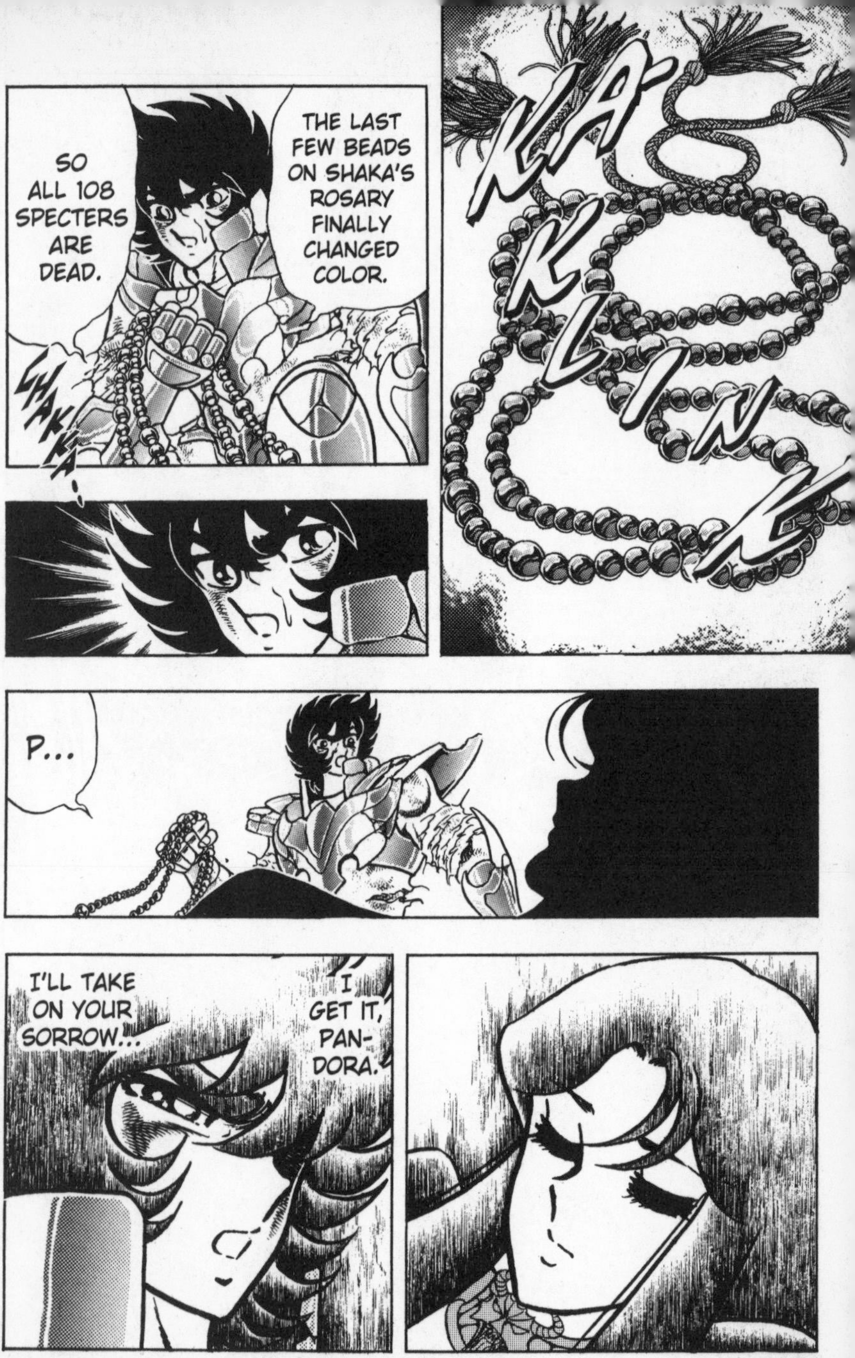
KA-KLINK
THE LAST FEW BEADS ON SHAKA'S ROSARY FINALLY CHANGED COLOR.
SO ALL 108 SPECTERS ARE DEAD.
SHAKA...
P...
I GET IT, PANDORA.
I'LL TAKE ON YOUR SORROW...

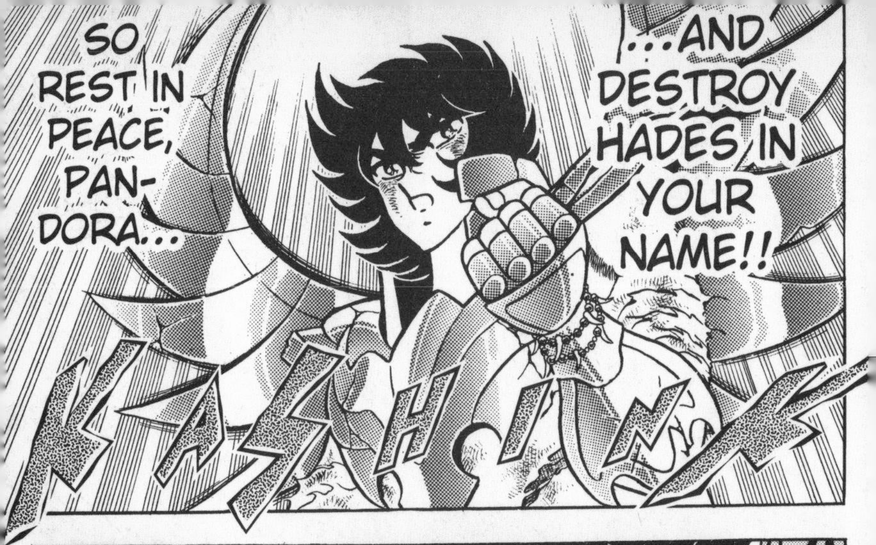
SO REST IN PEACE, PAN-DORA...
...AND DESTROY HADES IN YOUR NAME!!
KASHINK

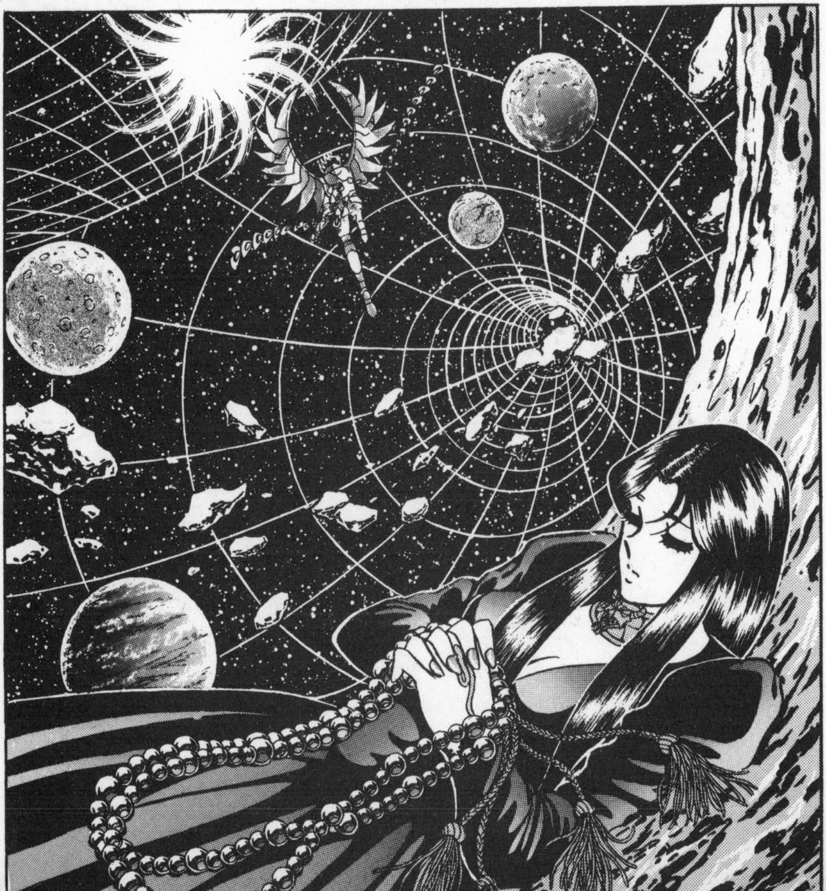

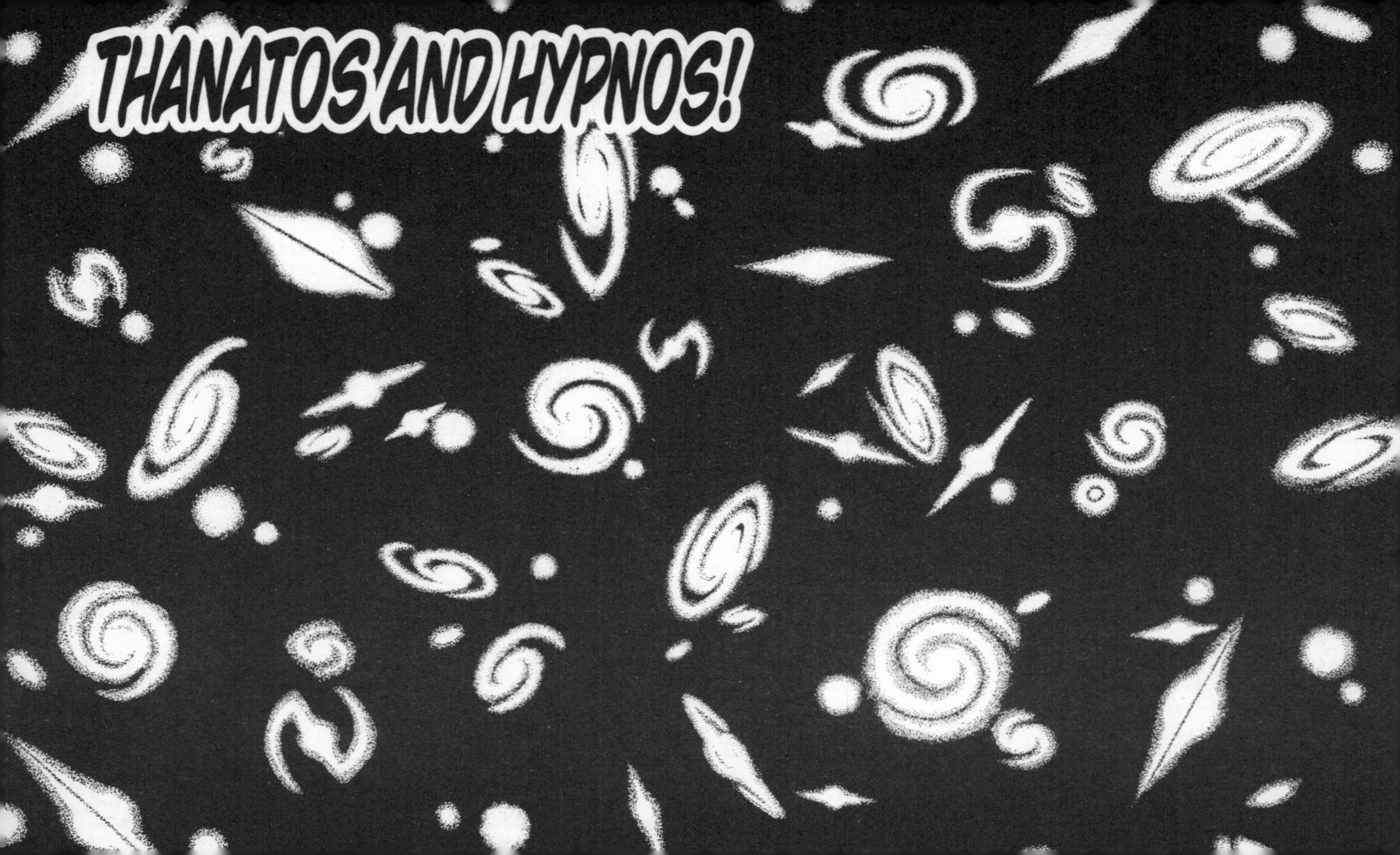
THANATOS AND HYPNOS!

READ THIS WAY

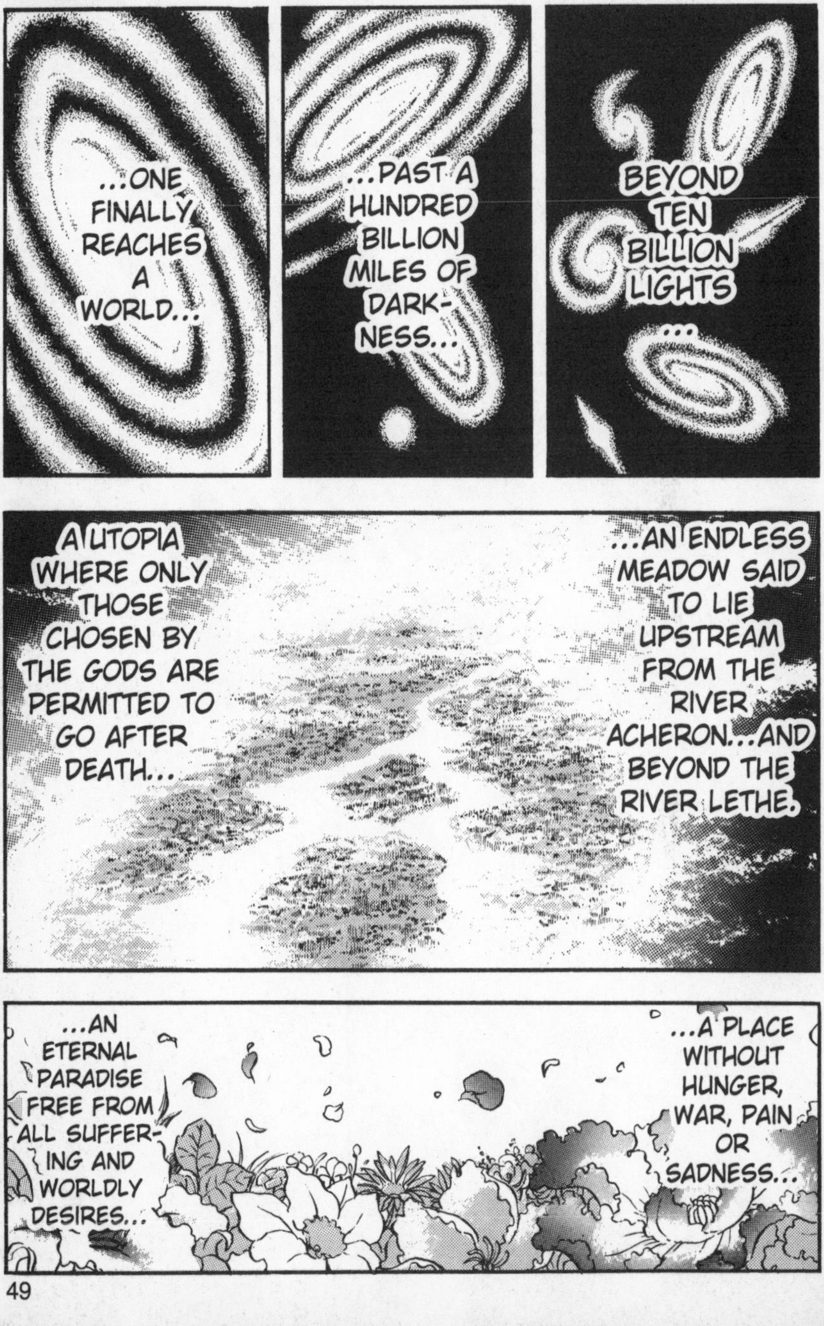
BEYOND TEN BILLION LIGHTS...
...PAST A HUNDRED BILLION MILES OF DARK-NESS...
...ONE FINALLY REACHES A WORLD...
...AN ENDLESS MEADOW SAID TO LIE UPSTREAM FROM THE RIVER ACHERON...AND BEYOND THE RIVER LETHE.
A UTOPIA WHERE ONLY THOSE CHOSEN BY THE GODS ARE PERMITTED TO GO AFTER DEATH...
...A PLACE WITHOUT HUNGER, WAR, PAIN OR SADNESS...
...AN ETERNAL PARADISE FREE FROM ALL SUFFER-ING AND WORLDLY DESIRES...

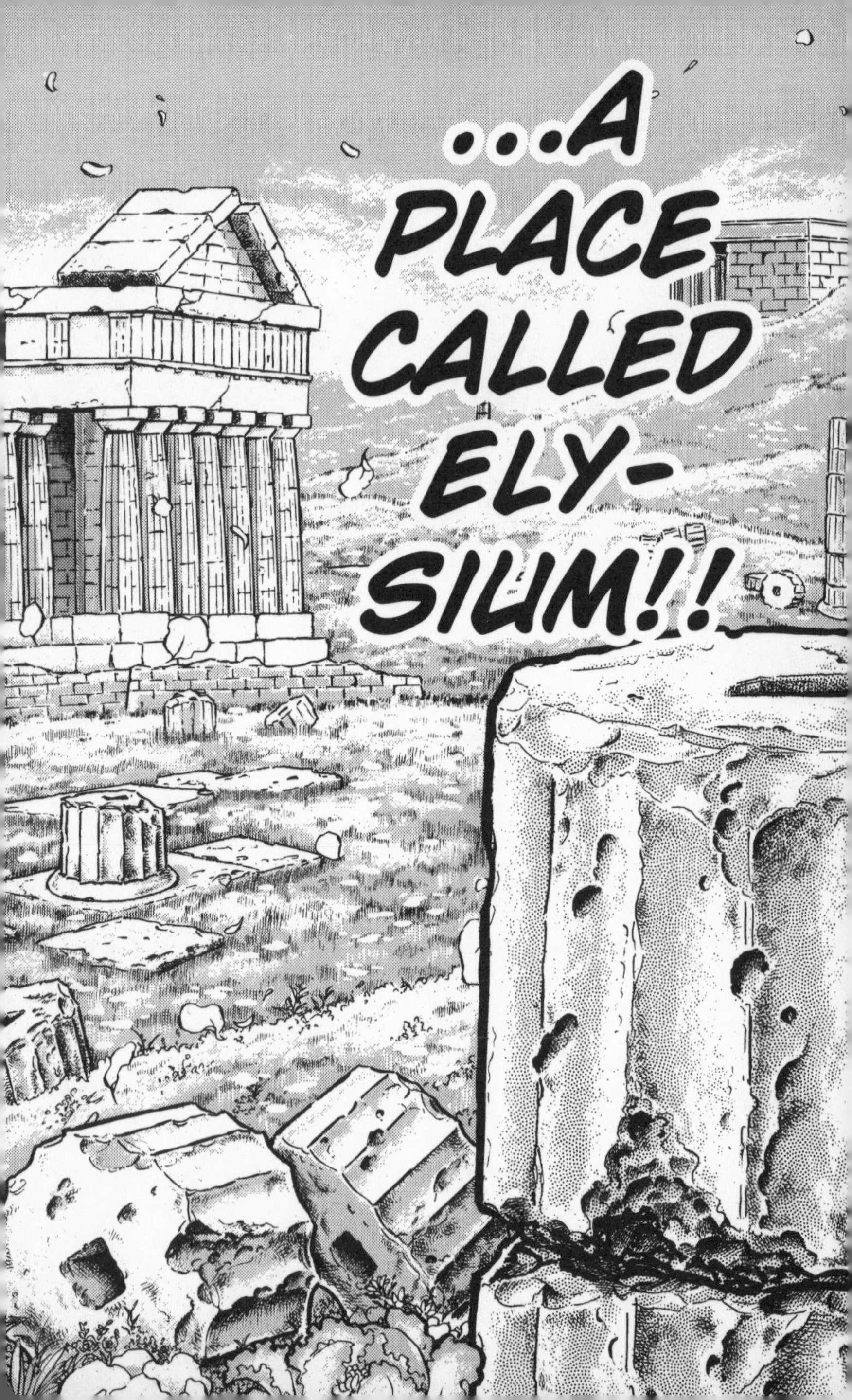
...A PLACE CALLED ELY-SIUM!!

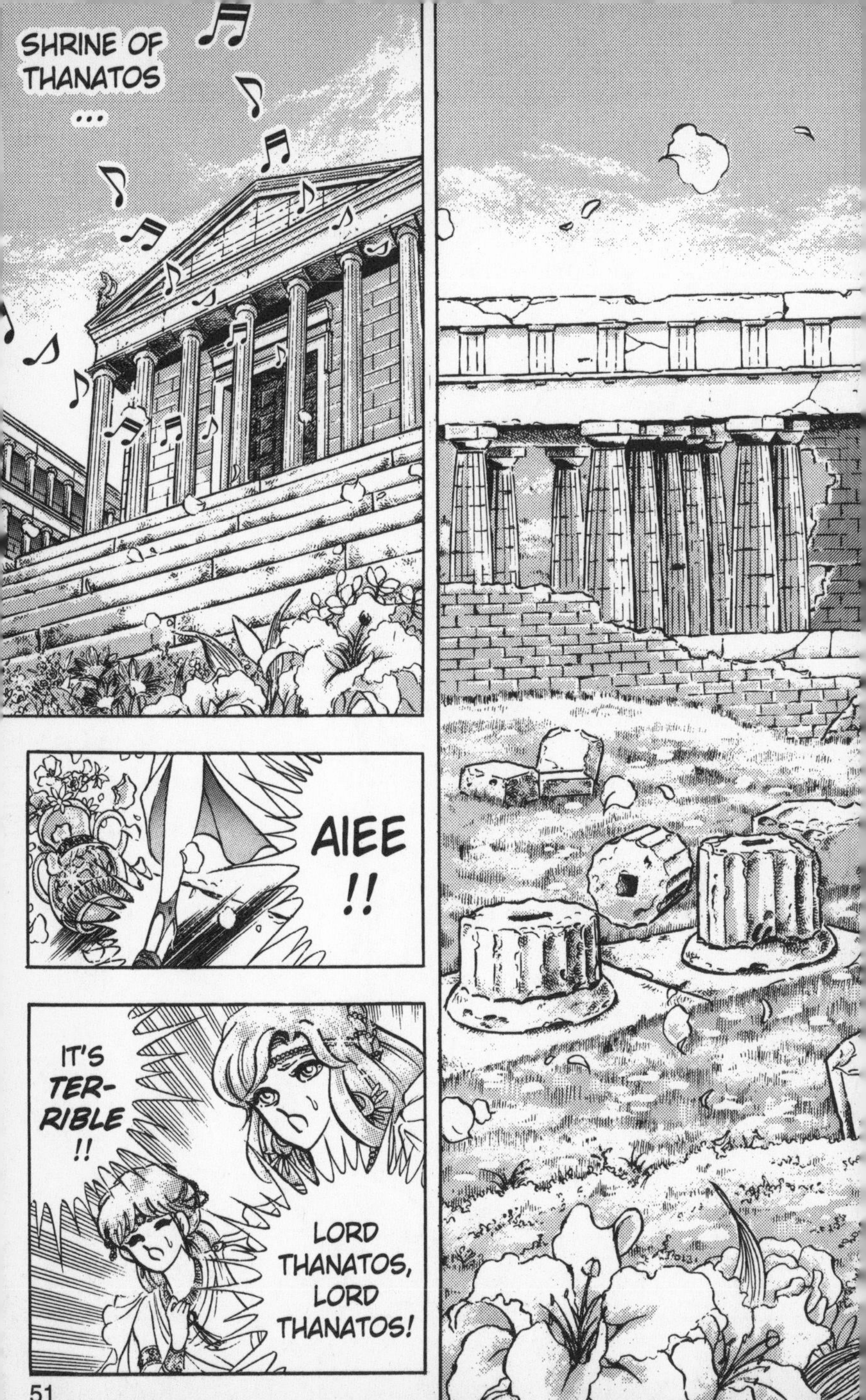
SHRINE OF THANATOS ...
AIEE !!
IT'S TER-RIBLE !!
LORD THANATOS, LORD THANATOS!

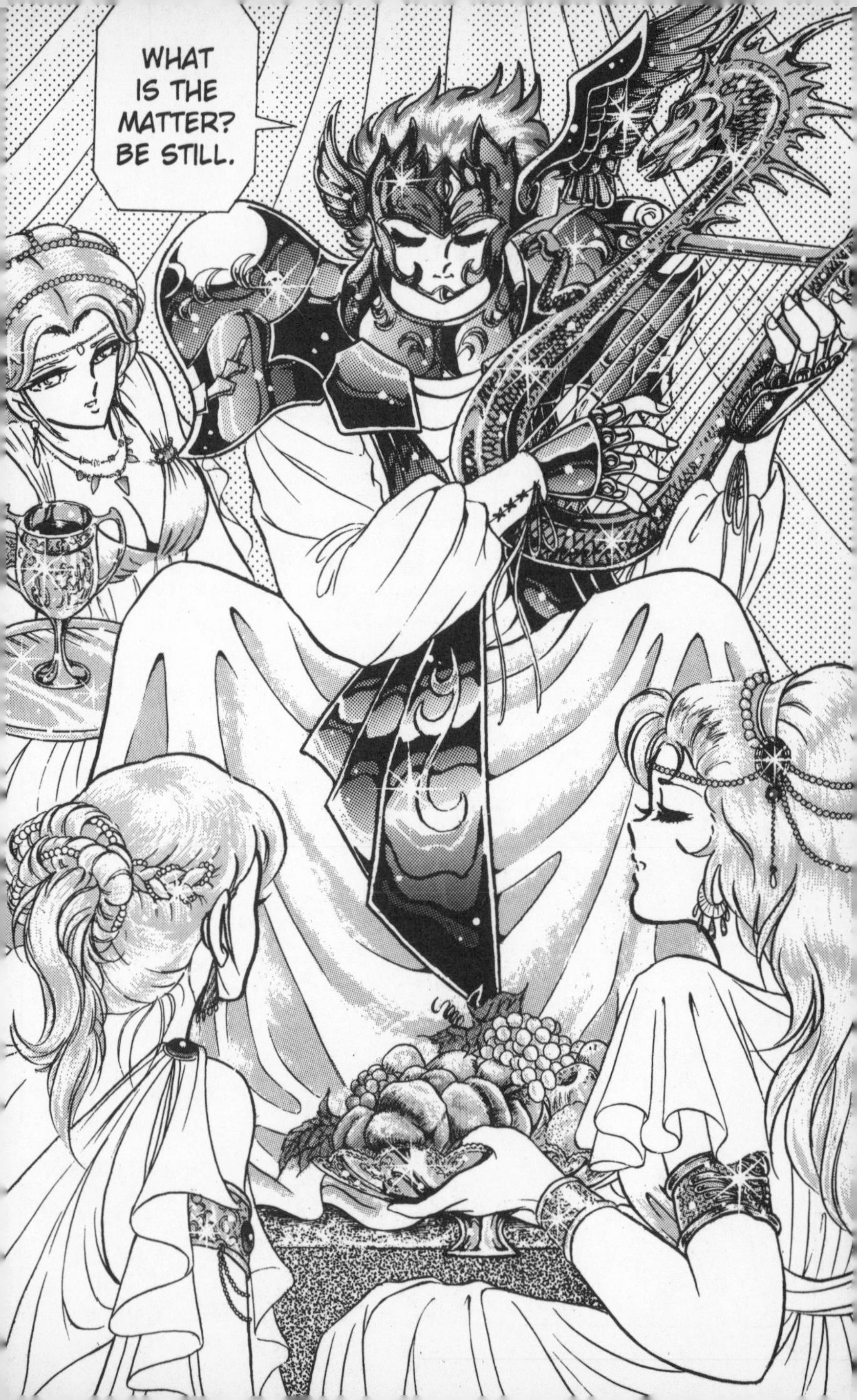
WHAT IS THE MATTER? BE STILL.

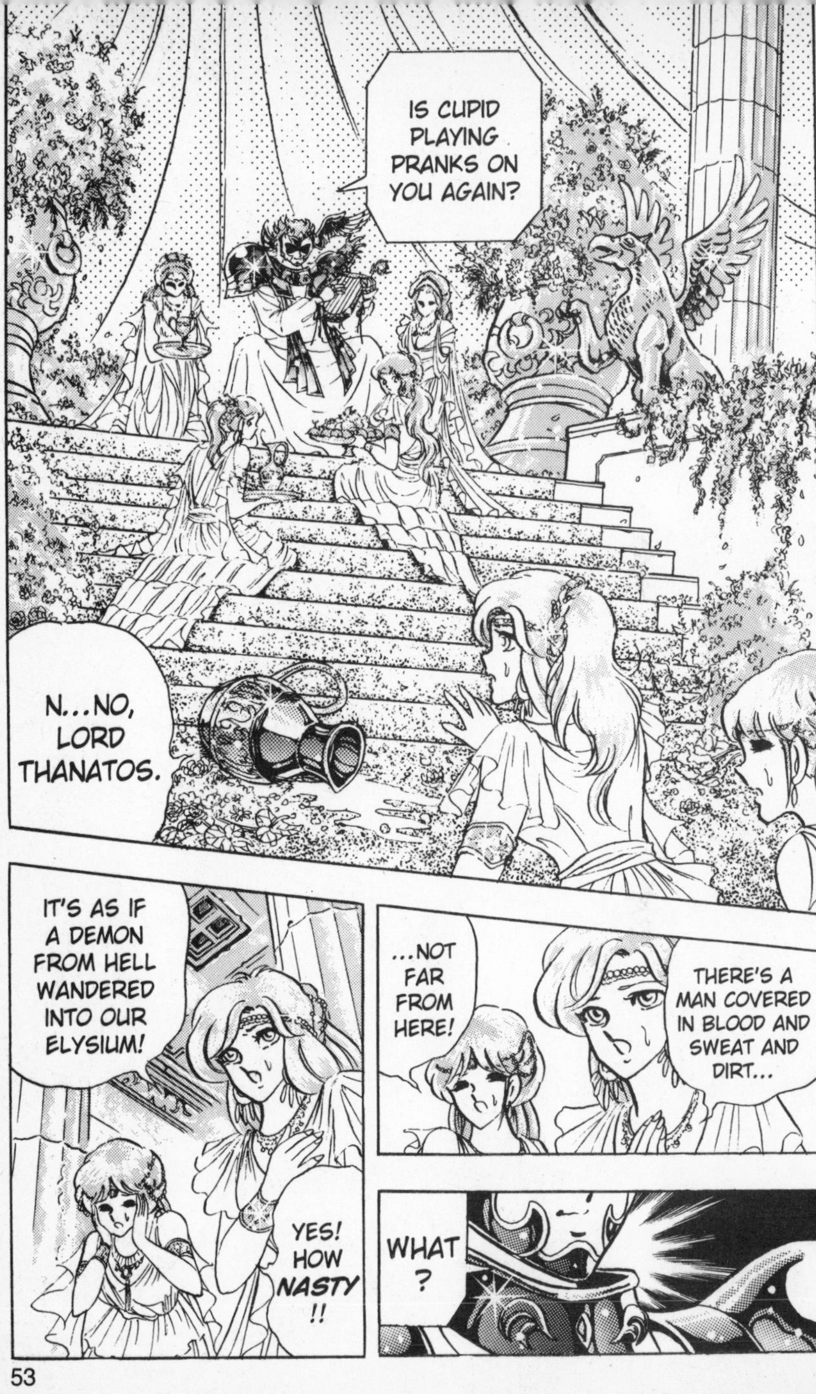
IS CUPID PLAYING PRANKS ON YOU AGAIN?
N...NO, LORD THANATOS.
THERE'S A MAN COVERED IN BLOOD AND SWEAT AND DIRT...
...NOT FAR FROM HERE!
WHAT?
IT'S AS IF A DEMON FROM HELL WANDERED INTO OUR ELYSIUM!
YES! HOW NASTY!!

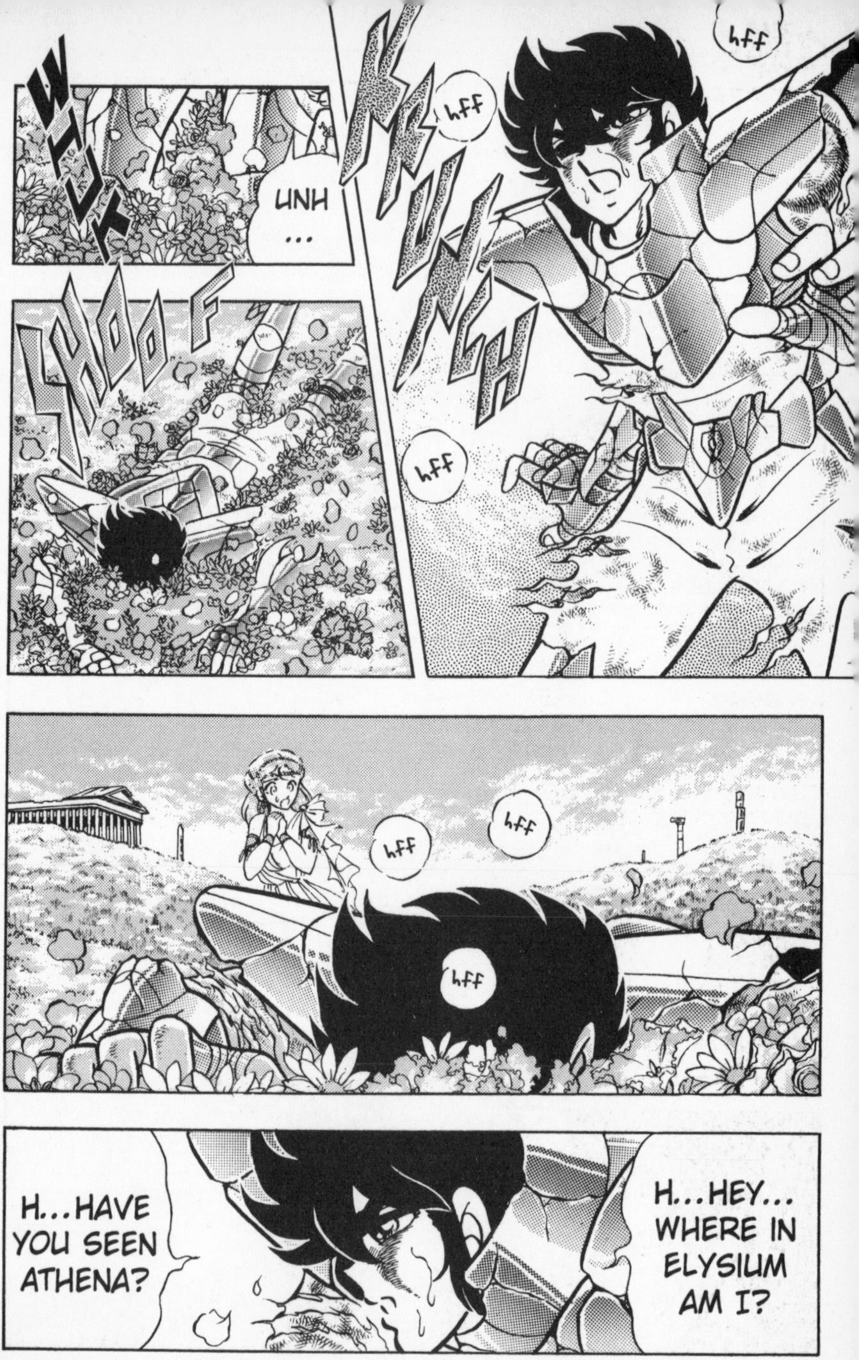
hff
KRUNCH
hff
hff
WHUK
UNH ...
WHOOF
hff
hff
hff
H...HEY... WHERE IN ELYSIUM AM I?
H...HAVE YOU SEEN ATHENA?

READ THIS WAY

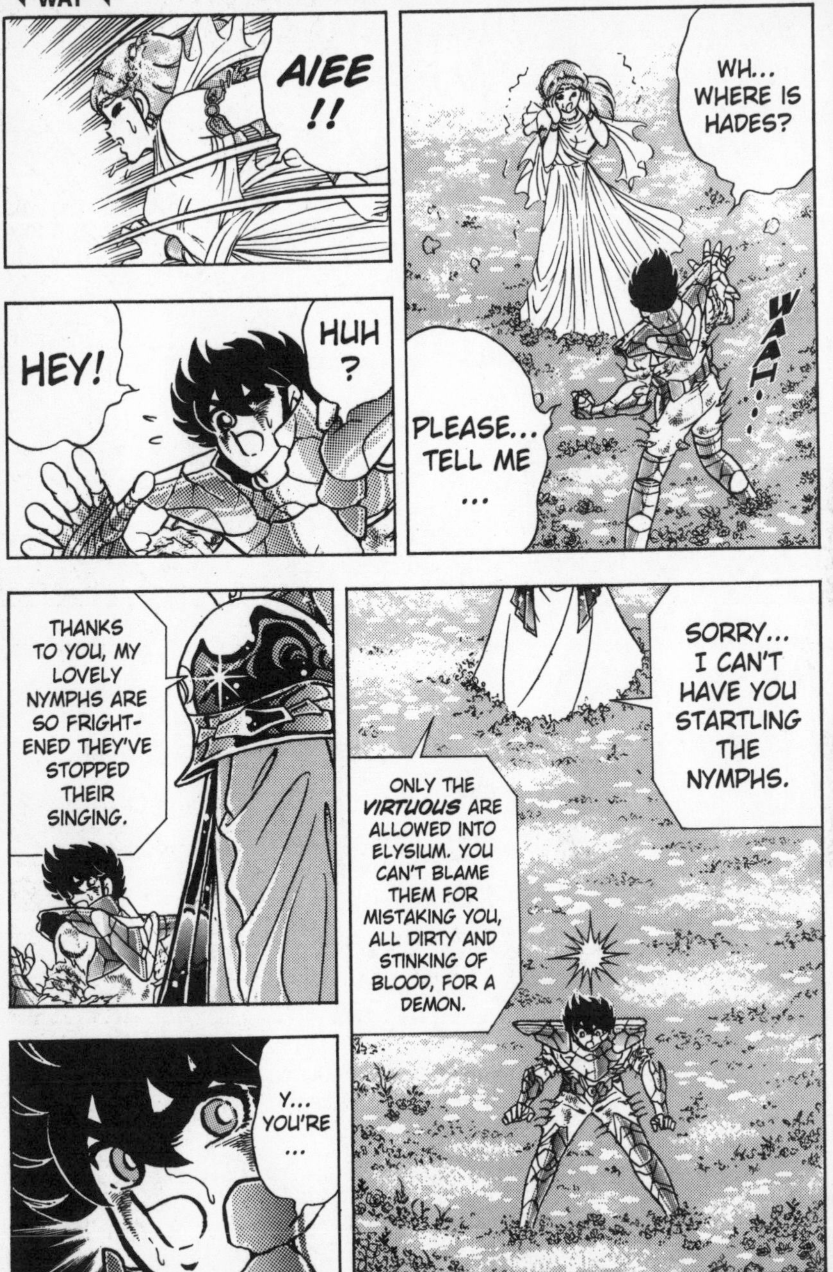
WH... WHERE IS HADES?
PLEASE... TELL ME ...
WAAH...
AIEE !!
HUH ?
HEY!
SORRY... I CAN'T HAVE YOU STARTLING THE NYMPHS.
ONLY THE *VIRTUOUS* ARE ALLOWED INTO ELYSIUM. YOU CAN'T BLAME THEM FOR MISTAKING YOU, ALL DIRTY AND STINKING OF BLOOD, FOR A DEMON.
THANKS TO YOU, MY LOVELY NYMPHS ARE SO FRIGHT-ENED THEY'VE STOPPED THEIR SINGING.
Y... YOU'RE ...

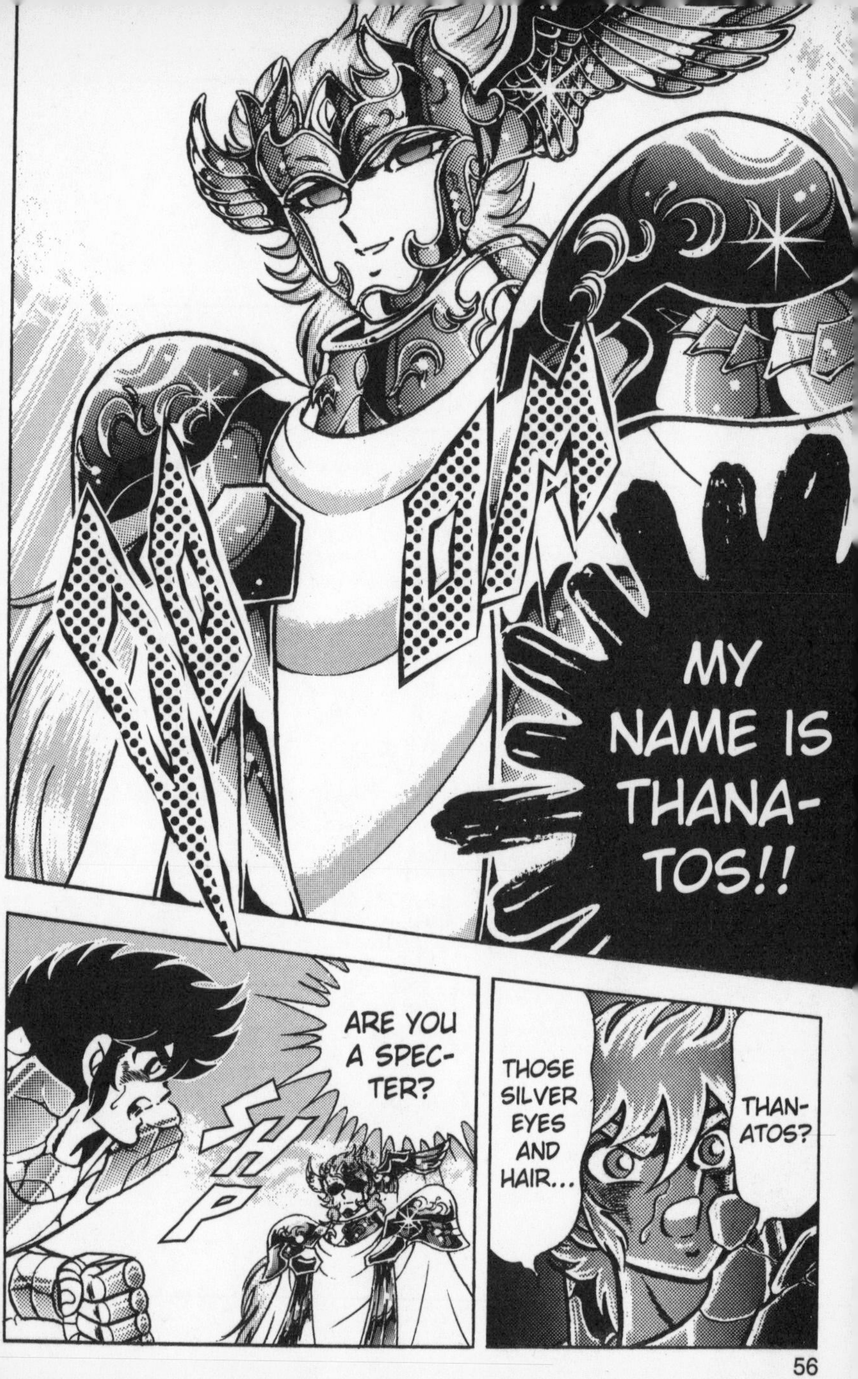
MY NAME IS THANATOS!!
THANATOS?
THOSE SILVER EYES AND HAIR...
ARE YOU A SPECTER?

READ THIS WAY

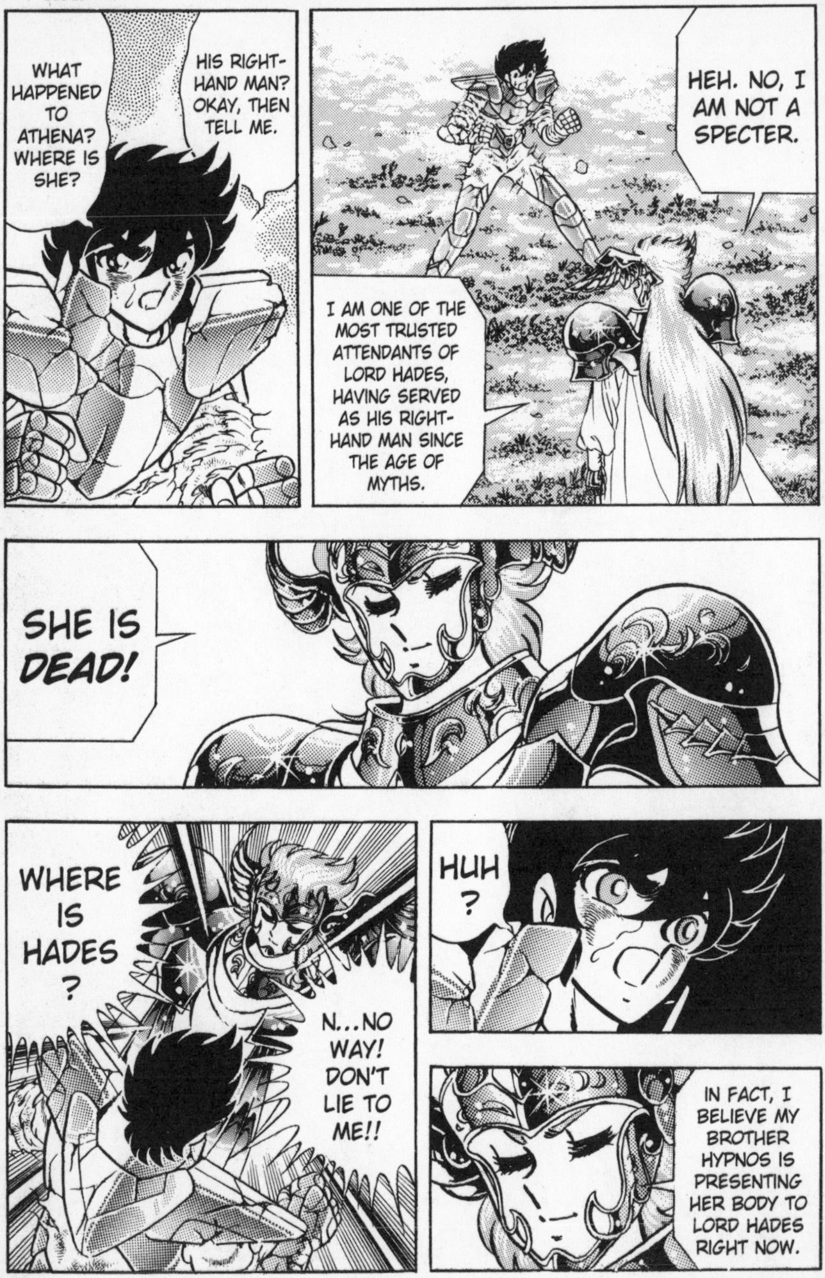

HEH. NO, I AM NOT A SPECTER.
I AM ONE OF THE MOST TRUSTED ATTENDANTS OF LORD HADES, HAVING SERVED AS HIS RIGHT-HAND MAN SINCE THE AGE OF MYTHS.
HIS RIGHT-HAND MAN? OKAY, THEN TELL ME.
WHAT HAPPENED TO ATHENA? WHERE IS SHE?
SHE IS *DEAD!*
HUH?
IN FACT, I BELIEVE MY BROTHER HYPNOS IS PRESENTING HER BODY TO LORD HADES RIGHT NOW.
WHERE IS HADES?
N...NO WAY! DON'T LIE TO ME!!

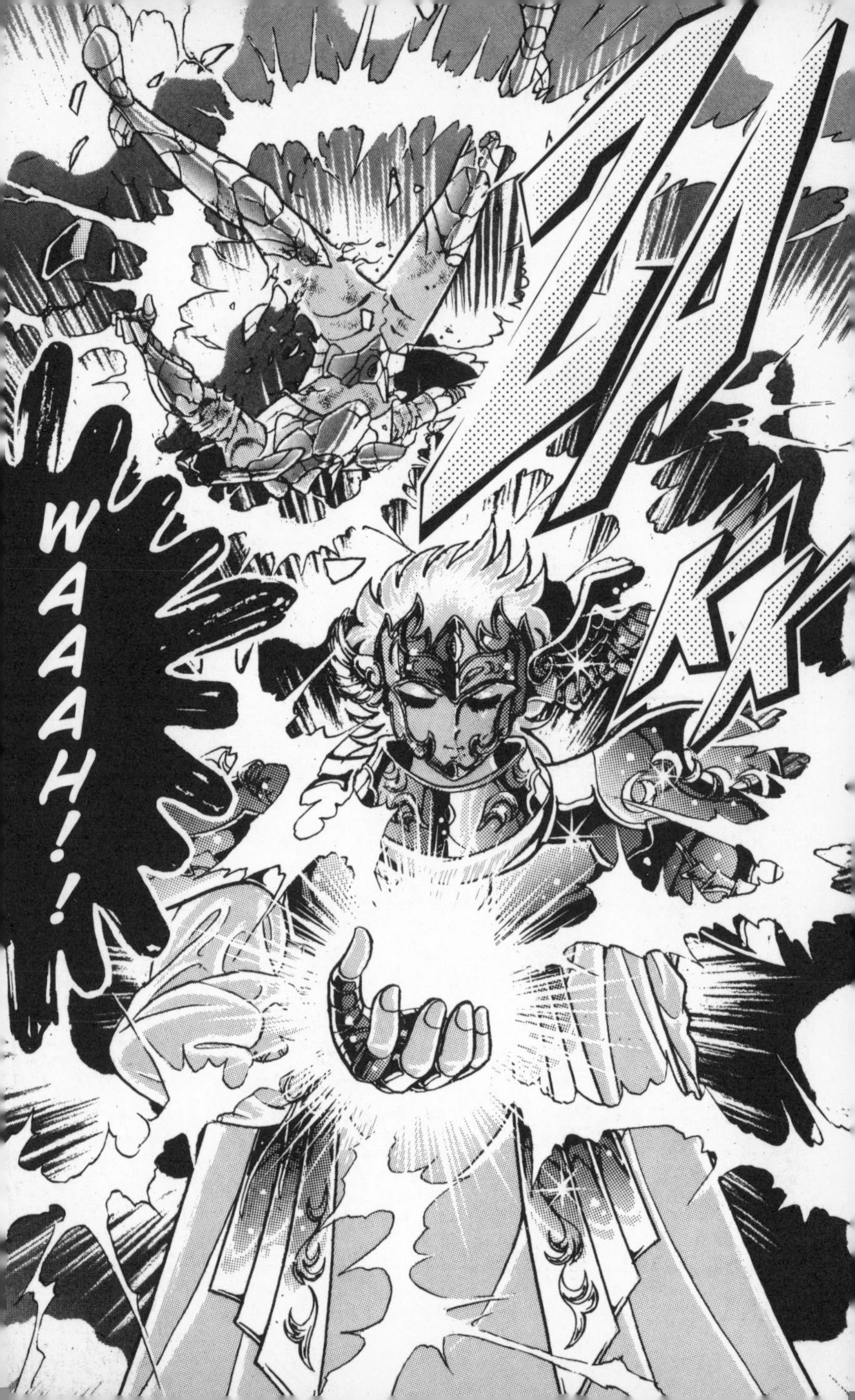
WAAAAH!!

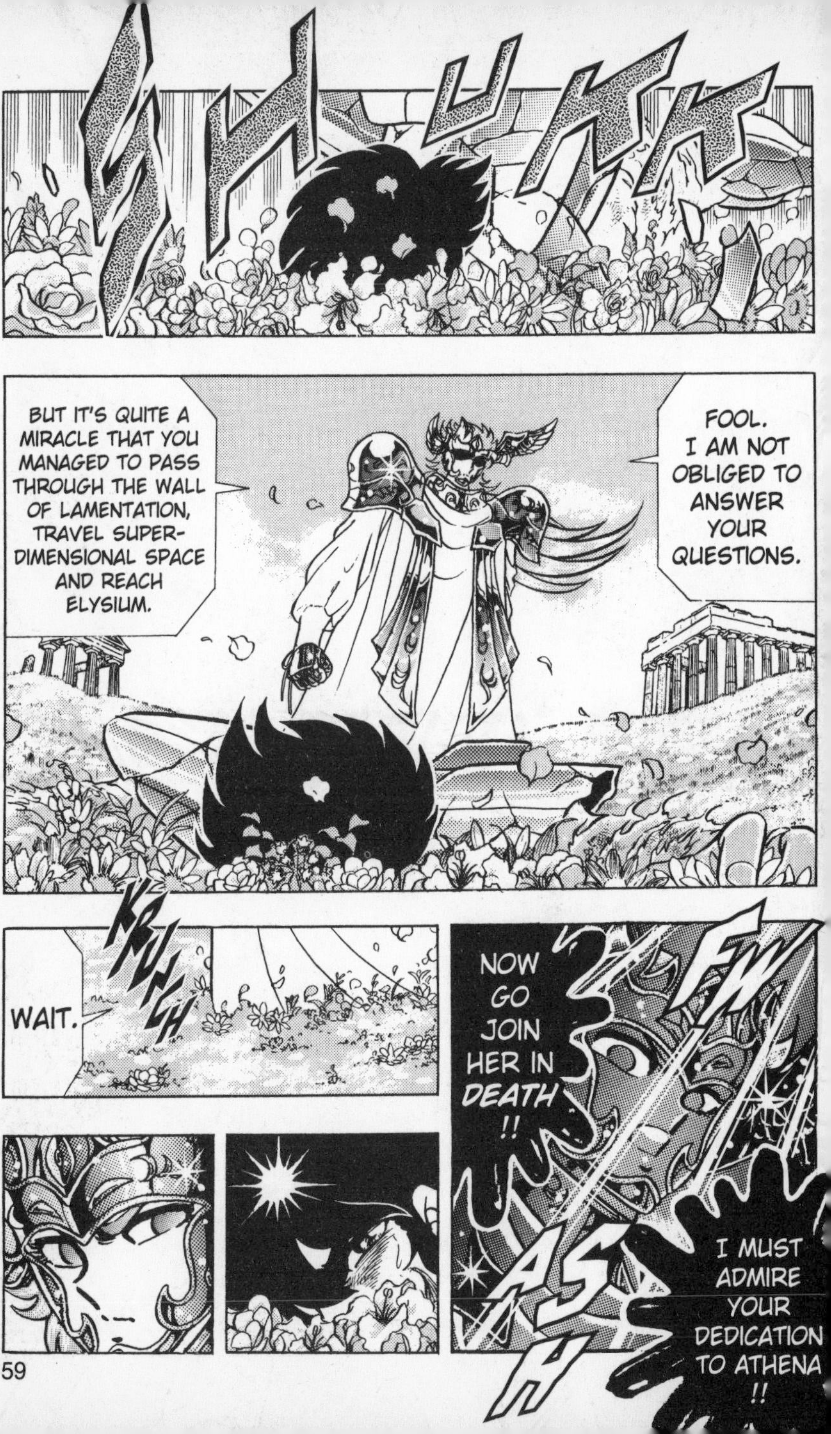
FOOL.
I AM NOT OBLIGED TO ANSWER YOUR QUESTIONS.
BUT IT'S QUITE A MIRACLE THAT YOU MANAGED TO PASS THROUGH THE WALL OF LAMENTATION, TRAVEL SUPER-DIMENSIONAL SPACE AND REACH ELYSIUM.
FWASH
I MUST ADMIRE YOUR DEDICATION TO ATHENA!!
NOW GO JOIN HER IN *DEATH*!!
KRUNCH
WAIT.

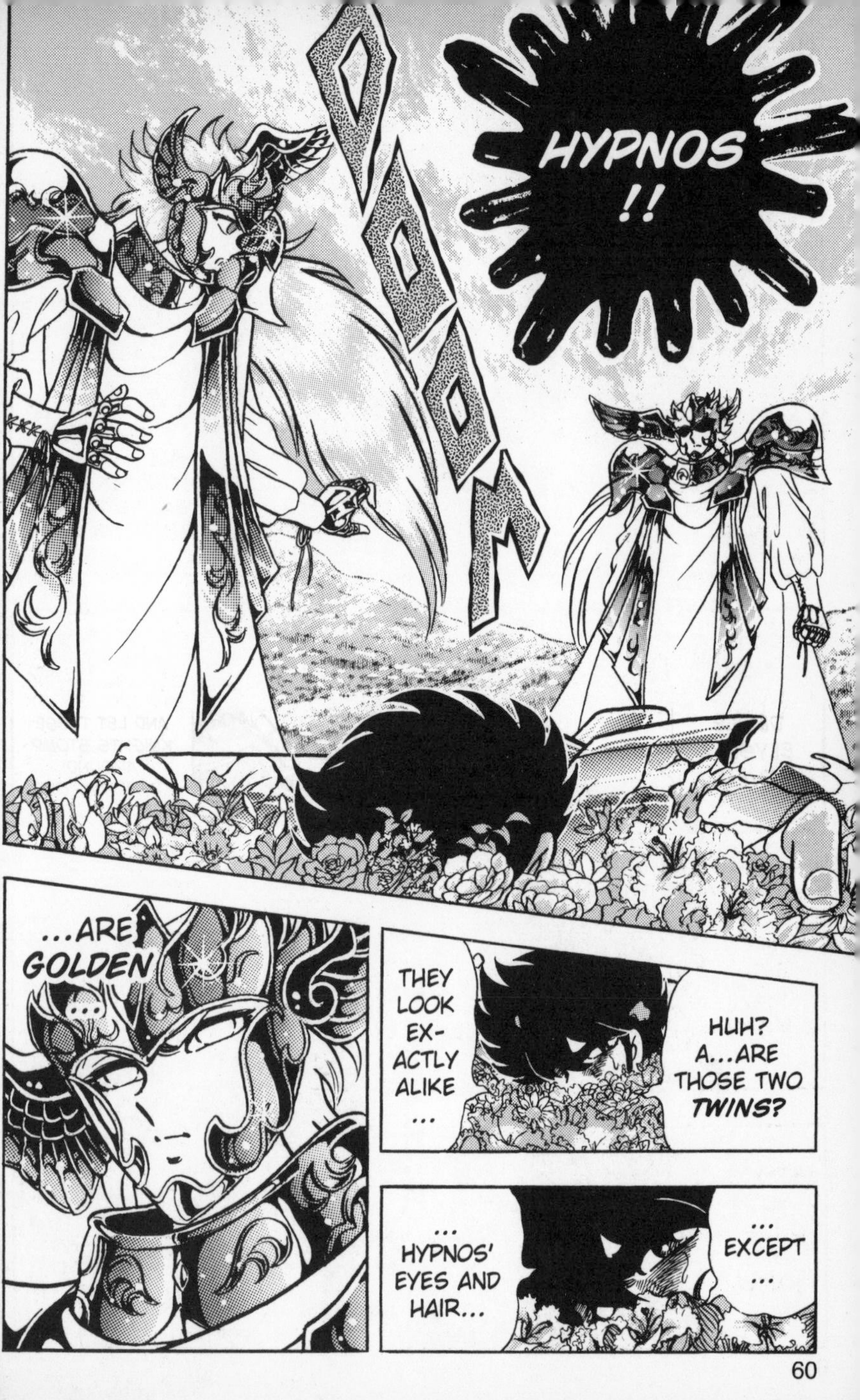
HYPNOS !!
HUH? A...ARE THOSE TWO TWINS?
THEY LOOK EX-ACTLY ALIKE ...
... EXCEPT ...
... HYPNOS' EYES AND HAIR...
...ARE GOLDEN
...

READ THIS WAY

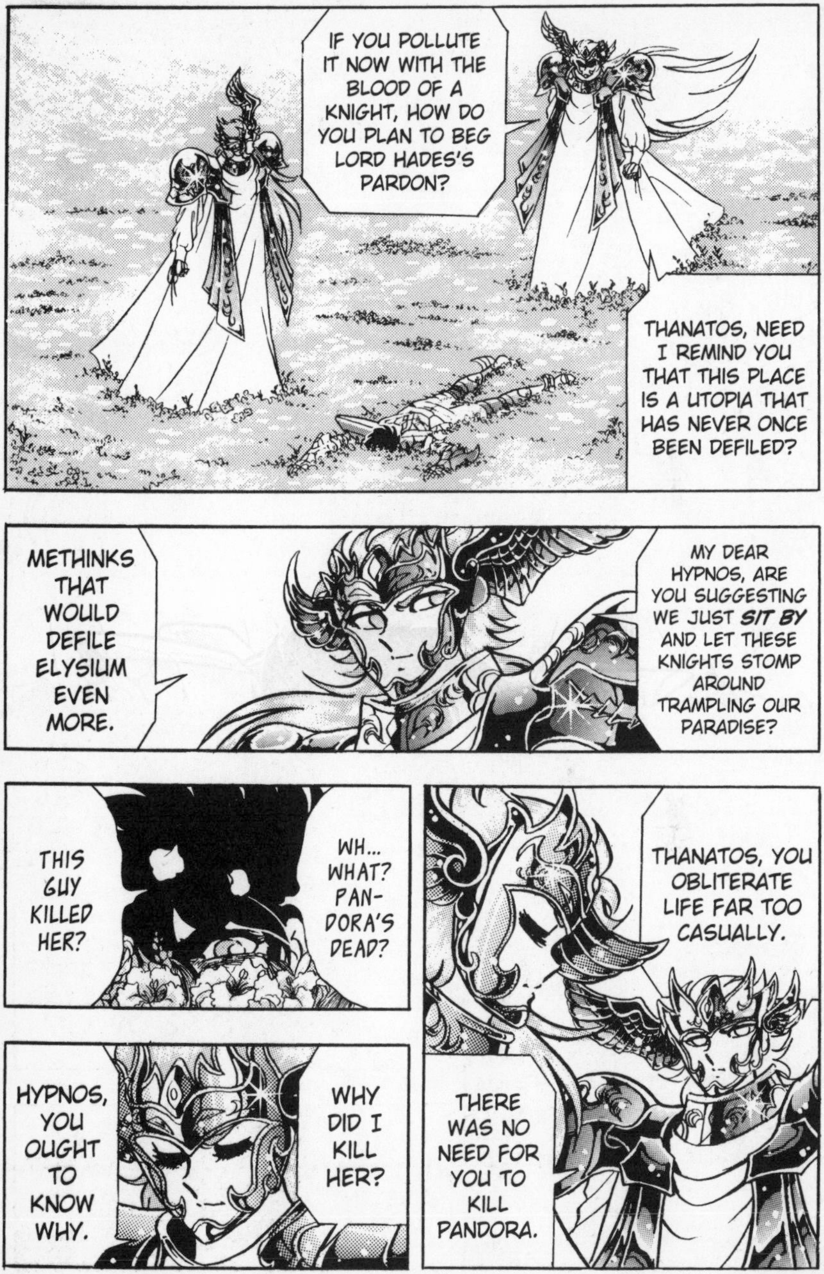
THANATOS, NEED I REMIND YOU THAT THIS PLACE IS A UTOPIA THAT HAS NEVER ONCE BEEN DEFILED?
IF YOU POLLUTE IT NOW WITH THE BLOOD OF A KNIGHT, HOW DO YOU PLAN TO BEG LORD HADES'S PARDON?
MY DEAR HYPNOS, ARE YOU SUGGESTING WE JUST *SIT BY* AND LET THESE KNIGHTS STOMP AROUND TRAMPLING OUR PARADISE?
METHINKS THAT WOULD DEFILE ELYSIUM EVEN MORE.
THANATOS, YOU OBLITERATE LIFE FAR TOO CASUALLY.
THERE WAS NO NEED FOR YOU TO KILL PANDORA.
WH... WHAT? PAN-DORA'S DEAD?
THIS GUY KILLED HER?
WHY DID I KILL HER?
HYPNOS, YOU OUGHT TO KNOW WHY.

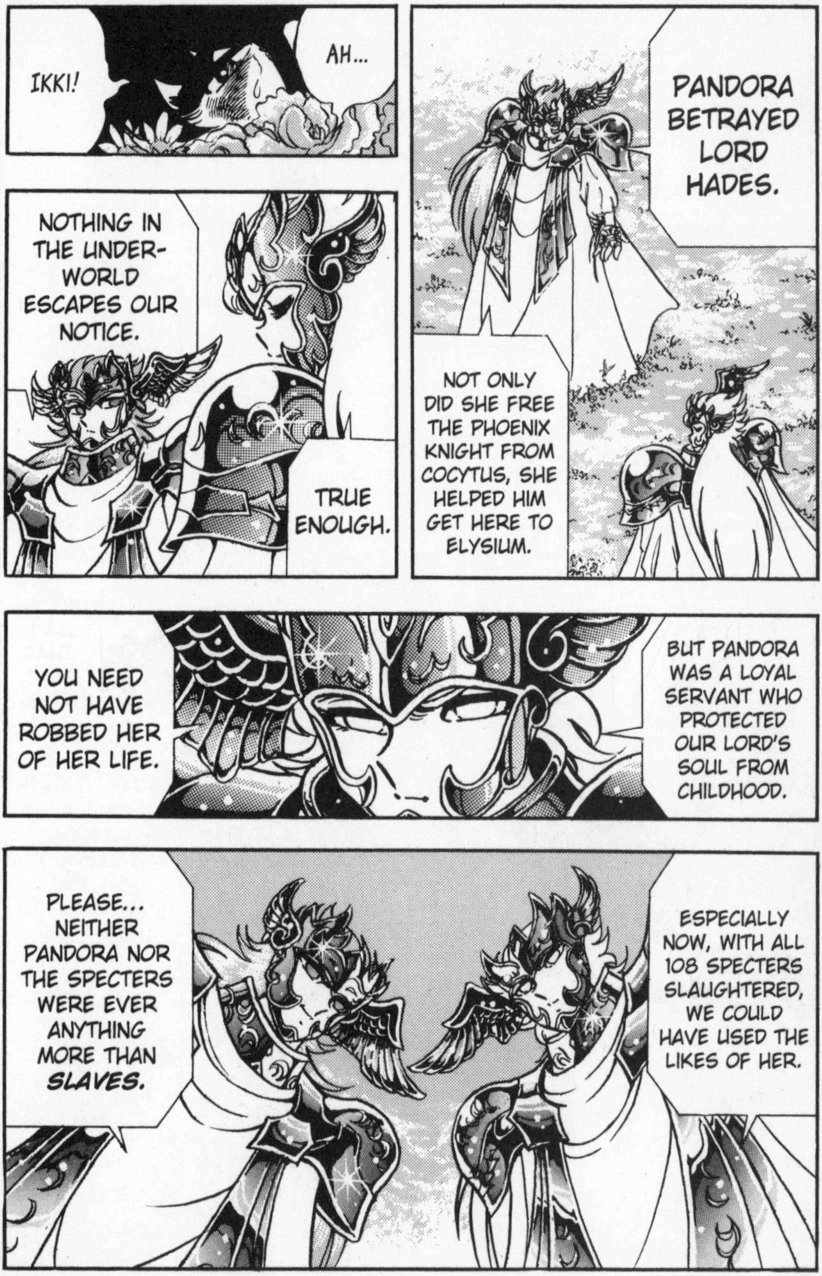
PANDORA BETRAYED LORD HADES.
NOT ONLY DID SHE FREE THE PHOENIX KNIGHT FROM COCYTUS, SHE HELPED HIM GET HERE TO ELYSIUM.
AH...
IKKI!
NOTHING IN THE UNDER-WORLD ESCAPES OUR NOTICE.
TRUE ENOUGH.
BUT PANDORA WAS A LOYAL SERVANT WHO PROTECTED OUR LORD'S SOUL FROM CHILDHOOD.
YOU NEED NOT HAVE ROBBED HER OF HER LIFE.
ESPECIALLY NOW, WITH ALL 108 SPECTERS SLAUGHTERED, WE COULD HAVE USED THE LIKES OF HER.
PLEASE... NEITHER PANDORA NOR THE SPECTERS WERE EVER ANYTHING MORE THAN *SLAVES.*

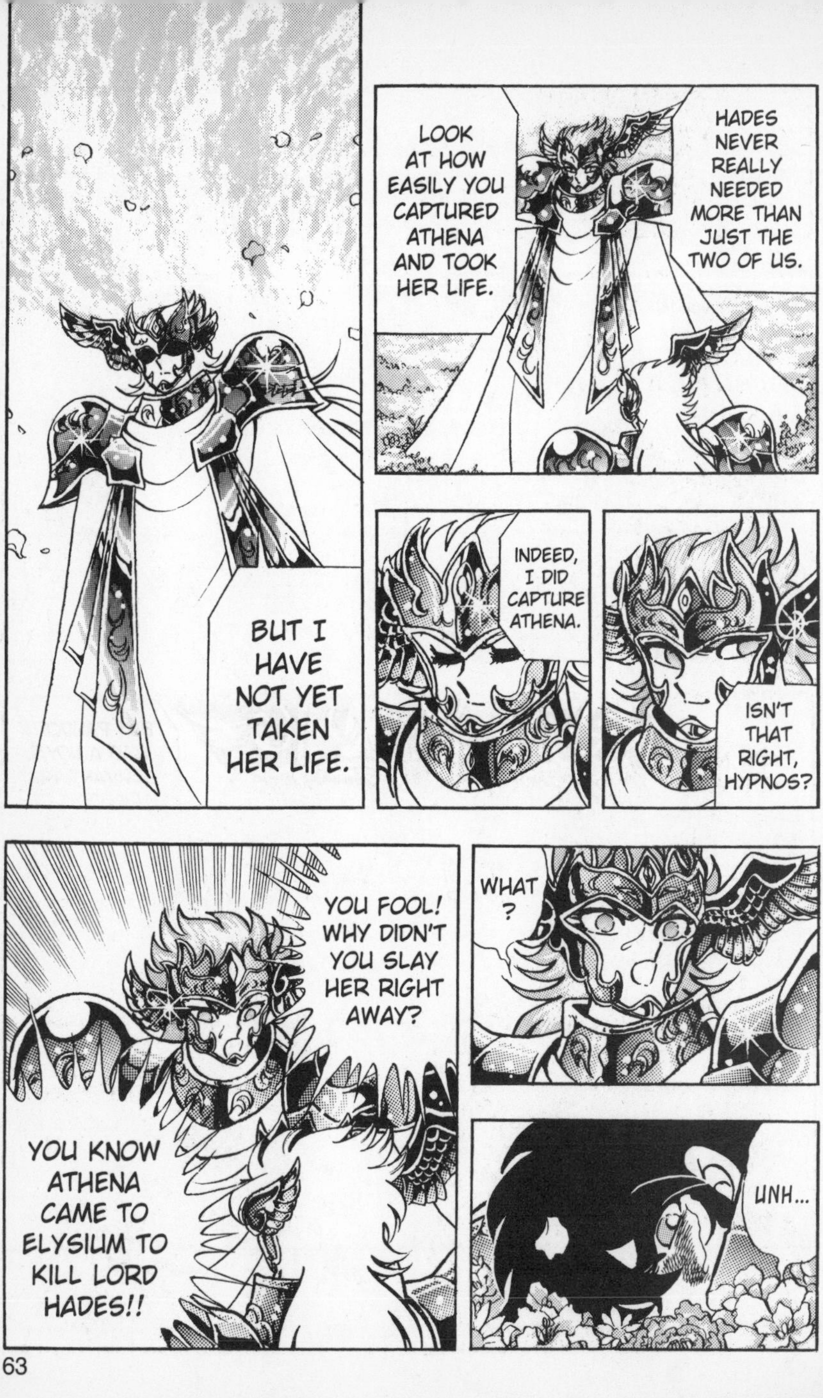
HADES NEVER REALLY NEEDED MORE THAN JUST THE TWO OF US.
LOOK AT HOW EASILY YOU CAPTURED ATHENA AND TOOK HER LIFE.
ISN'T THAT RIGHT, HYPNOS?
INDEED, I DID CAPTURE ATHENA.
BUT I HAVE NOT YET TAKEN HER LIFE.
WHAT?
UNH...
YOU FOOL! WHY DIDN'T YOU SLAY HER RIGHT AWAY?
YOU KNOW ATHENA CAME TO ELYSIUM TO KILL LORD HADES!!

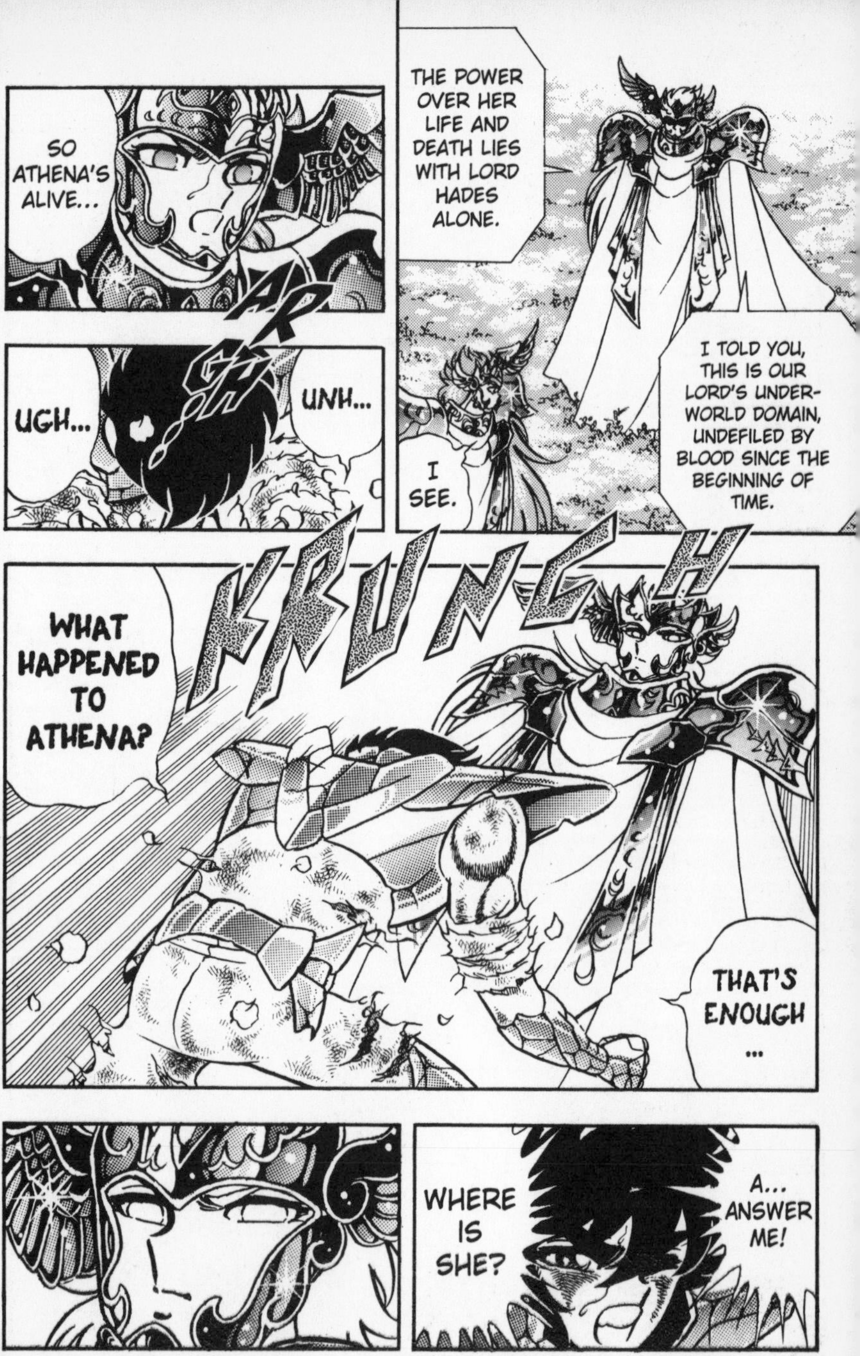
THE POWER OVER HER LIFE AND DEATH LIES WITH LORD HADES ALONE.
I TOLD YOU, THIS IS OUR LORD'S UNDER-WORLD DOMAIN, UNDEFILED BY BLOOD SINCE THE BEGINNING OF TIME.
I SEE.
SO ATHENA'S ALIVE...
ARGH
UNH...
UGH...
KRUNCH
WHAT HAPPENED TO ATHENA?
THAT'S ENOUGH ...
A... ANSWER ME!
WHERE IS SHE?

READ THIS WAY

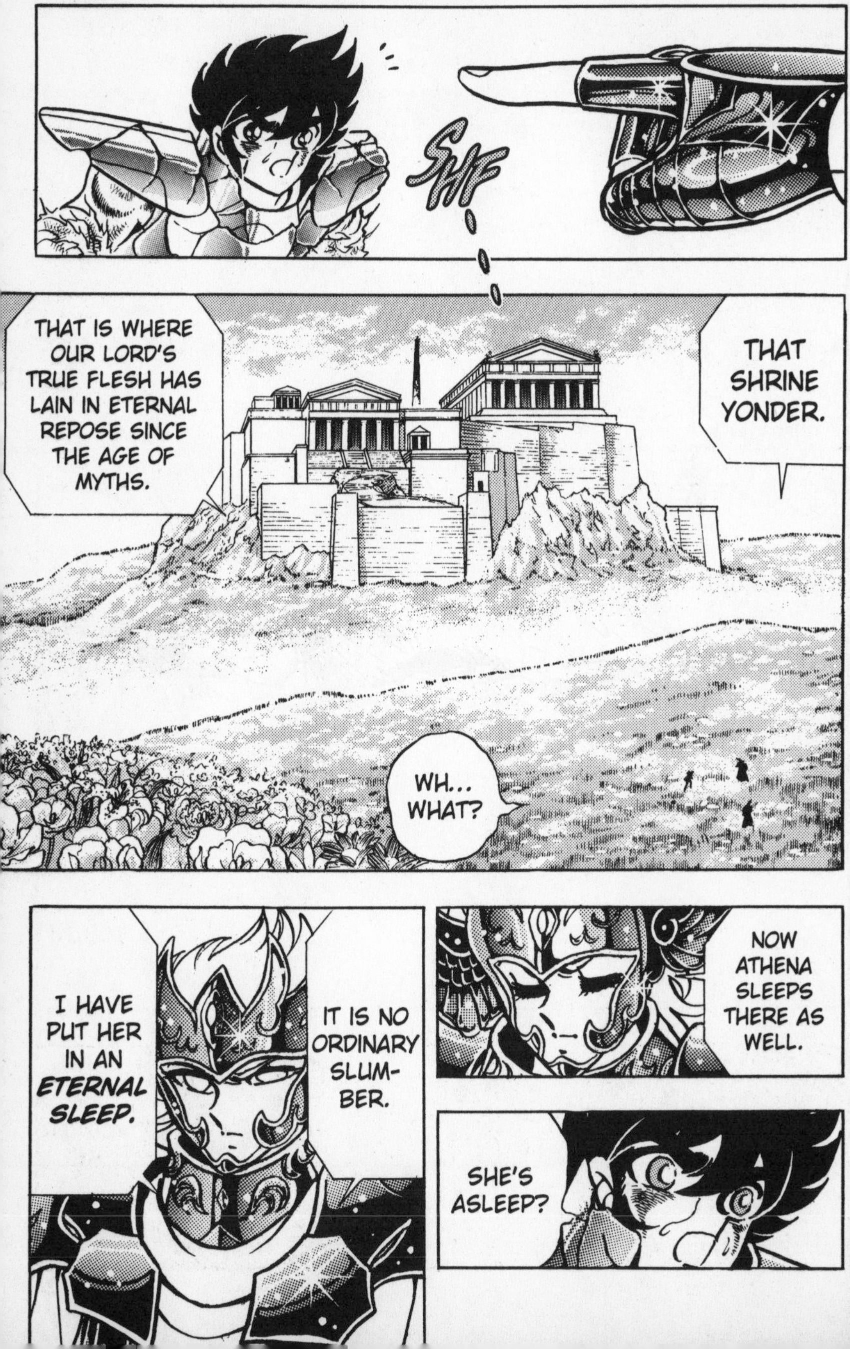
SHF
THAT SHRINE YONDER.
THAT IS WHERE OUR LORD'S TRUE FLESH HAS LAIN IN ETERNAL REPOSE SINCE THE AGE OF MYTHS.
WH... WHAT?
NOW ATHENA SLEEPS THERE AS WELL.
SHE'S ASLEEP?
IT IS NO ORDINARY SLUMBER.
I HAVE PUT HER IN AN *ETERNAL SLEEP.*

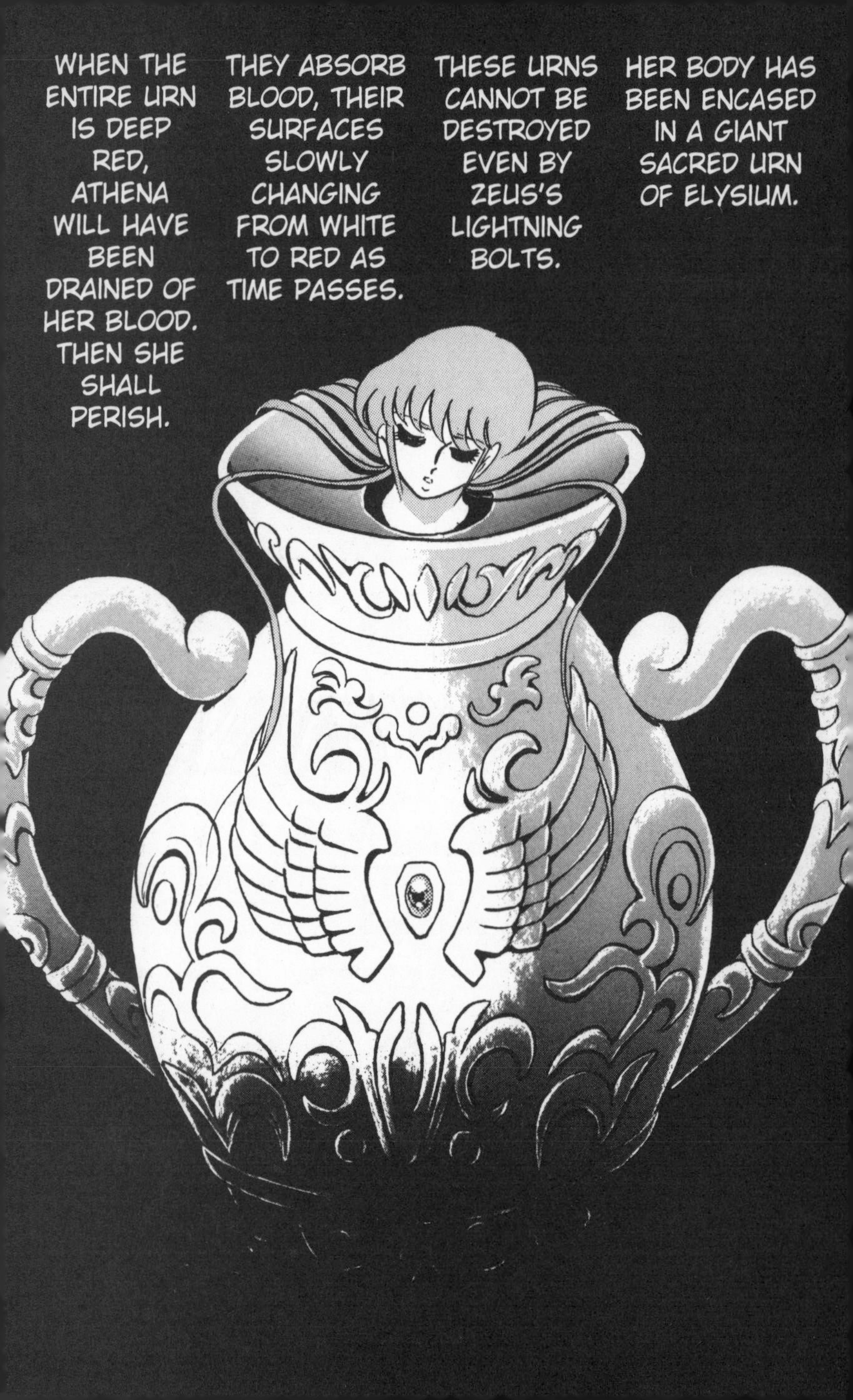
HER BODY HAS BEEN ENCASED IN A GIANT SACRED URN OF ELYSIUM.
THESE URNS CANNOT BE DESTROYED EVEN BY ZEUS'S LIGHTNING BOLTS.
THEY ABSORB BLOOD, THEIR SURFACES SLOWLY CHANGING FROM WHITE TO RED AS TIME PASSES.
WHEN THE ENTIRE URN IS DEEP RED, ATHENA WILL HAVE BEEN DRAINED OF HER BLOOD. THEN SHE SHALL PERISH.

READ THIS WAY

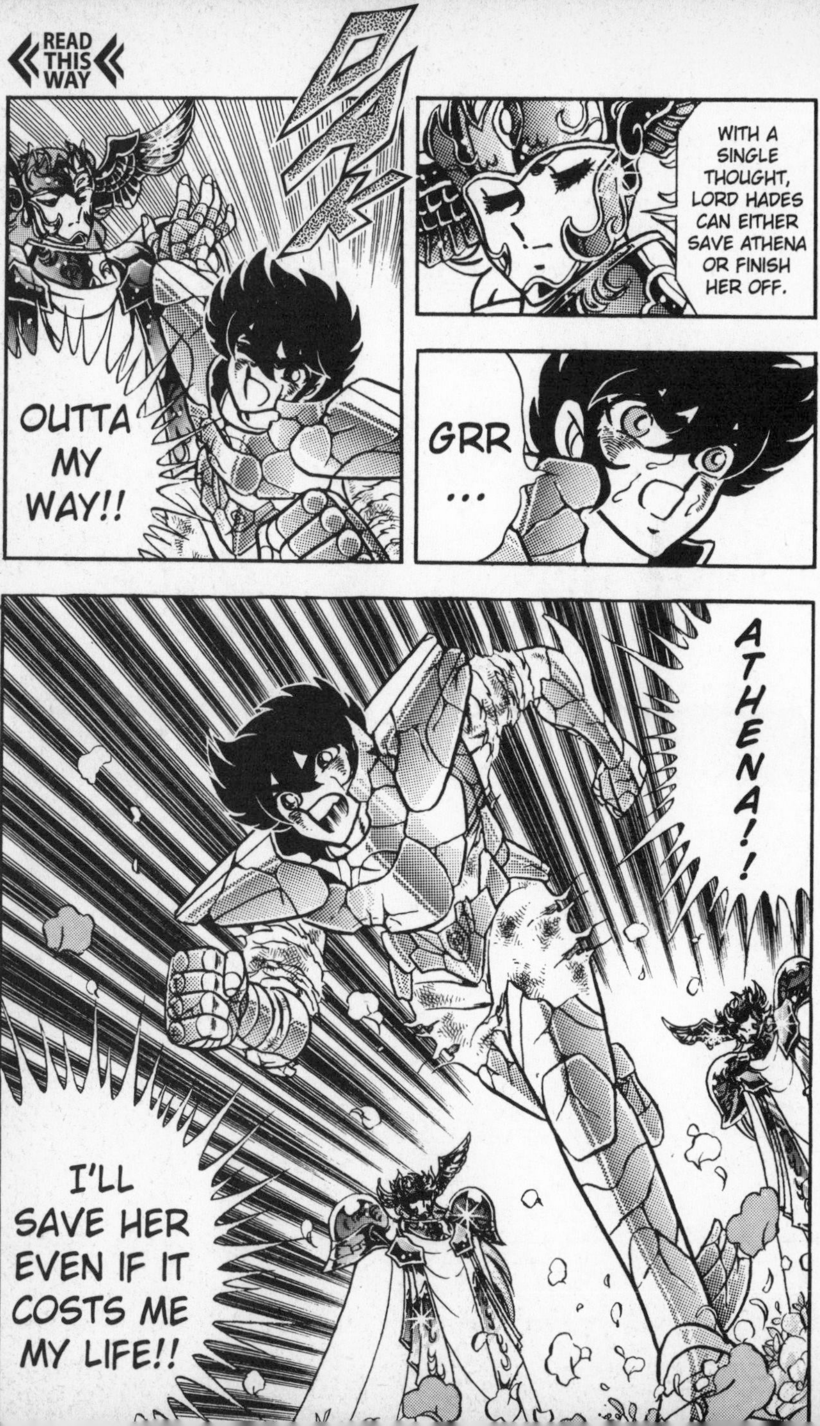
WITH A SINGLE THOUGHT, LORD HADES CAN EITHER SAVE ATHENA OR FINISH HER OFF.
GRR ...
OUTTA MY WAY!!
ATHENA!!
I'LL SAVE HER EVEN IF IT COSTS ME MY LIFE!!

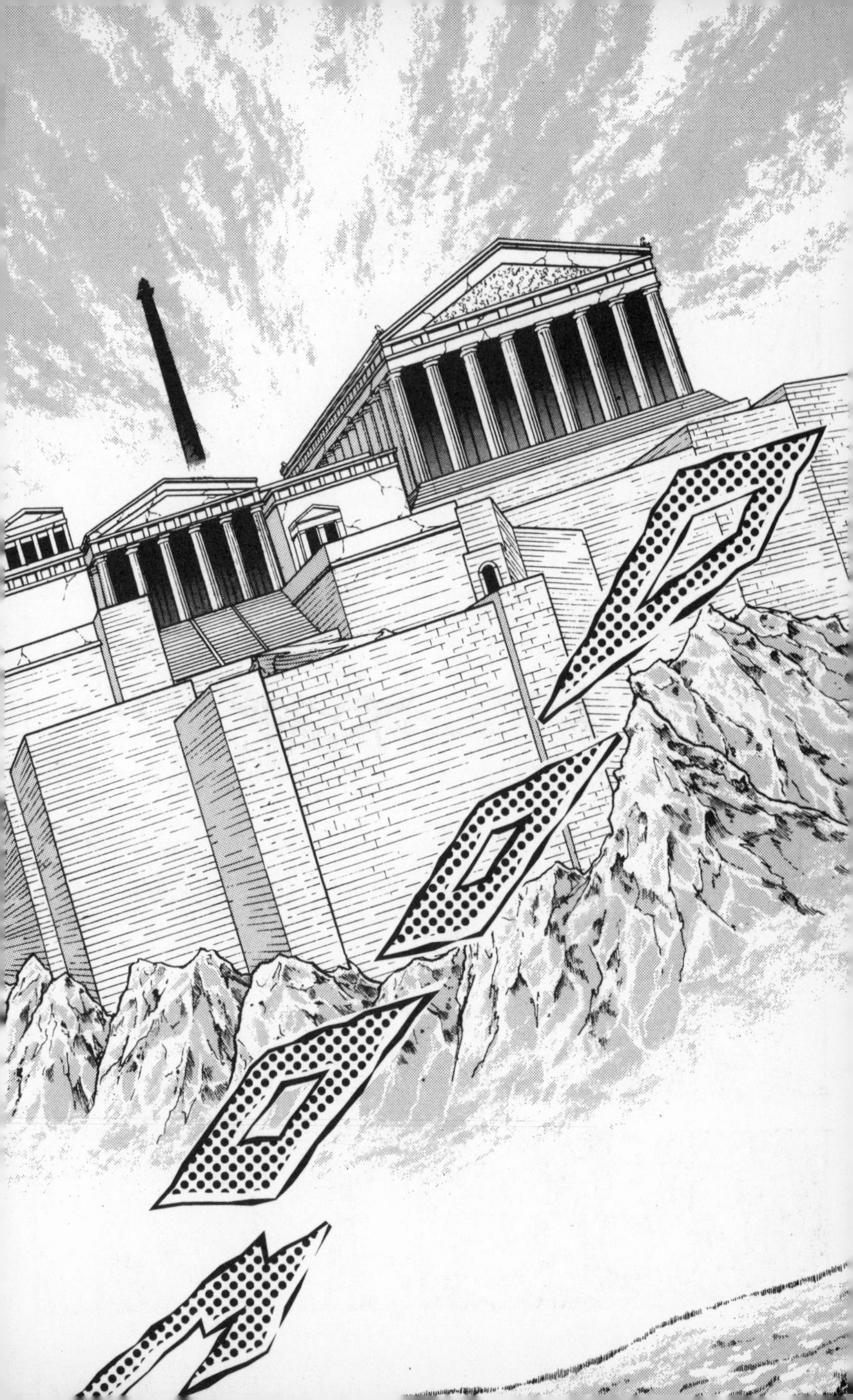

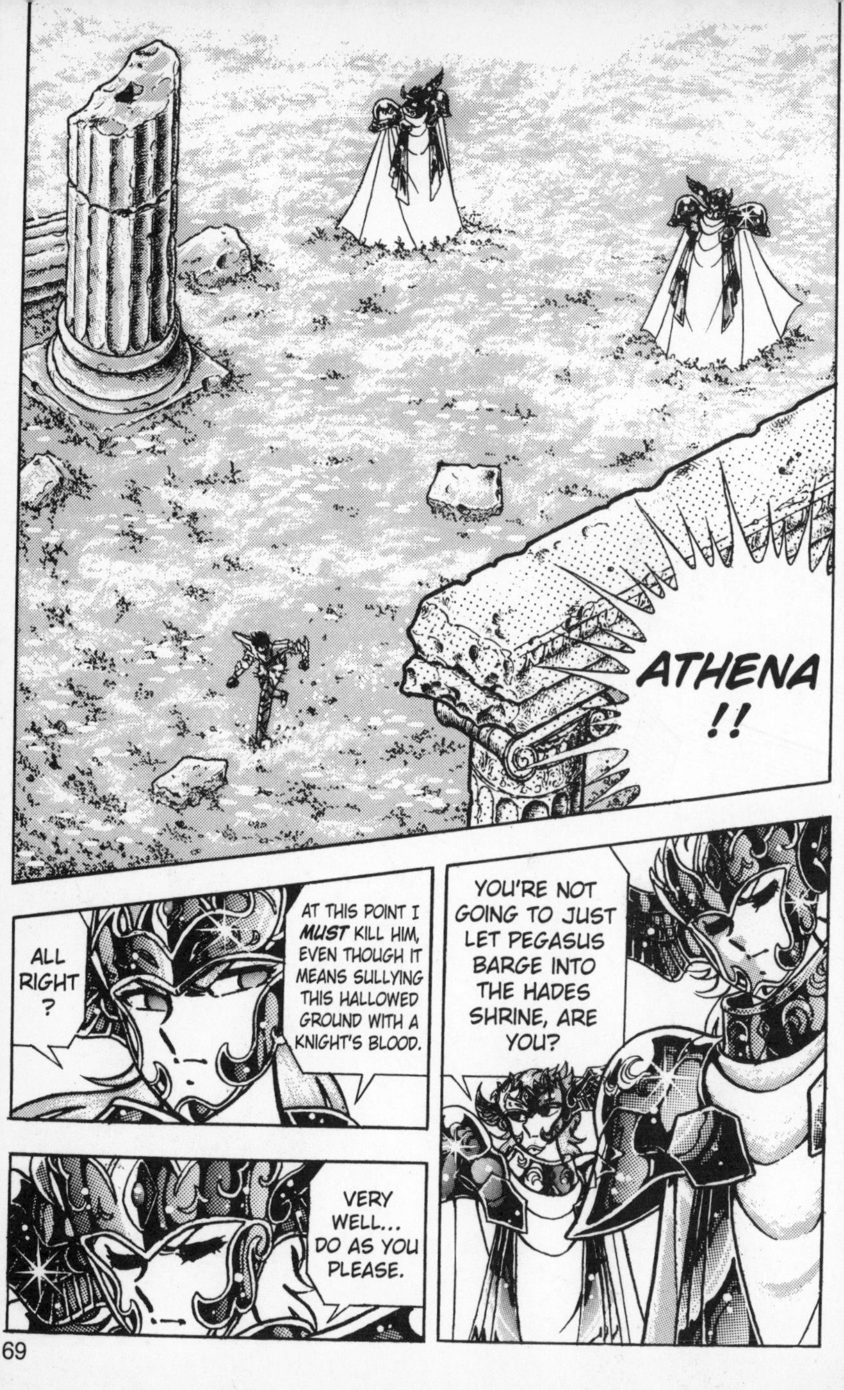
ATHENA !!
YOU'RE NOT GOING TO JUST LET PEGASUS BARGE INTO THE HADES SHRINE, ARE YOU?
AT THIS POINT I **MUST** KILL HIM, EVEN THOUGH IT MEANS SULLYING THIS HALLOWED GROUND WITH A KNIGHT'S BLOOD.
ALL RIGHT?
VERY WELL... DO AS YOU PLEASE.

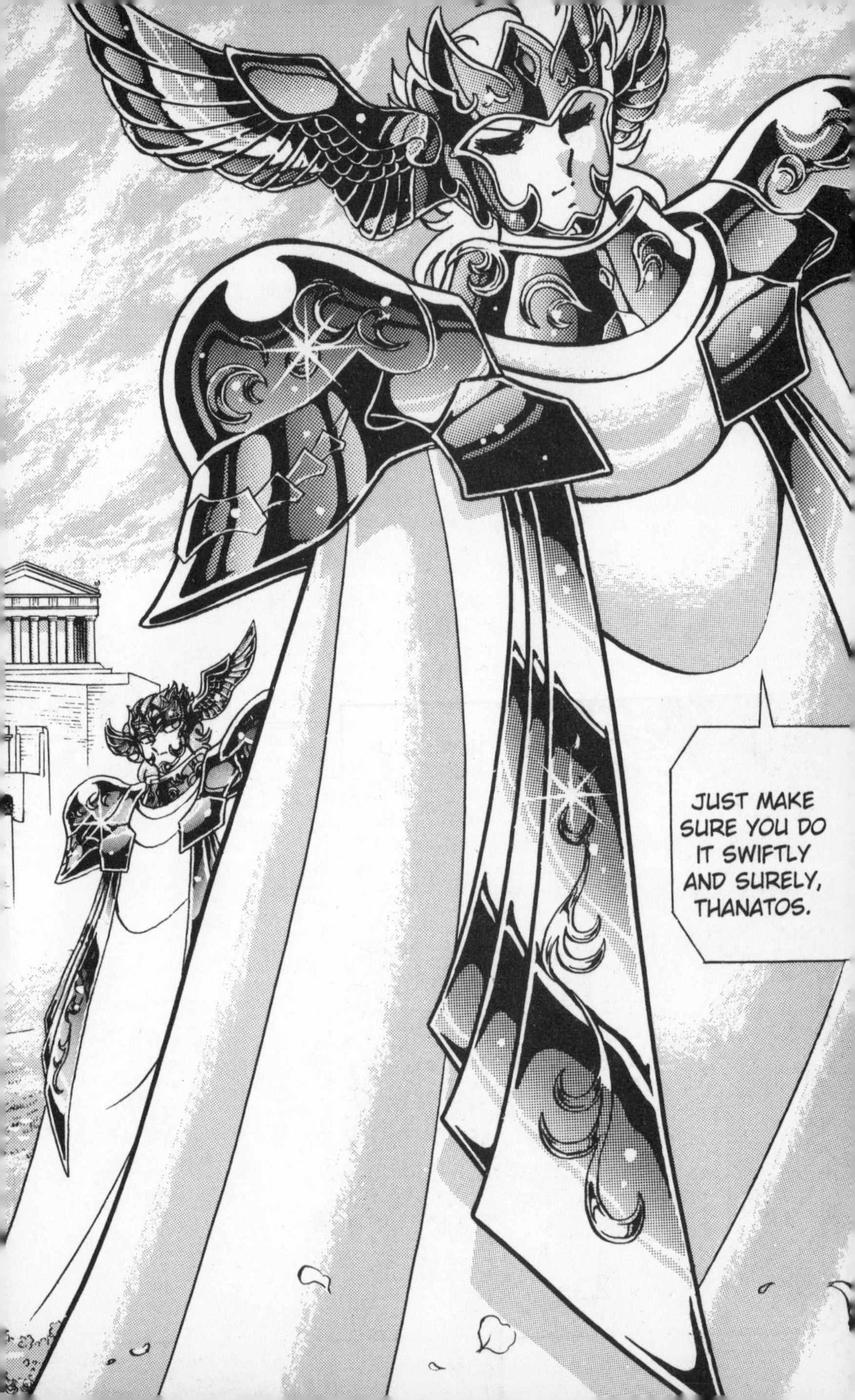
JUST MAKE SURE YOU DO IT SWIFTLY AND SURELY, THANATOS.

READ THIS WAY

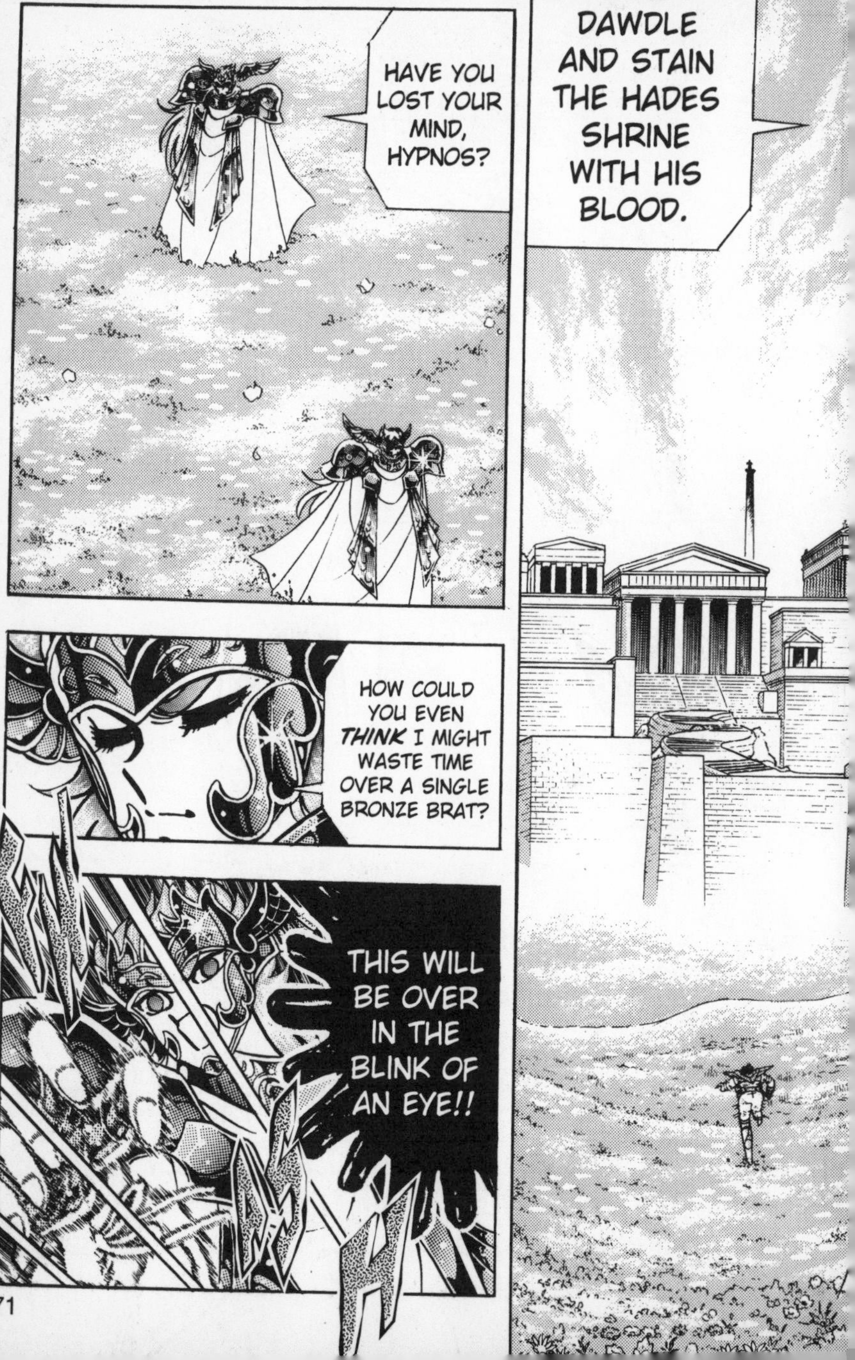
DO NOT DAWDLE AND STAIN THE HADES SHRINE WITH HIS BLOOD.
HAVE YOU LOST YOUR MIND, HYPNOS?
HOW COULD YOU EVEN *THINK* I MIGHT WASTE TIME OVER A SINGLE BRONZE BRAT?
THIS WILL BE OVER IN THE BLINK OF AN EYE!!

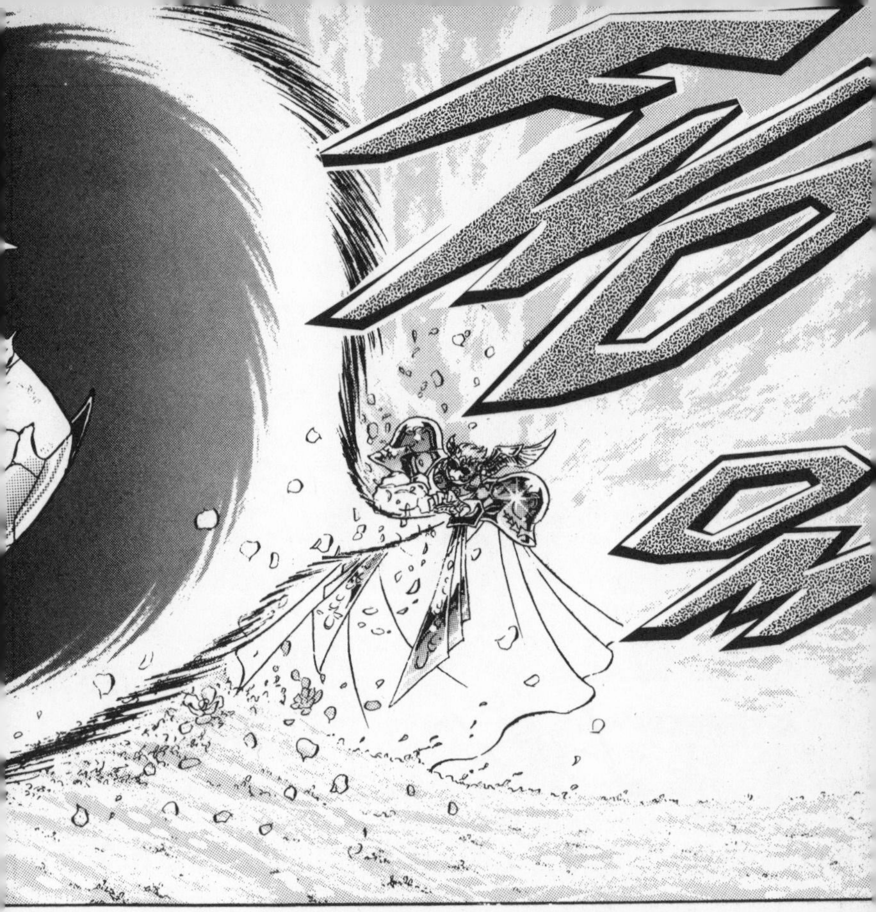

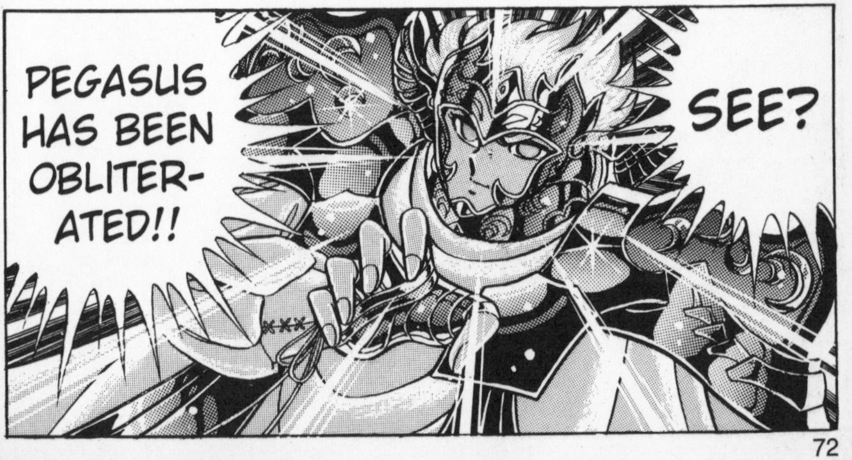
SEE?
PEGASUS HAS BEEN OBLITER-ATED!!

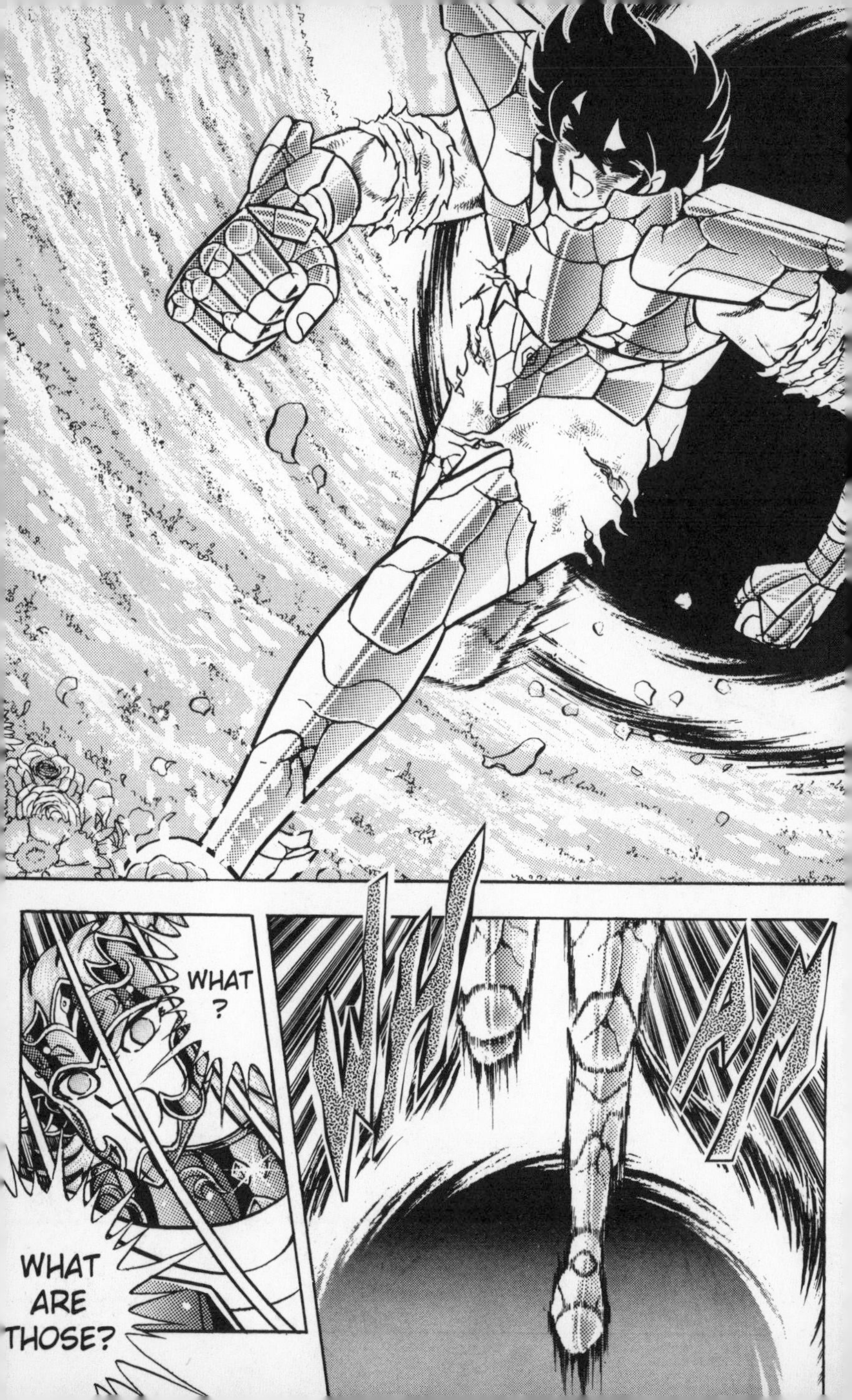
WHAM
WHAT ?
WHAT ARE THOSE?

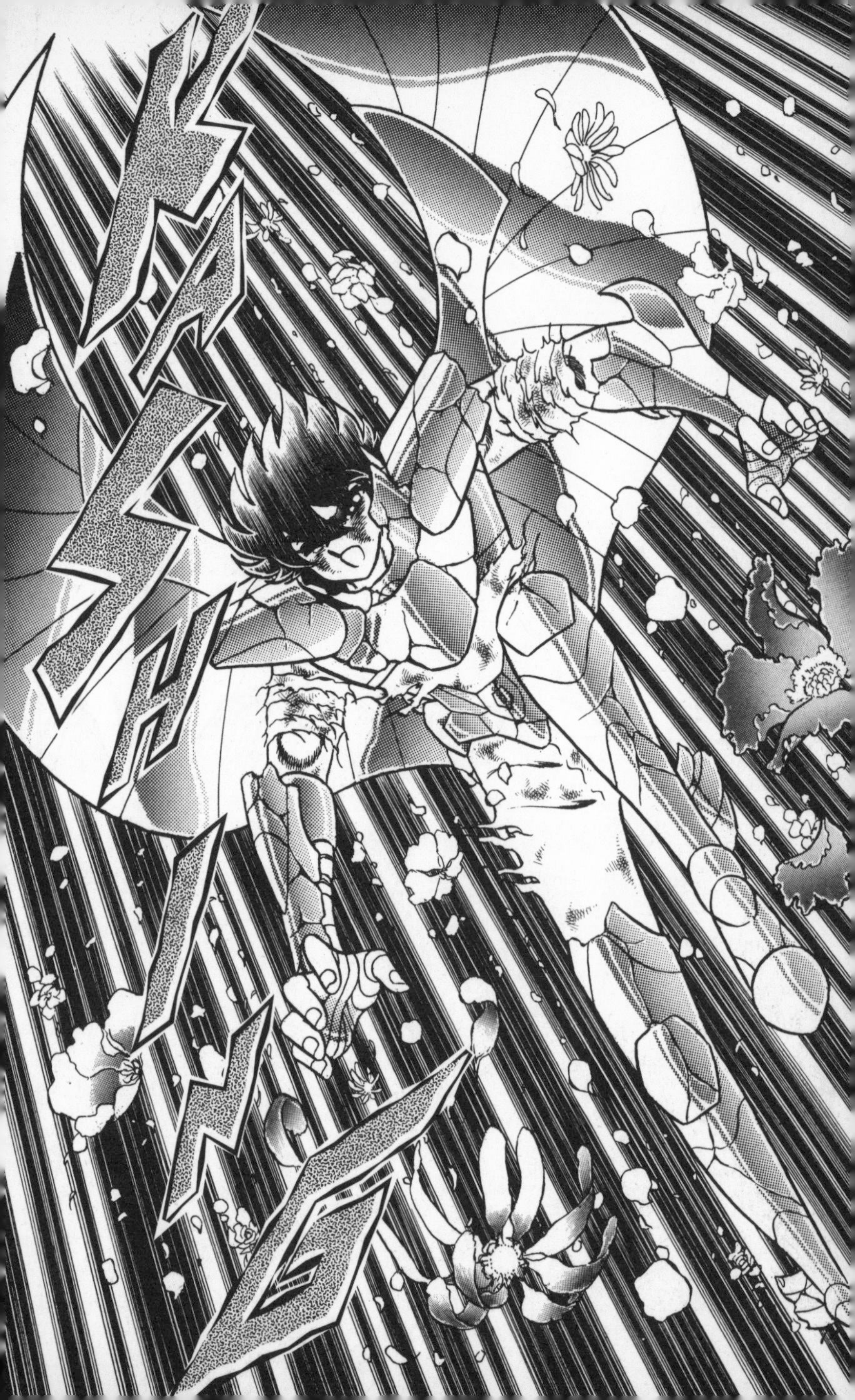

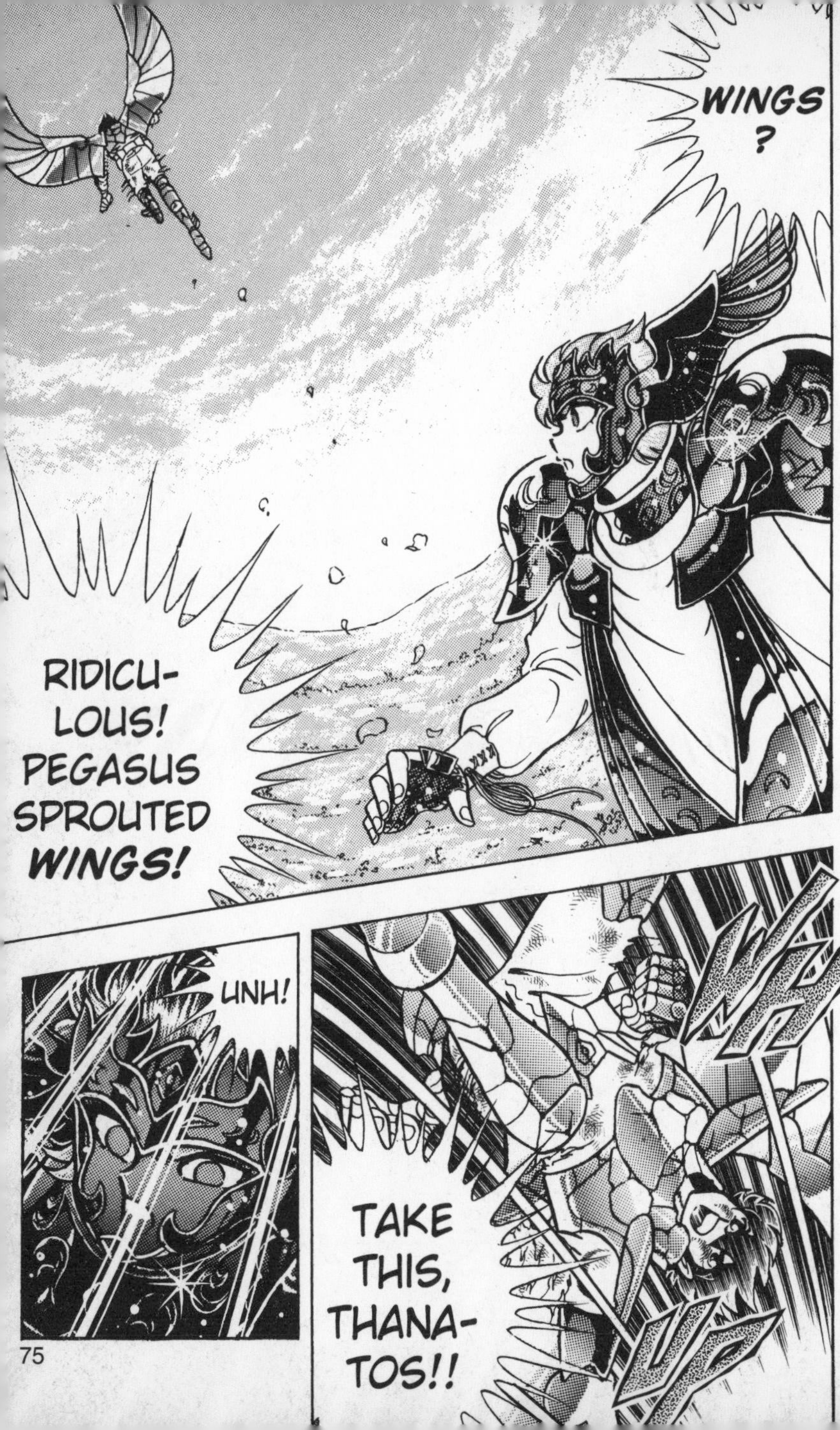
WINGS ?
RIDICU-LOUS! PEGASUS SPROUTED WINGS!
TAKE THIS, THANA-TOS!!
UNH!

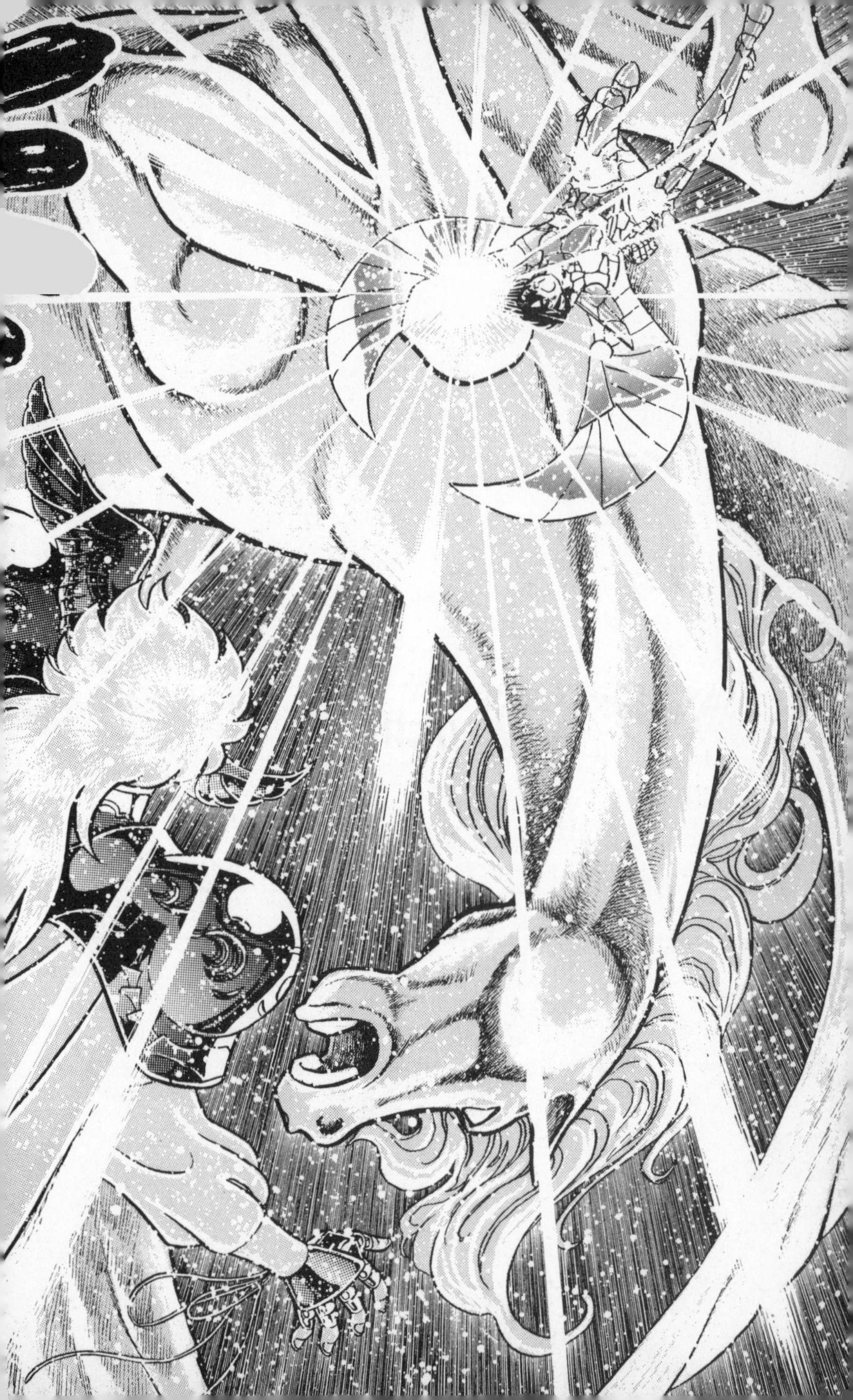

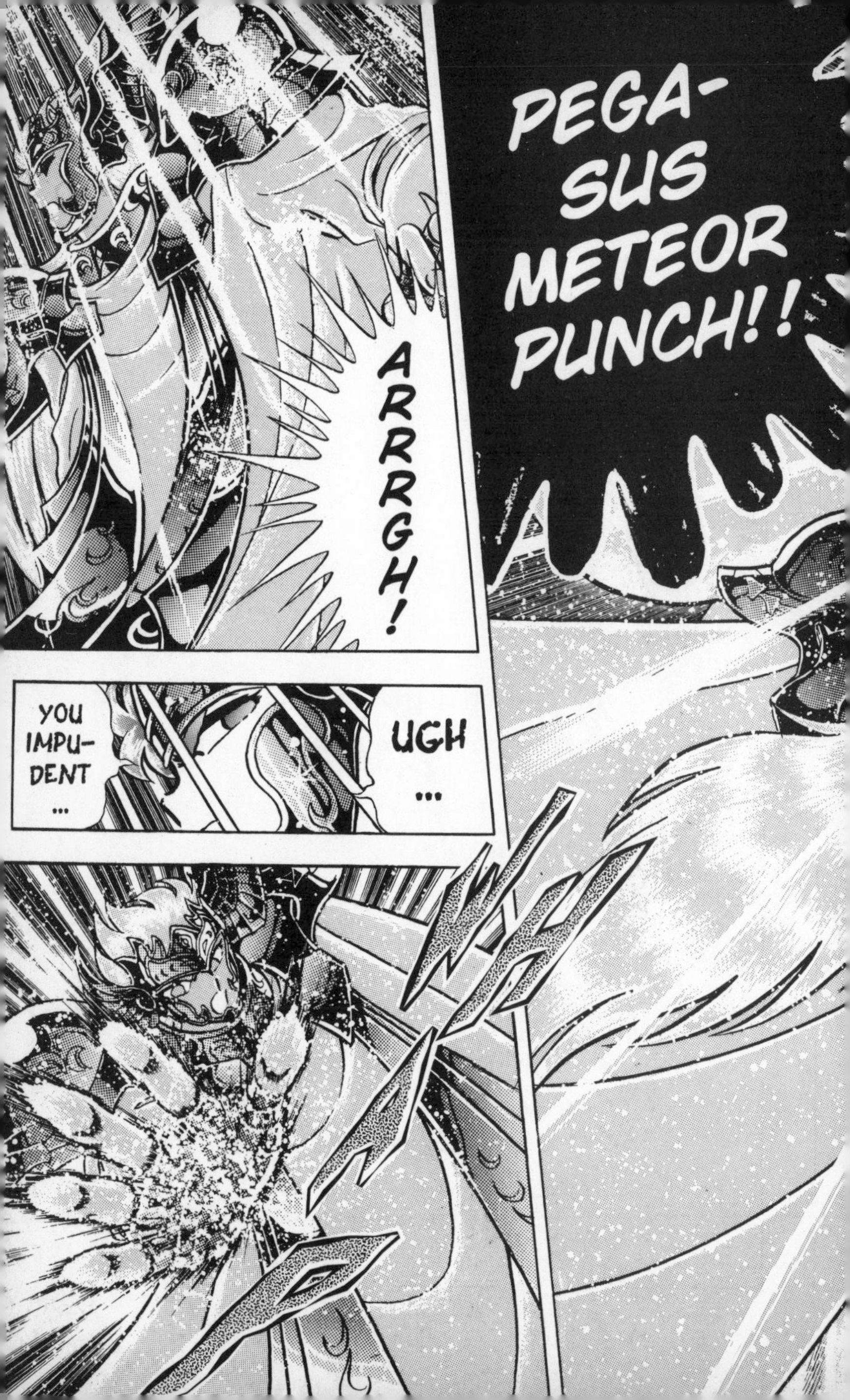
PEGA-SUS METEOR PUNCH!!
ARRRGH!
UGH ...
YOU IMPU-DENT ...

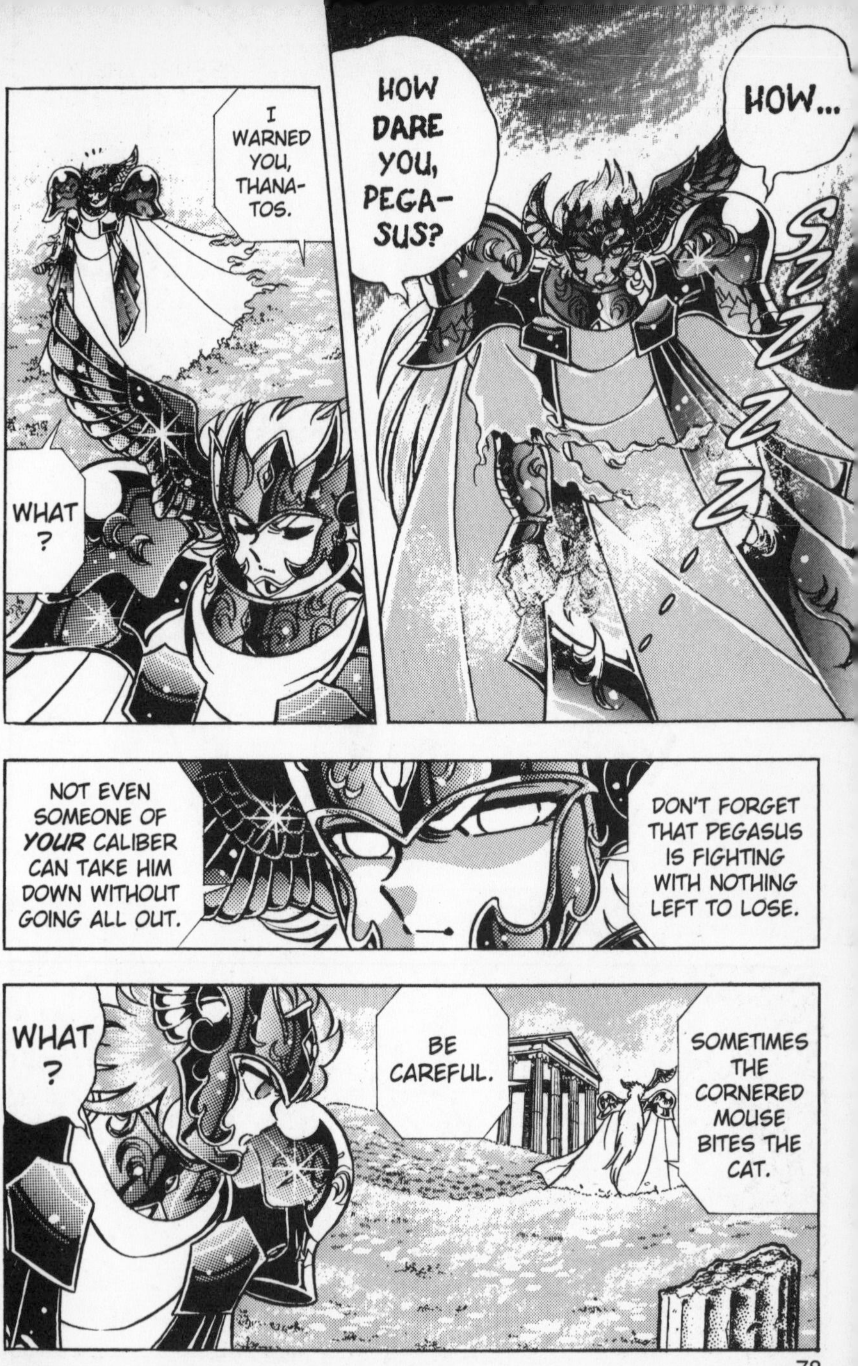
HOW...
HOW DARE YOU, PEGASUS?
I WARNED YOU, THANATOS.
WHAT?
DON'T FORGET THAT PEGASUS IS FIGHTING WITH NOTHING LEFT TO LOSE.
NOT EVEN SOMEONE OF YOUR CALIBER CAN TAKE HIM DOWN WITHOUT GOING ALL OUT.
SOMETIMES THE CORNERED MOUSE BITES THE CAT.
BE CAREFUL.
WHAT?

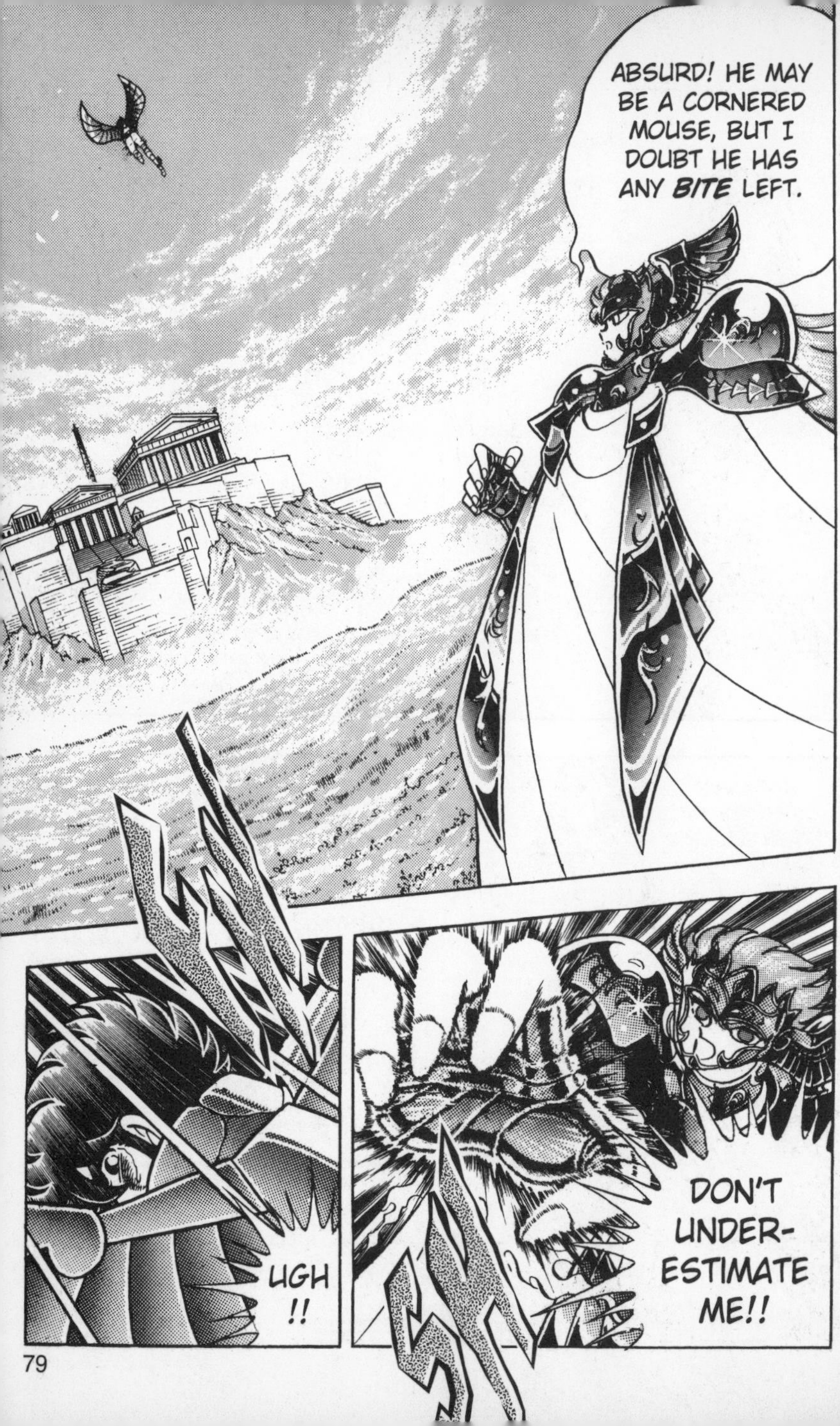
ABSURD! HE MAY BE A CORNERED MOUSE, BUT I DOUBT HE HAS ANY BITE LEFT.
DON'T UNDER-ESTIMATE ME!!
UGH !!

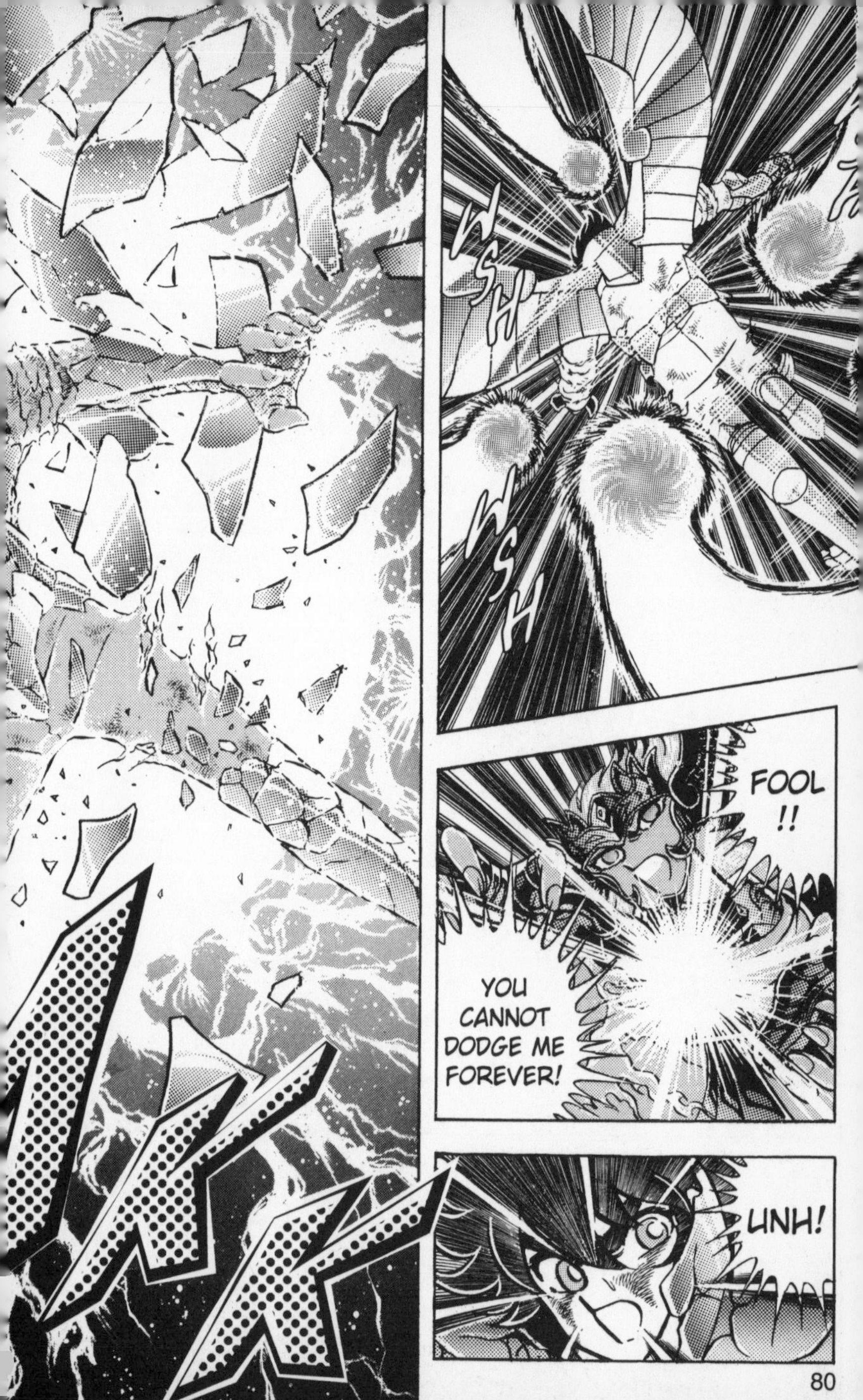
WSH
WSH
FOOL!!
YOU CANNOT DODGE ME FOREVER!
UNH!

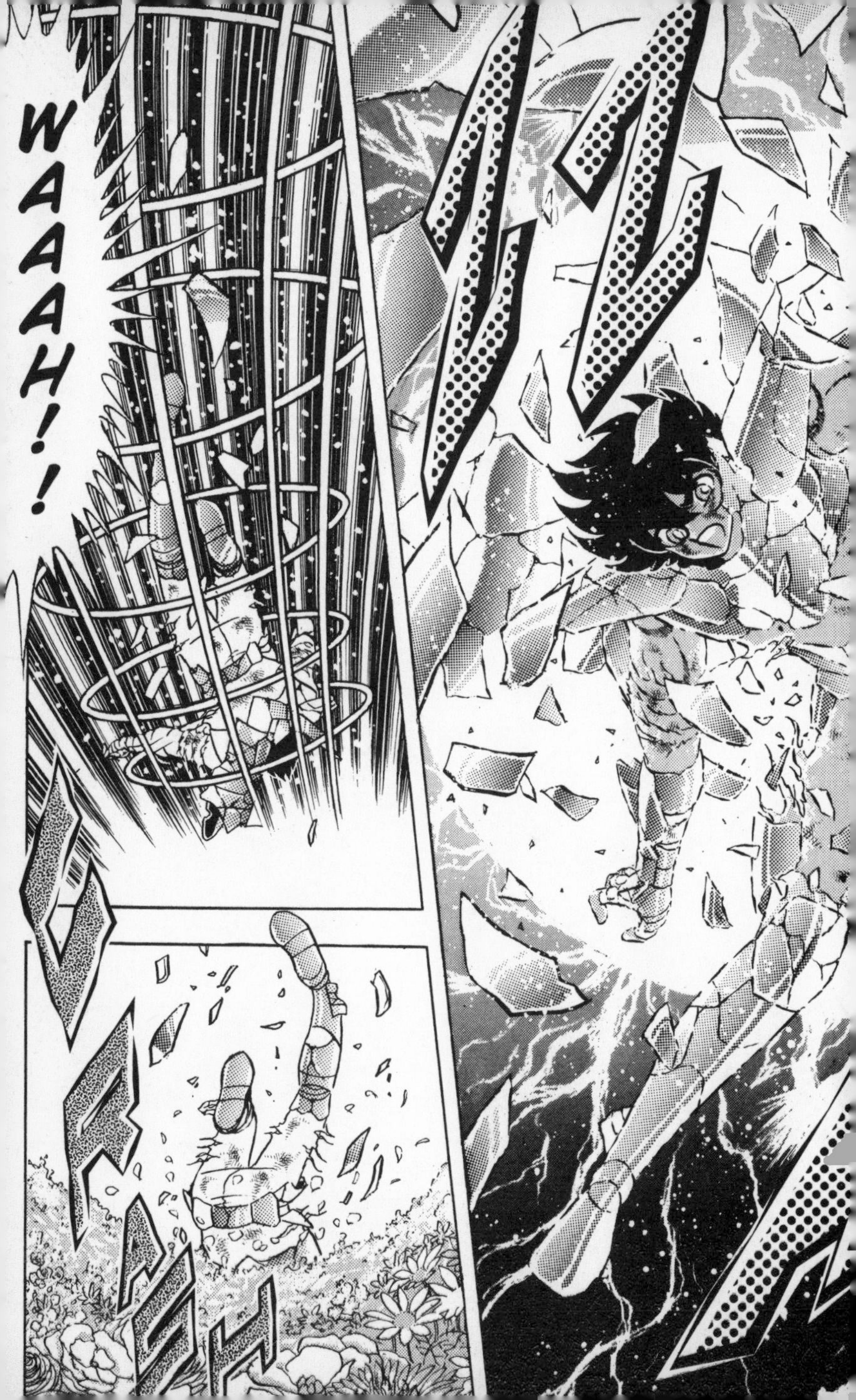
WAAAAH!!!

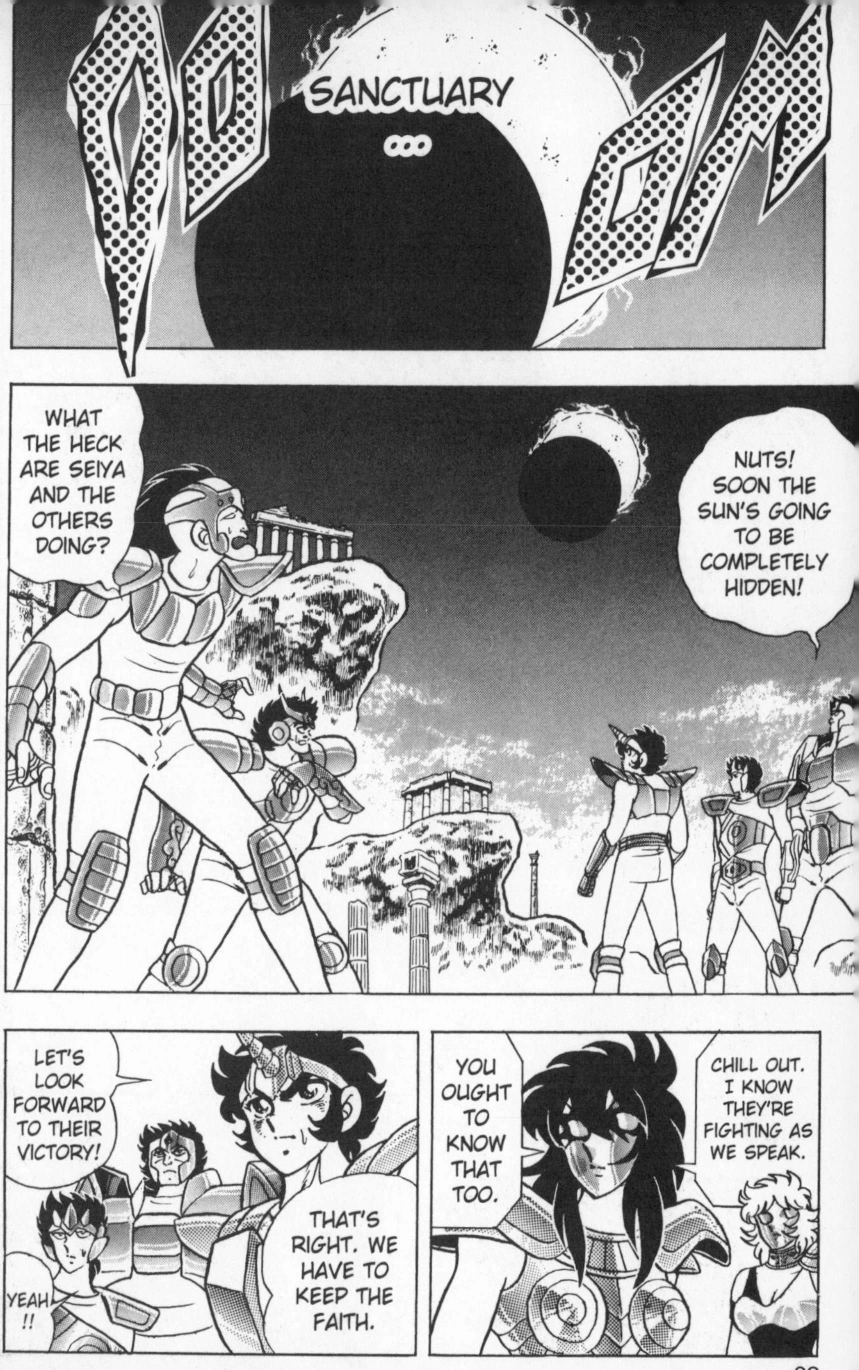
SANCTUARY
...
NUTS! SOON THE SUN'S GOING TO BE COMPLETELY HIDDEN!
WHAT THE HECK ARE SEIYA AND THE OTHERS DOING?
CHILL OUT. I KNOW THEY'RE FIGHTING AS WE SPEAK.
YOU OUGHT TO KNOW THAT TOO.
LET'S LOOK FORWARD TO THEIR VICTORY!
THAT'S RIGHT. WE HAVE TO KEEP THE FAITH.
YEAH!!

READ THIS WAY

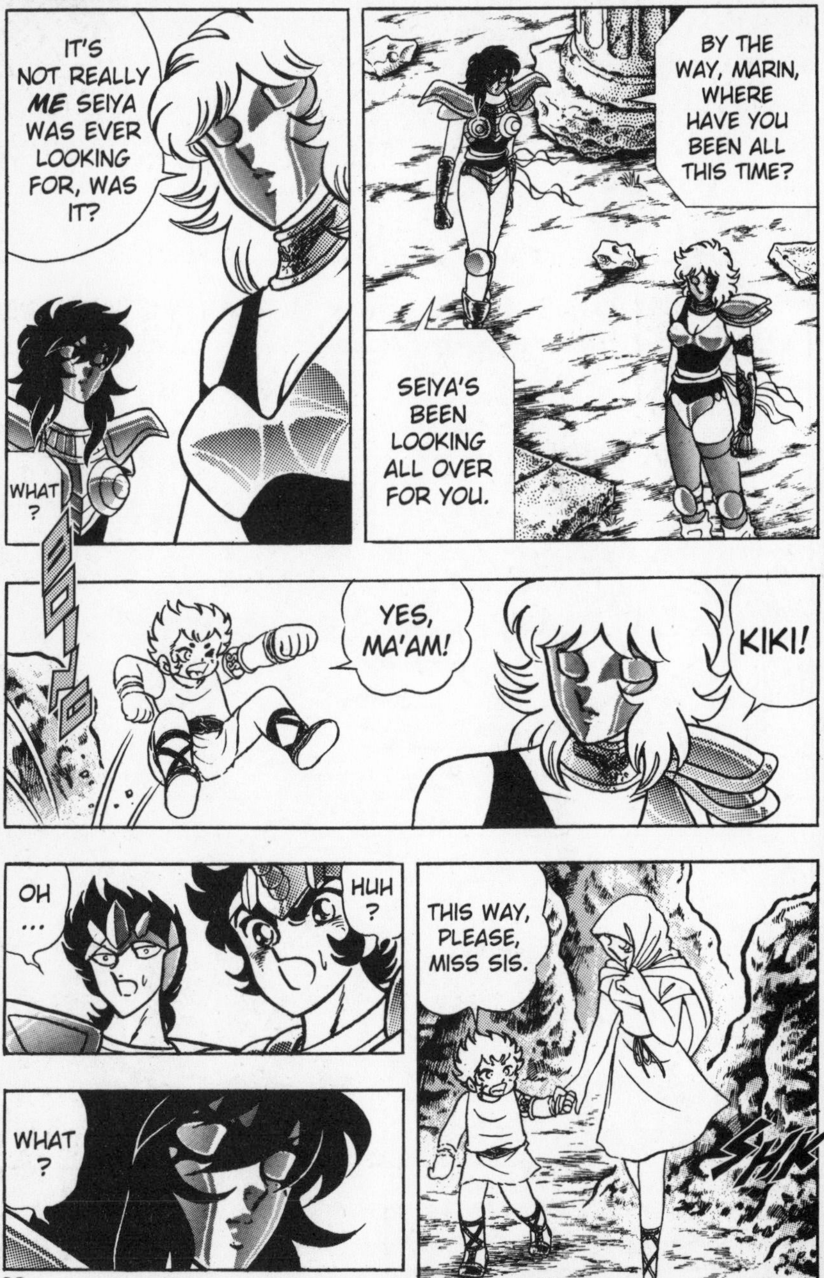

BY THE WAY, MARIN, WHERE HAVE YOU BEEN ALL THIS TIME?
SEIYA'S BEEN LOOKING ALL OVER FOR YOU.
IT'S NOT REALLY *ME* SEIYA WAS EVER LOOKING FOR, WAS IT?
WHAT?
KIKI!
YES, MA'AM!
THIS WAY, PLEASE, MISS SIS.
HUH?
OH ...
WHAT?

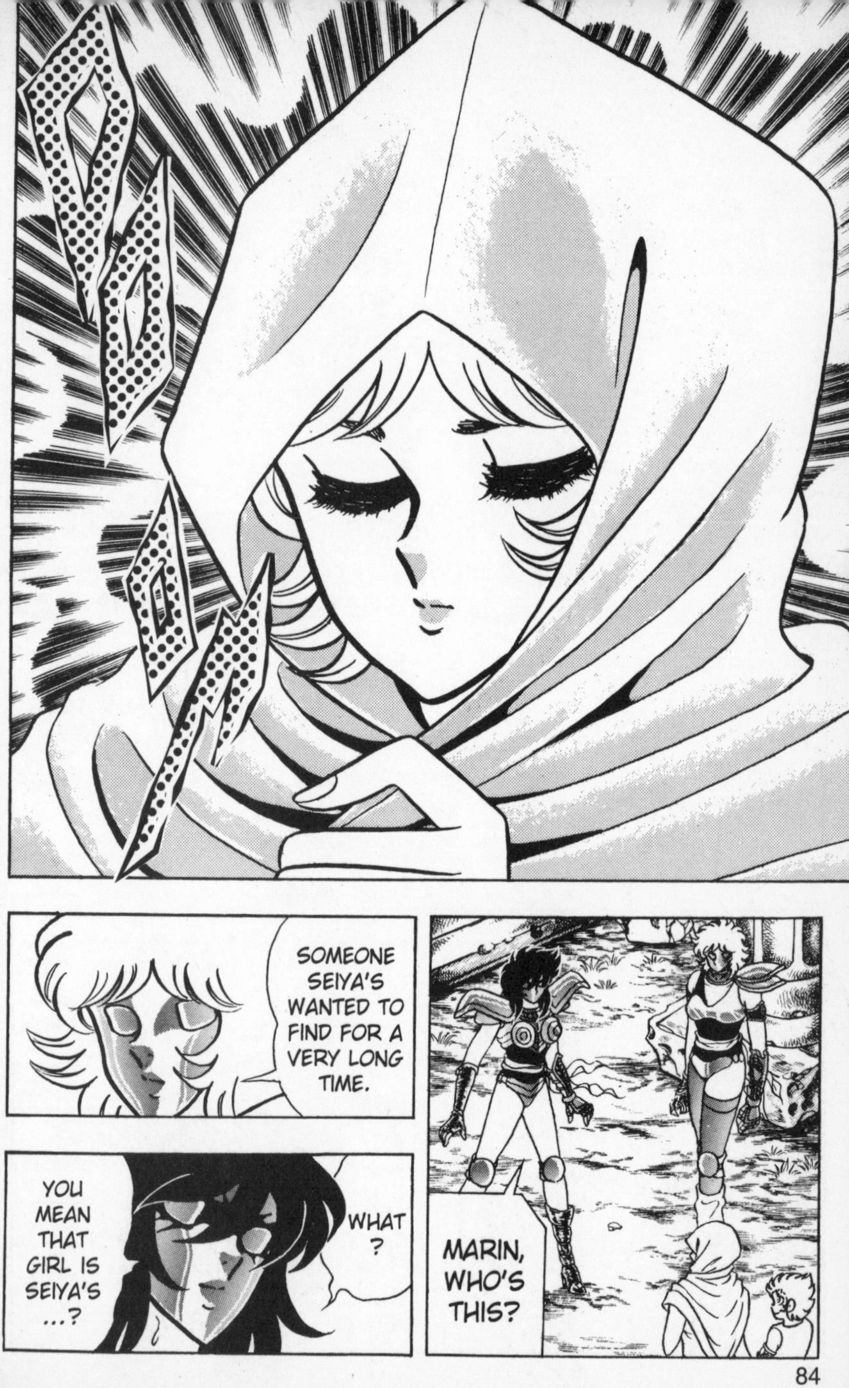
MARIN, WHO'S THIS?
SOMEONE SEIYA'S WANTED TO FIND FOR A VERY LONG TIME.
WHAT?
YOU MEAN THAT GIRL IS SEIYA'S ...?

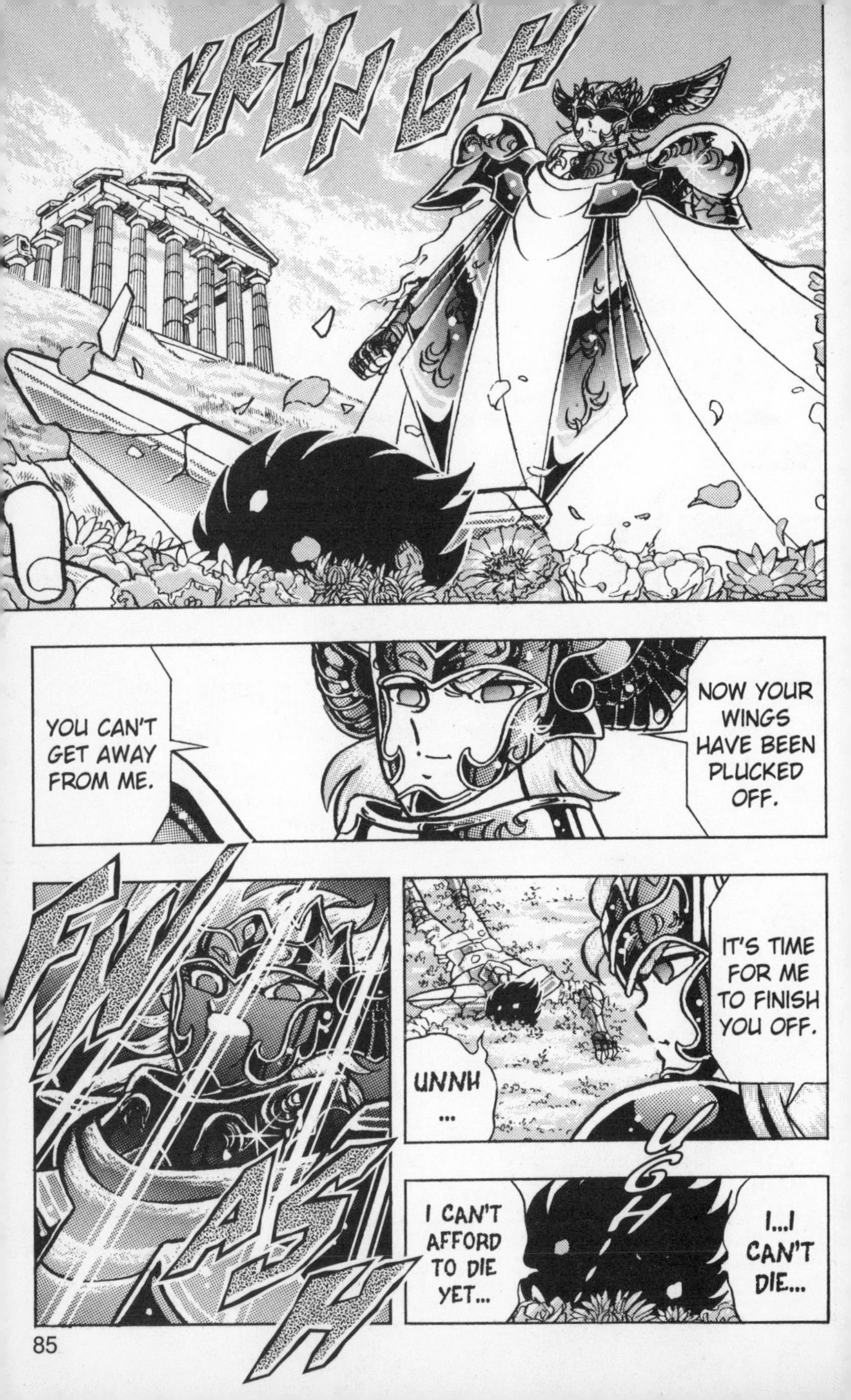
KRUNCH
NOW YOUR WINGS HAVE BEEN PLUCKED OFF.
YOU CAN'T GET AWAY FROM ME.
IT'S TIME FOR ME TO FINISH YOU OFF.
UNNH ...
UGH
I...I CAN'T DIE...
I CAN'T AFFORD TO DIE YET...
FWASH

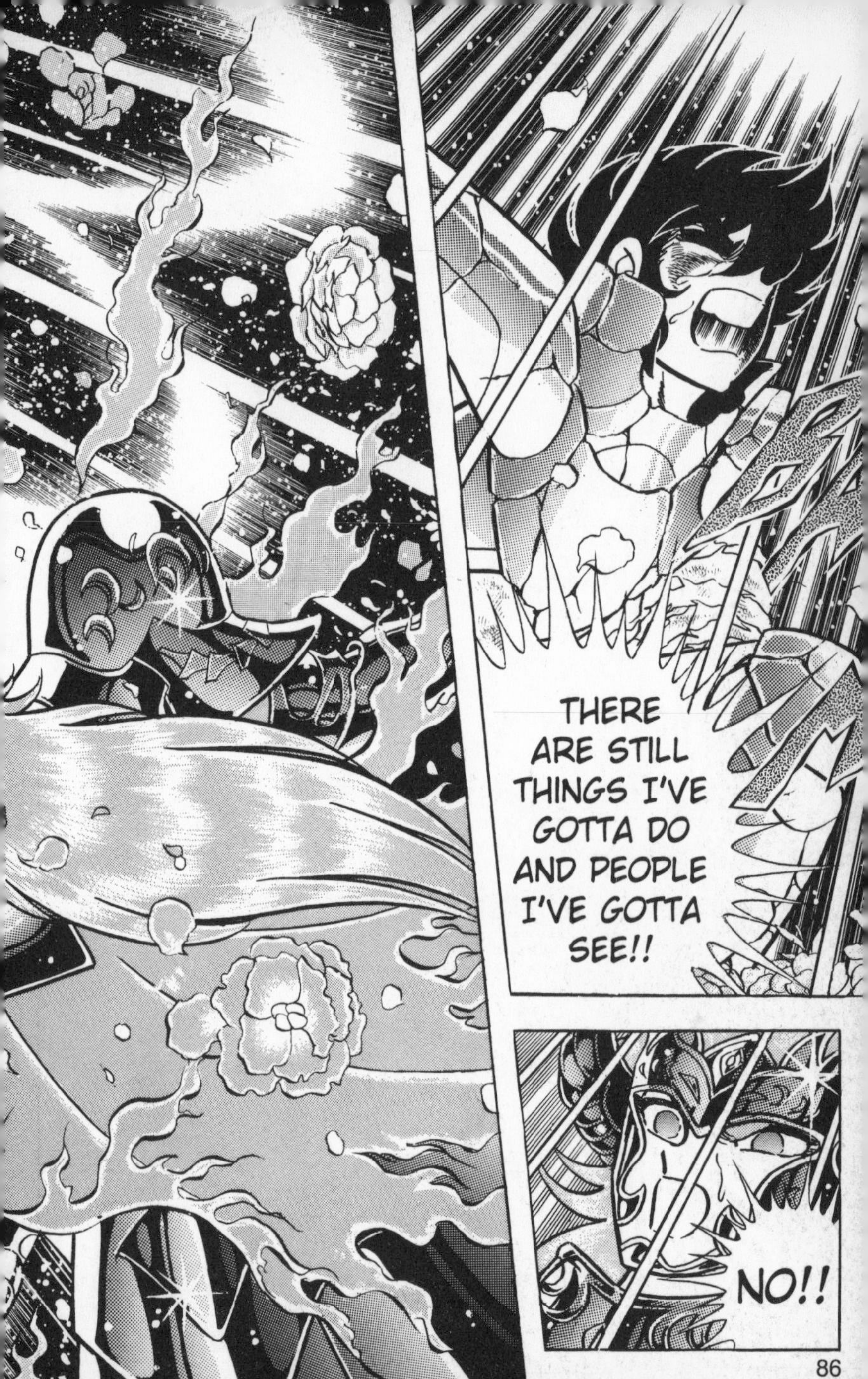
THERE ARE STILL THINGS I'VE GOTTA DO AND PEOPLE I'VE GOTTA SEE!!
NO!!

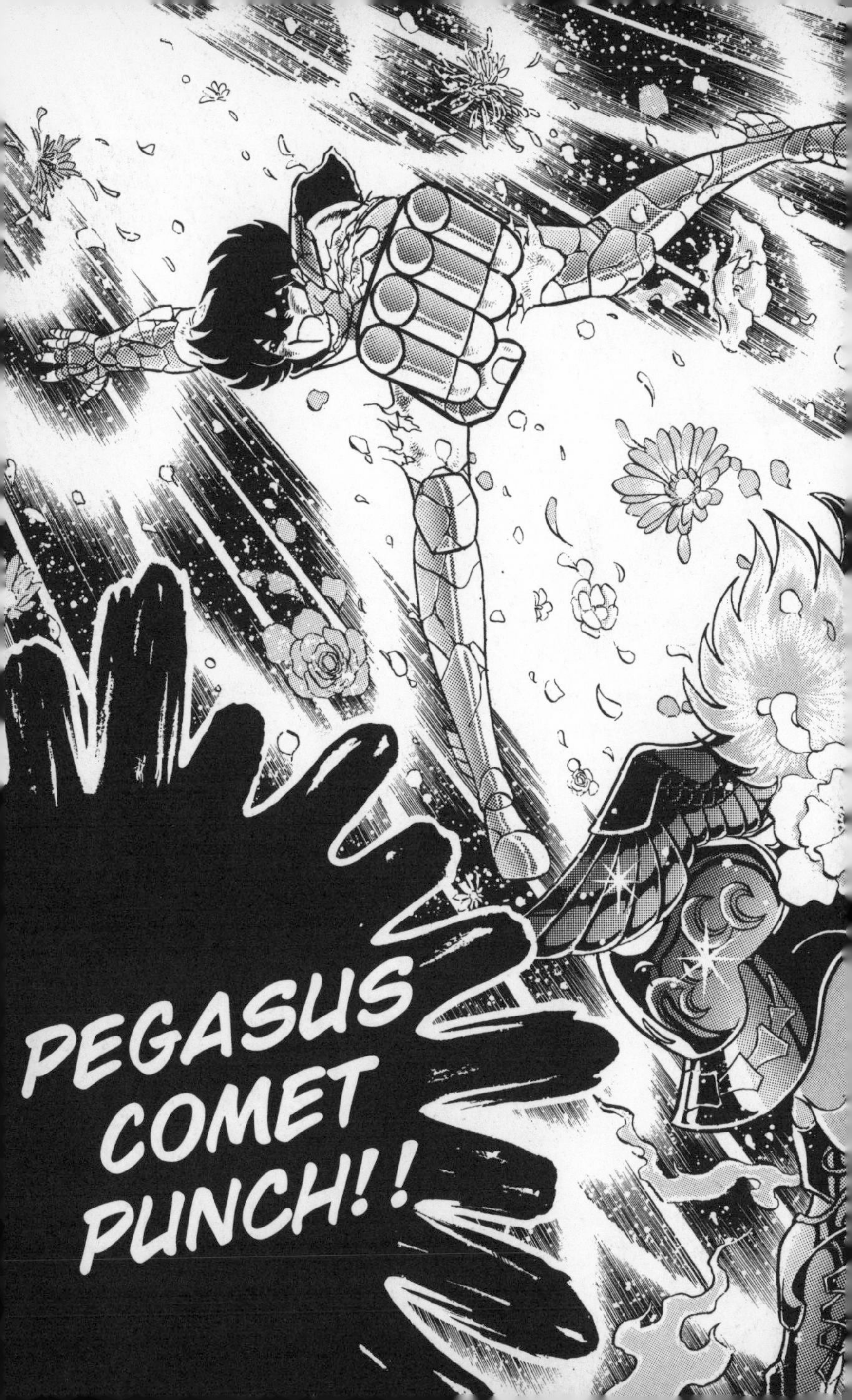
PEGASUS COMET PUNCH!!

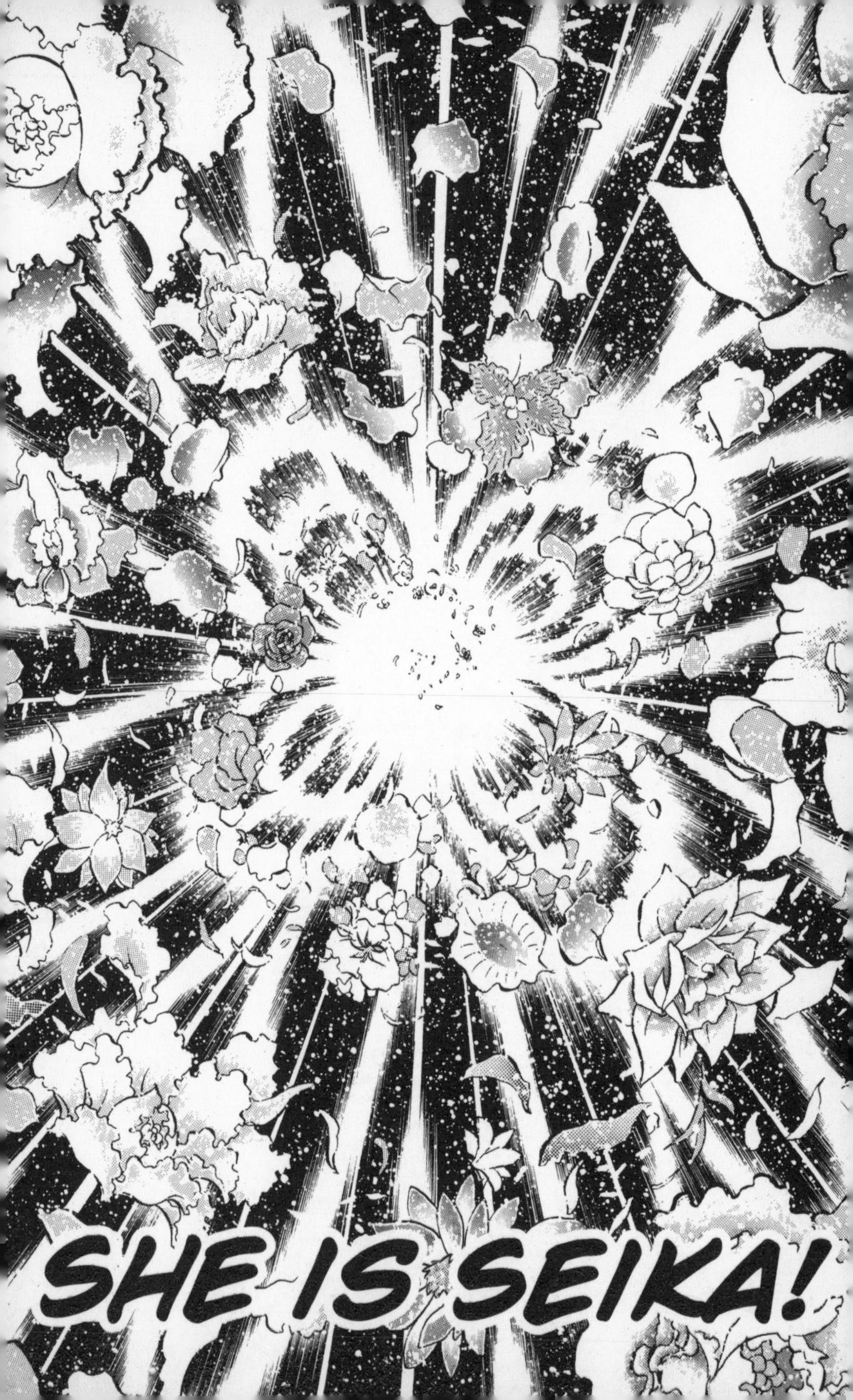
SHE IS SEIKA!

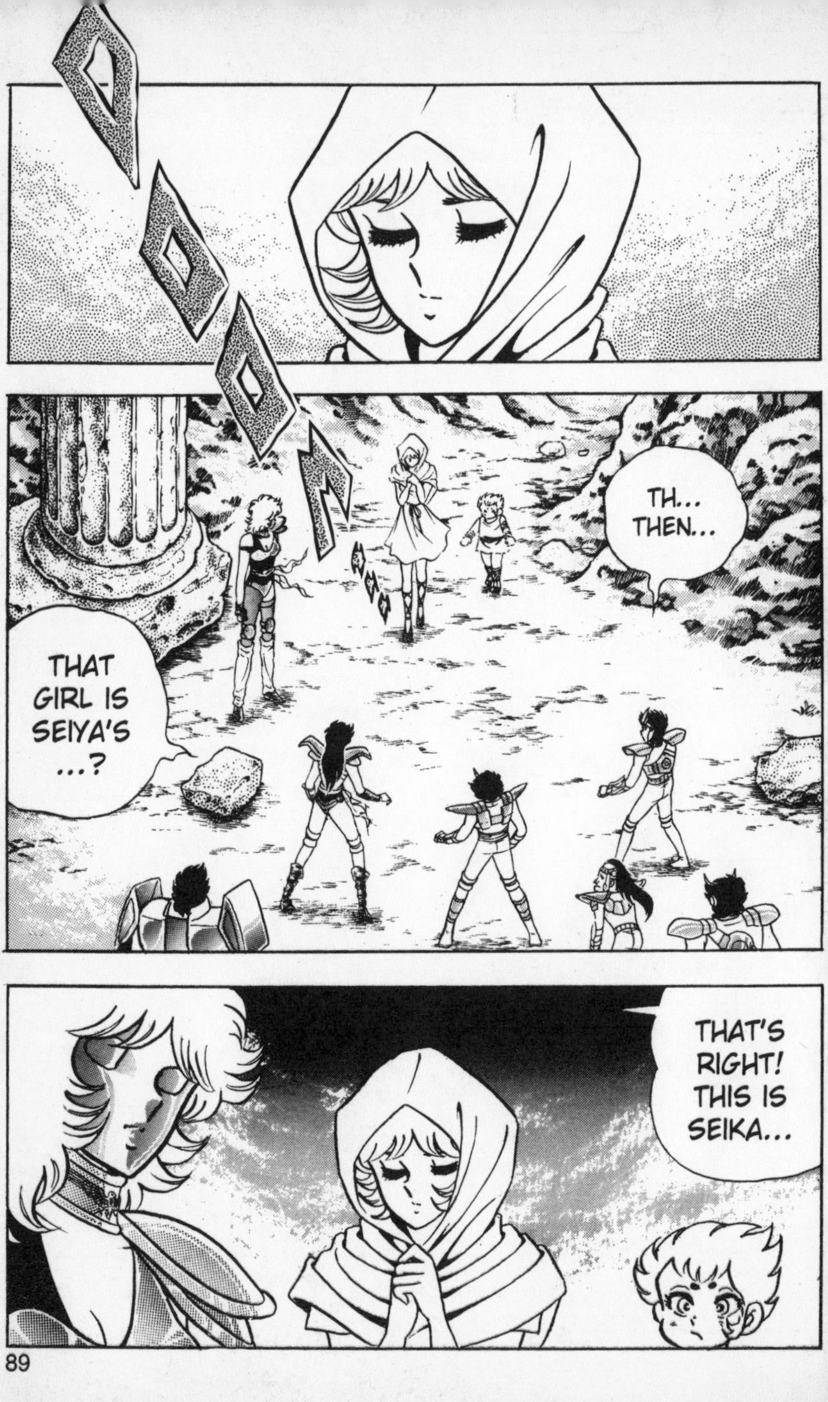
TH... THEN...
THAT GIRL IS SEIYA'S ...?
THAT'S RIGHT! THIS IS SEIKA...

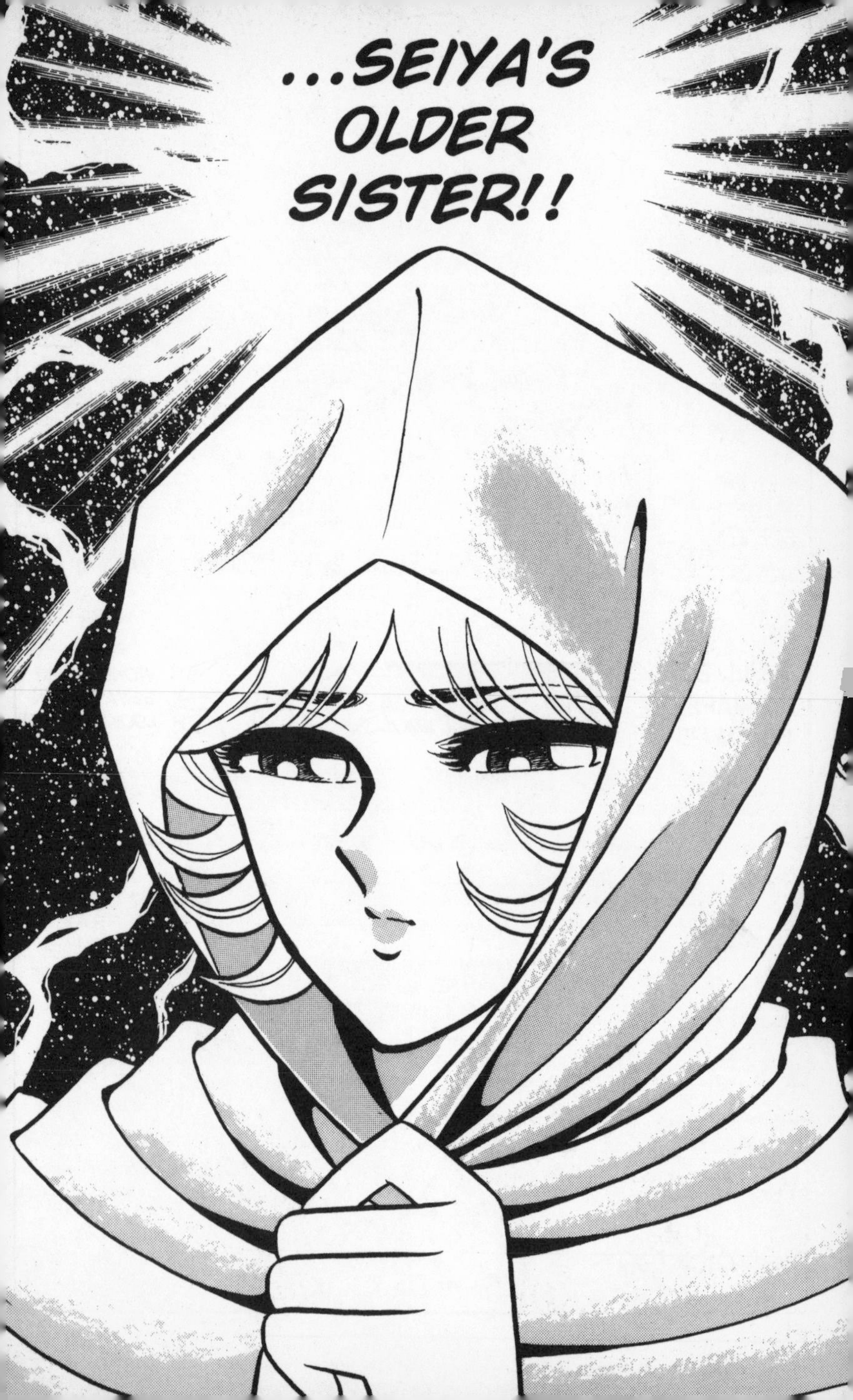
...SEIYA'S OLDER SISTER!!

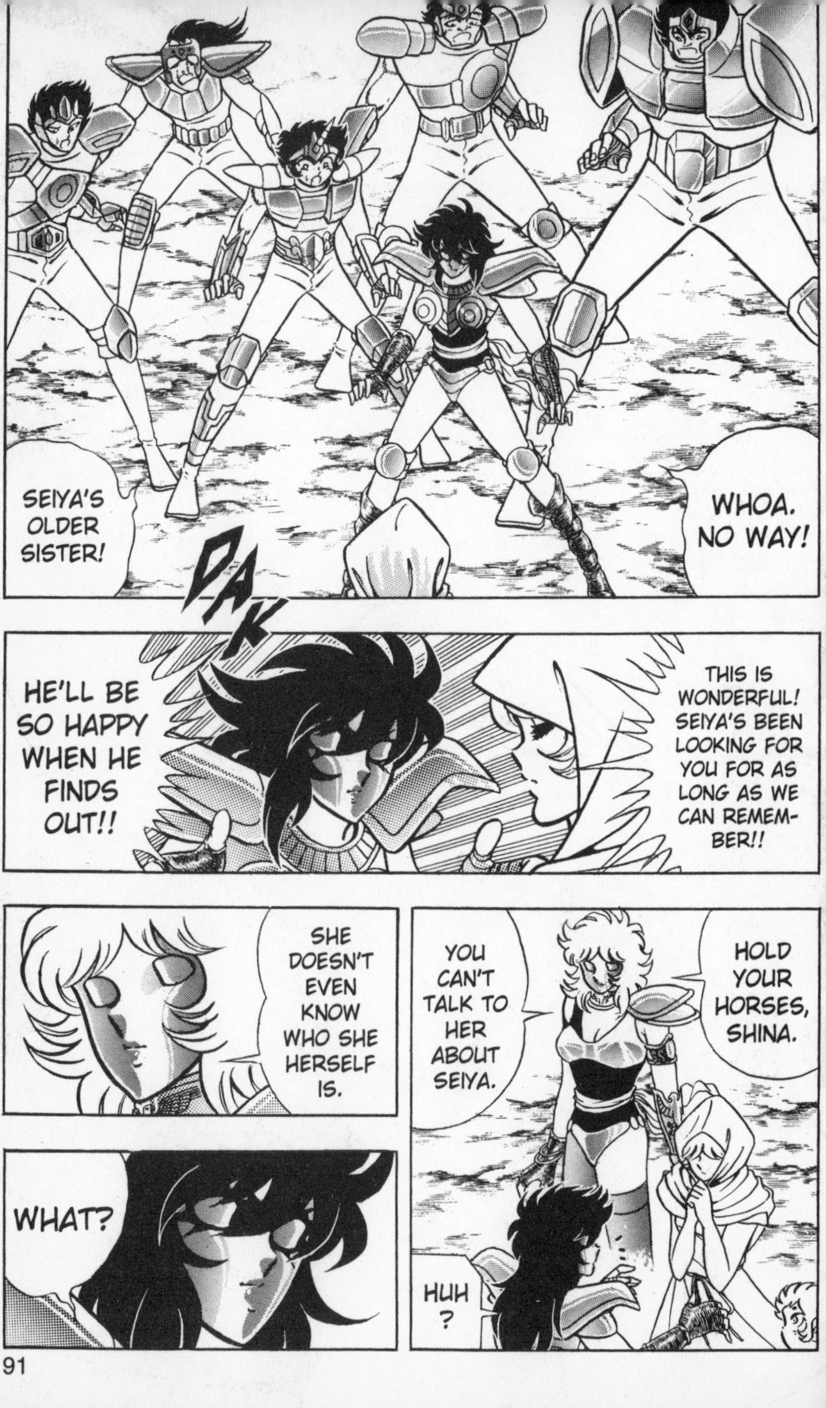
WHOA. NO WAY!
SEIYA'S OLDER SISTER!
DAK
THIS IS WONDERFUL! SEIYA'S BEEN LOOKING FOR YOU FOR AS LONG AS WE CAN REMEMBER!!
HE'LL BE SO HAPPY WHEN HE FINDS OUT!!
HOLD YOUR HORSES, SHINA.
YOU CAN'T TALK TO HER ABOUT SEIYA.
HUH ?
SHE DOESN'T EVEN KNOW WHO SHE HERSELF IS.
WHAT?

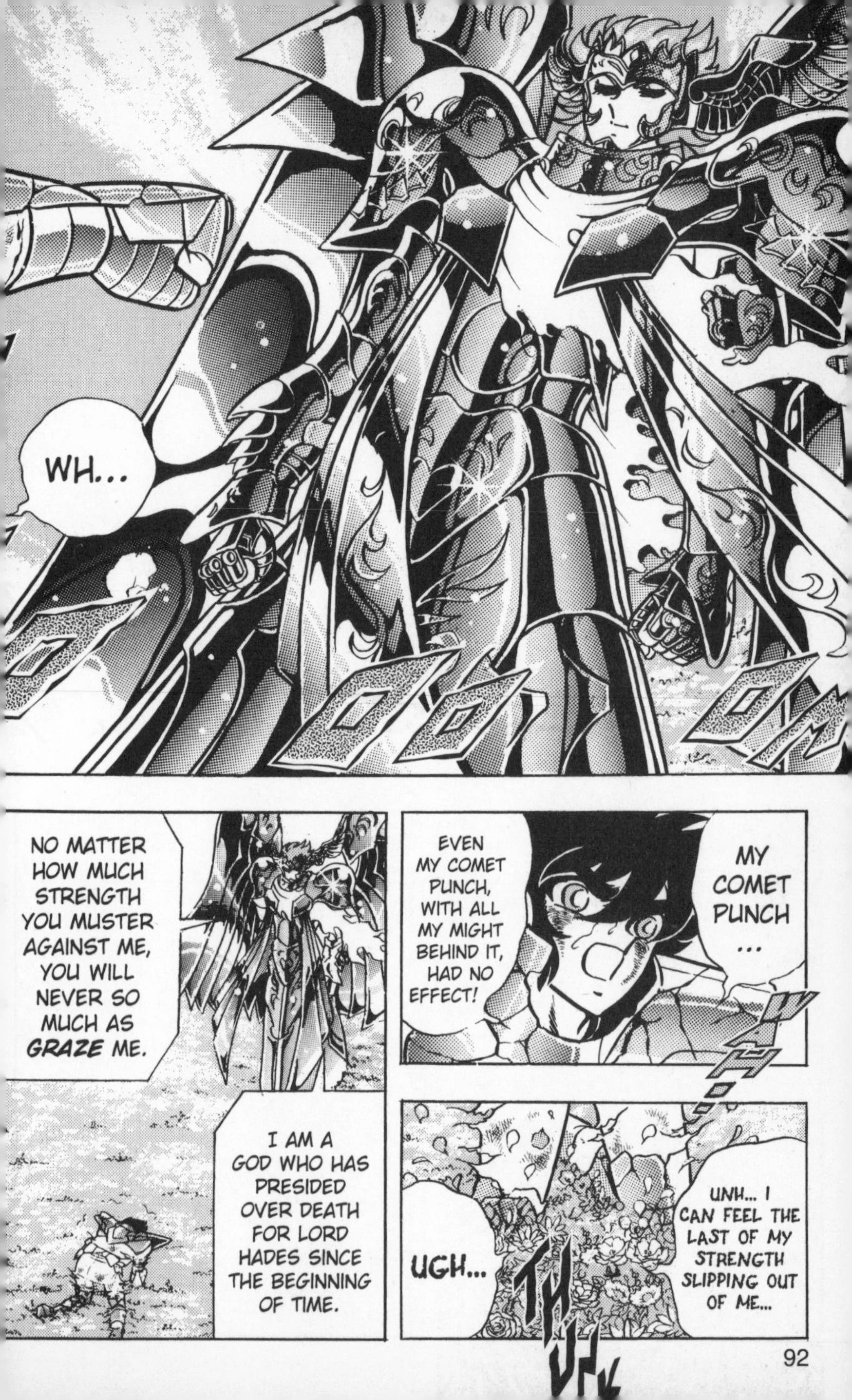
WH...
MY COMET PUNCH ...
EVEN MY COMET PUNCH, WITH ALL MY MIGHT BEHIND IT, HAD NO EFFECT!
UNH... I CAN FEEL THE LAST OF MY STRENGTH SLIPPING OUT OF ME...
UGH...
THUD
NO MATTER HOW MUCH STRENGTH YOU MUSTER AGAINST ME, YOU WILL NEVER SO MUCH AS ***GRAZE*** ME.
I AM A GOD WHO HAS PRESIDED OVER DEATH FOR LORD HADES SINCE THE BEGINNING OF TIME.

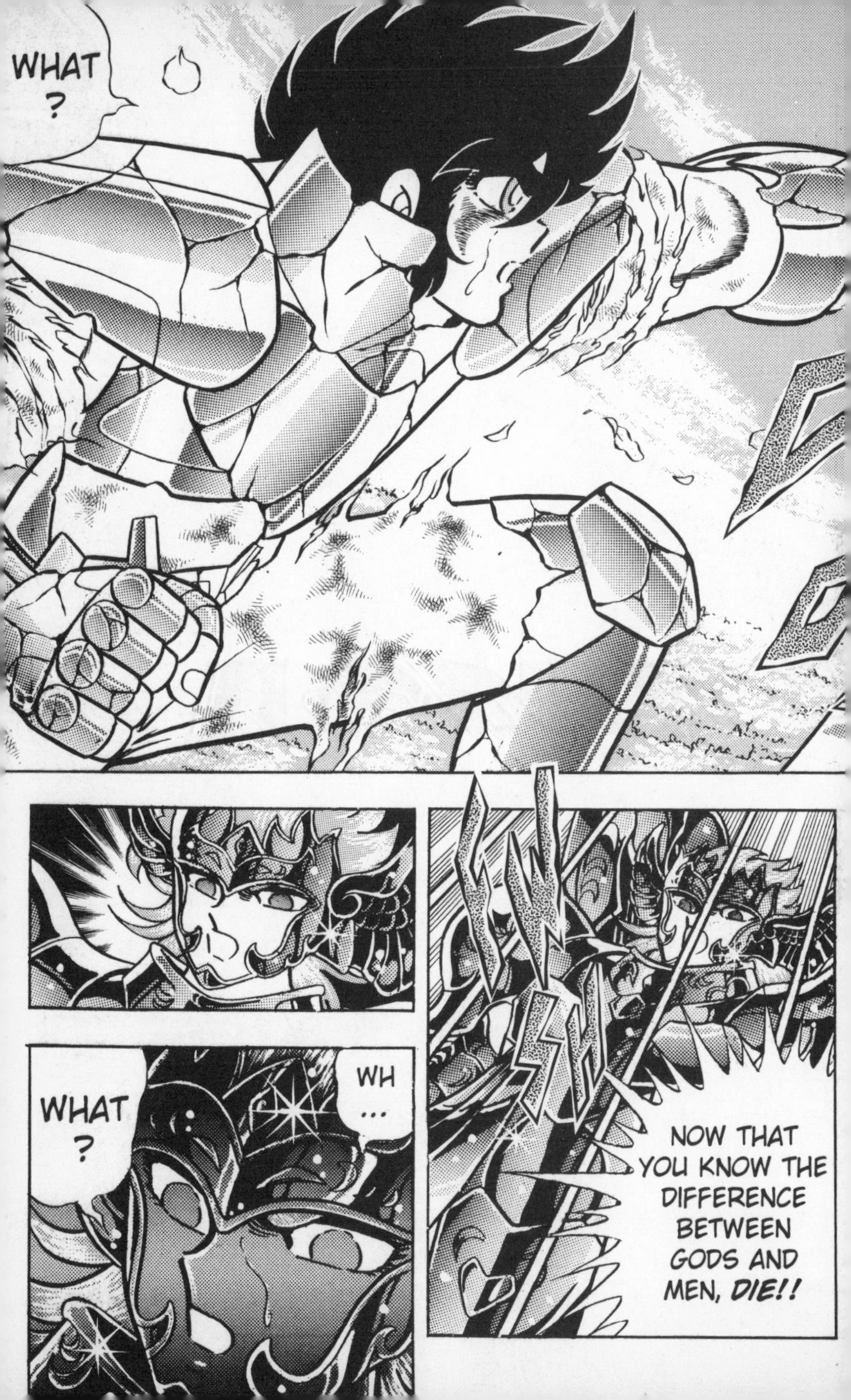
WHAT ?
NOW THAT YOU KNOW THE DIFFERENCE BETWEEN GODS AND MEN, *DIE!!*
WH ...
WHAT ?

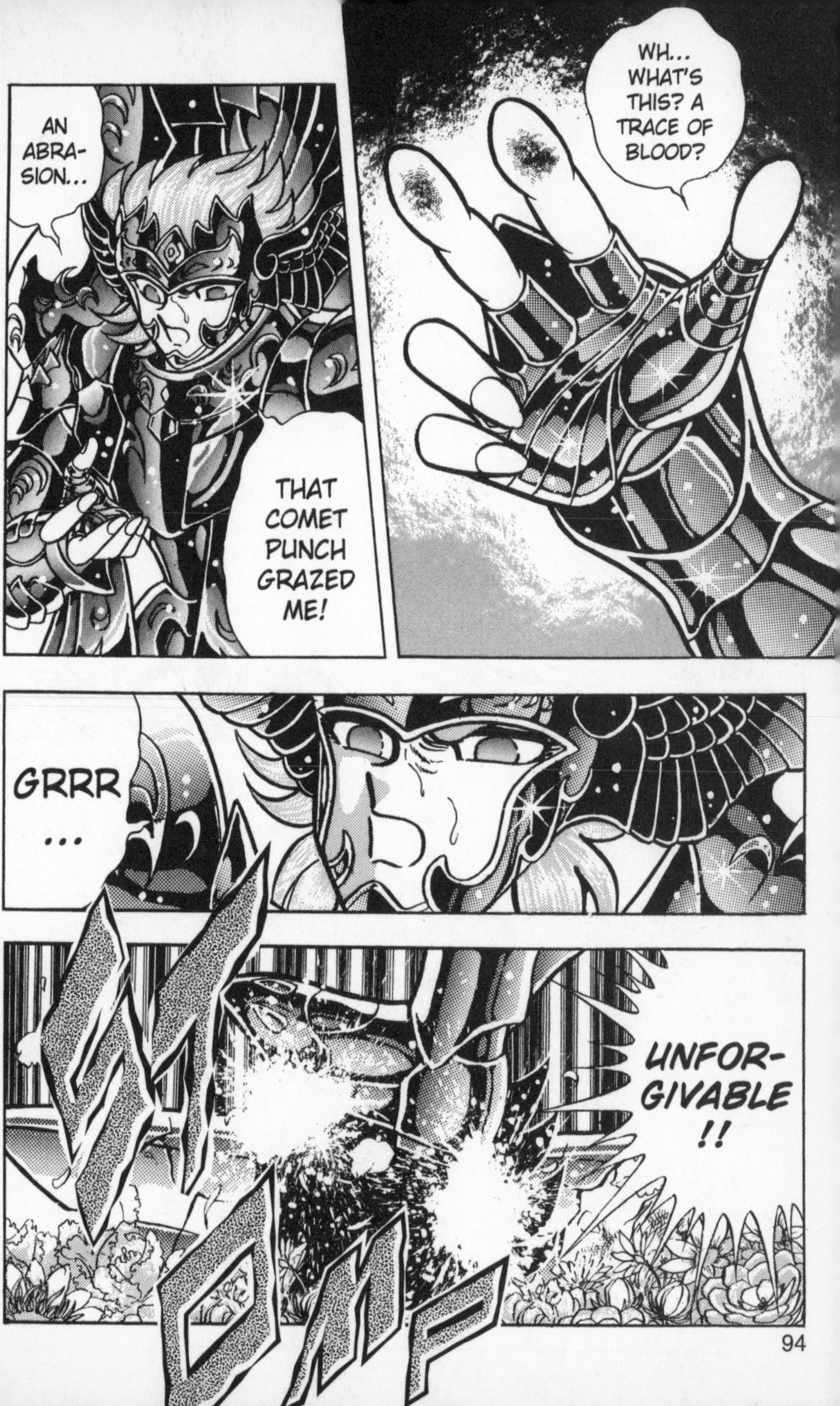
WH... WHAT'S THIS? A TRACE OF BLOOD?
AN ABRASION...
THAT COMET PUNCH GRAZED ME!
GRRR ...
UNFORGIVABLE !!

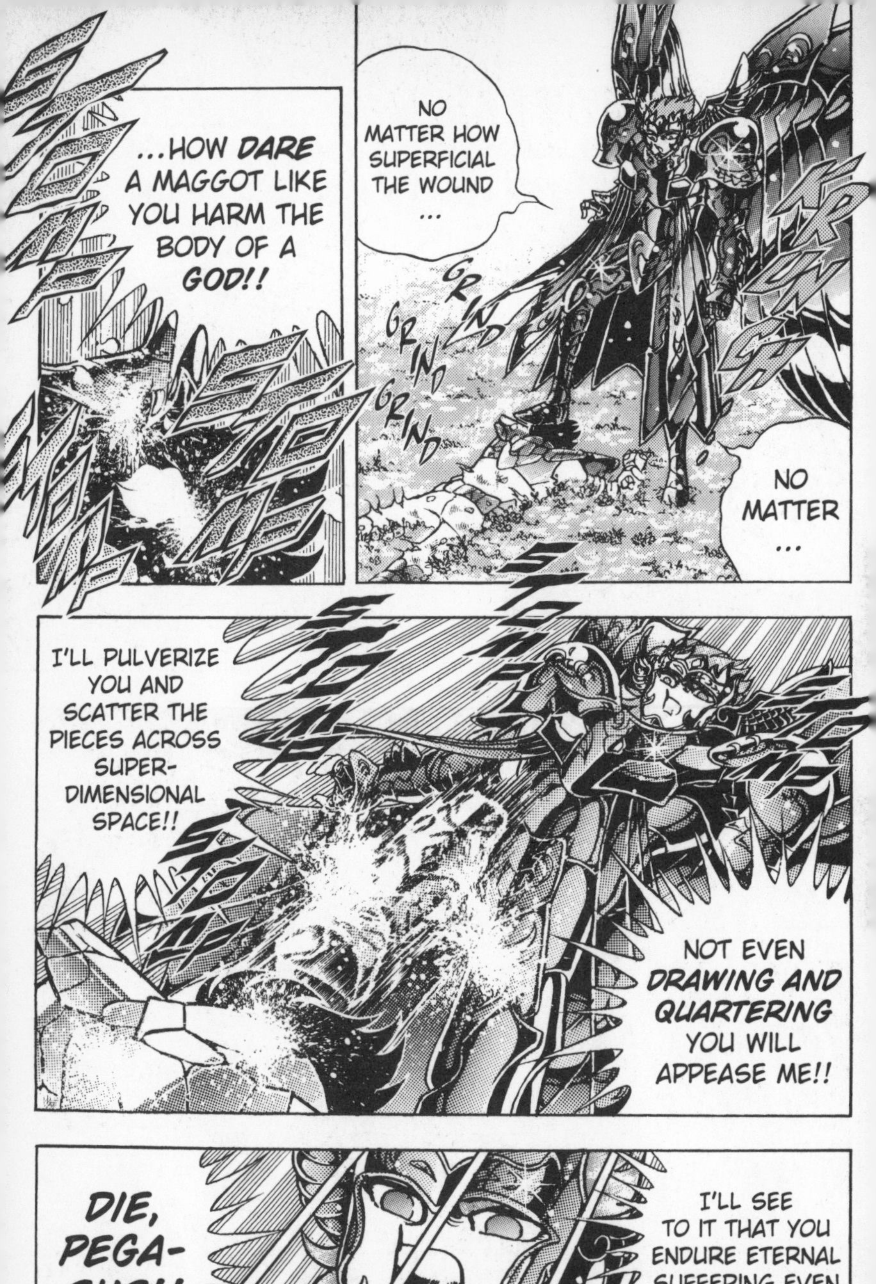
NO MATTER HOW SUPERFICIAL THE WOUND ...
GRIND GRIND GRIND
NO MATTER ...
...HOW DARE A MAGGOT LIKE YOU HARM THE BODY OF A GOD!!
NOT EVEN DRAWING AND QUARTERING YOU WILL APPEASE ME!!
I'LL PULVERIZE YOU AND SCATTER THE PIECES ACROSS SUPER-DIMENSIONAL SPACE!!
I'LL SEE TO IT THAT YOU ENDURE ETERNAL SUFFERING EVEN AFTER DEATH!!
DIE, PEGA-SUS!!

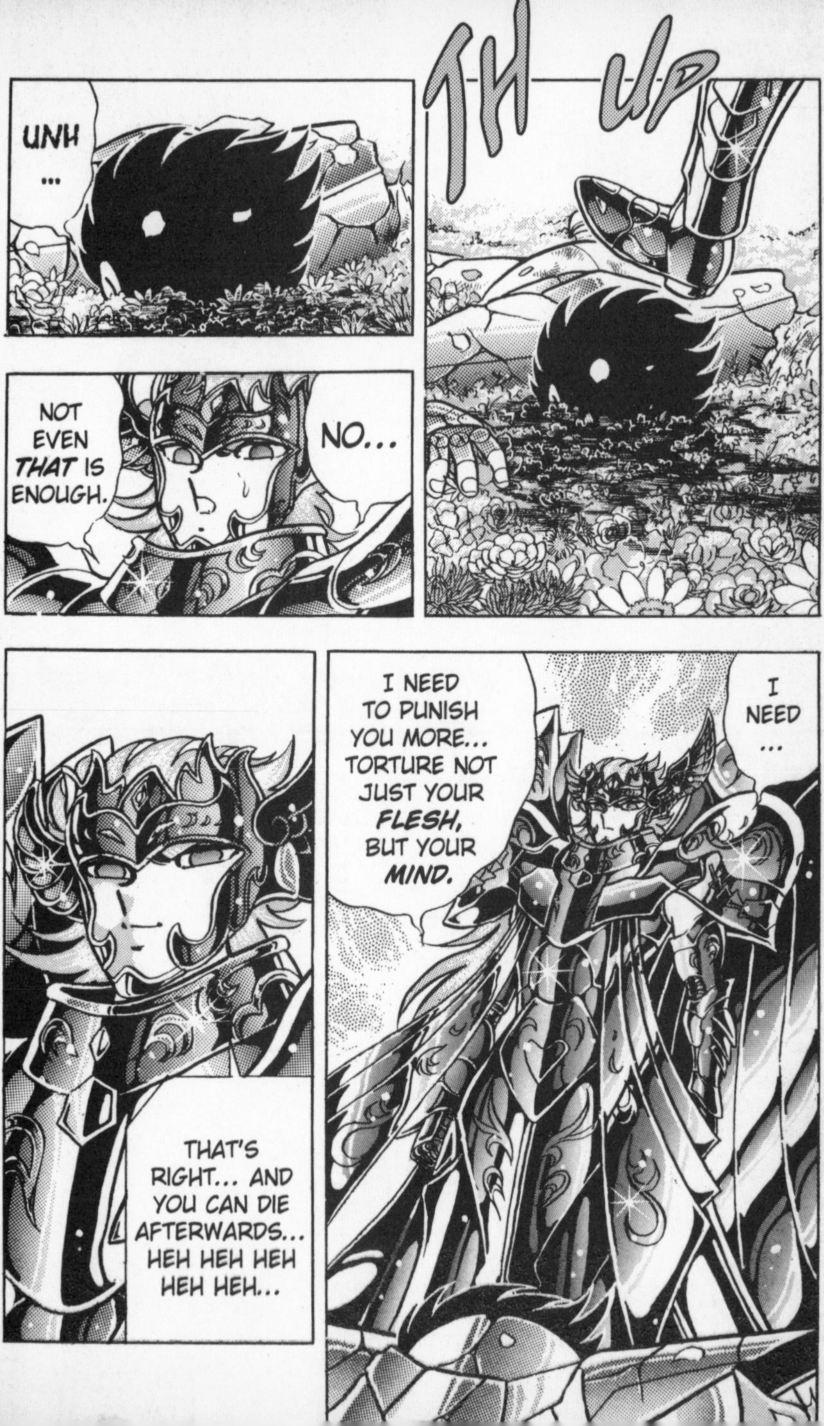
THUD
UNH ...
NO...
NOT EVEN THAT IS ENOUGH.
I NEED ...
I NEED TO PUNISH YOU MORE... TORTURE NOT JUST YOUR FLESH, BUT YOUR MIND.
THAT'S RIGHT... AND YOU CAN DIE AFTERWARDS... HEH HEH HEH HEH HEH...

READ THIS WAY

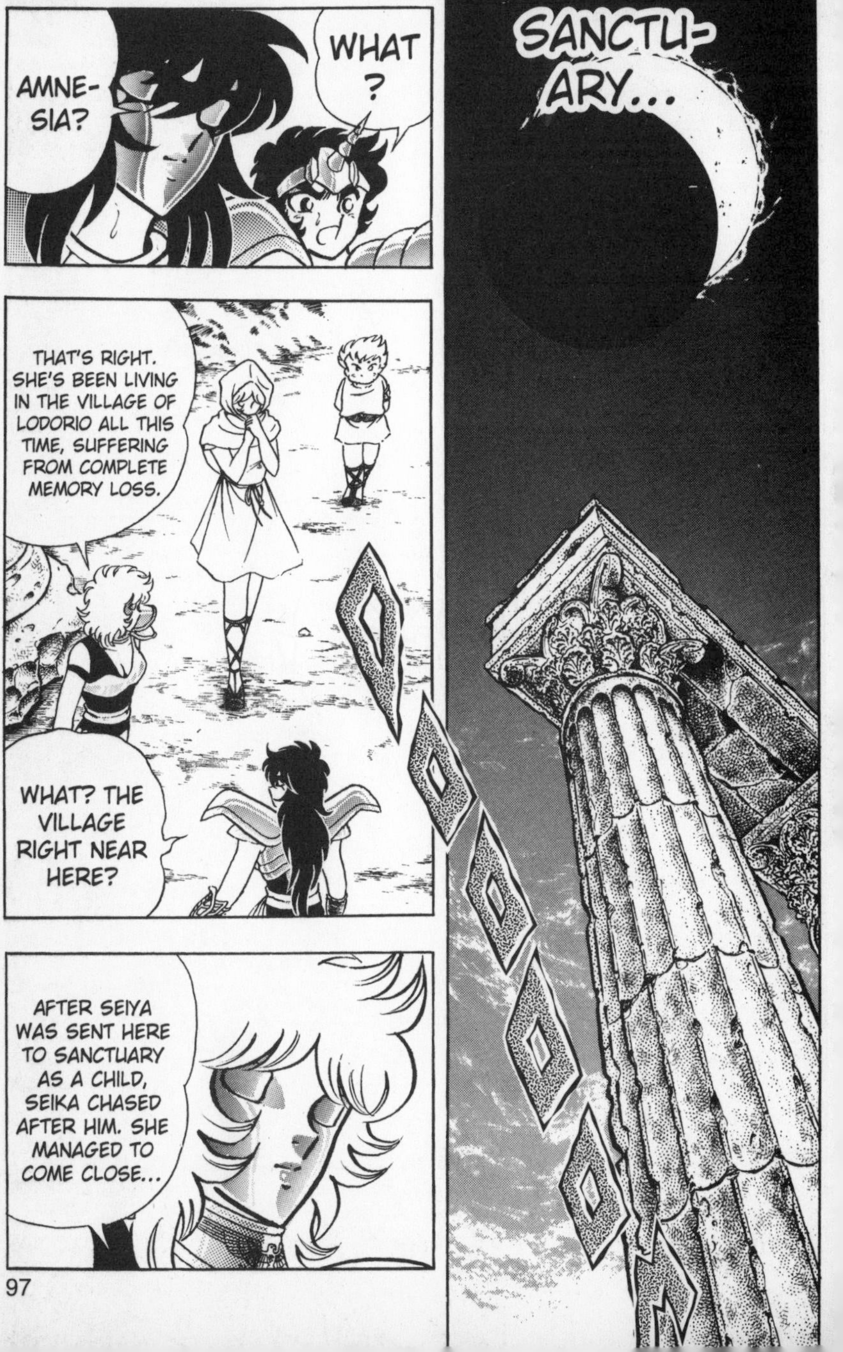
SANCTU-ARY...
AMNE-SIA?
WHAT?
THAT'S RIGHT. SHE'S BEEN LIVING IN THE VILLAGE OF LODORIO ALL THIS TIME, SUFFERING FROM COMPLETE MEMORY LOSS.
WHAT? THE VILLAGE RIGHT NEAR HERE?
AFTER SEIYA WAS SENT HERE TO SANCTUARY AS A CHILD, SEIKA CHASED AFTER HIM. SHE MANAGED TO COME CLOSE...

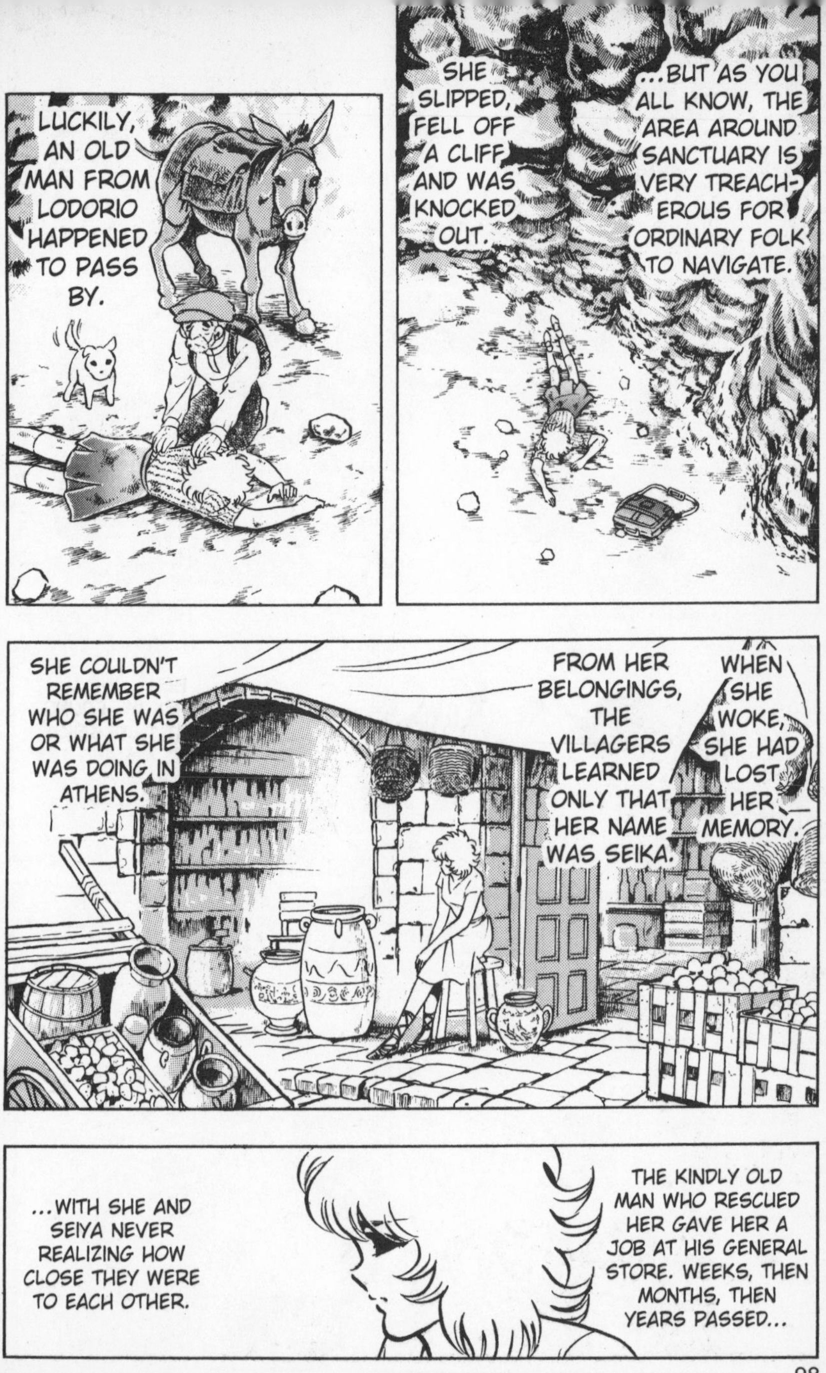
...BUT AS YOU ALL KNOW, THE AREA AROUND SANCTUARY IS VERY TREACHEROUS FOR ORDINARY FOLK TO NAVIGATE.
SHE SLIPPED, FELL OFF A CLIFF AND WAS KNOCKED OUT.
LUCKILY, AN OLD MAN FROM LODORIO HAPPENED TO PASS BY.
WHEN SHE WOKE, SHE HAD LOST HER MEMORY.
FROM HER BELONGINGS, THE VILLAGERS LEARNED ONLY THAT HER NAME WAS SEIKA.
SHE COULDN'T REMEMBER WHO SHE WAS OR WHAT SHE WAS DOING IN ATHENS.
THE KINDLY OLD MAN WHO RESCUED HER GAVE HER A JOB AT HIS GENERAL STORE. WEEKS, THEN MONTHS, THEN YEARS PASSED...
...WITH SHE AND SEIYA NEVER REALIZING HOW CLOSE THEY WERE TO EACH OTHER.

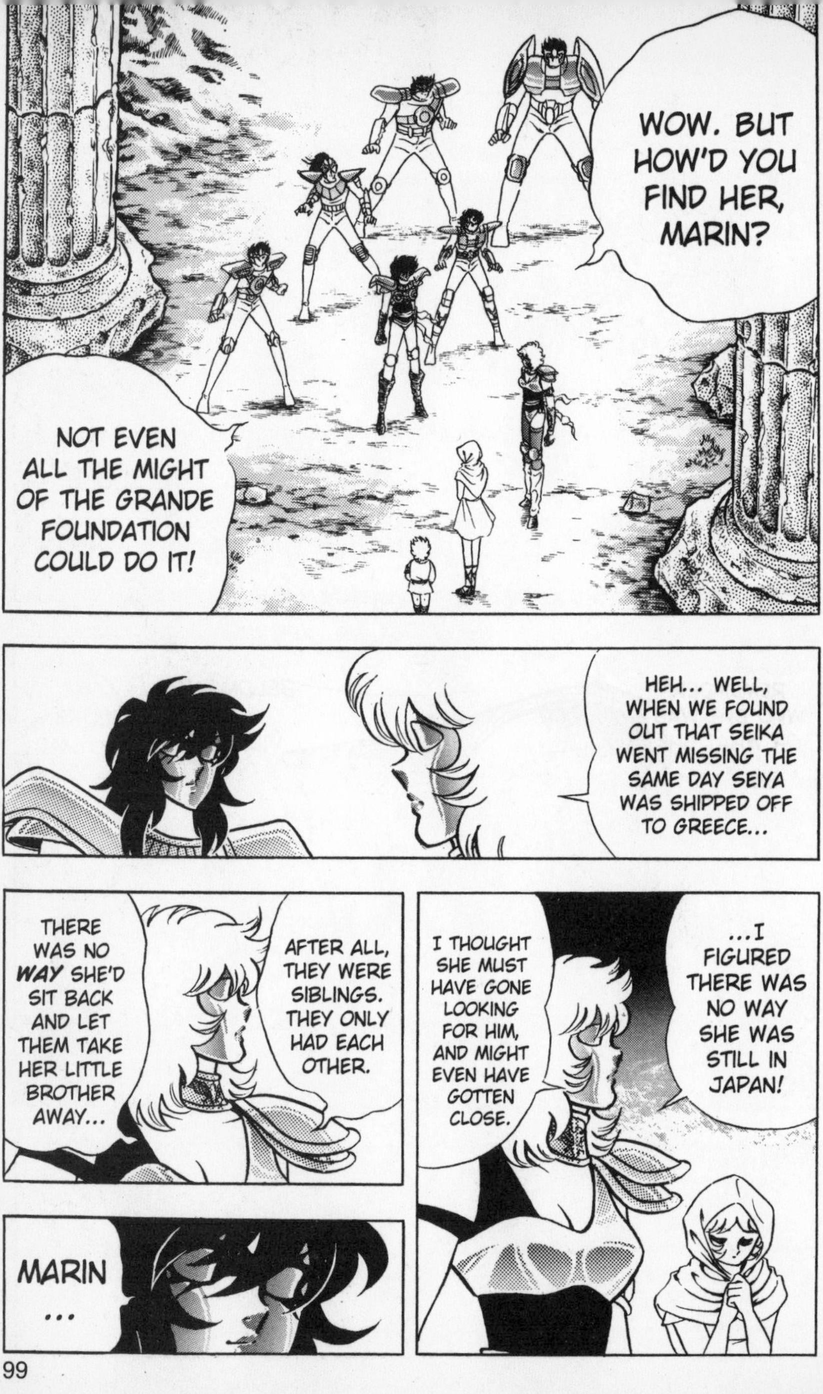
WOW. BUT HOW'D YOU FIND HER, MARIN?
NOT EVEN ALL THE MIGHT OF THE GRANDE FOUNDATION COULD DO IT!
HEH... WELL, WHEN WE FOUND OUT THAT SEIKA WENT MISSING THE SAME DAY SEIYA WAS SHIPPED OFF TO GREECE...
...I FIGURED THERE WAS NO WAY SHE WAS STILL IN JAPAN!
I THOUGHT SHE MUST HAVE GONE LOOKING FOR HIM, AND MIGHT EVEN HAVE GOTTEN CLOSE.
AFTER ALL, THEY WERE SIBLINGS. THEY ONLY HAD EACH OTHER.
THERE WAS NO ***WAY*** SHE'D SIT BACK AND LET THEM TAKE HER LITTLE BROTHER AWAY...
MARIN ...

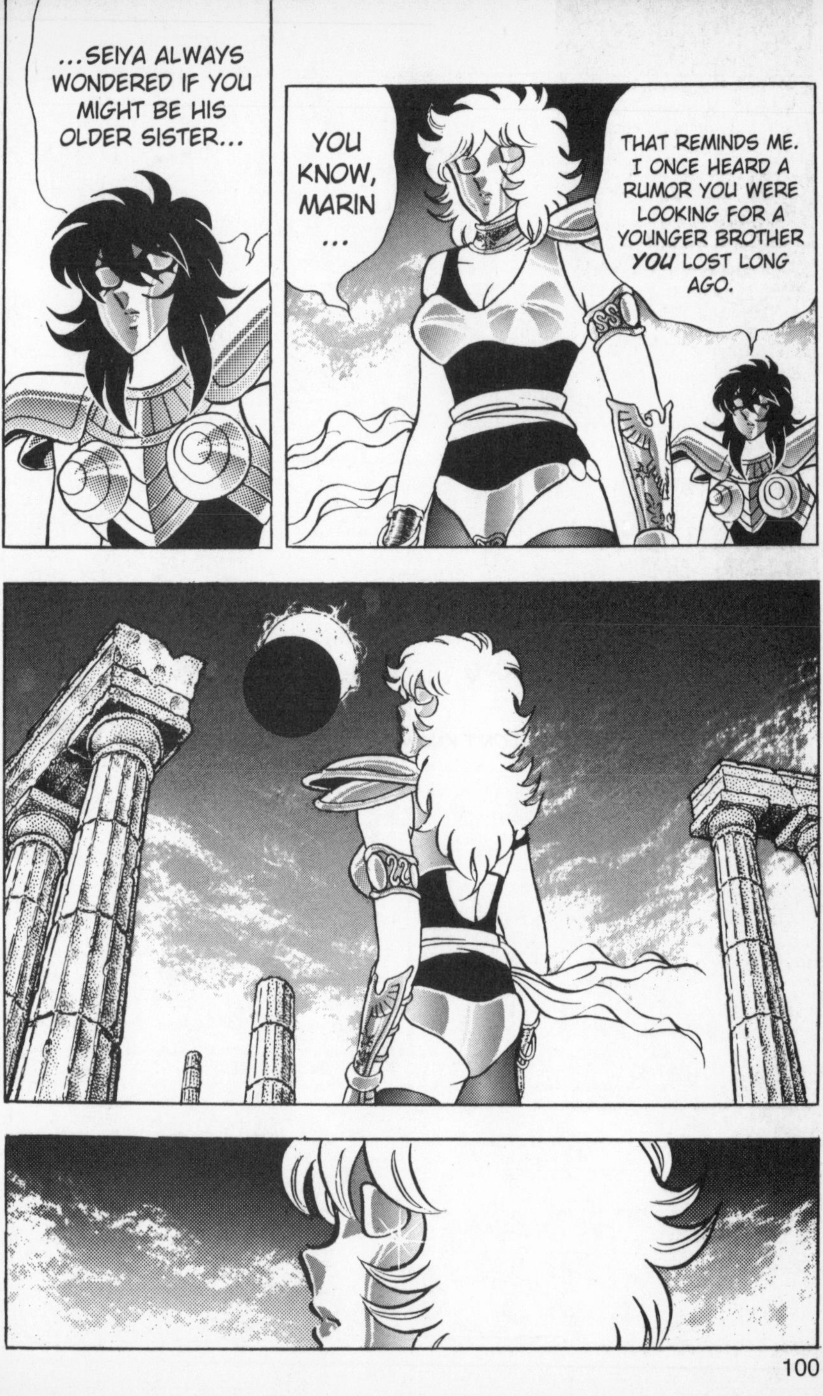
THAT REMINDS ME. I ONCE HEARD A RUMOR YOU WERE LOOKING FOR A YOUNGER BROTHER *YOU* LOST LONG AGO.
YOU KNOW, MARIN ...
...SEIYA ALWAYS WONDERED IF YOU MIGHT BE HIS OLDER SISTER...

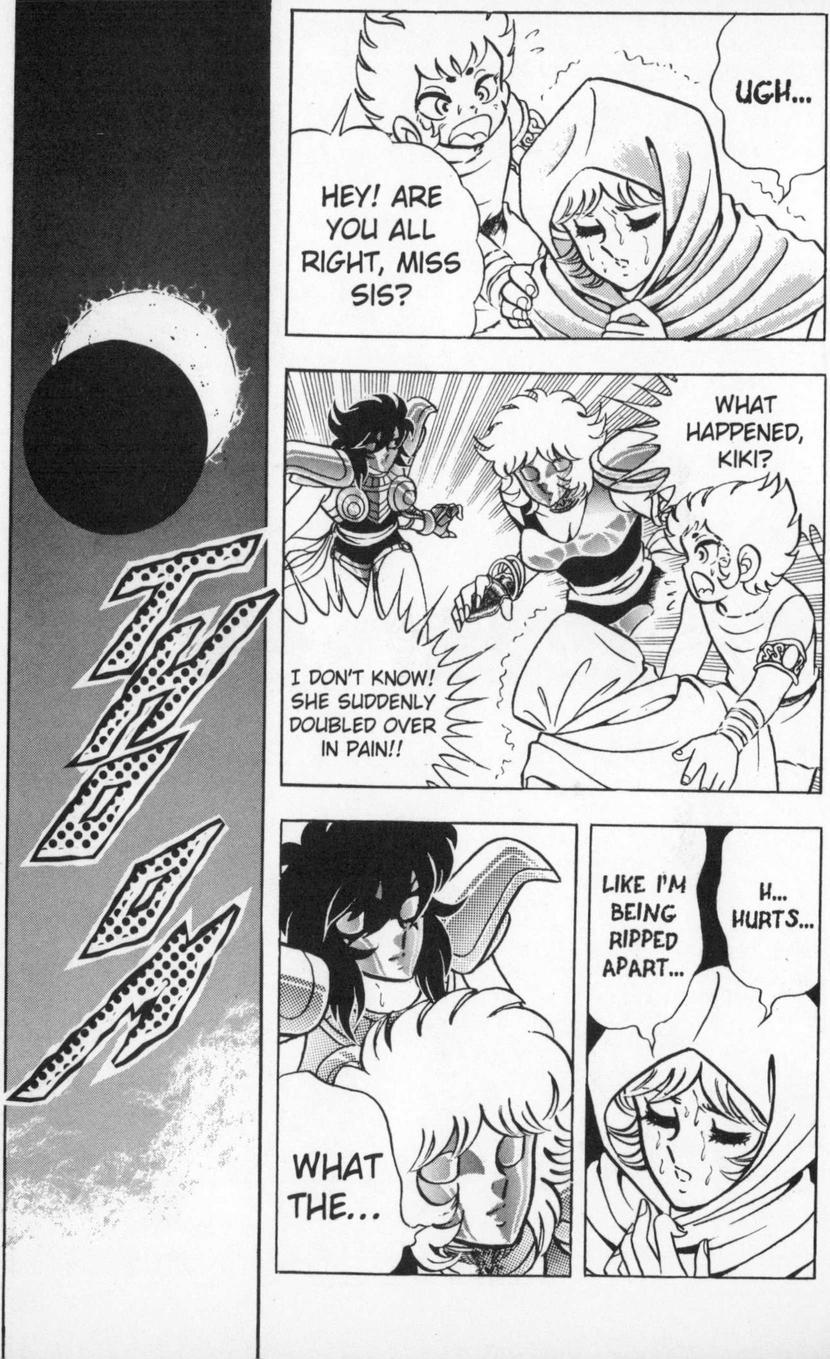
UGH...
HEY! ARE YOU ALL RIGHT, MISS SIS?
WHAT HAPPENED, KIKI?
I DON'T KNOW! SHE SUDDENLY DOUBLED OVER IN PAIN!!
H... HURTS...
LIKE I'M BEING RIPPED APART...
WHAT THE...

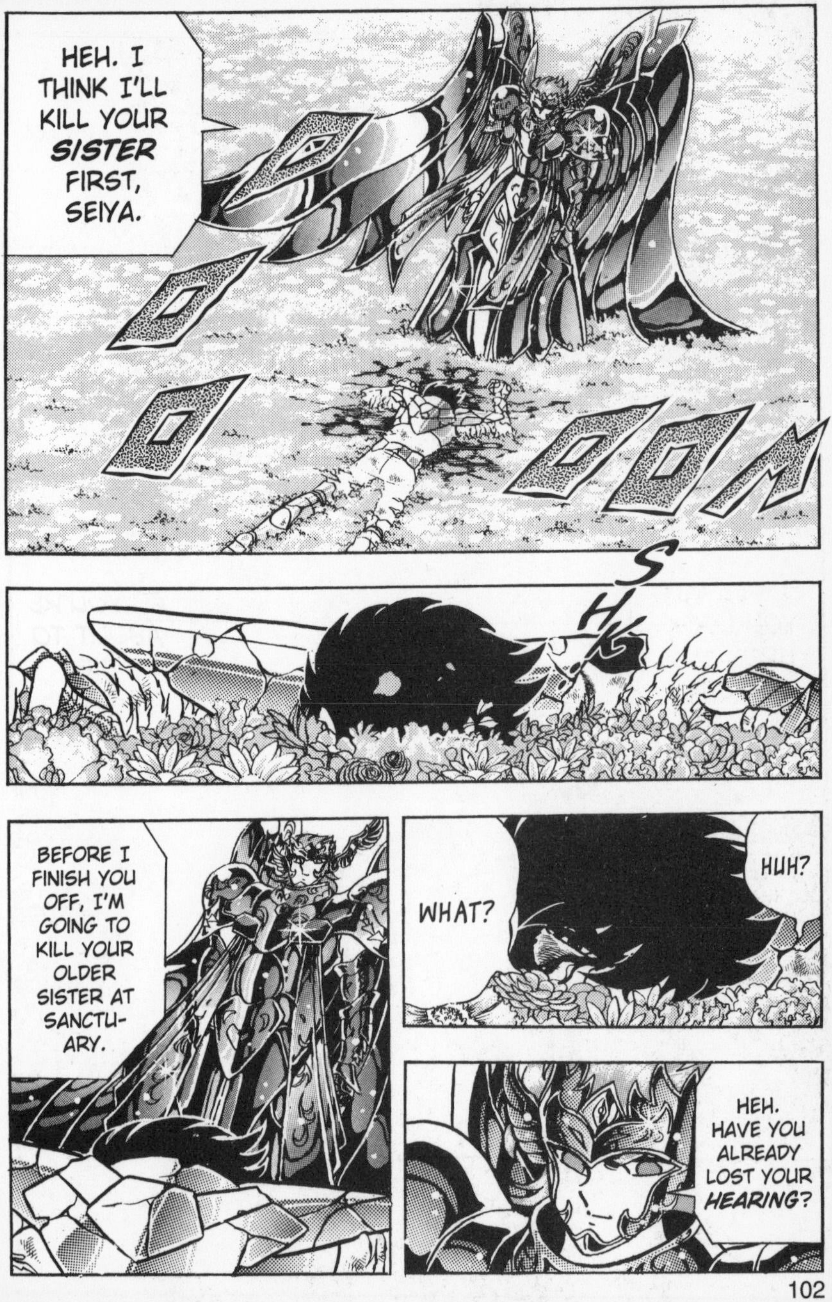
HEH. I THINK I'LL KILL YOUR SISTER FIRST, SEIYA.
DOOOM
SHK
HUH?
WHAT?
HEH. HAVE YOU ALREADY LOST YOUR HEARING?
BEFORE I FINISH YOU OFF, I'M GOING TO KILL YOUR OLDER SISTER AT SANCTUARY.

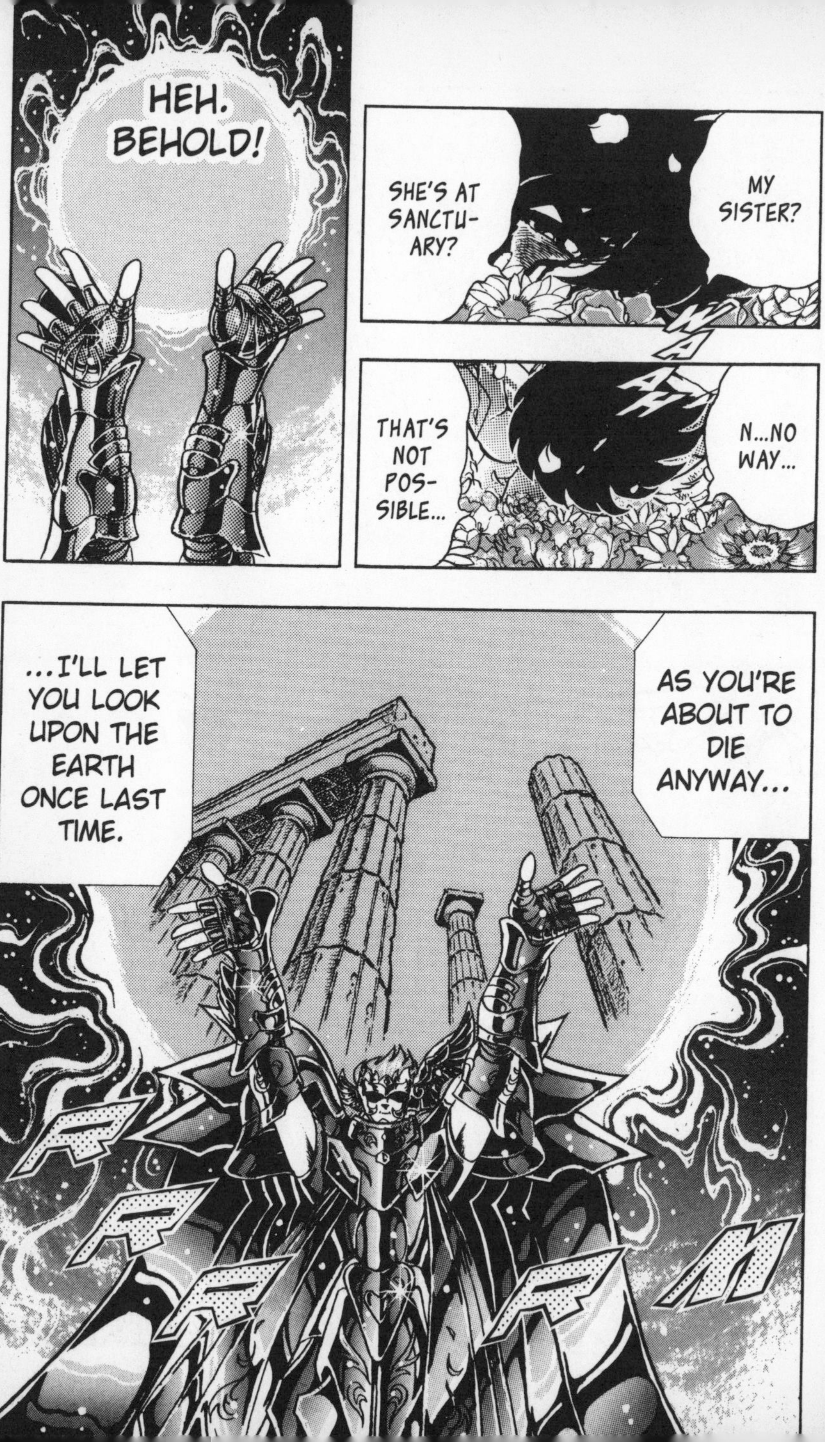
MY SISTER?
SHE'S AT SANCTUARY?
N...NO WAY...
THAT'S NOT POSSIBLE...
WAAH
HEH. BEHOLD!
AS YOU'RE ABOUT TO DIE ANYWAY...
...I'LL LET YOU LOOK UPON THE EARTH ONCE LAST TIME.
FFFFM

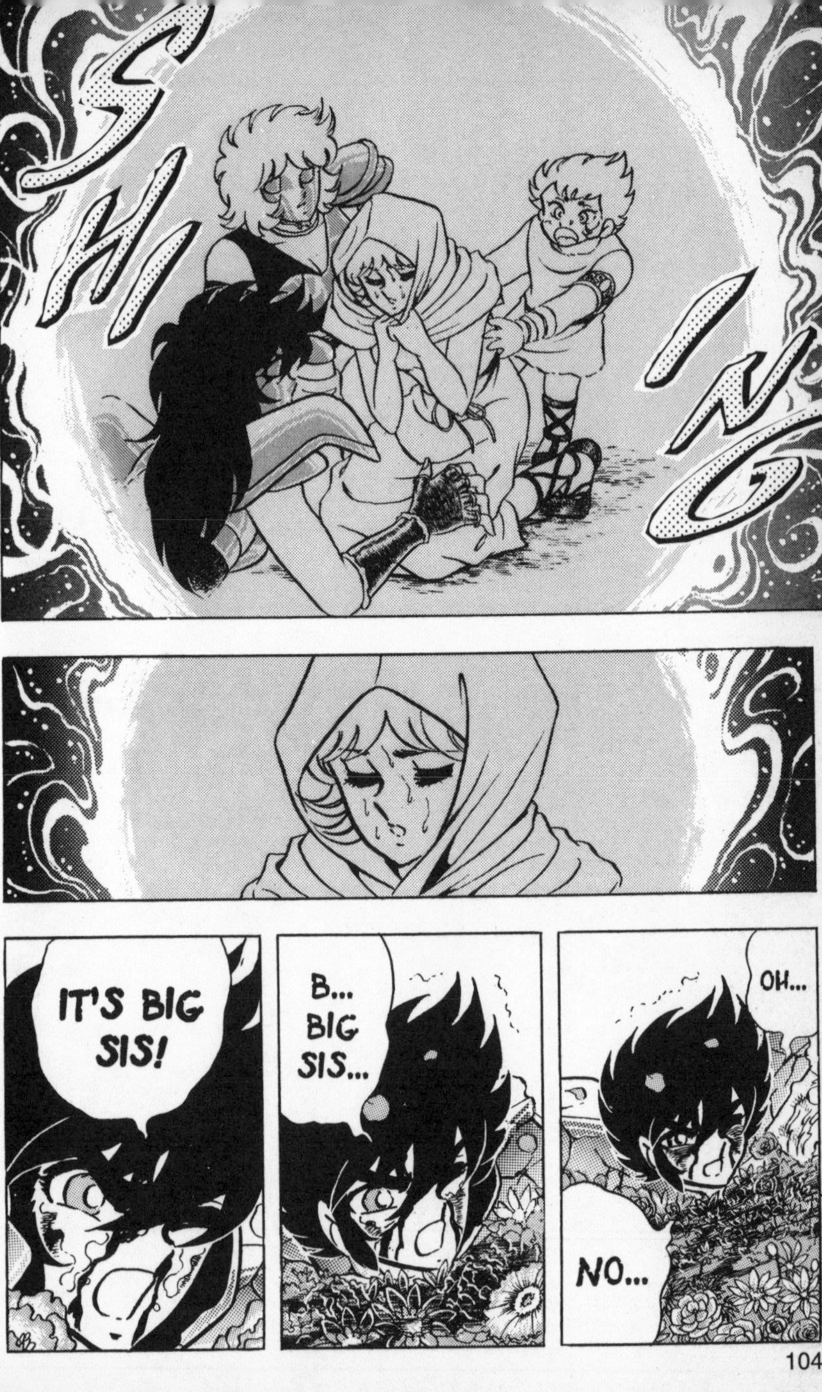
SHIING
OH...
NO...
B... BIG SIS...
IT'S BIG SIS!

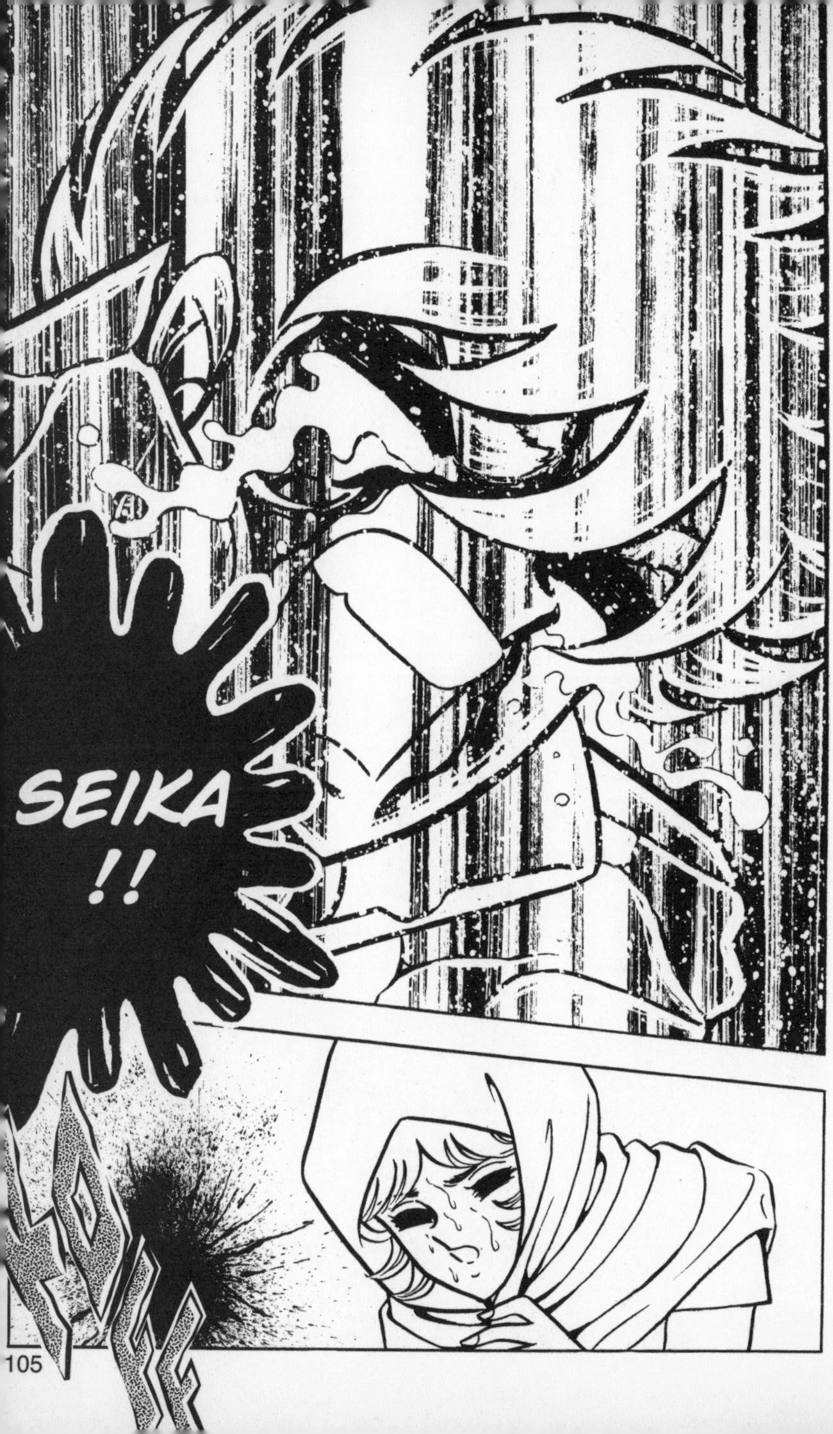
SEIKA !!

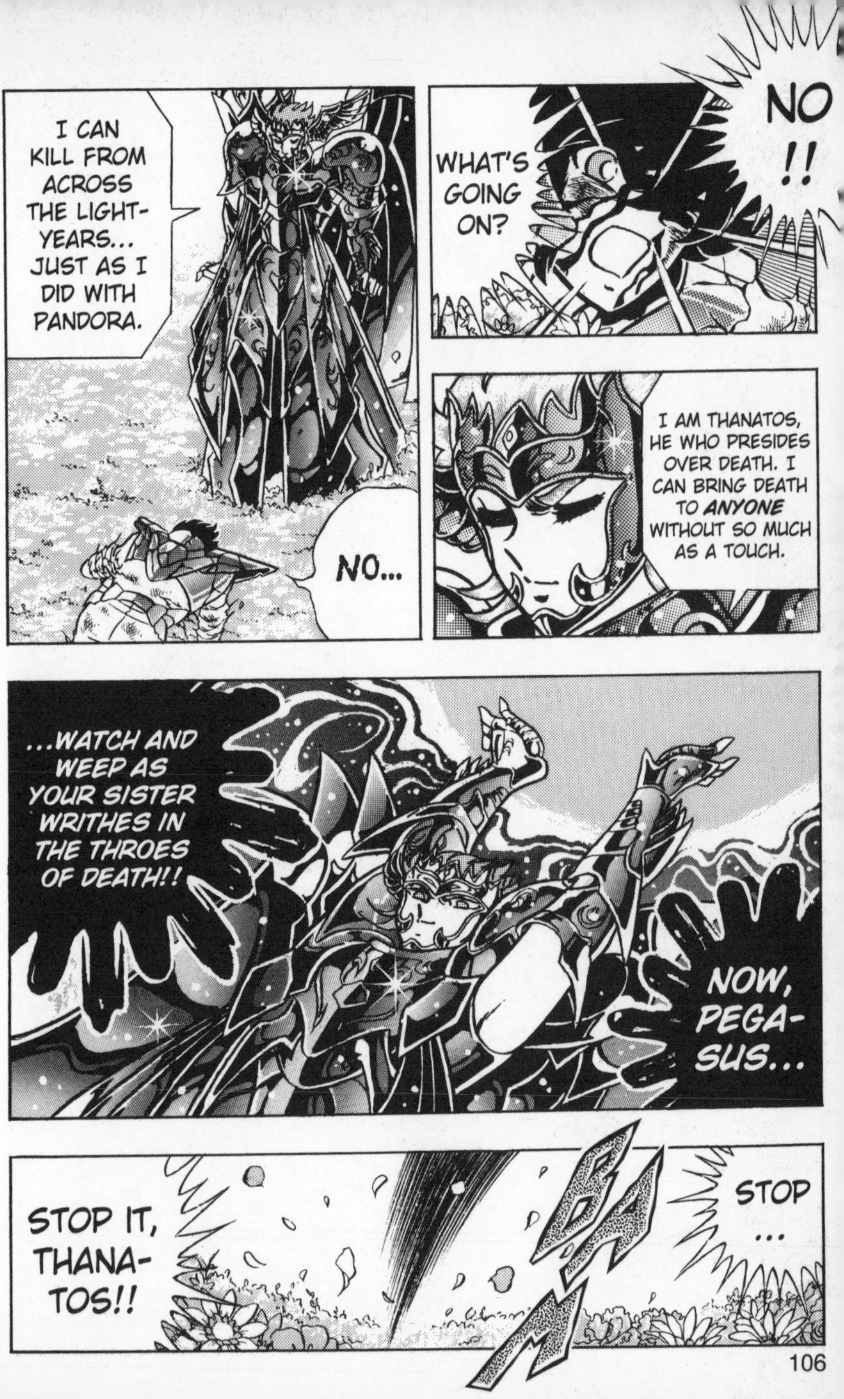
NO !!
WHAT'S GOING ON?
I AM THANATOS, HE WHO PRESIDES OVER DEATH. I CAN BRING DEATH TO *ANYONE* WITHOUT SO MUCH AS A TOUCH.
I CAN KILL FROM ACROSS THE LIGHT-YEARS... JUST AS I DID WITH PANDORA.
NO...
NOW, PEGA-SUS...
...WATCH AND WEEP AS YOUR SISTER WRITHES IN THE THROES OF DEATH!!
STOP ...
STOP IT, THANA-TOS!!

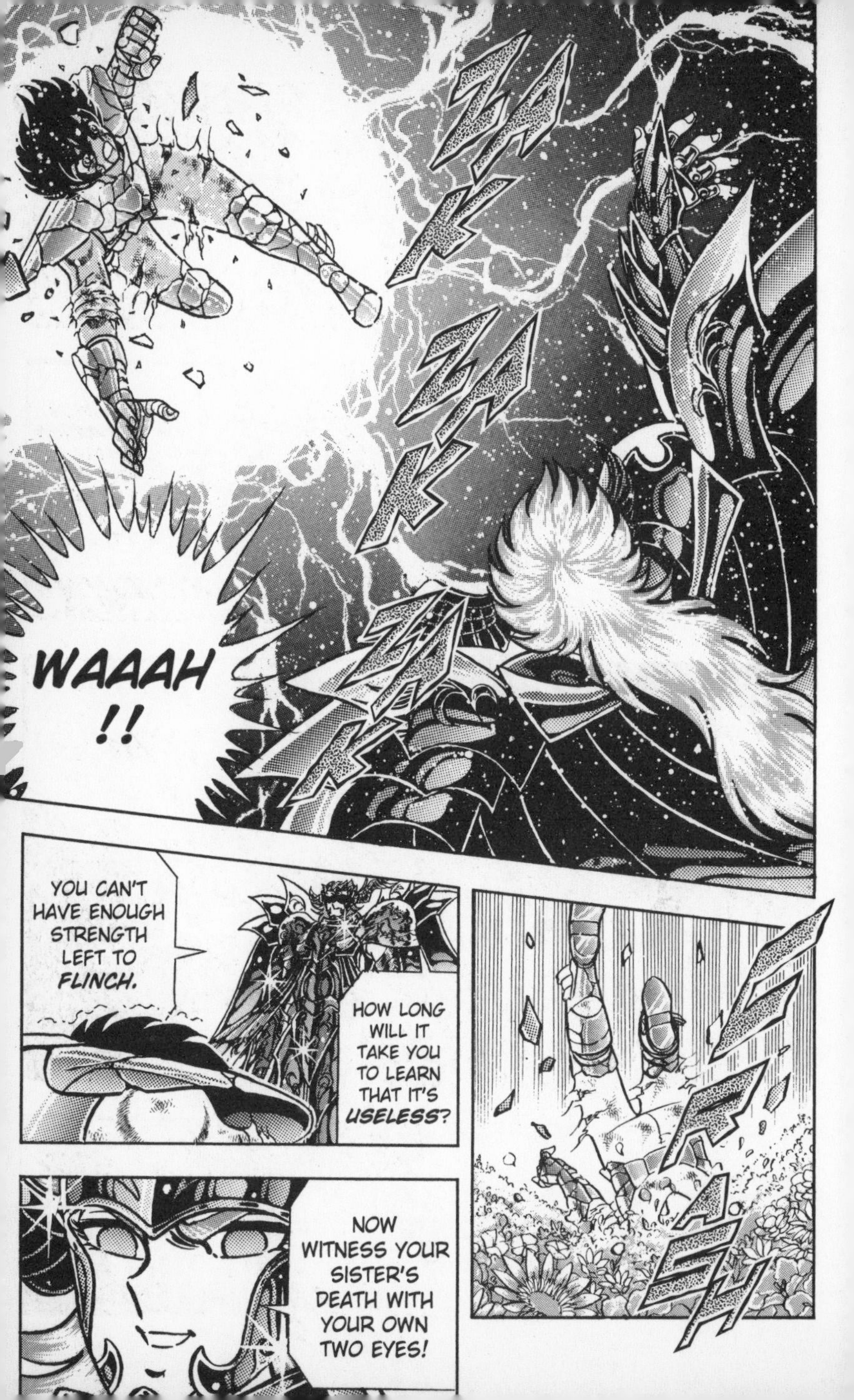
WAAAH !!
YOU CAN'T HAVE ENOUGH STRENGTH LEFT TO FLINCH.
HOW LONG WILL IT TAKE YOU TO LEARN THAT IT'S USELESS?
NOW WITNESS YOUR SISTER'S DEATH WITH YOUR OWN TWO EYES!

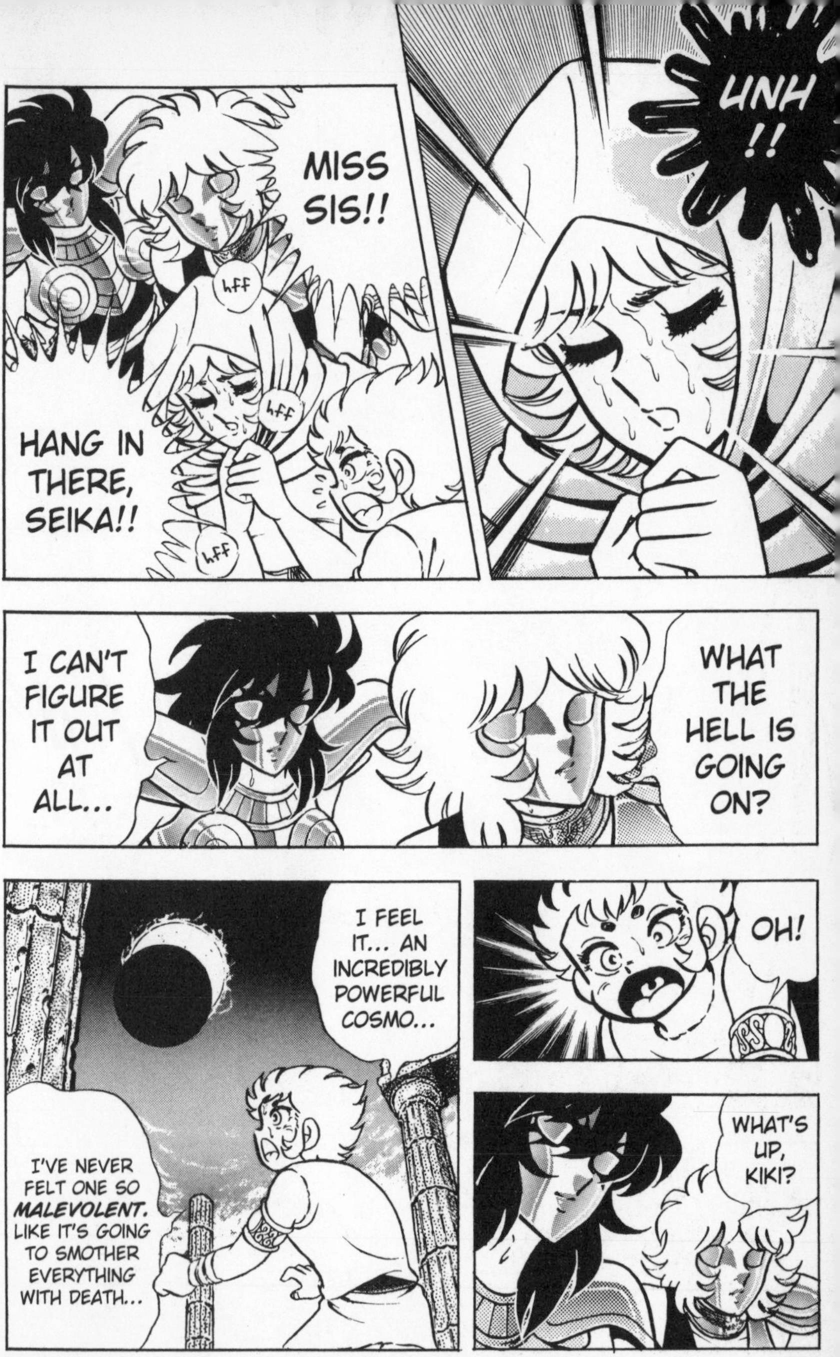
UNH!!
MISS SIS!!
hff
hff
hff
HANG IN THERE, SEIKA!!
WHAT THE HELL IS GOING ON?
I CAN'T FIGURE IT OUT AT ALL...
OH!
WHAT'S UP, KIKI?
I FEEL IT... AN INCREDIBLY POWERFUL COSMO...
I'VE NEVER FELT ONE SO ***MALEVOLENT.*** LIKE IT'S GOING TO SMOTHER EVERYTHING WITH DEATH...

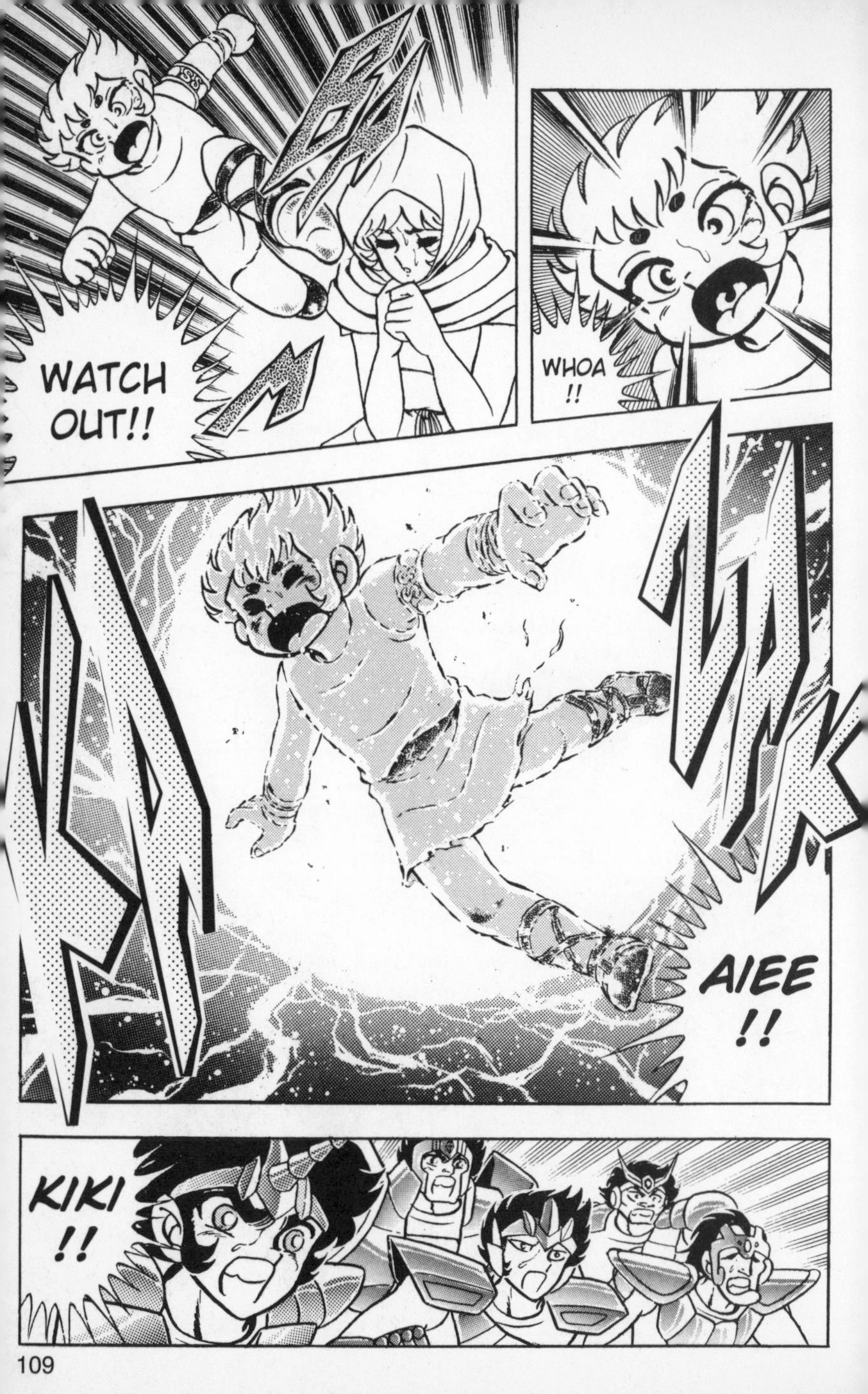
WHOA !!
WATCH OUT!!
AIEE !!
KIKI !!

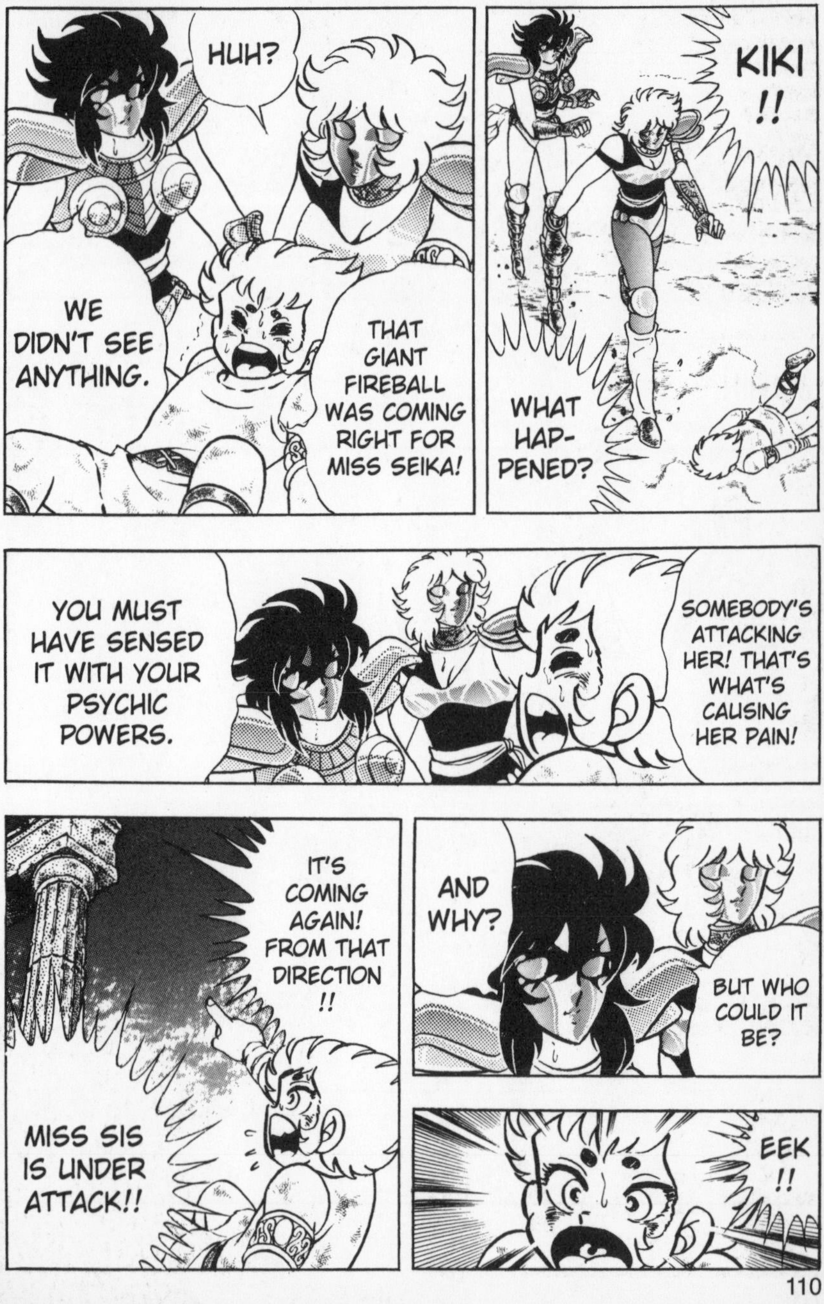
KIKI!!
WHAT HAP-PENED?
HUH?
THAT GIANT FIREBALL WAS COMING RIGHT FOR MISS SEIKA!
WE DIDN'T SEE ANYTHING.
SOMEBODY'S ATTACKING HER! THAT'S WHAT'S CAUSING HER PAIN!
YOU MUST HAVE SENSED IT WITH YOUR PSYCHIC POWERS.
BUT WHO COULD IT BE?
AND WHY?
EEK!!
IT'S COMING AGAIN! FROM THAT DIRECTION!!
MISS SIS IS UNDER ATTACK!!

READ THIS WAY

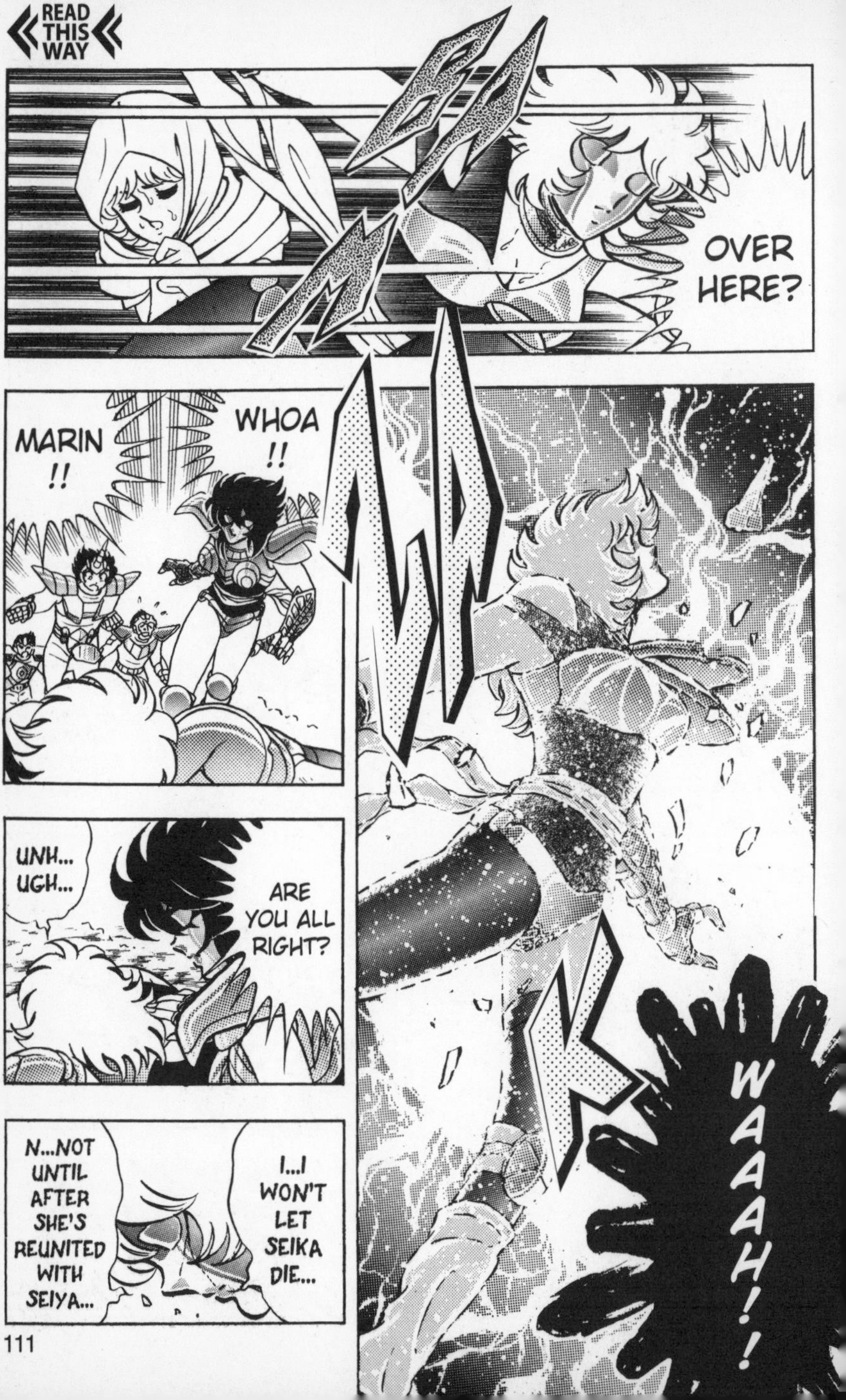
OVER HERE?
WAAAH!!
WHOA!!
MARIN!!
ARE YOU ALL RIGHT?
UNH... UGH...
I...I WON'T LET SEIKA DIE...
N...NOT UNTIL AFTER SHE'S REUNITED WITH SEIYA...

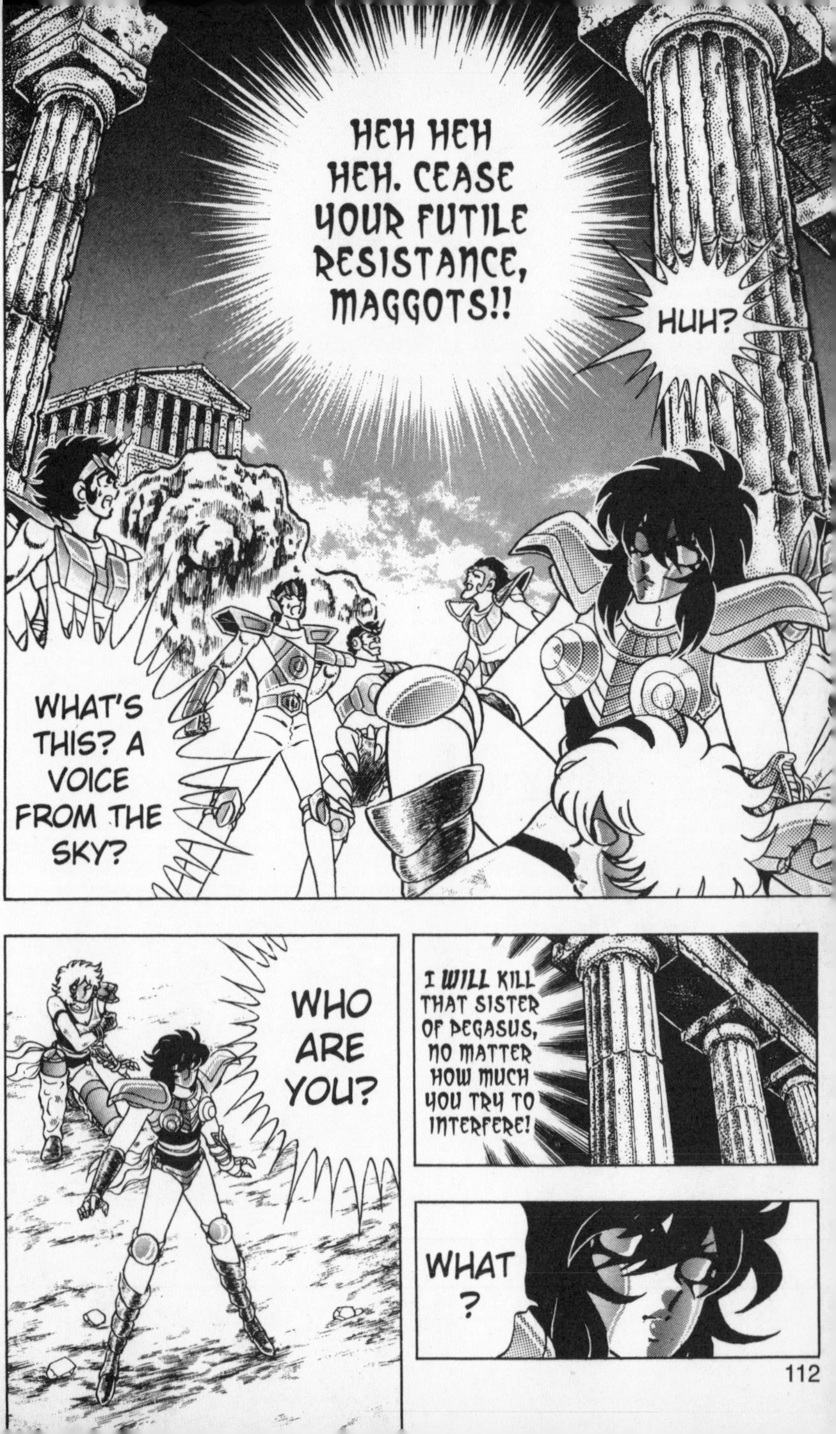
HEH HEH HEH. CEASE YOUR FUTILE RESISTANCE, MAGGOTS!!
HUH?
WHAT'S THIS? A VOICE FROM THE SKY?
I WILL KILL THAT SISTER OF PEGASUS, NO MATTER HOW MUCH YOU TRY TO INTERFERE!
WHAT ?
WHO ARE YOU?

READ THIS WAY

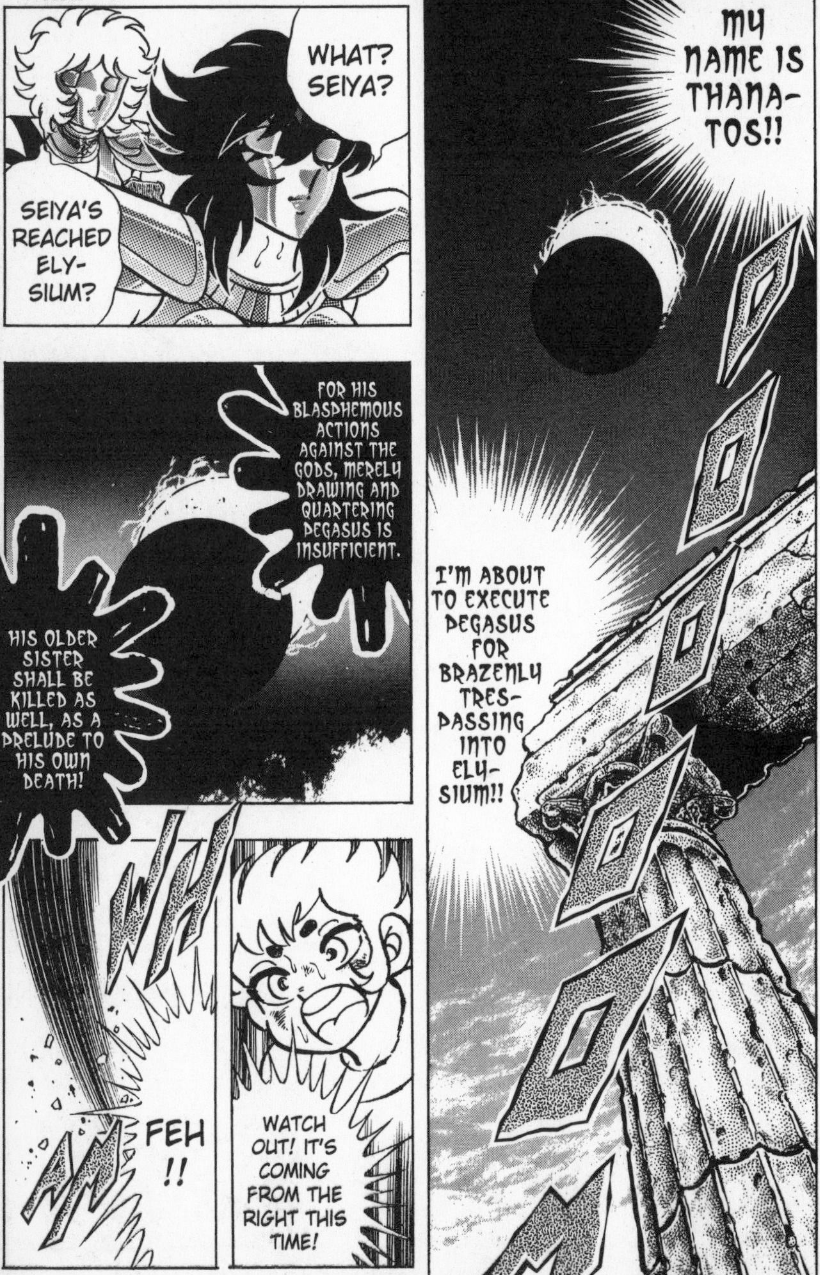

MY NAME IS THANATOS!!
I'M ABOUT TO EXECUTE PEGASUS FOR BRAZENLY TRESPASSING INTO ELYSIUM!!
WHAT? SEIYA?
SEIYA'S REACHED ELYSIUM?
FOR HIS BLASPHEMOUS ACTIONS AGAINST THE GODS, MERELY DRAWING AND QUARTERING PEGASUS IS INSUFFICIENT.
HIS OLDER SISTER SHALL BE KILLED AS WELL, AS A PRELUDE TO HIS OWN DEATH!
WATCH OUT! IT'S COMING FROM THE RIGHT THIS TIME!
FEH !!

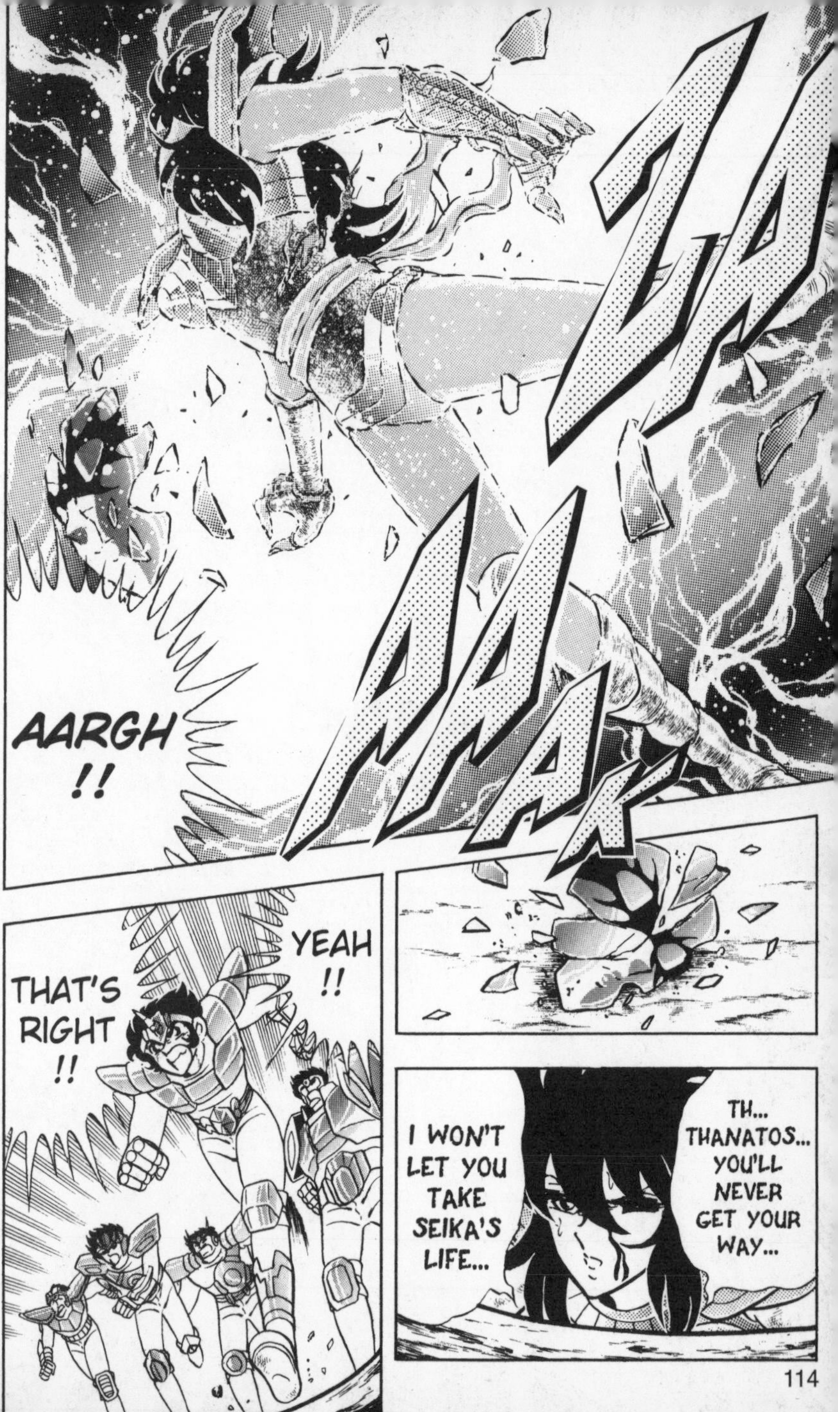
AARGH!!
TH... THANATOS... YOU'LL NEVER GET YOUR WAY...
I WON'T LET YOU TAKE SEIKA'S LIFE...
YEAH!!
THAT'S RIGHT!!

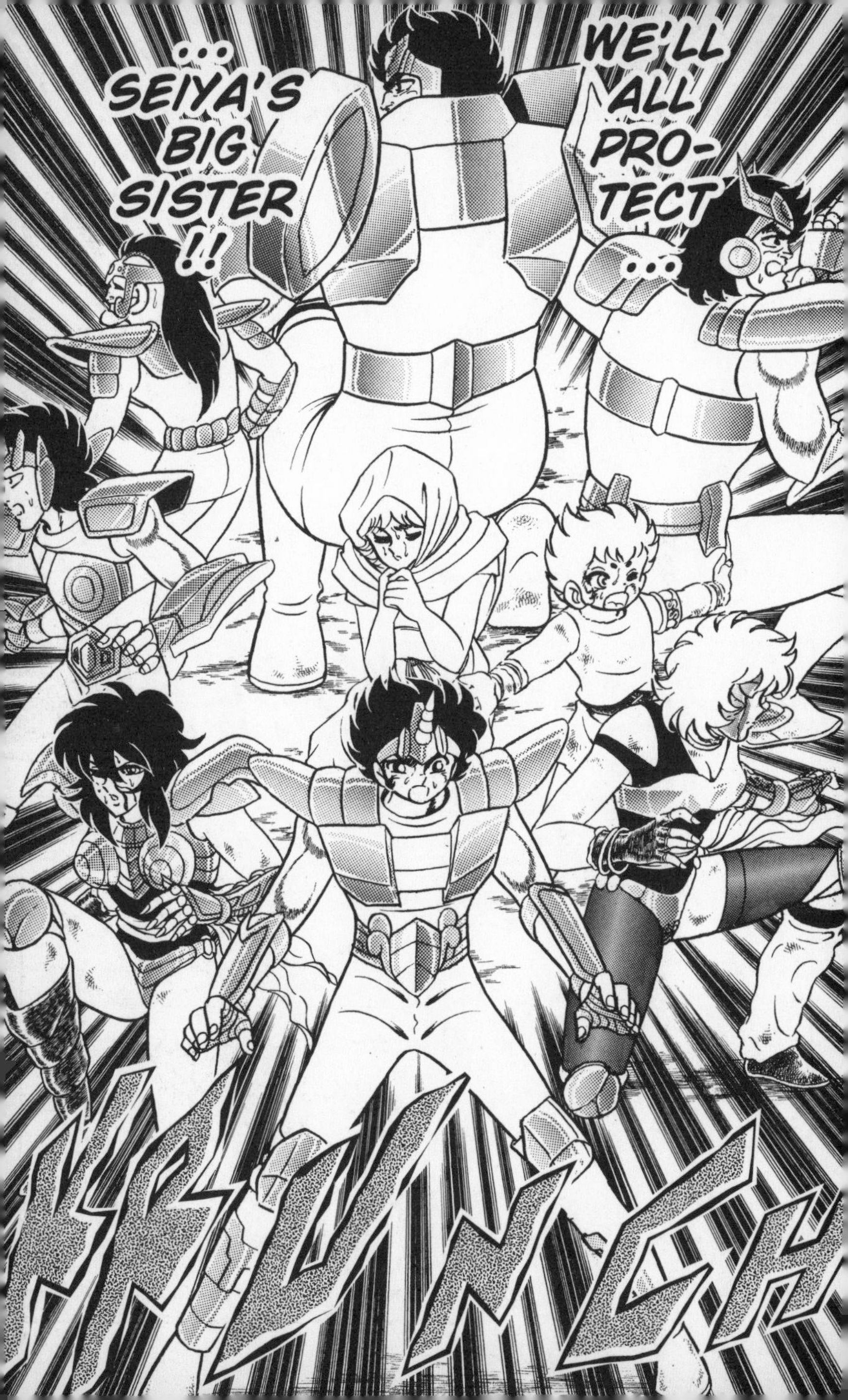
WE'LL ALL PRO-TECT ...
... SEIYA'S BIG SISTER!!

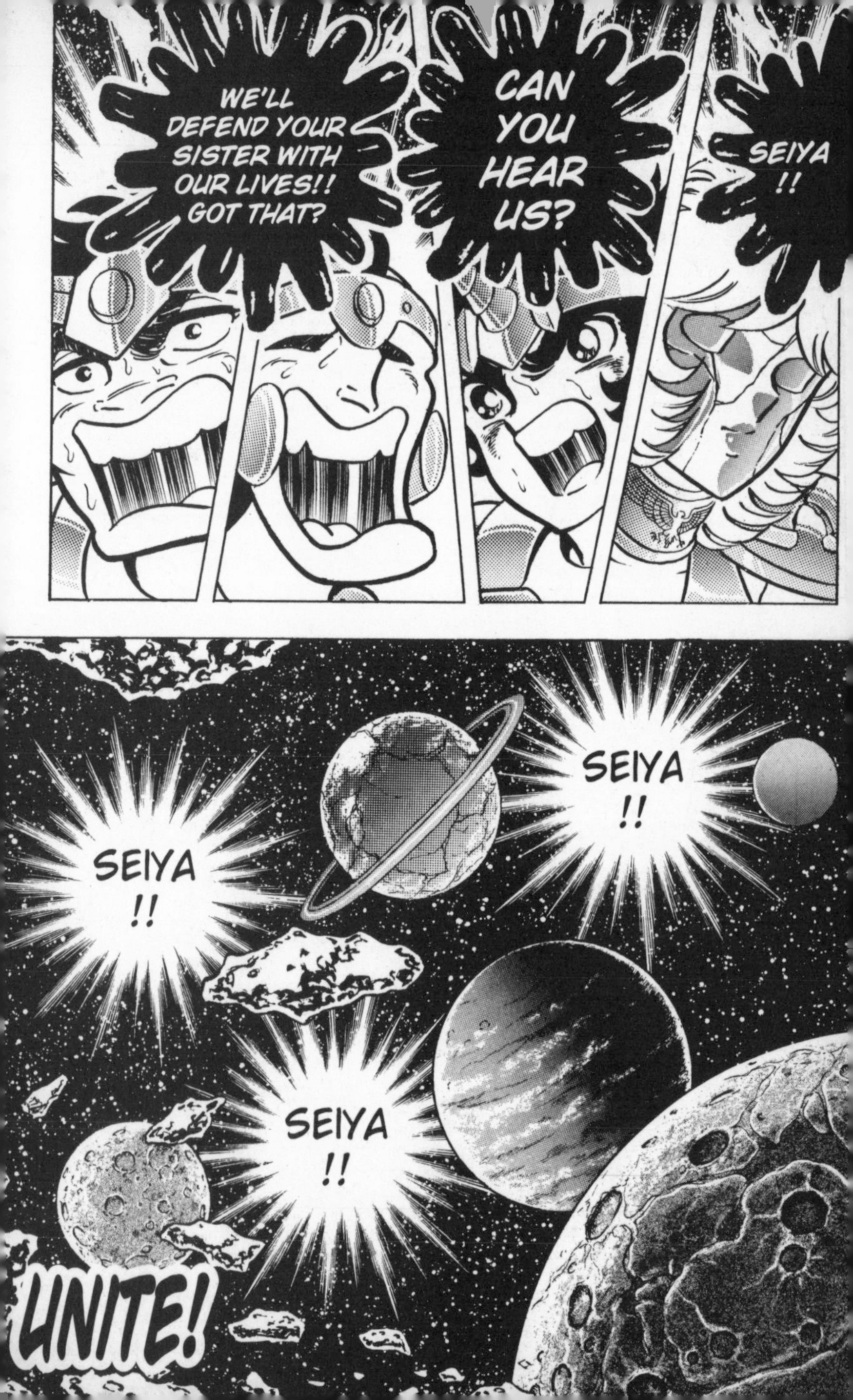
SEIYA !!
CAN YOU HEAR US?
WE'LL DEFEND YOUR SISTER WITH OUR LIVES!! GOT THAT?
SEIYA !!
SEIYA !!
SEIYA !!
UNITE!

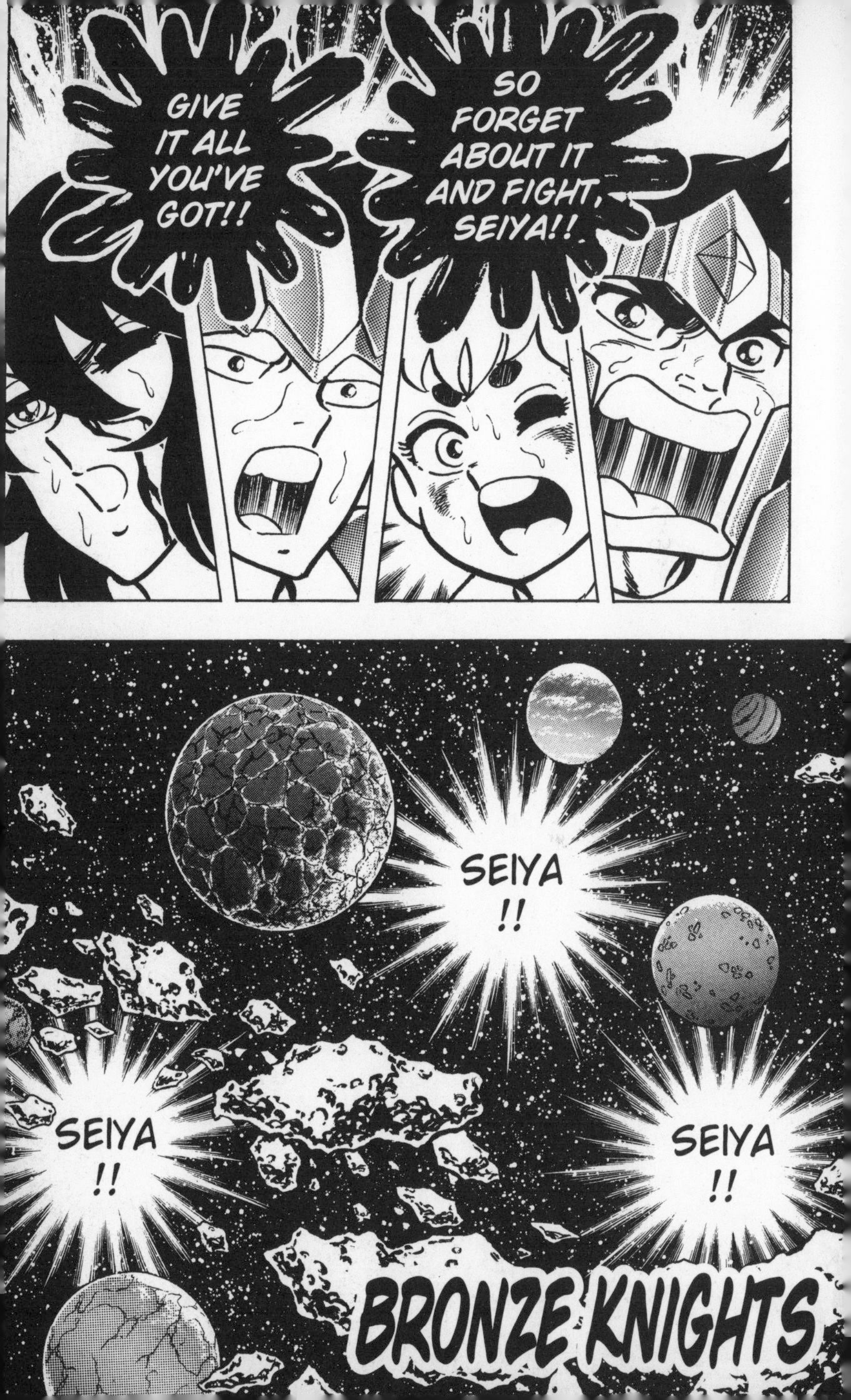
SO FORGET ABOUT IT AND FIGHT, SEIYA!!
GIVE IT ALL YOU'VE GOT!!
SEIYA!!
SEIYA!!
SEIYA!!
BRONZE KNIGHTS

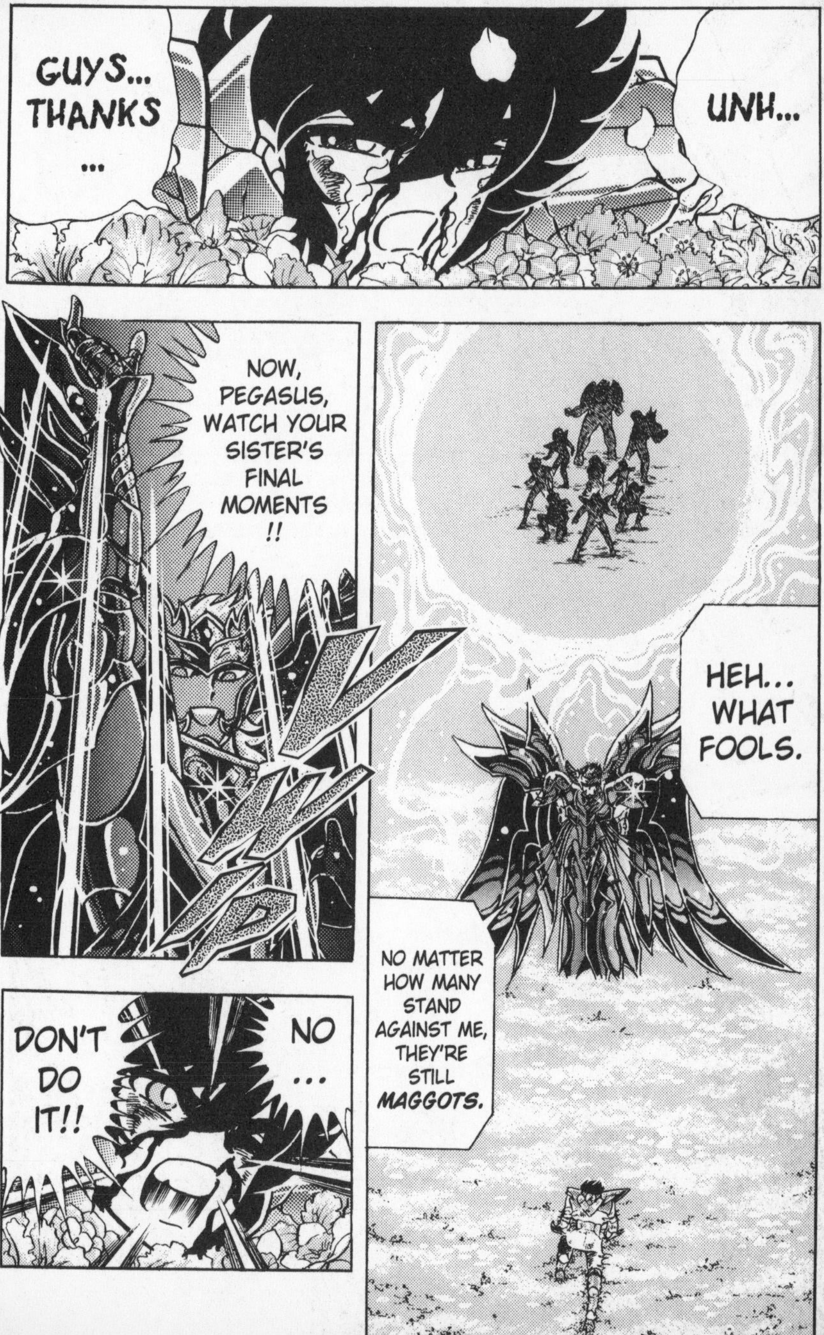
UNH...
GUYS... THANKS ...
HEH... WHAT FOOLS.
NO MATTER HOW MANY STAND AGAINST ME, THEY'RE STILL *MAGGOTS.*
NOW, PEGASUS, WATCH YOUR SISTER'S FINAL MOMENTS !!
NO ...
DON'T DO IT!!

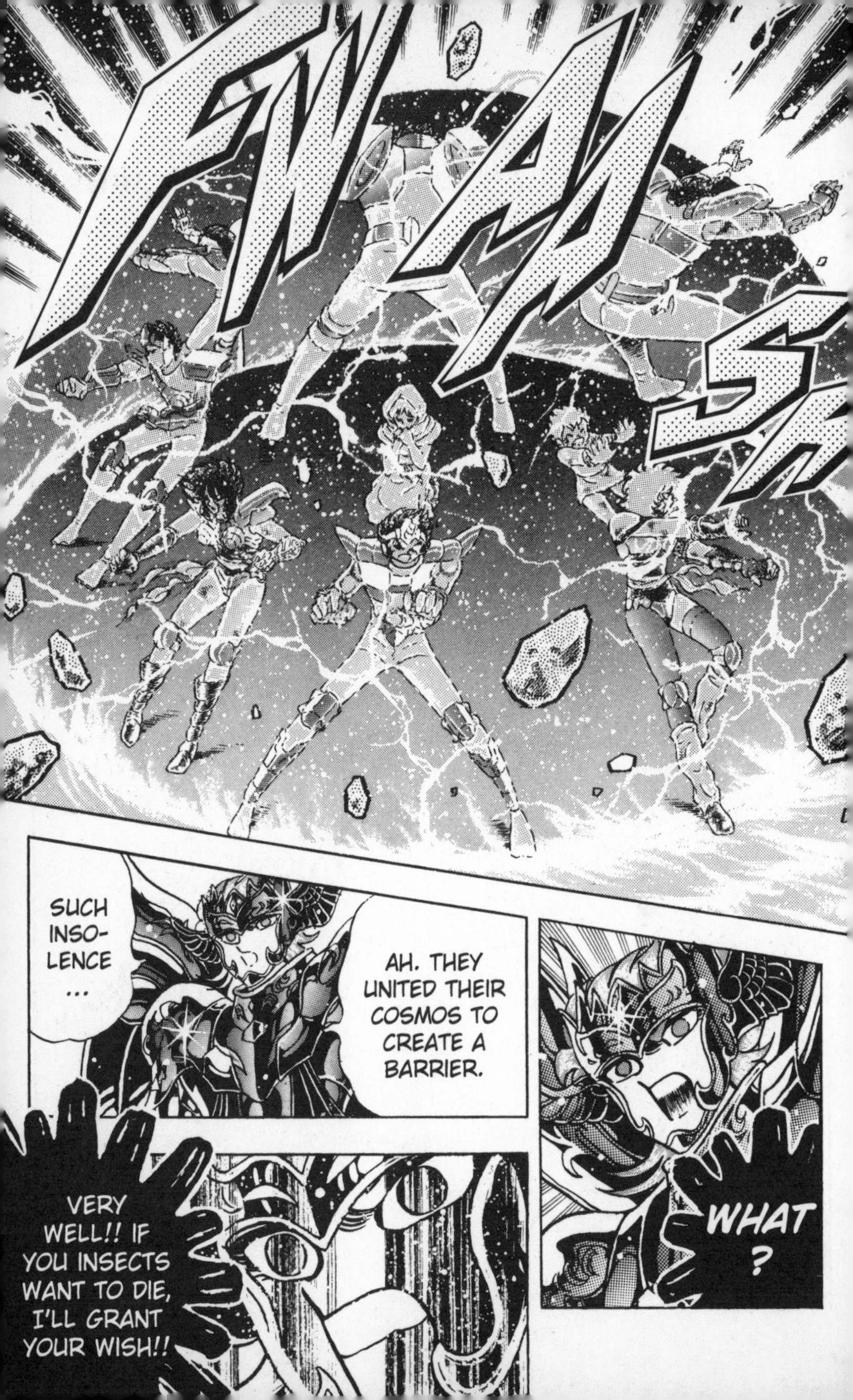
WHAT?
AH. THEY UNITED THEIR COSMOS TO CREATE A BARRIER.
SUCH INSOLENCE...
VERY WELL!! IF YOU INSECTS WANT TO DIE, I'LL GRANT YOUR WISH!!

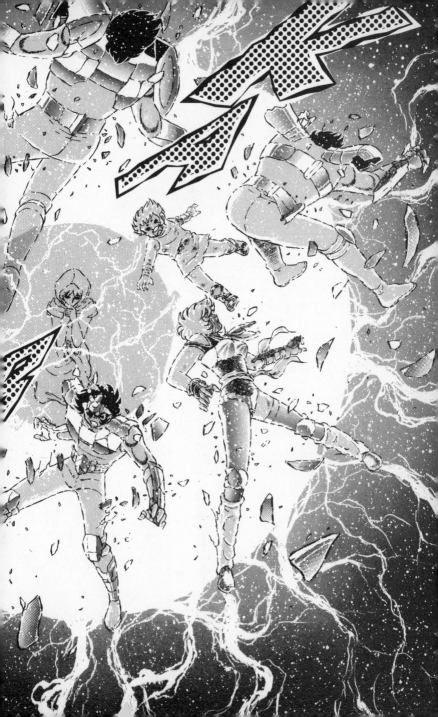

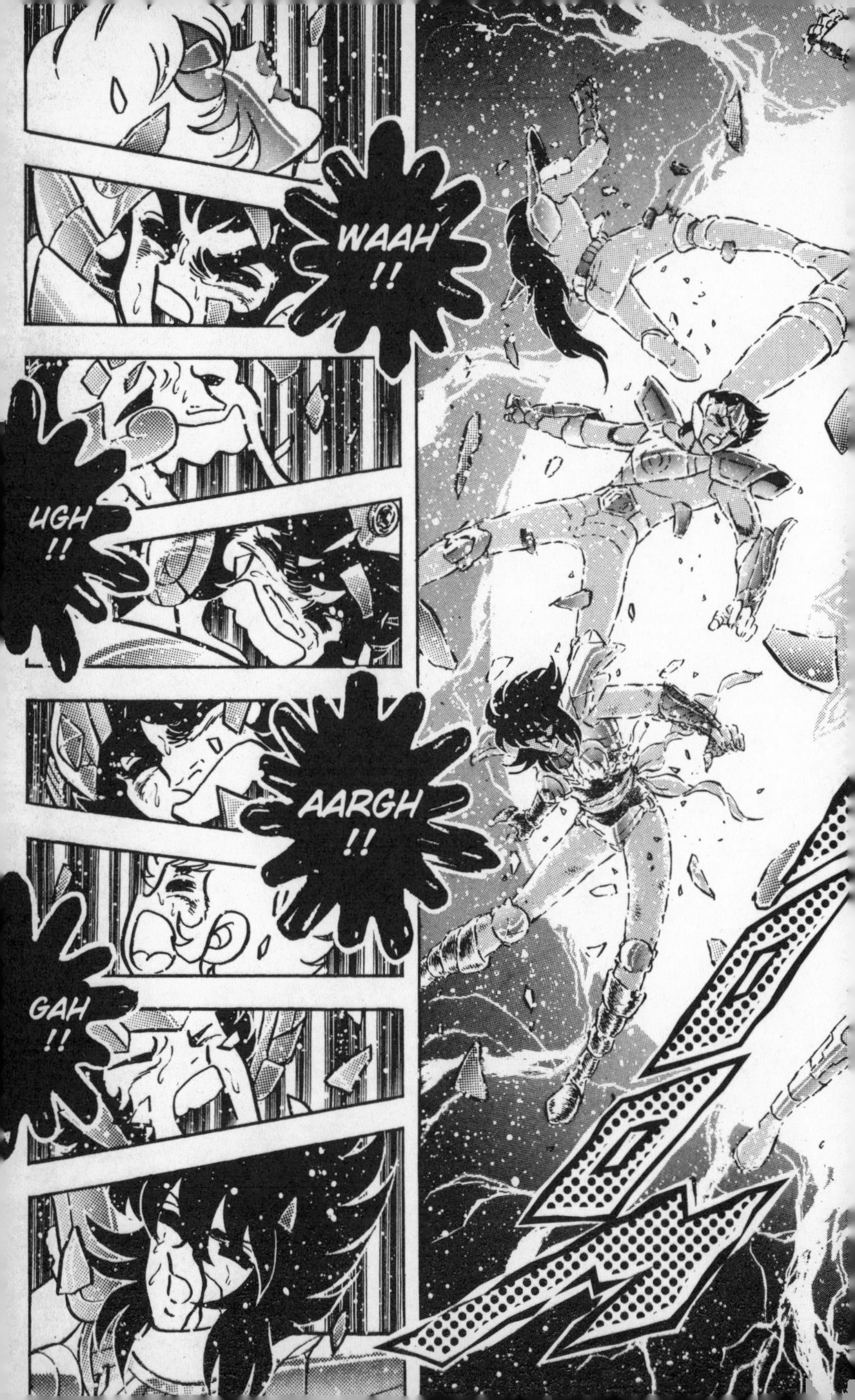
WAAH !!
UGH !!
AARGH !!
GAH !!

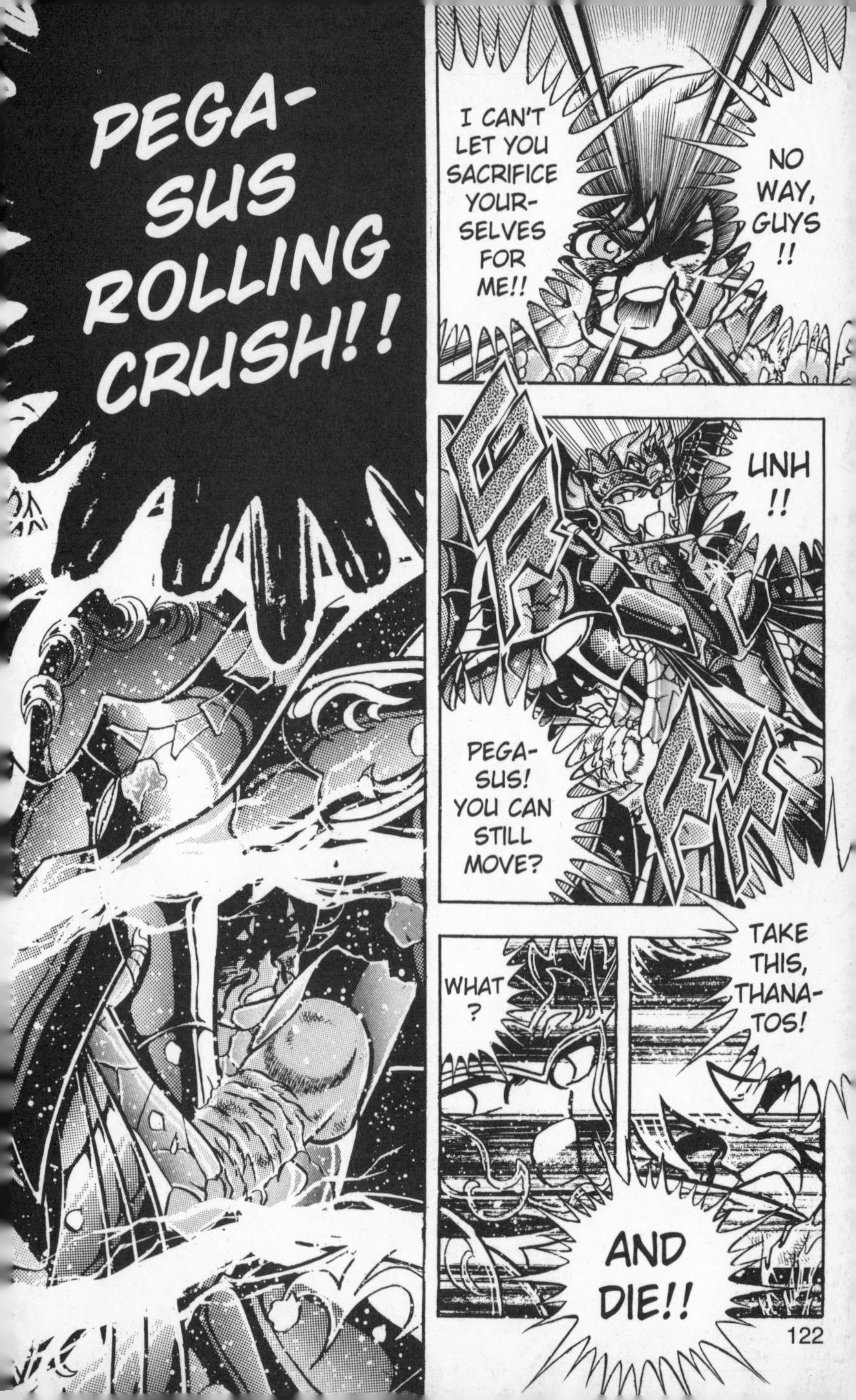
NO WAY, GUYS !!
I CAN'T LET YOU SACRIFICE YOURSELVES FOR ME!!
UNH !!
PEGASUS! YOU CAN STILL MOVE?
TAKE THIS, THANATOS!
WHAT ?
AND DIE!!
PEGASUS ROLLING CRUSH!!

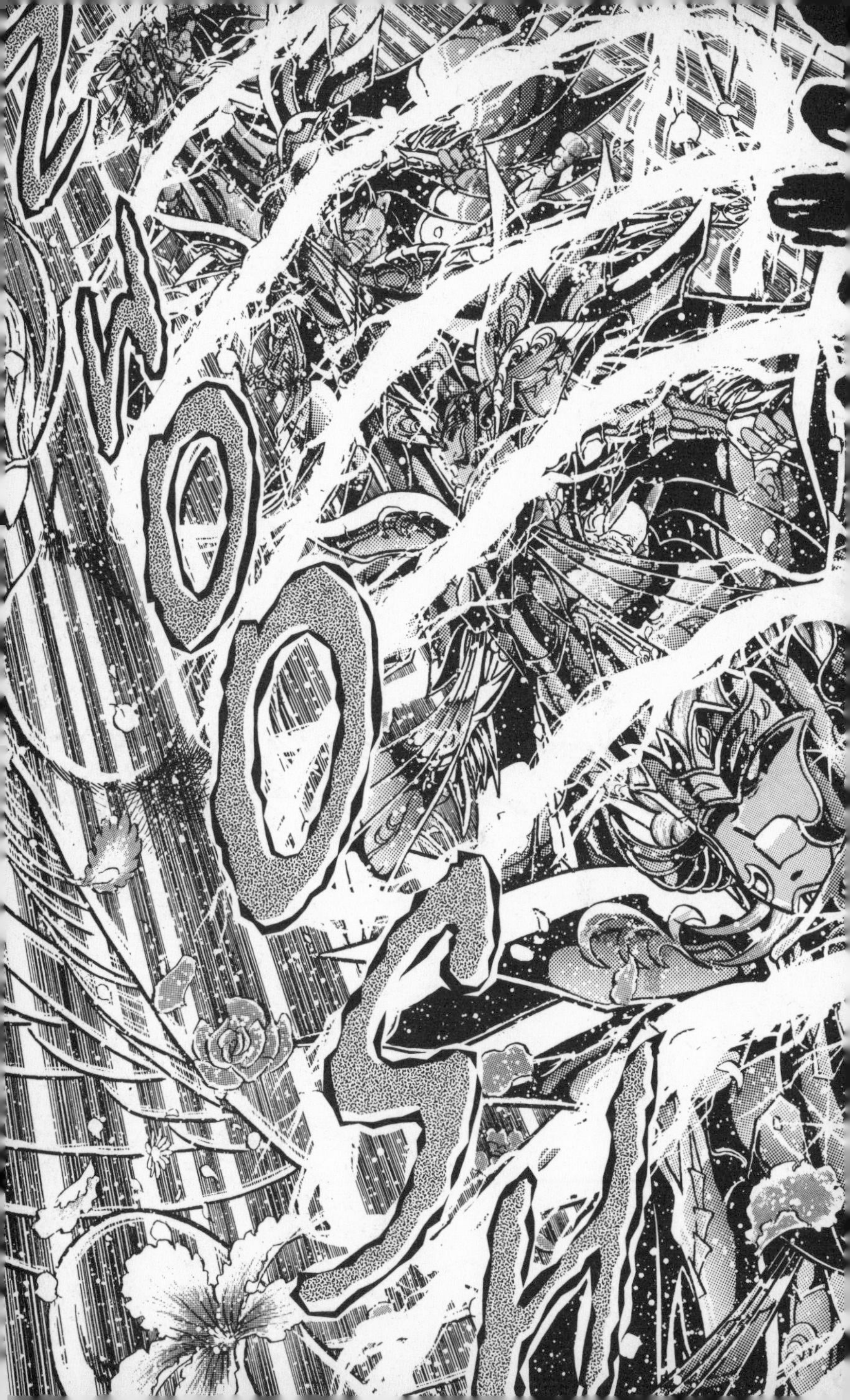
WOOSH

ARE YOU TRYING TO KILL YOURSELF, PEGASUS?

HEH.

WHAT?

HEY!!

FWA

SH

WHERE'D THANATOS GO?

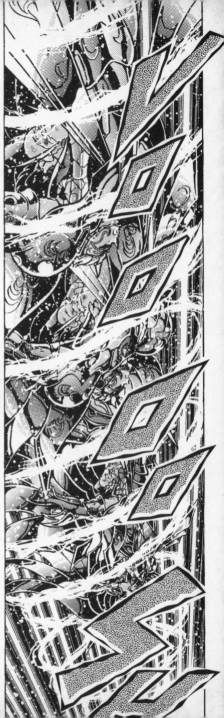

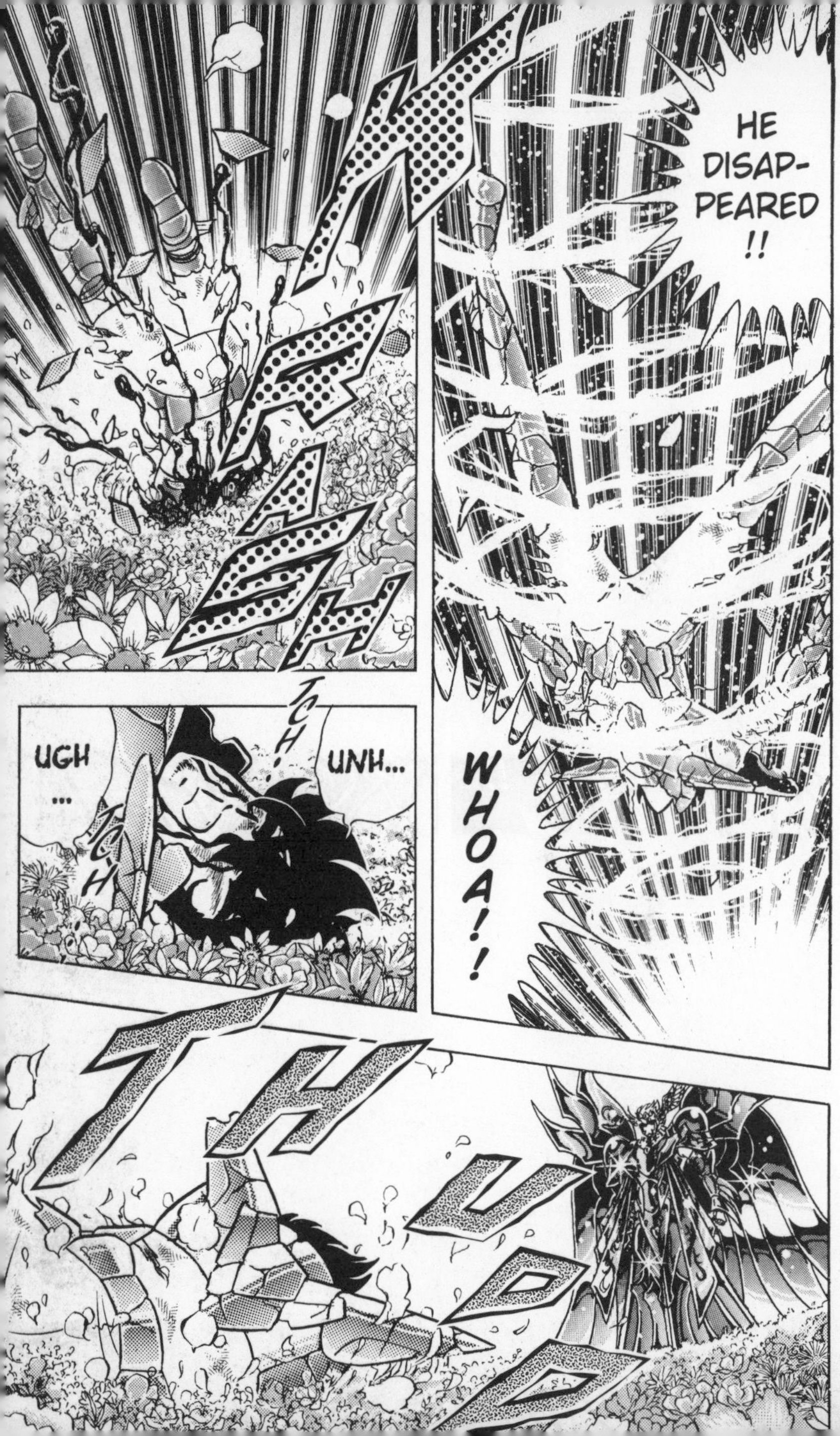
HE DISAPPEARED!!
WHOA!!
FASH
TCH!
UNH...
UGH ...
TCH
THUD

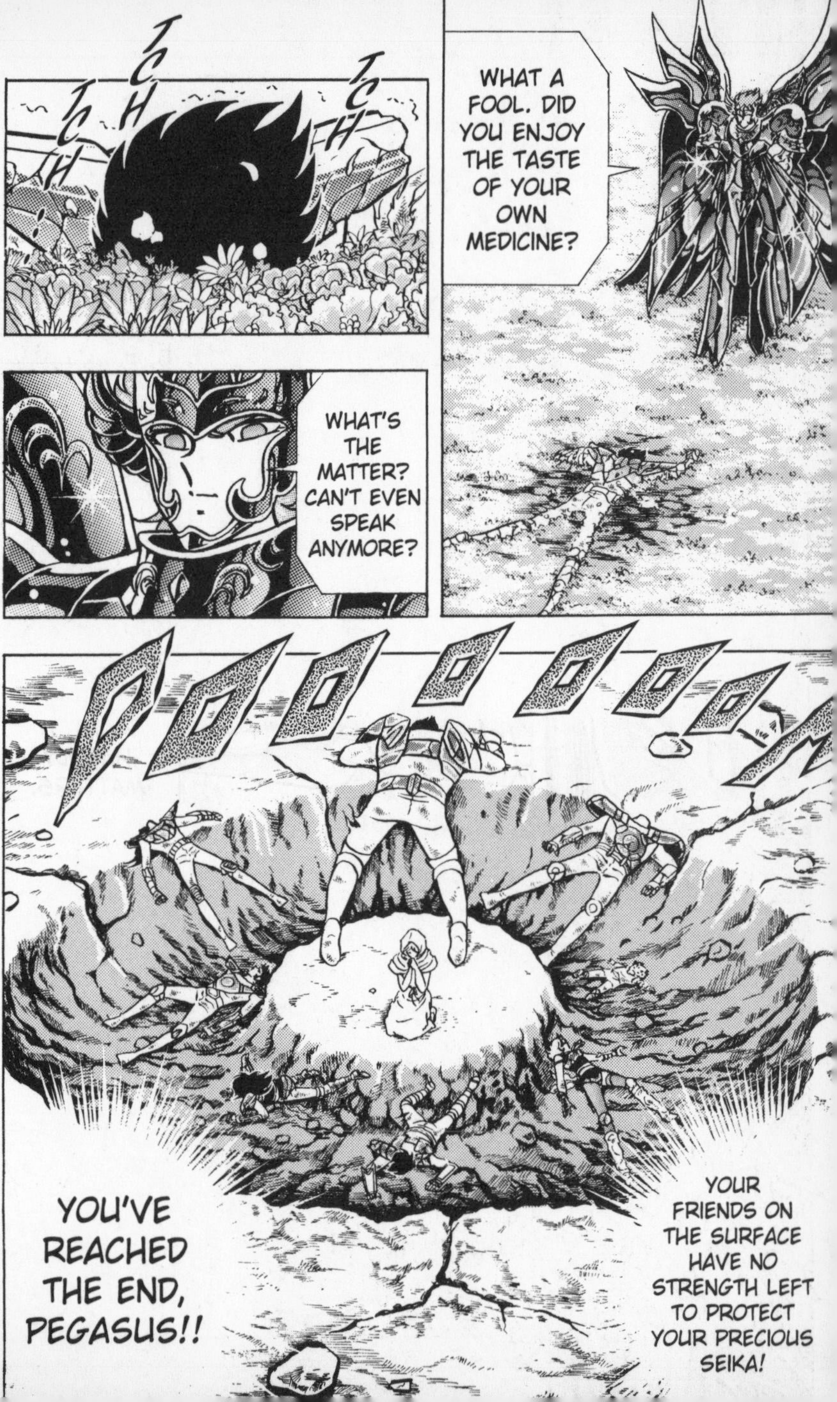
WHAT A FOOL. DID YOU ENJOY THE TASTE OF YOUR OWN MEDICINE?
ICH
ICH
ICH
WHAT'S THE MATTER? CAN'T EVEN SPEAK ANYMORE?
DOOOOOOM
YOUR FRIENDS ON THE SURFACE HAVE NO STRENGTH LEFT TO PROTECT YOUR PRECIOUS SEIKA!
YOU'VE REACHED THE END, PEGASUS!!

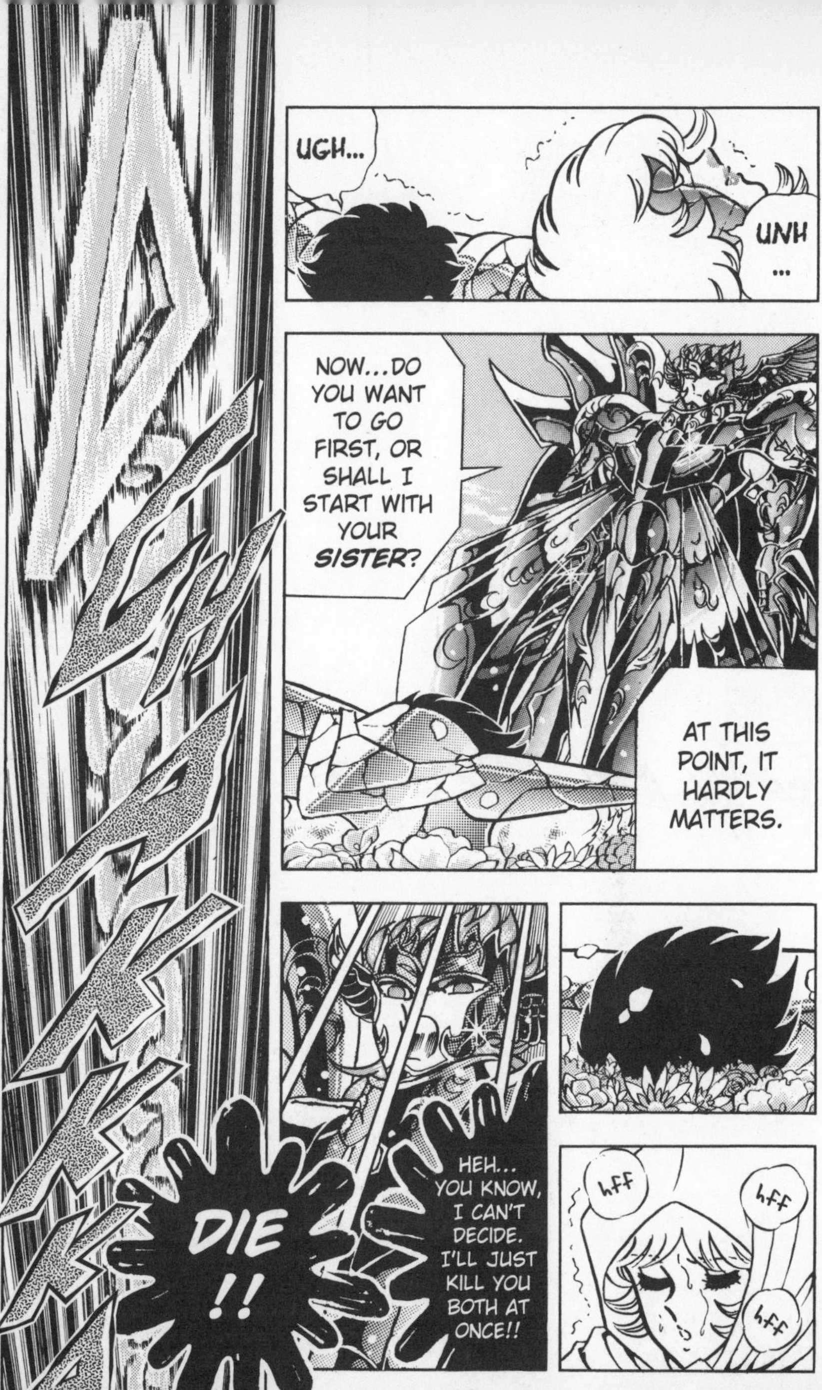
UGH...
UNH ...
NOW...DO YOU WANT TO GO FIRST, OR SHALL I START WITH YOUR *SISTER*?
AT THIS POINT, IT HARDLY MATTERS.
hff
hff
hff
HEH... YOU KNOW, I CAN'T DECIDE. I'LL JUST KILL YOU BOTH AT ONCE!!
DIE !!

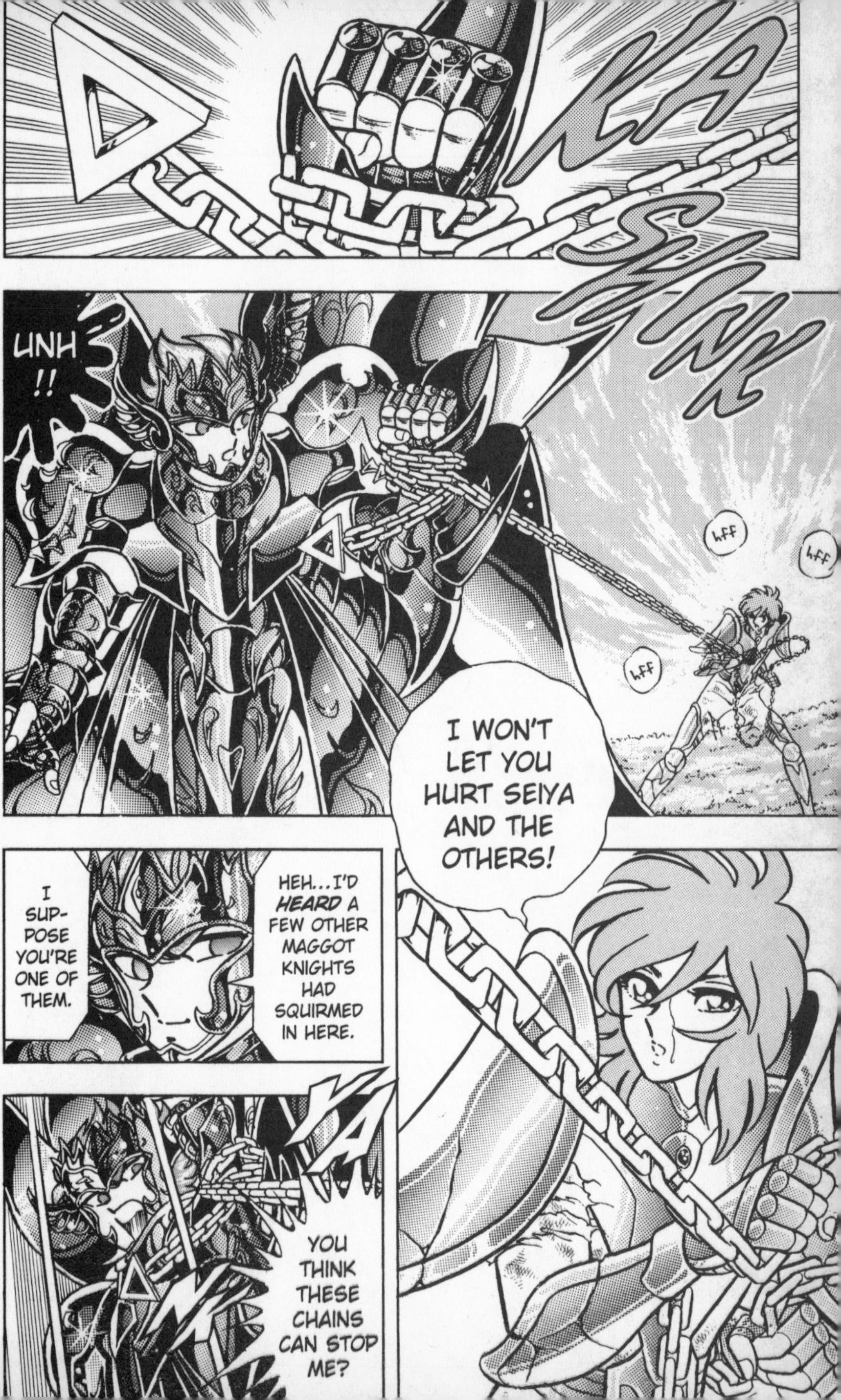
KA
SHINK
UNH !!
hff
hff
hff
I WON'T LET YOU HURT SEIYA AND THE OTHERS!
HEH...I'D *HEARD* A FEW OTHER MAGGOT KNIGHTS HAD SQUIRMED IN HERE.
I SUP-POSE YOU'RE ONE OF THEM.
YOU THINK THESE CHAINS CAN STOP ME?

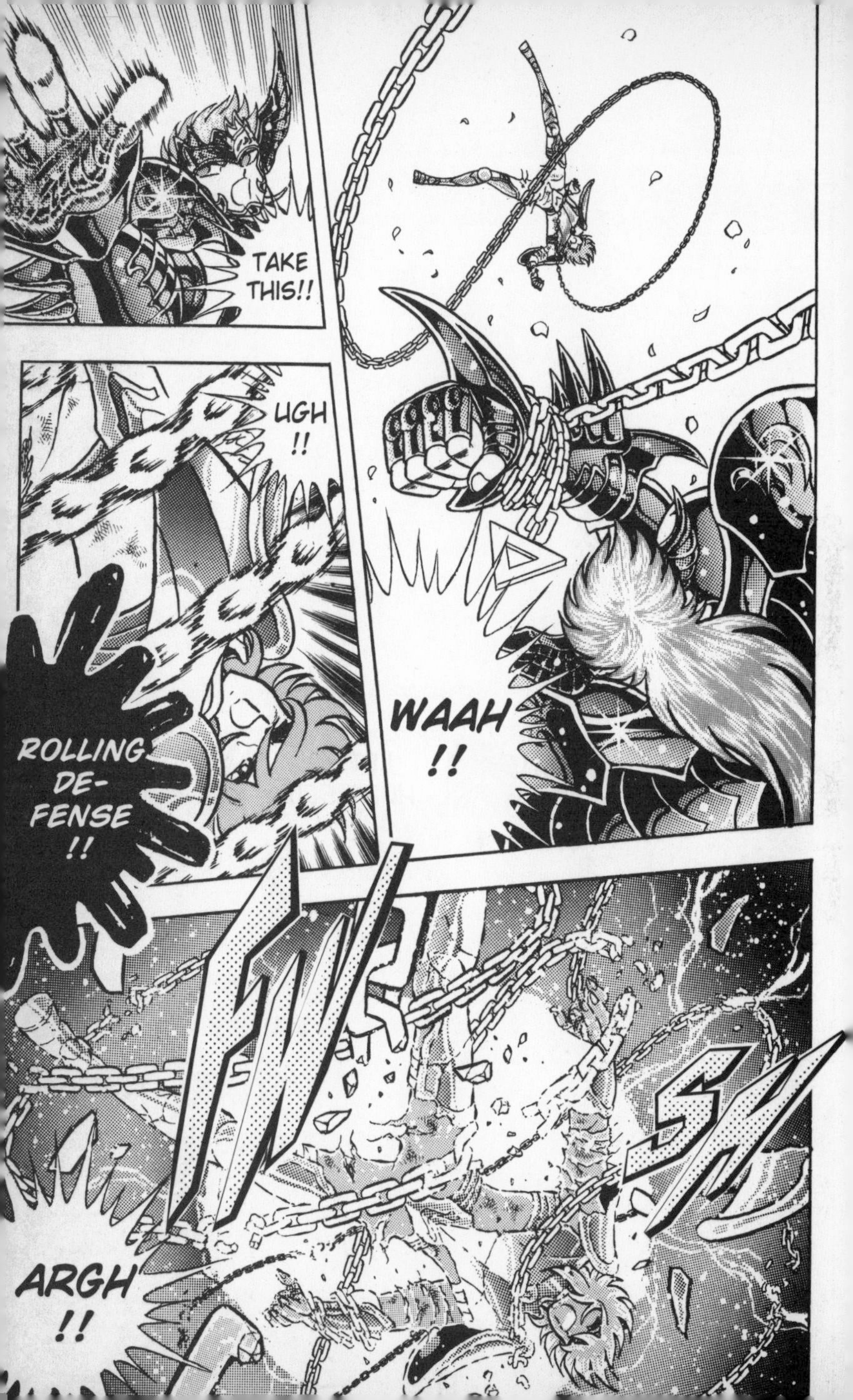
WAAH !!
TAKE THIS!!
UGH !!
ROLLING DE-FENSE !!
ARGH !!

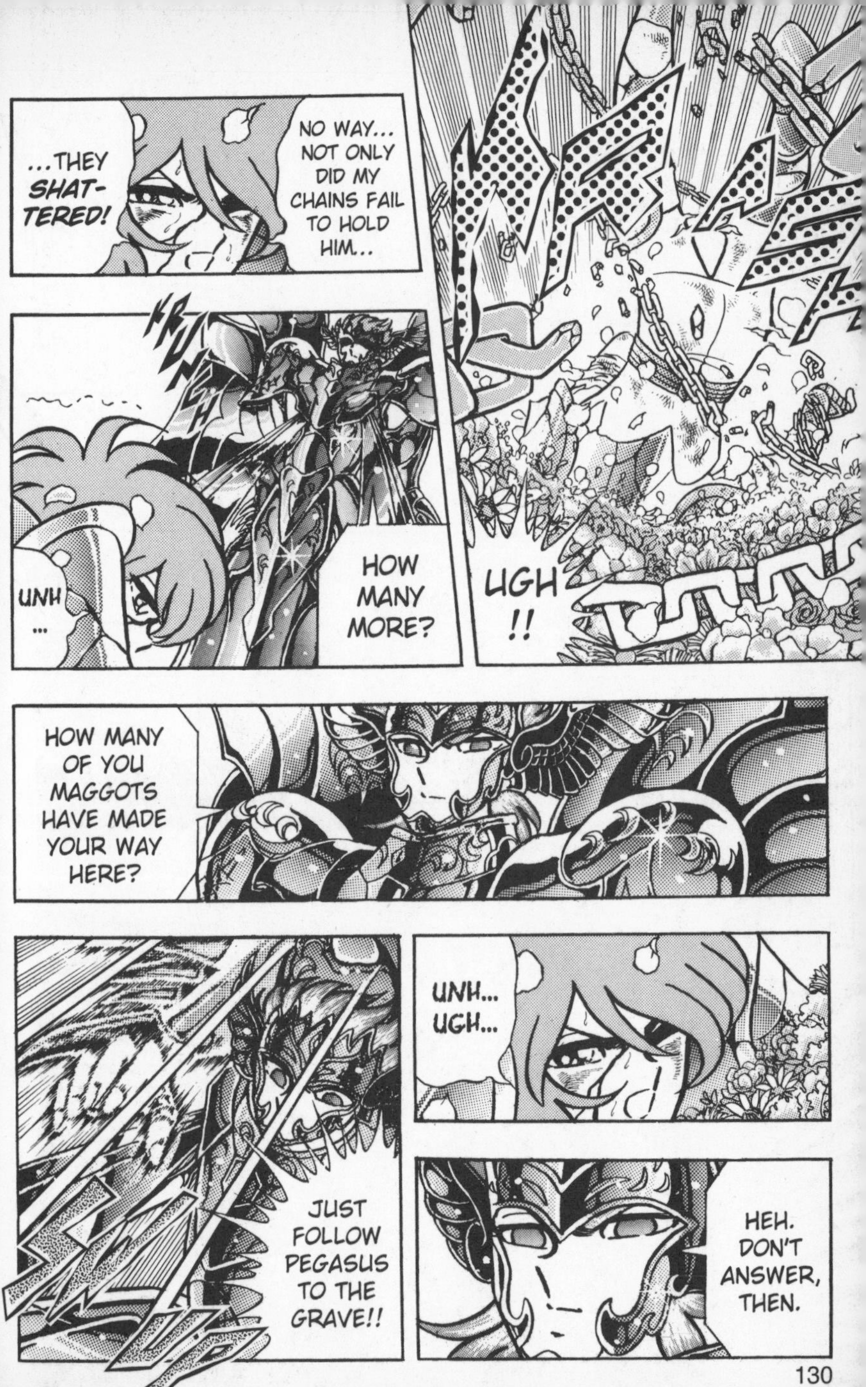
UGH!!
NO WAY... NOT ONLY DID MY CHAINS FAIL TO HOLD HIM...
...THEY SHATTERED!
HOW MANY MORE?
UNH...
HOW MANY OF YOU MAGGOTS HAVE MADE YOUR WAY HERE?
UNH... UGH...
HEH. DON'T ANSWER, THEN.
JUST FOLLOW PEGASUS TO THE GRAVE!!

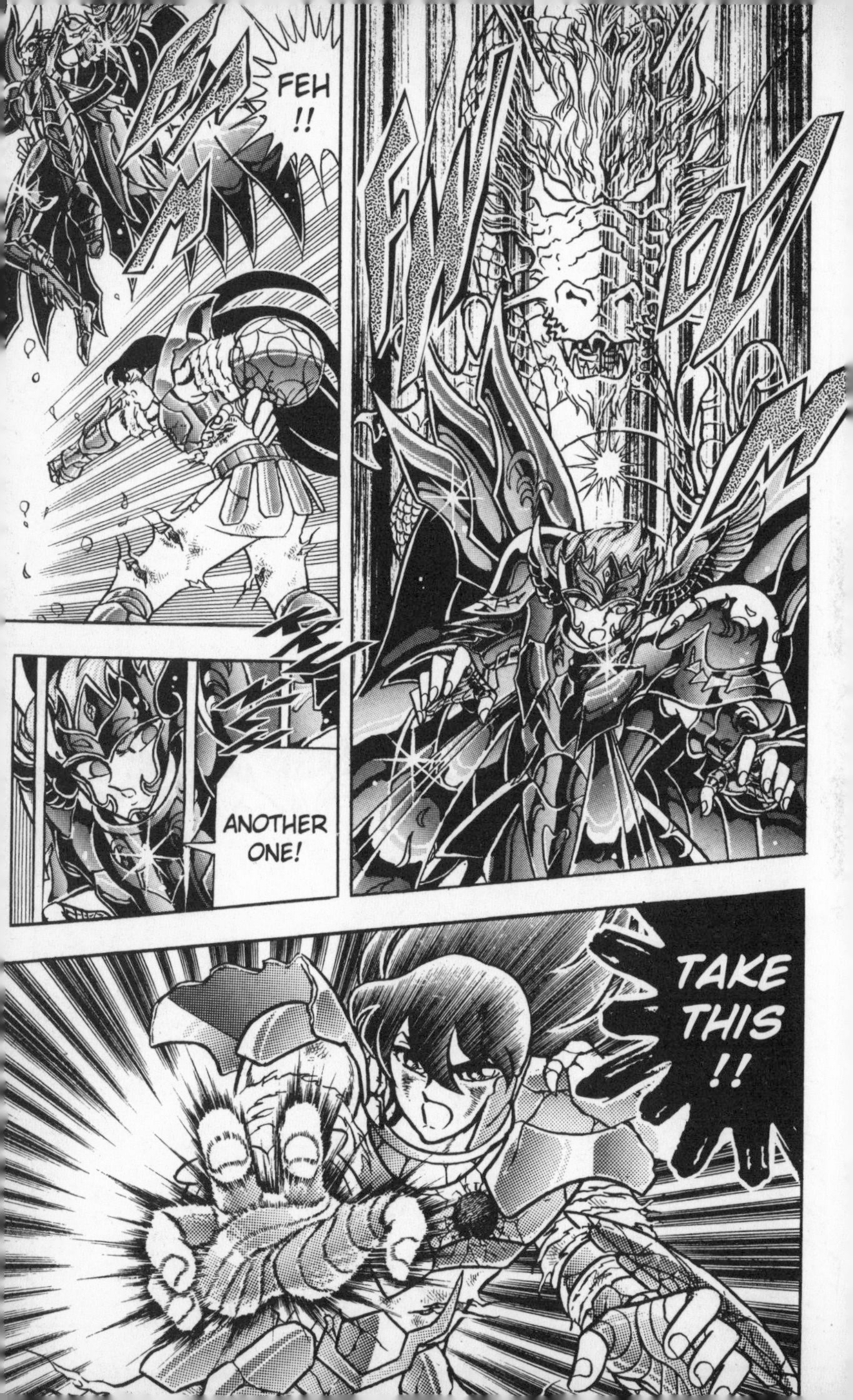
FEH !!
ANOTHER ONE!
TAKE THIS !!

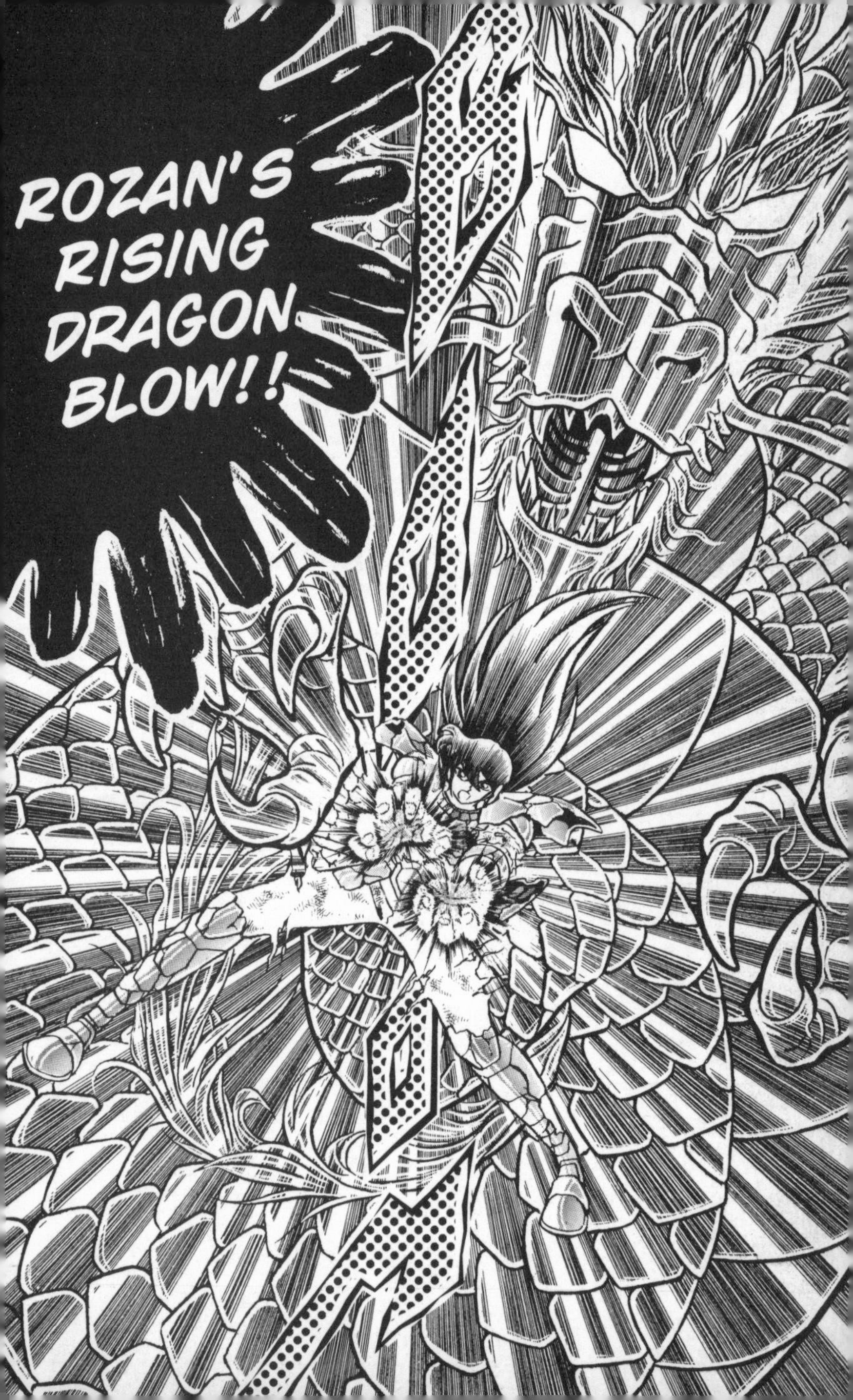
ROZAN'S RISING DRAGON BLOW!!

READ THIS WAY

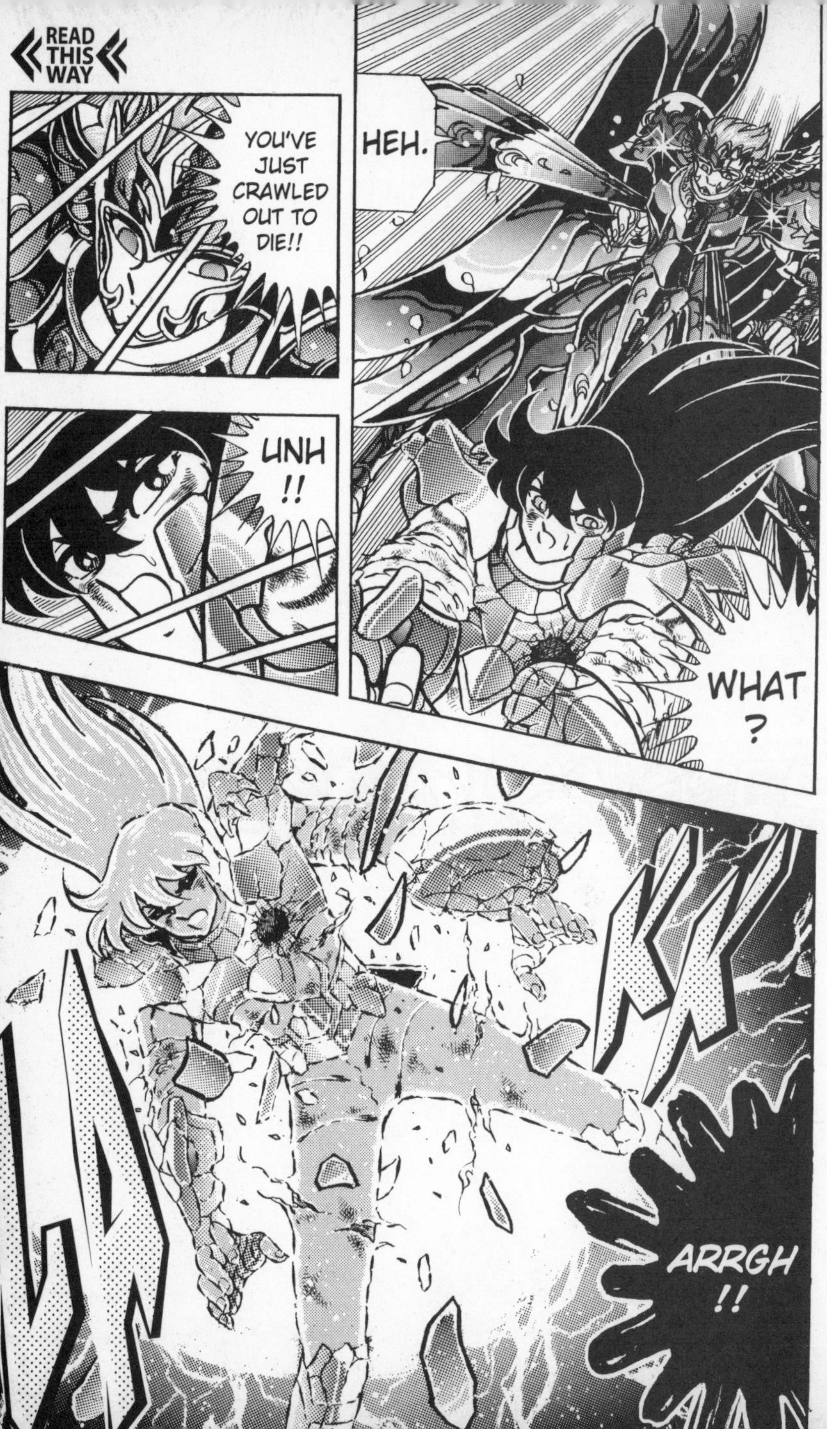
HEH.
WHAT?
YOU'VE JUST CRAWLED OUT TO DIE!!
UNH!!
ARRGH!!

ARE YOU THE LAST ONE?

UGH...

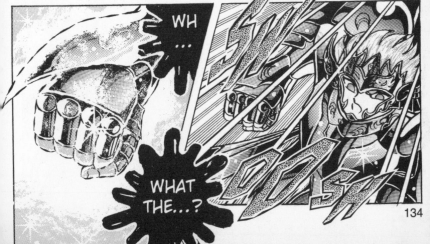

WH...

WHAT THE...?

134

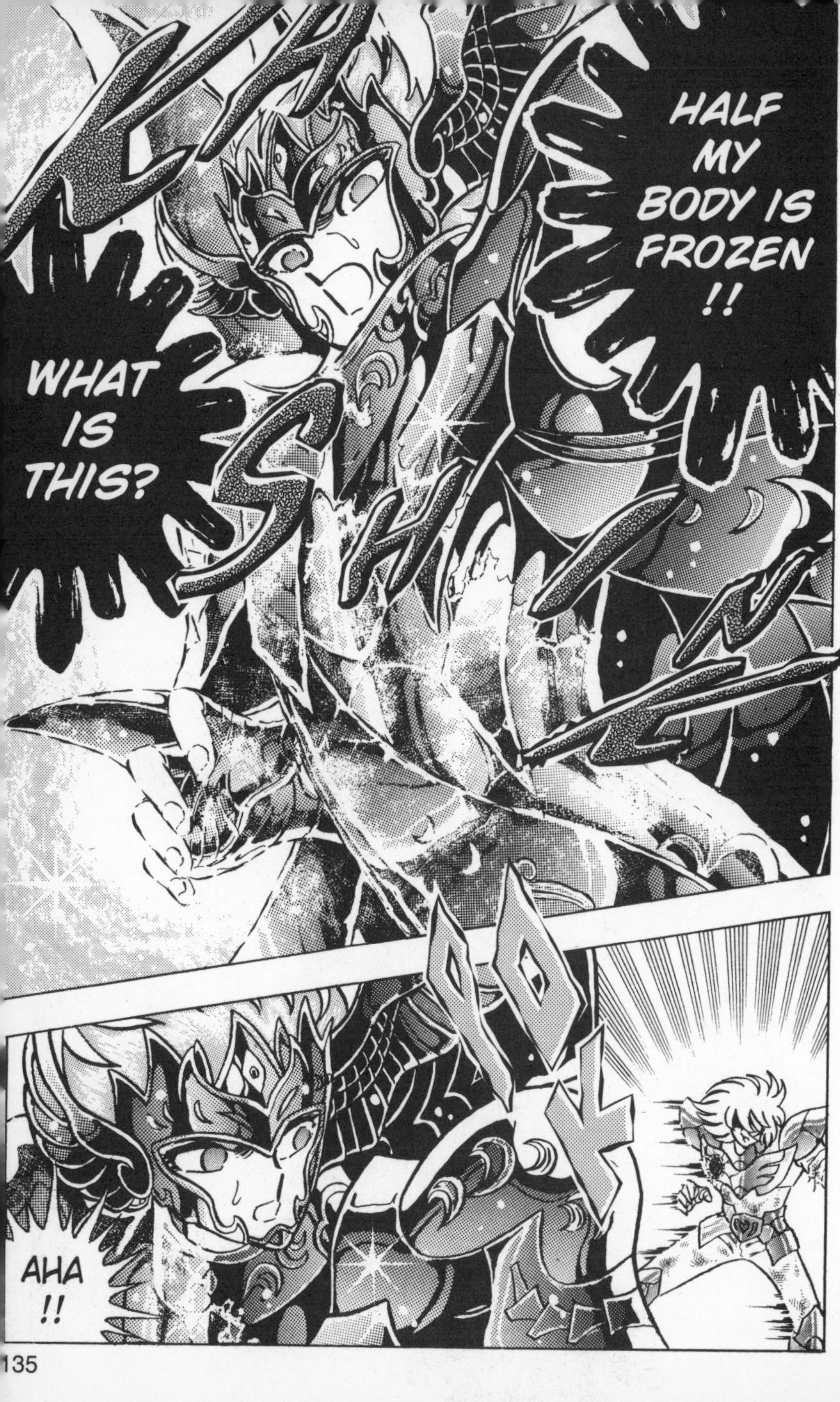
HALF MY BODY IS FROZEN!!
WHAT IS THIS?
AHA!!

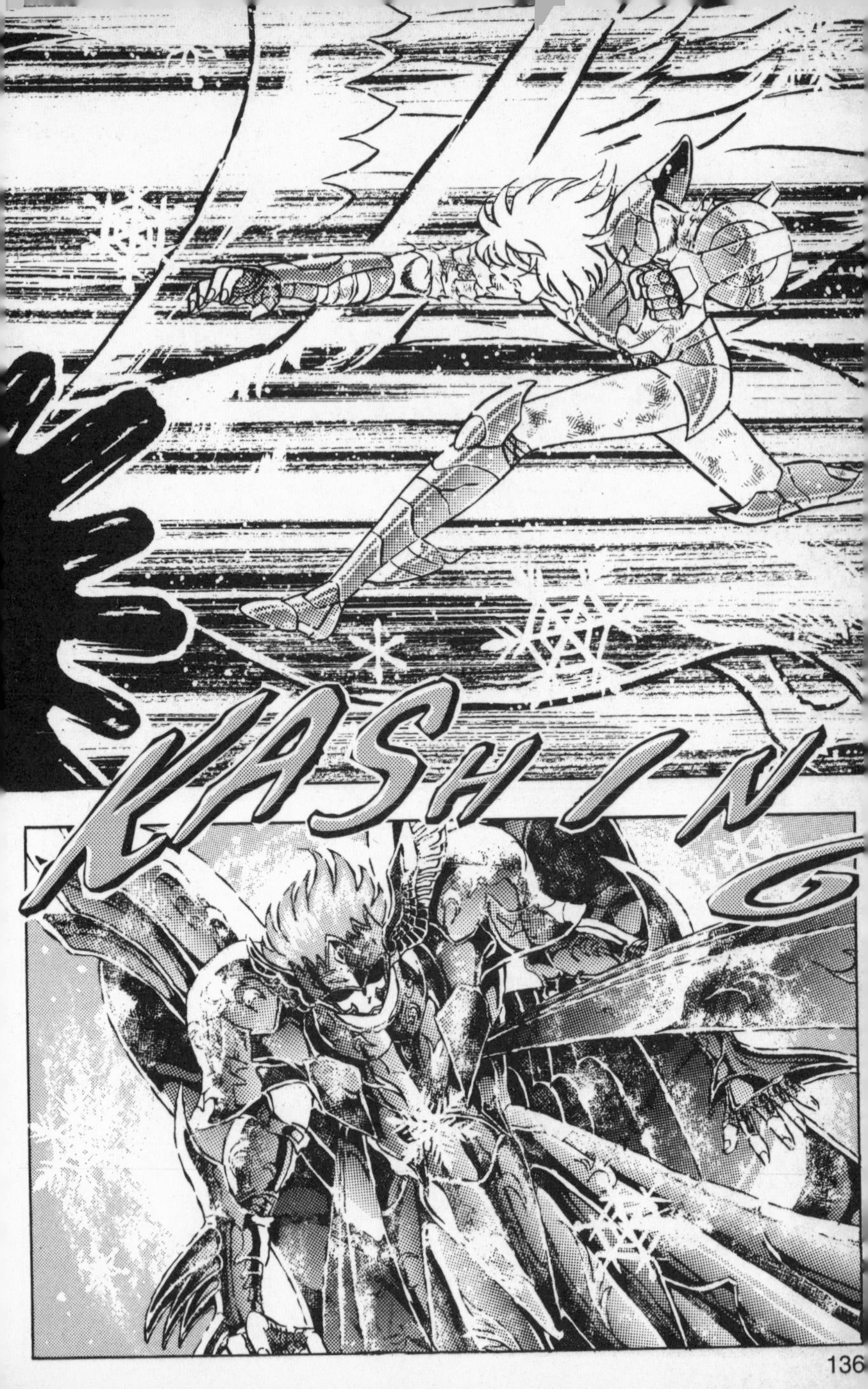
KASHING

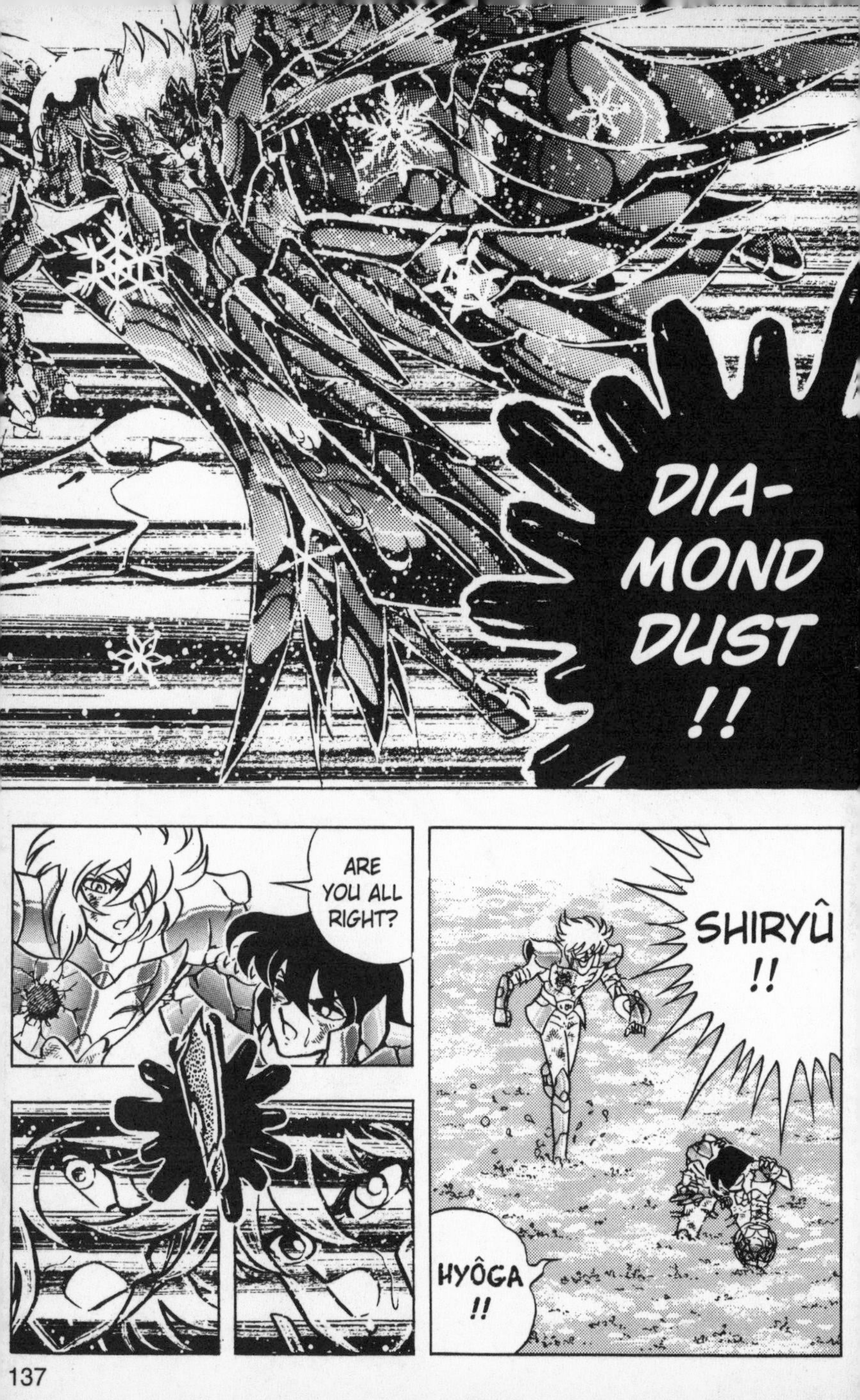
DIA-MOND DUST!!
SHIRYÛ!!
HYÔGA!!
ARE YOU ALL RIGHT?

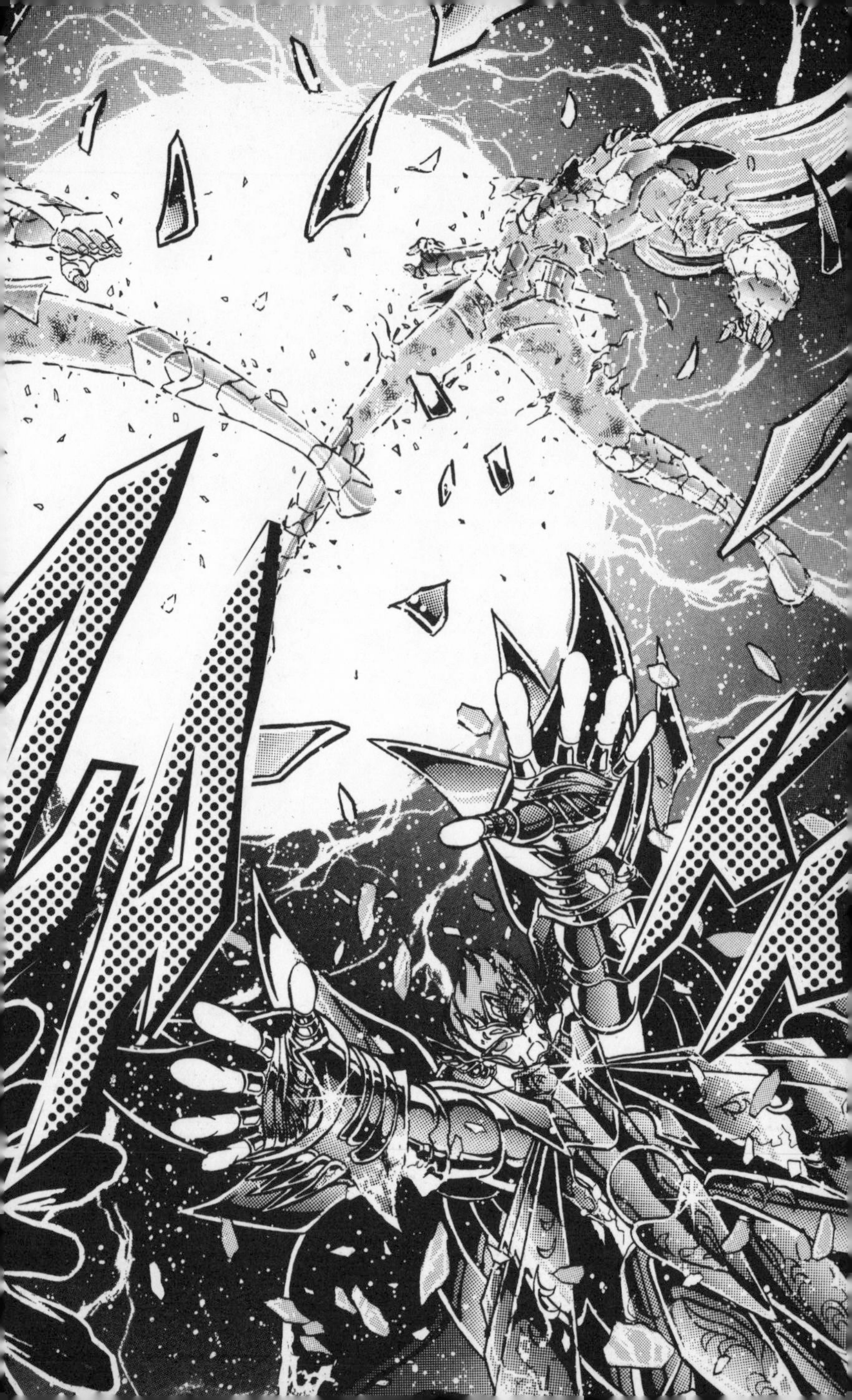

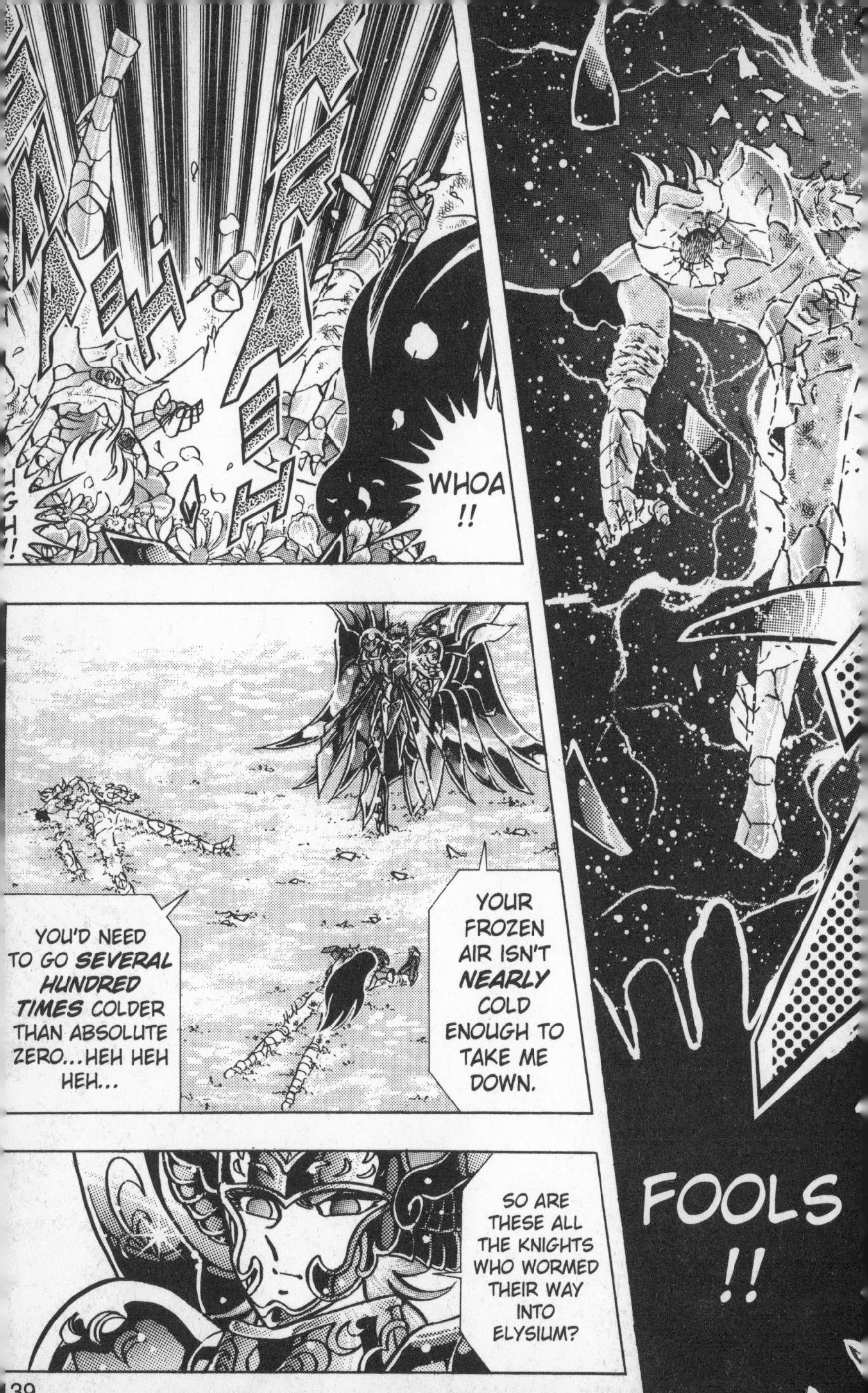
FOOLS!!
WHOA!!
YOUR FROZEN AIR ISN'T **NEARLY** COLD ENOUGH TO TAKE ME DOWN.
YOU'D NEED TO GO **SEVERAL HUNDRED TIMES** COLDER THAN ABSOLUTE ZERO...HEH HEH HEH...
SO ARE THESE ALL THE KNIGHTS WHO WORMED THEIR WAY INTO ELYSIUM?

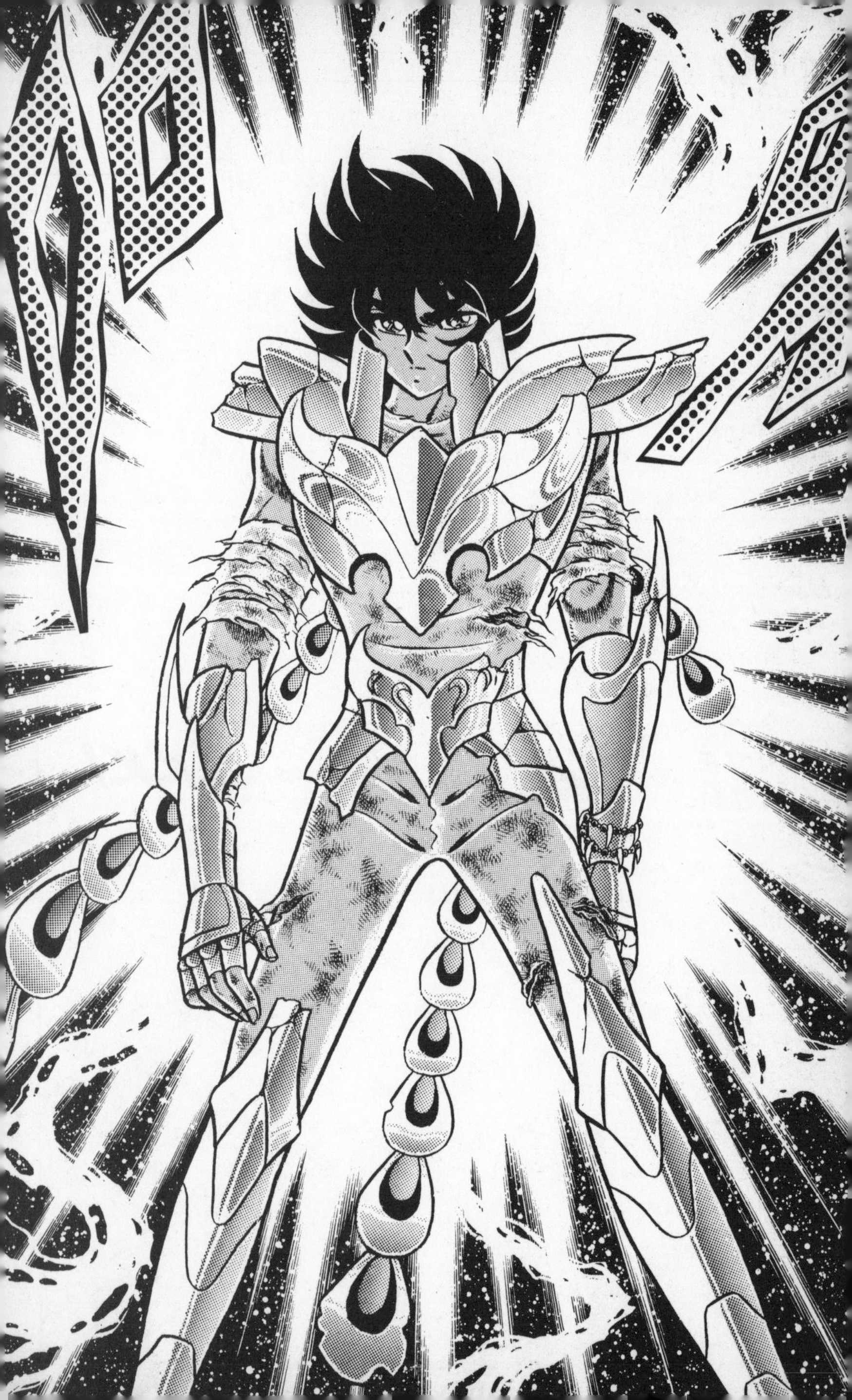

READ THIS WAY

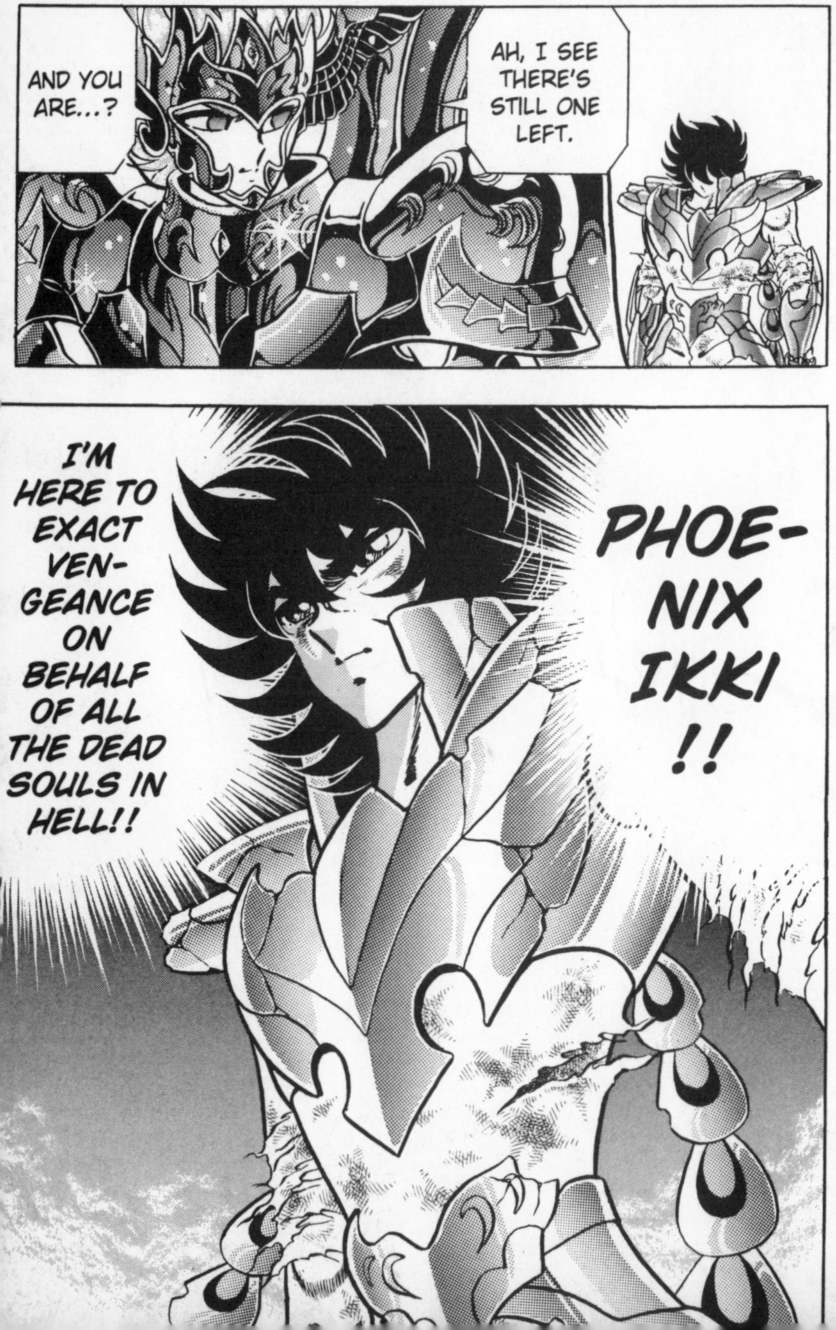
AH, I SEE THERE'S STILL ONE LEFT.
AND YOU ARE...?
PHOENIX IKKI!!
I'M HERE TO EXACT VENGEANCE ON BEHALF OF ALL THE DEAD SOULS IN HELL!!

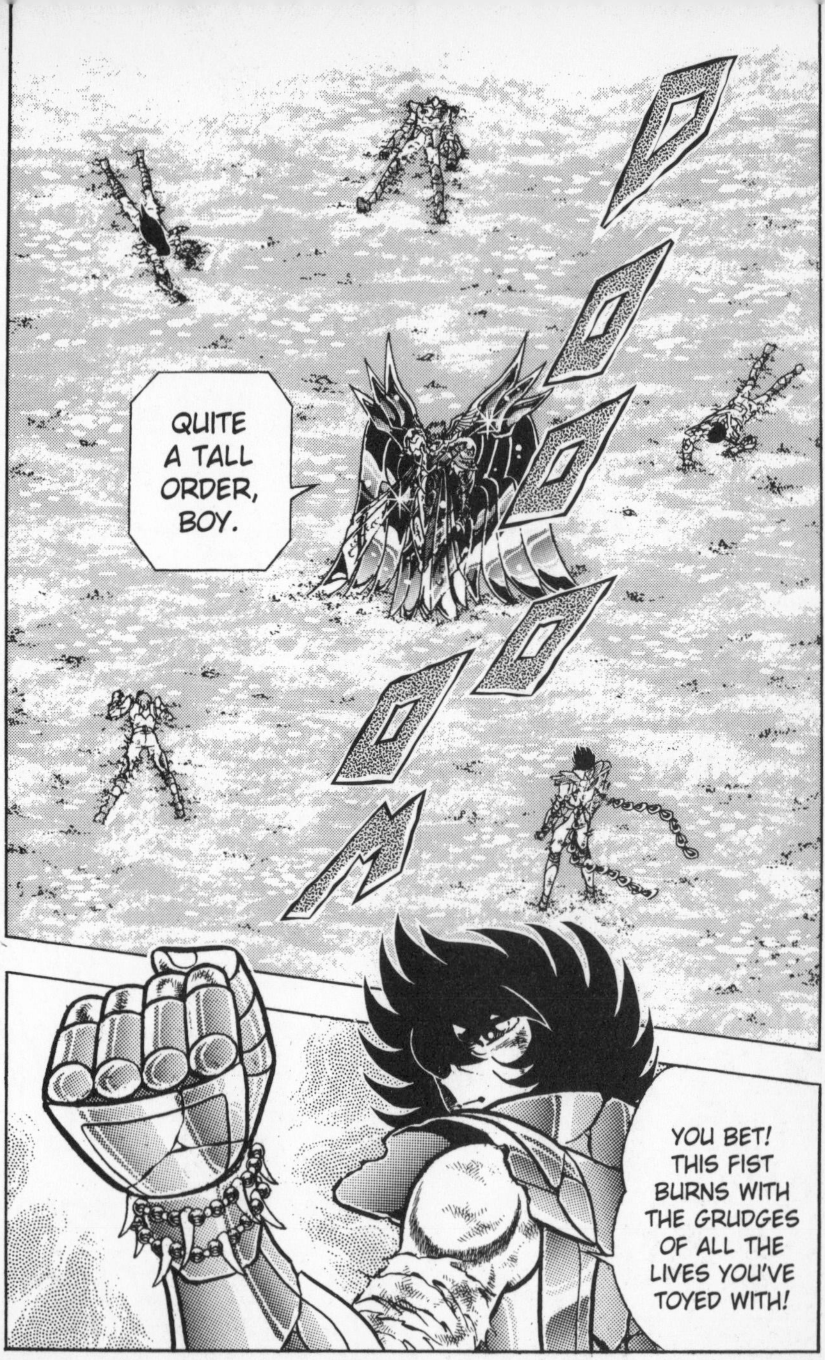
QUITE A TALL ORDER, BOY.
YOU BET! THIS FIST BURNS WITH THE GRUDGES OF ALL THE LIVES YOU'VE TOYED WITH!

READ THIS WAY

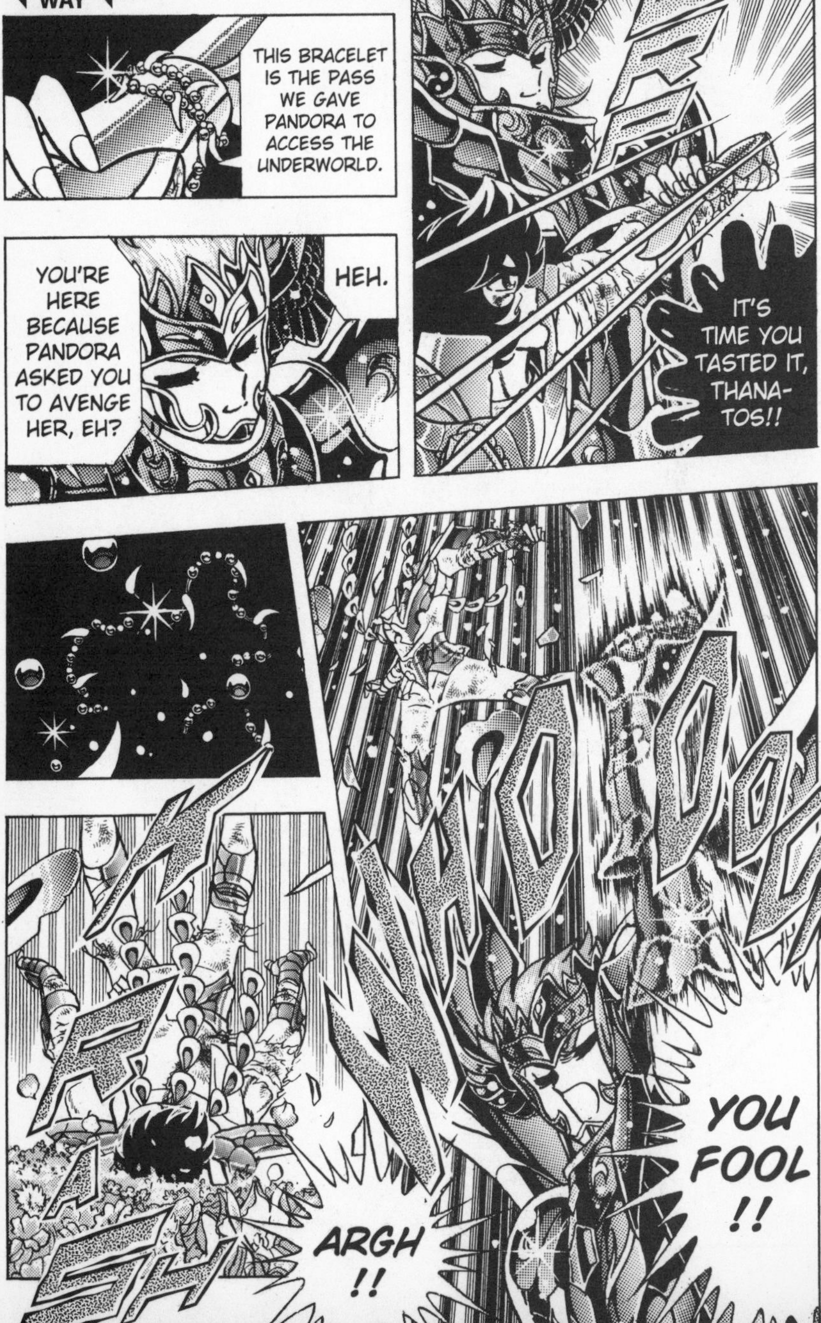
IT'S TIME YOU TASTED IT, THANATOS!!
THIS BRACELET IS THE PASS WE GAVE PANDORA TO ACCESS THE UNDERWORLD.
HEH.
YOU'RE HERE BECAUSE PANDORA ASKED YOU TO AVENGE HER, EH?
YOU FOOL !!
ARGH !!

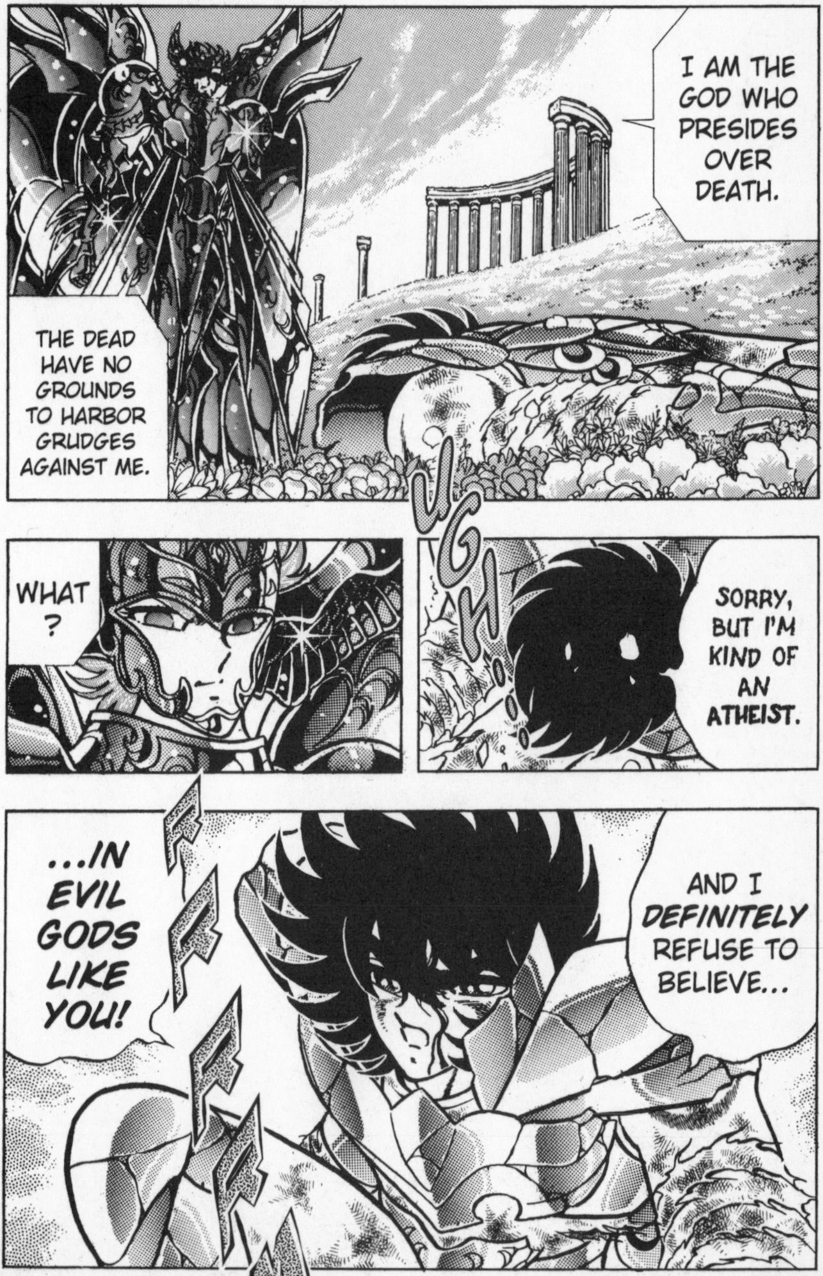
I AM THE GOD WHO PRESIDES OVER DEATH.
THE DEAD HAVE NO GROUNDS TO HARBOR GRUDGES AGAINST ME.
UGH...!
SORRY, BUT I'M KIND OF AN ATHEIST.
WHAT ?
AND I *DEFINITELY* REFUSE TO BELIEVE...
...IN EVIL GODS LIKE YOU!

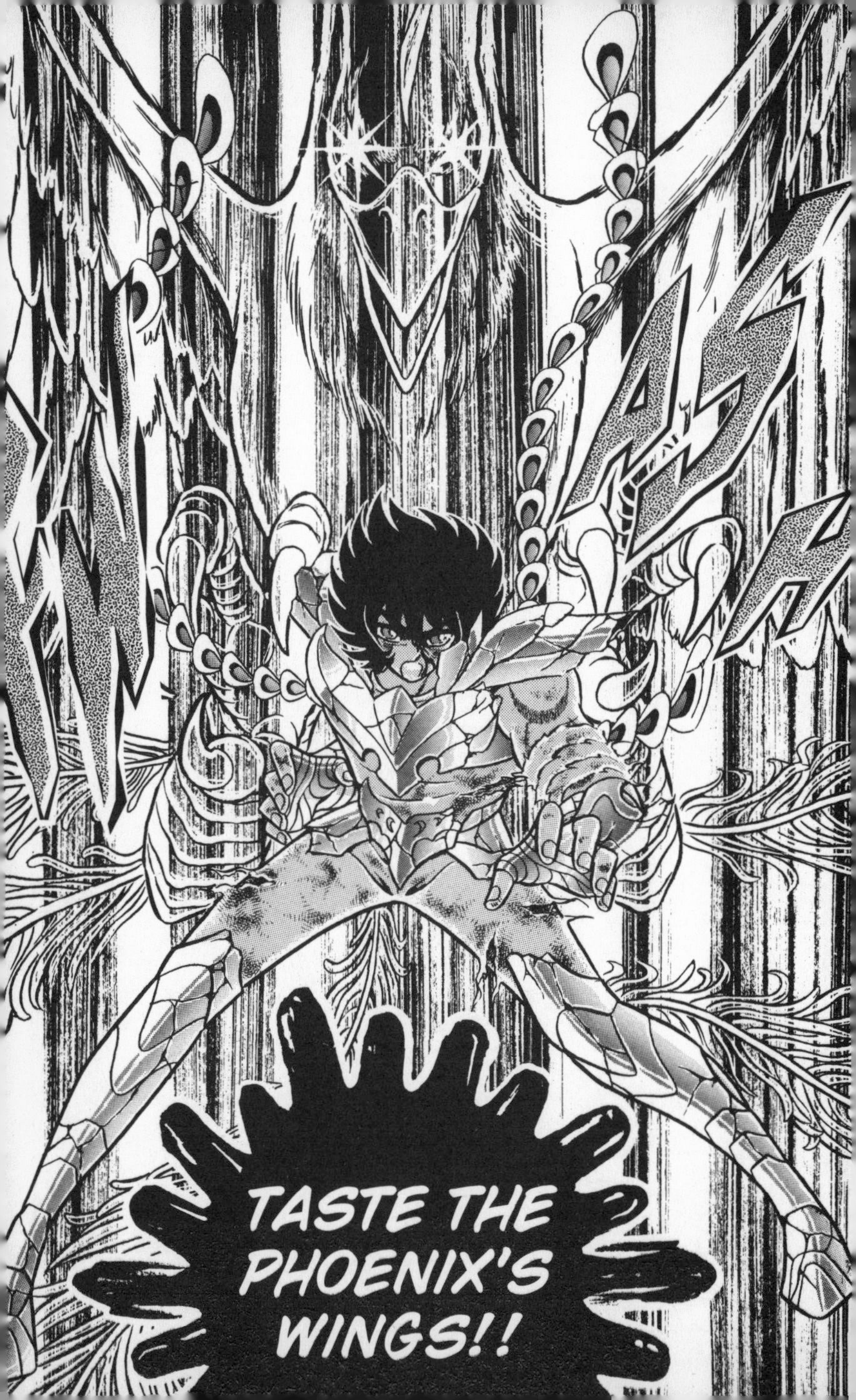
TASTE THE PHOENIX'S WINGS!!

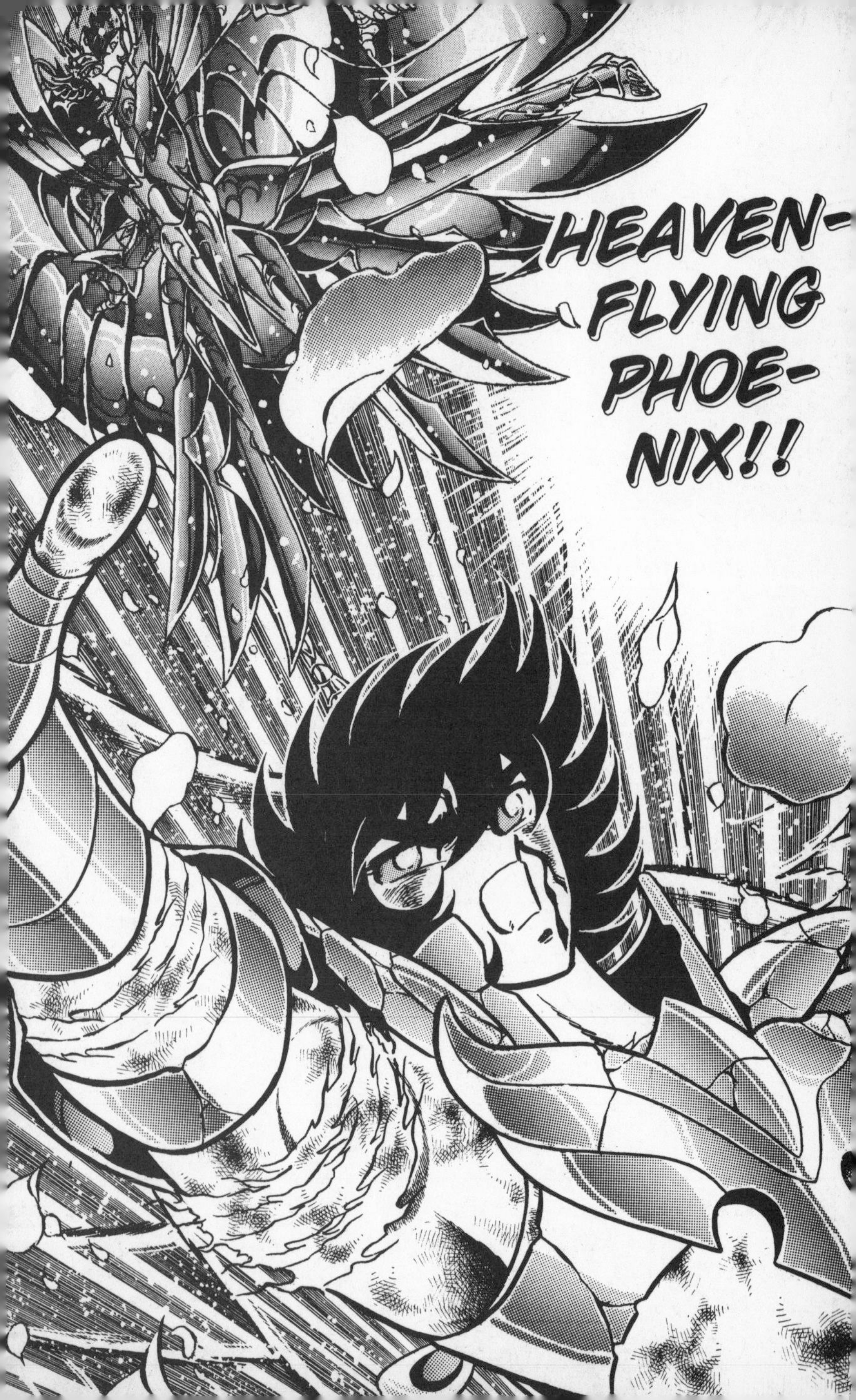
HEAVEN-FLYING PHOE-NIX!!

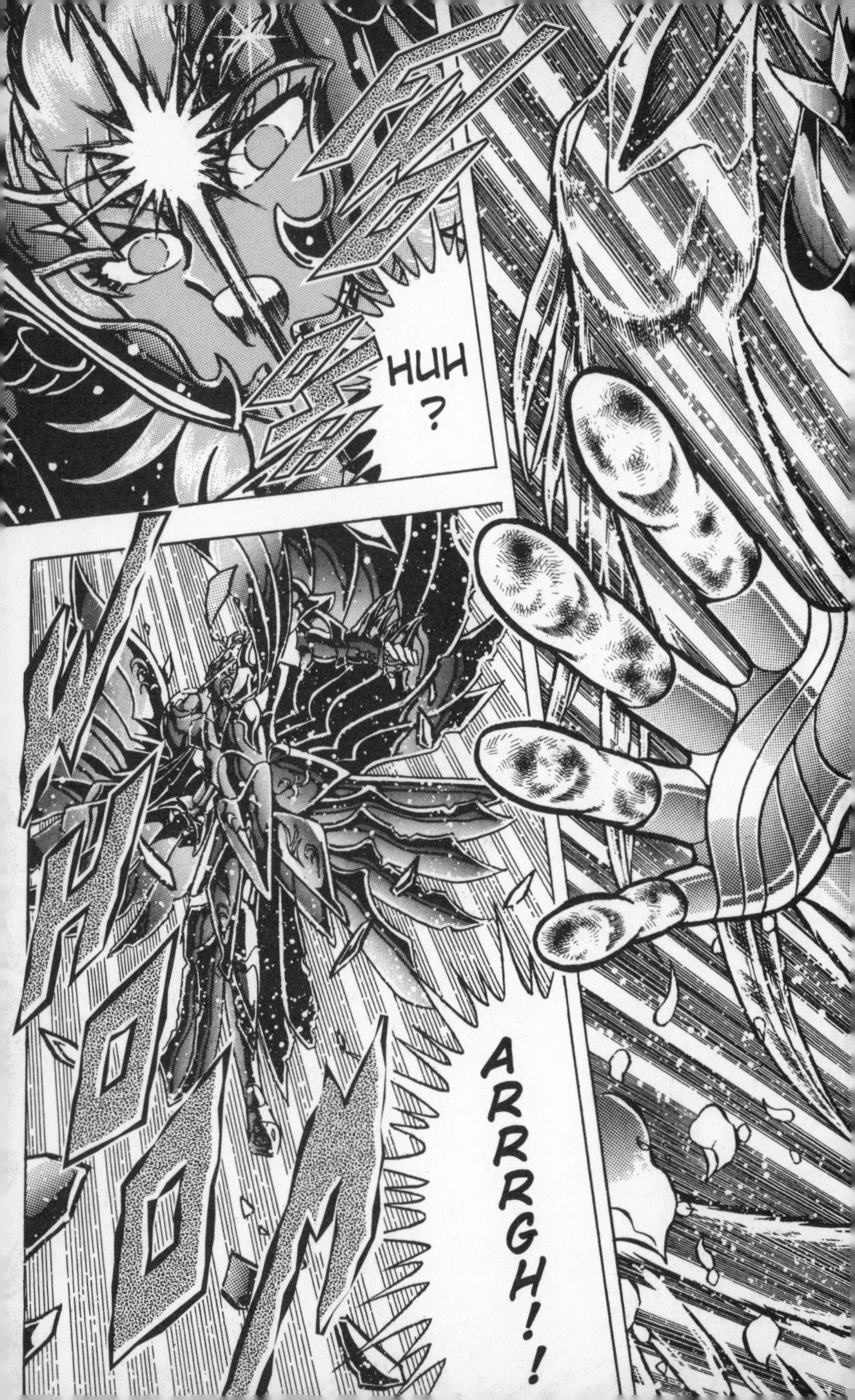
HUH
?
ARRRGH!!

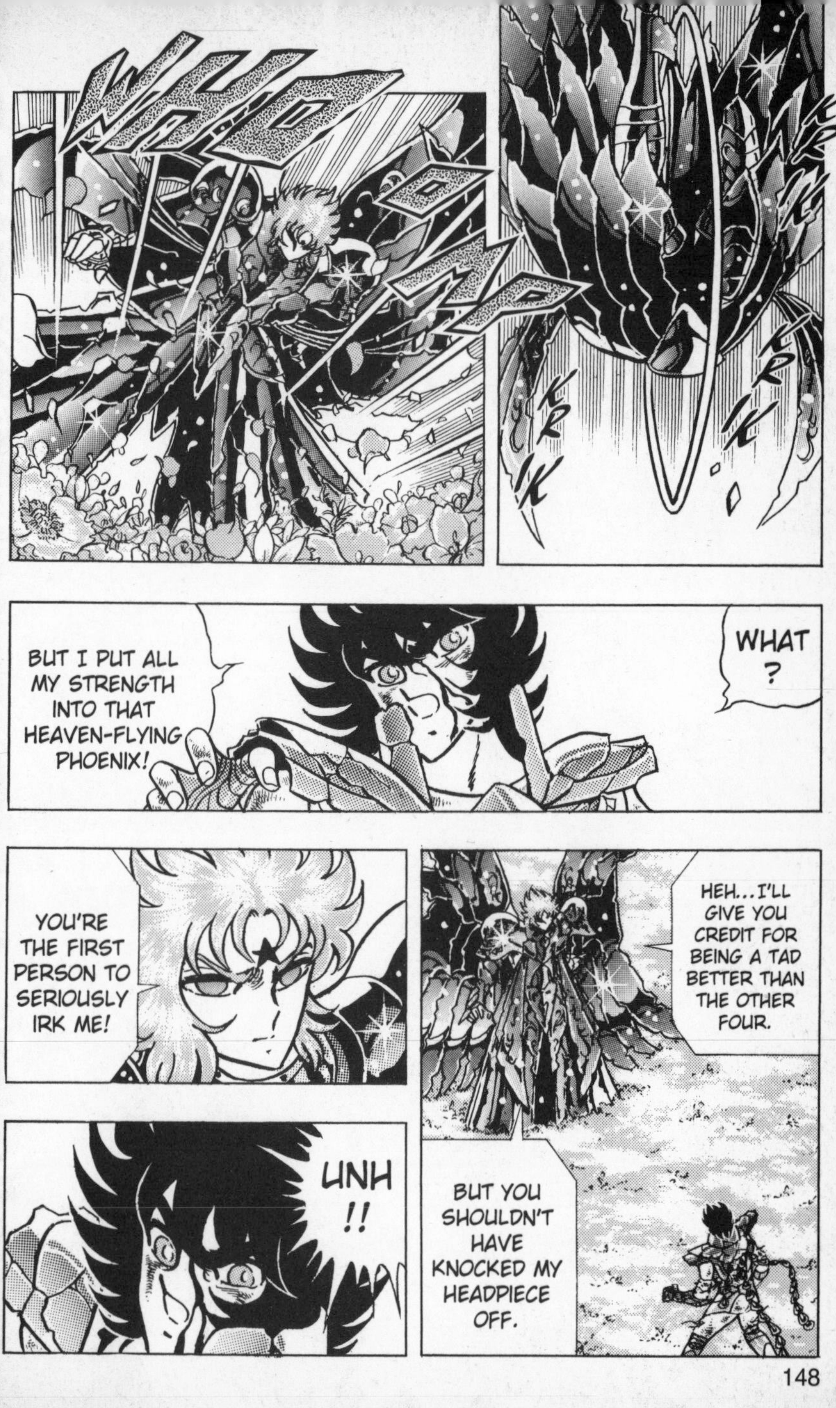
KRIK
KRIK
KRIK
WHOOMP
WHAT?
BUT I PUT ALL MY STRENGTH INTO THAT HEAVEN-FLYING PHOENIX!
HEH...I'LL GIVE YOU CREDIT FOR BEING A TAD BETTER THAN THE OTHER FOUR.
BUT YOU SHOULDN'T HAVE KNOCKED MY HEADPIECE OFF.
YOU'RE THE FIRST PERSON TO SERIOUSLY IRK ME!
UNH!!

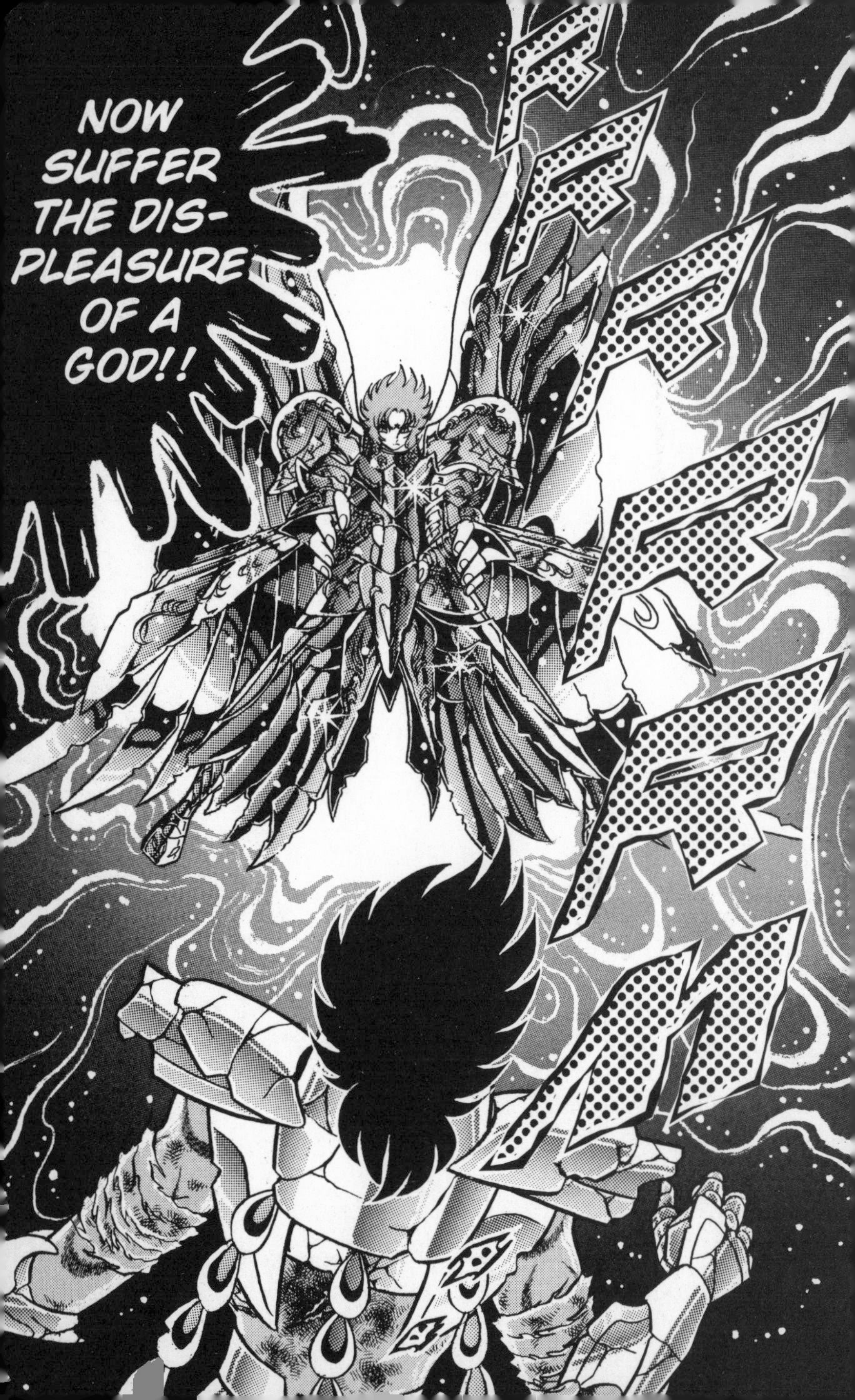
NOW SUFFER THE DIS- PLEASURE OF A GOD!!

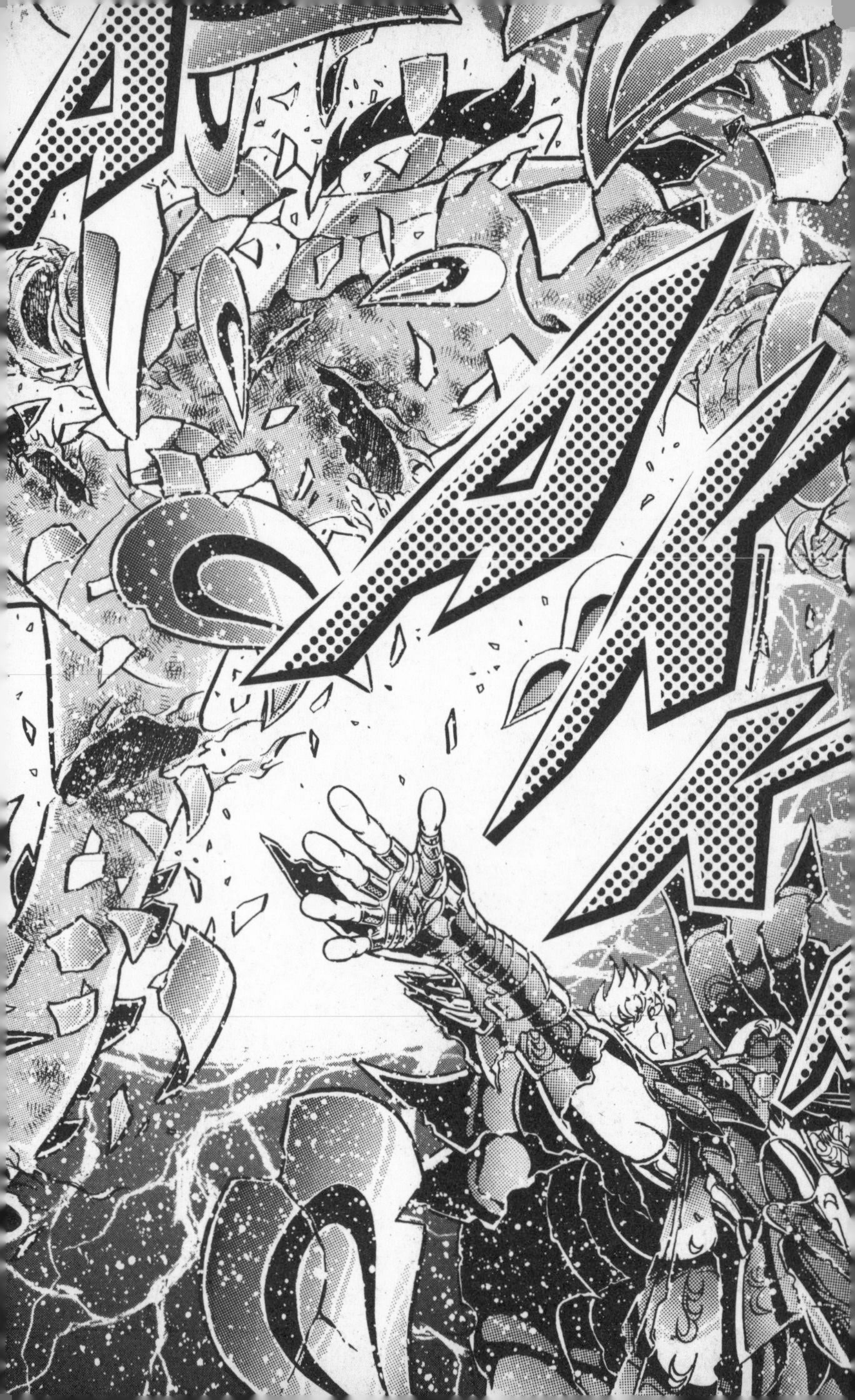

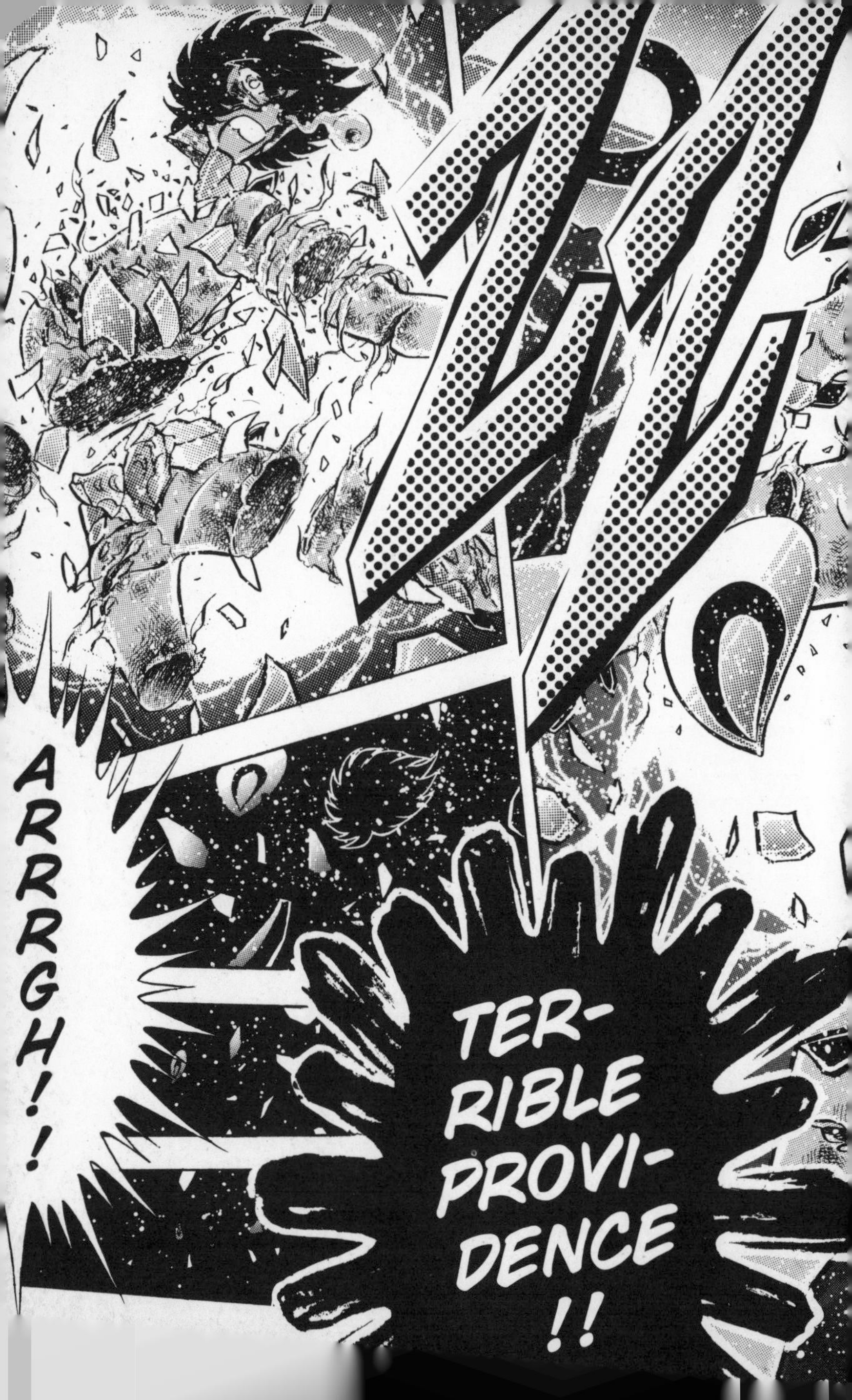
TER-RIBLE PROVI-DENCE!!
ARRRGH!!

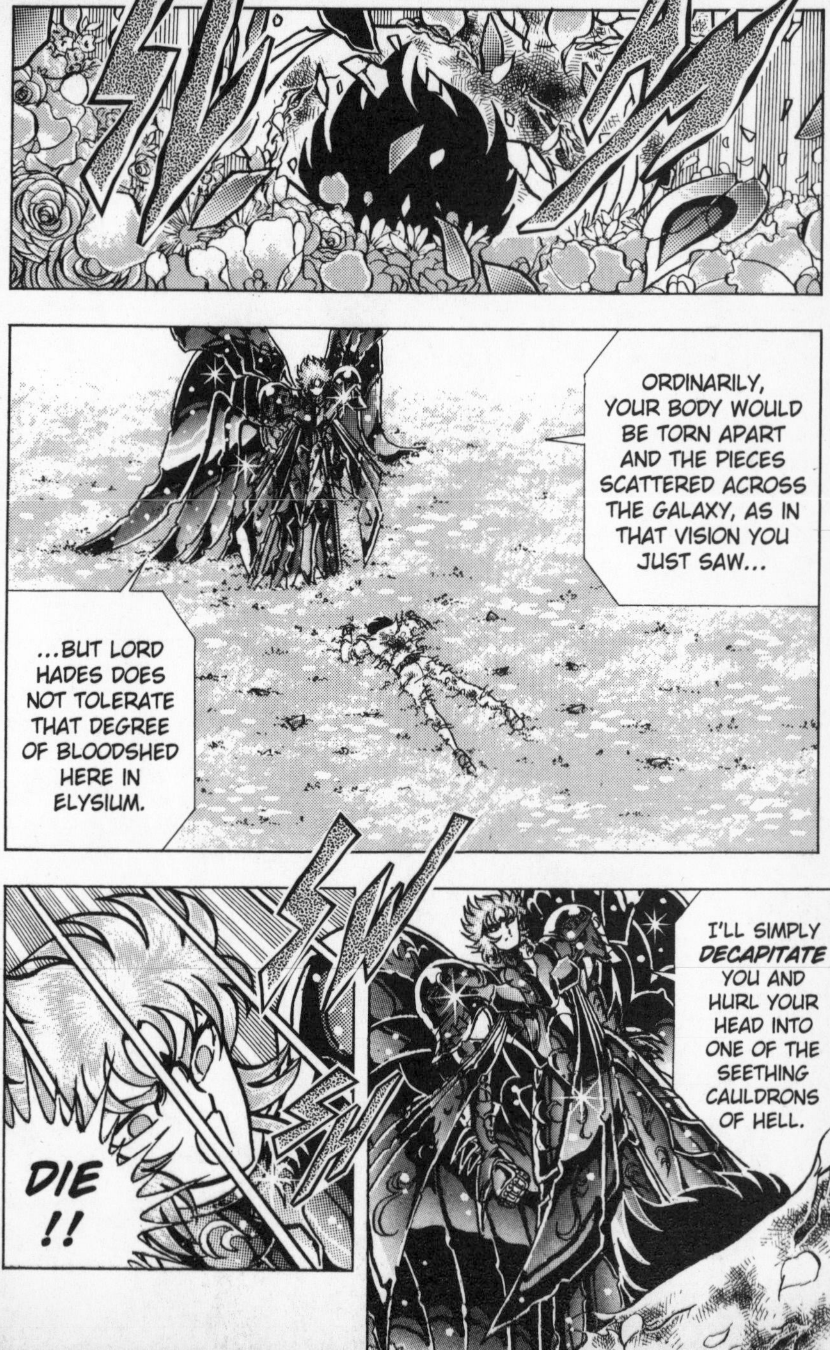
ORDINARILY, YOUR BODY WOULD BE TORN APART AND THE PIECES SCATTERED ACROSS THE GALAXY, AS IN THAT VISION YOU JUST SAW...
...BUT LORD HADES DOES NOT TOLERATE THAT DEGREE OF BLOODSHED HERE IN ELYSIUM.
I'LL SIMPLY *DECAPITATE* YOU AND HURL YOUR HEAD INTO ONE OF THE SEETHING CAULDRONS OF HELL.
DIE !!

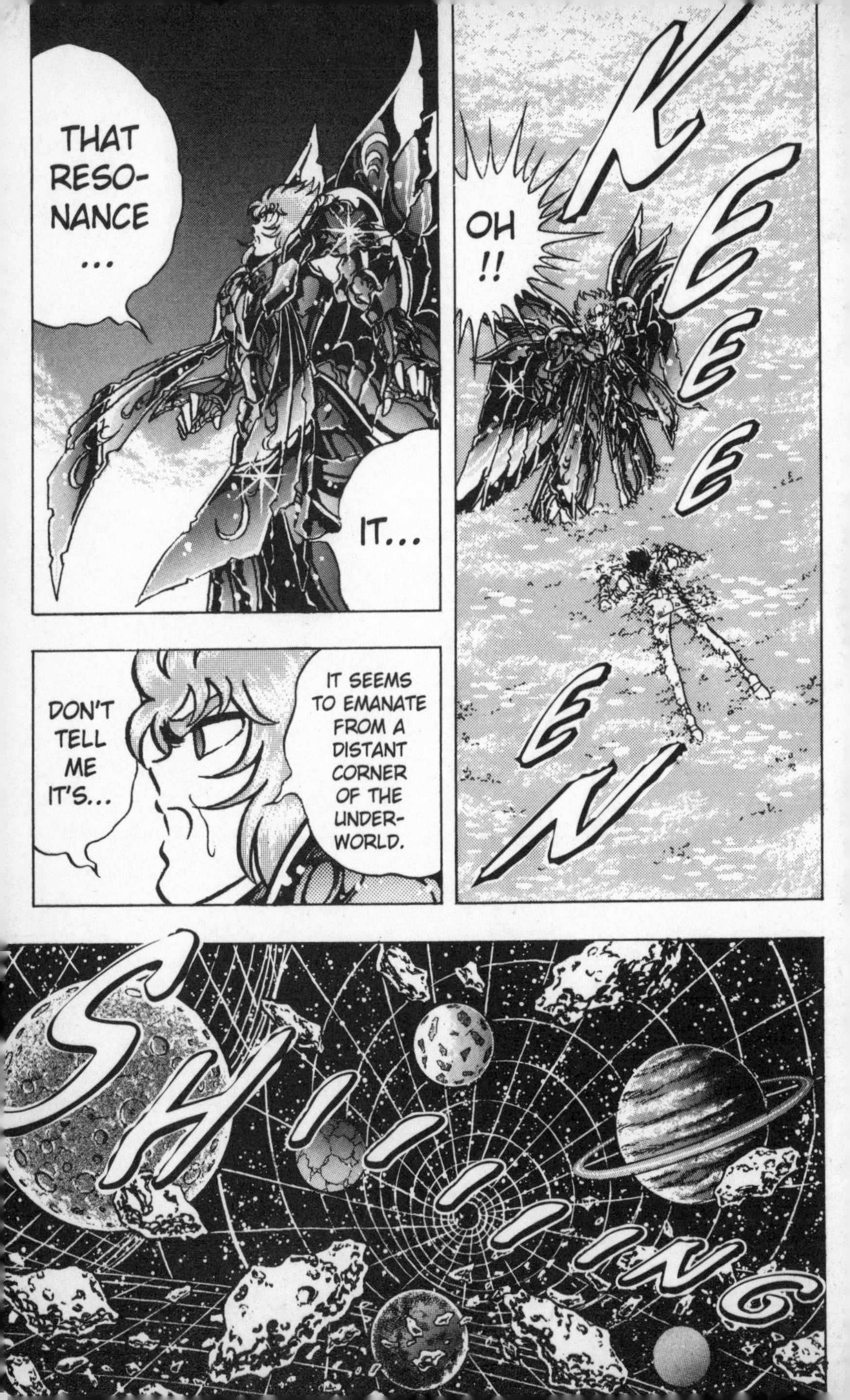
KEEEEN
OH !!
THAT RESONANCE...
IT...
IT SEEMS TO EMANATE FROM A DISTANT CORNER OF THE UNDERWORLD.
DON'T TELL ME IT'S...
SHIIIIING

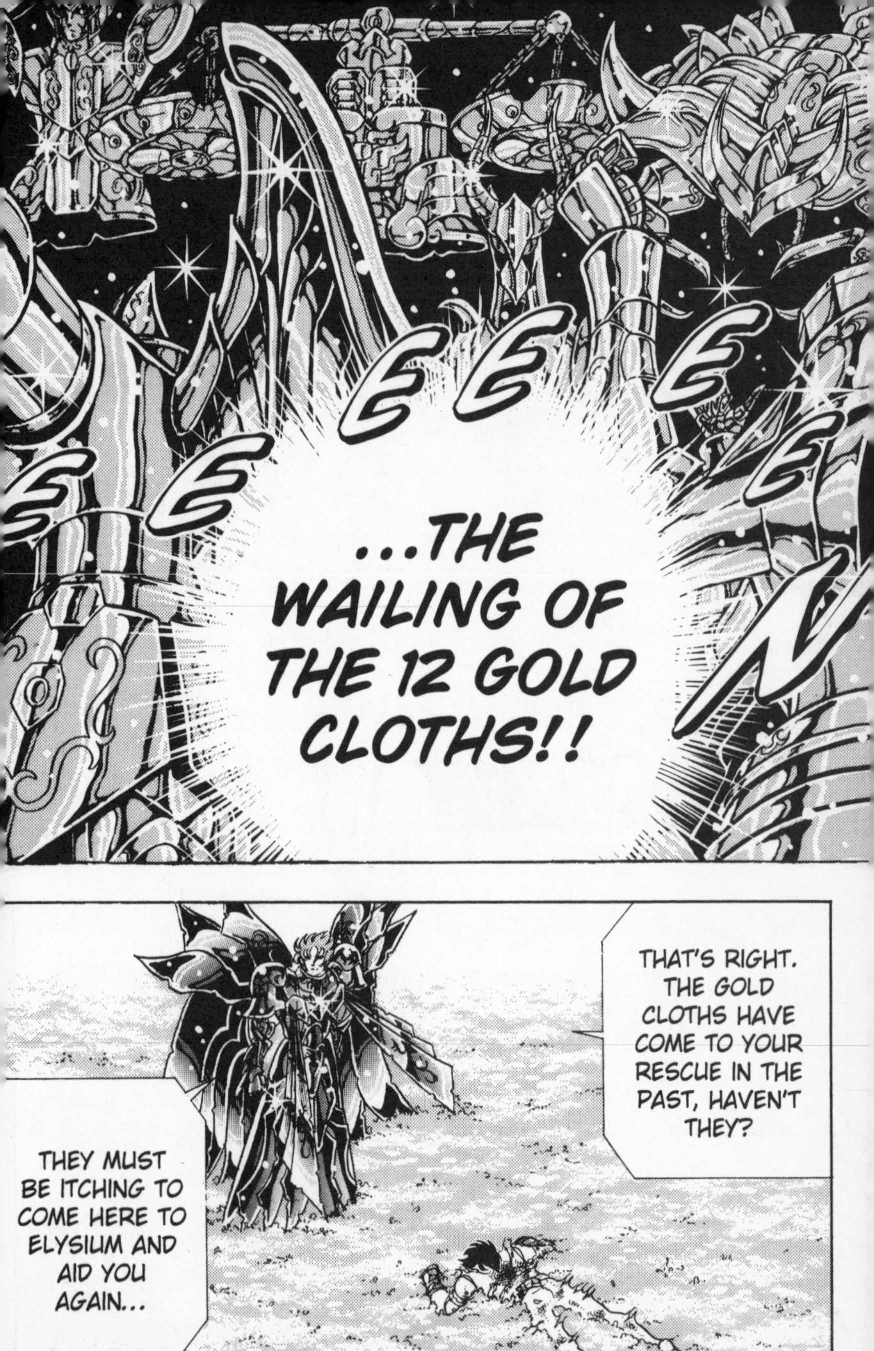
EEEEEEEEEEN
...THE WAILING OF THE 12 GOLD CLOTHS!!
THAT'S RIGHT. THE GOLD CLOTHS HAVE COME TO YOUR RESCUE IN THE PAST, HAVEN'T THEY?
THEY MUST BE ITCHING TO COME HERE TO ELYSIUM AND AID YOU AGAIN...

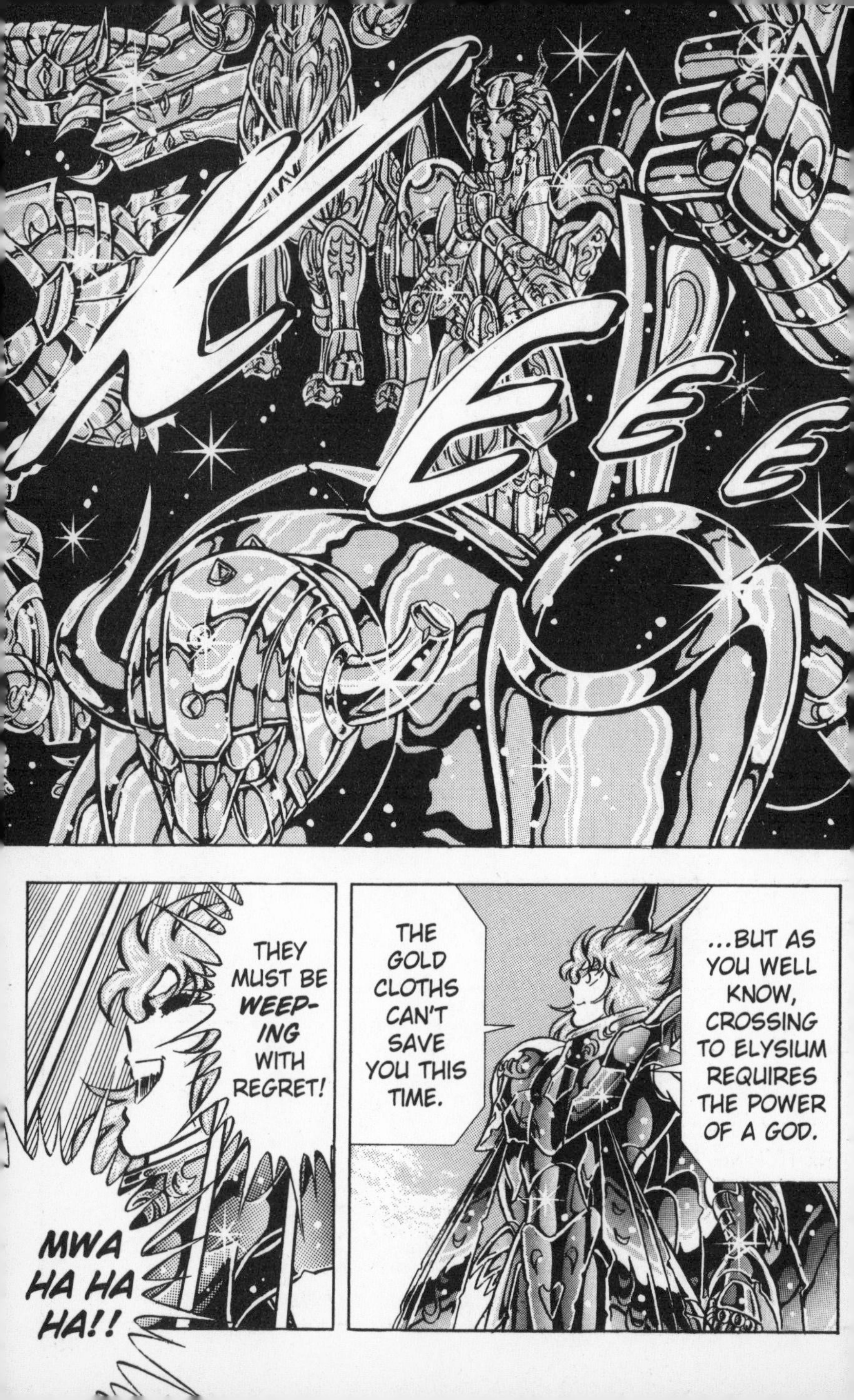
THE GOLD CLOTHS CAN'T SAVE YOU THIS TIME.
...BUT AS YOU WELL KNOW, CROSSING TO ELYSIUM REQUIRES THE POWER OF A GOD.
THEY MUST BE *WEEPING* WITH REGRET!
MWA HA HA HA!!

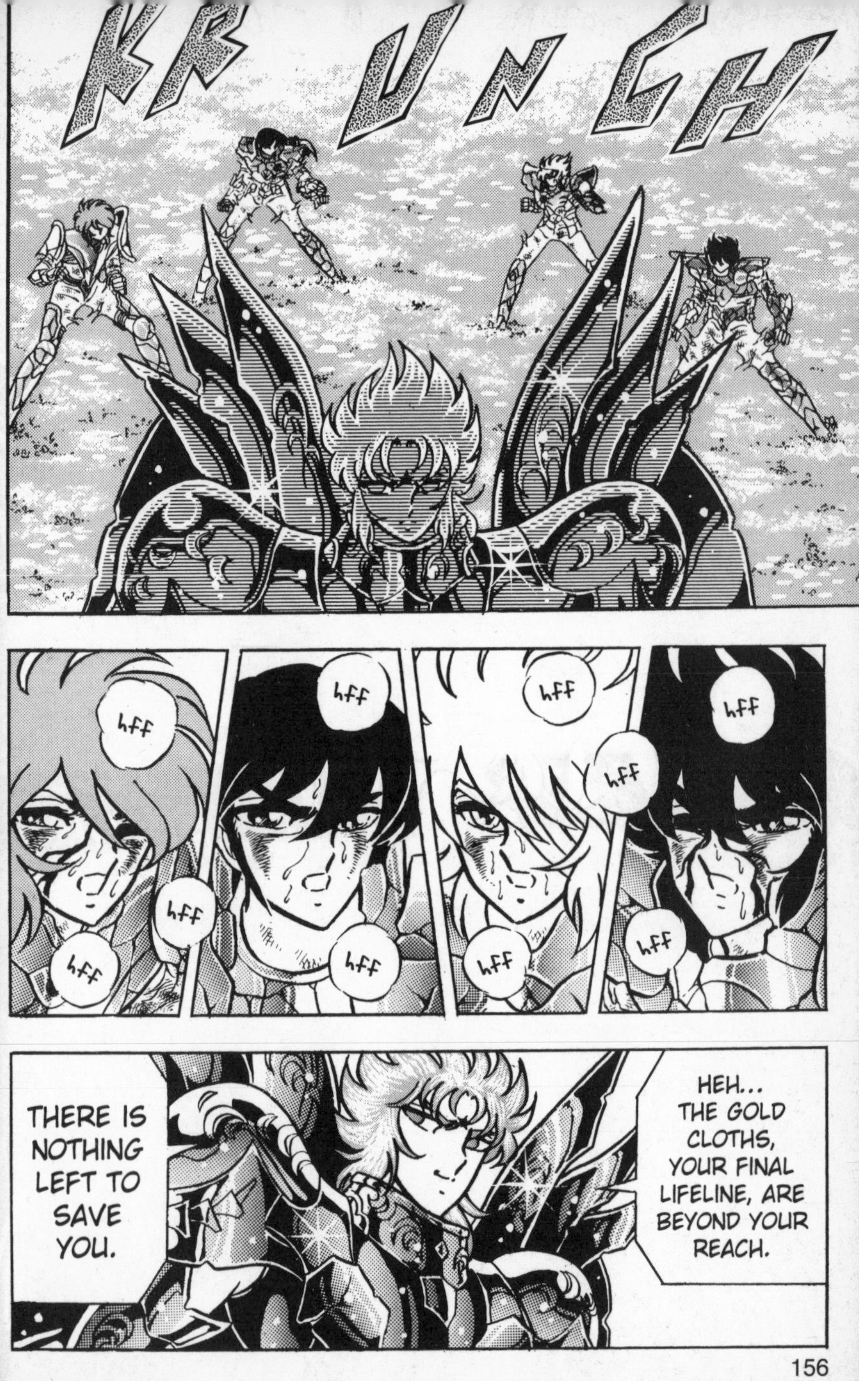
KRUNCH
hff
hff
hff
hff
hff
hff
hff
hff
hff
hff
HEH... THE GOLD CLOTHS, YOUR FINAL LIFELINE, ARE BEYOND YOUR REACH.
THERE IS NOTHING LEFT TO SAVE YOU.

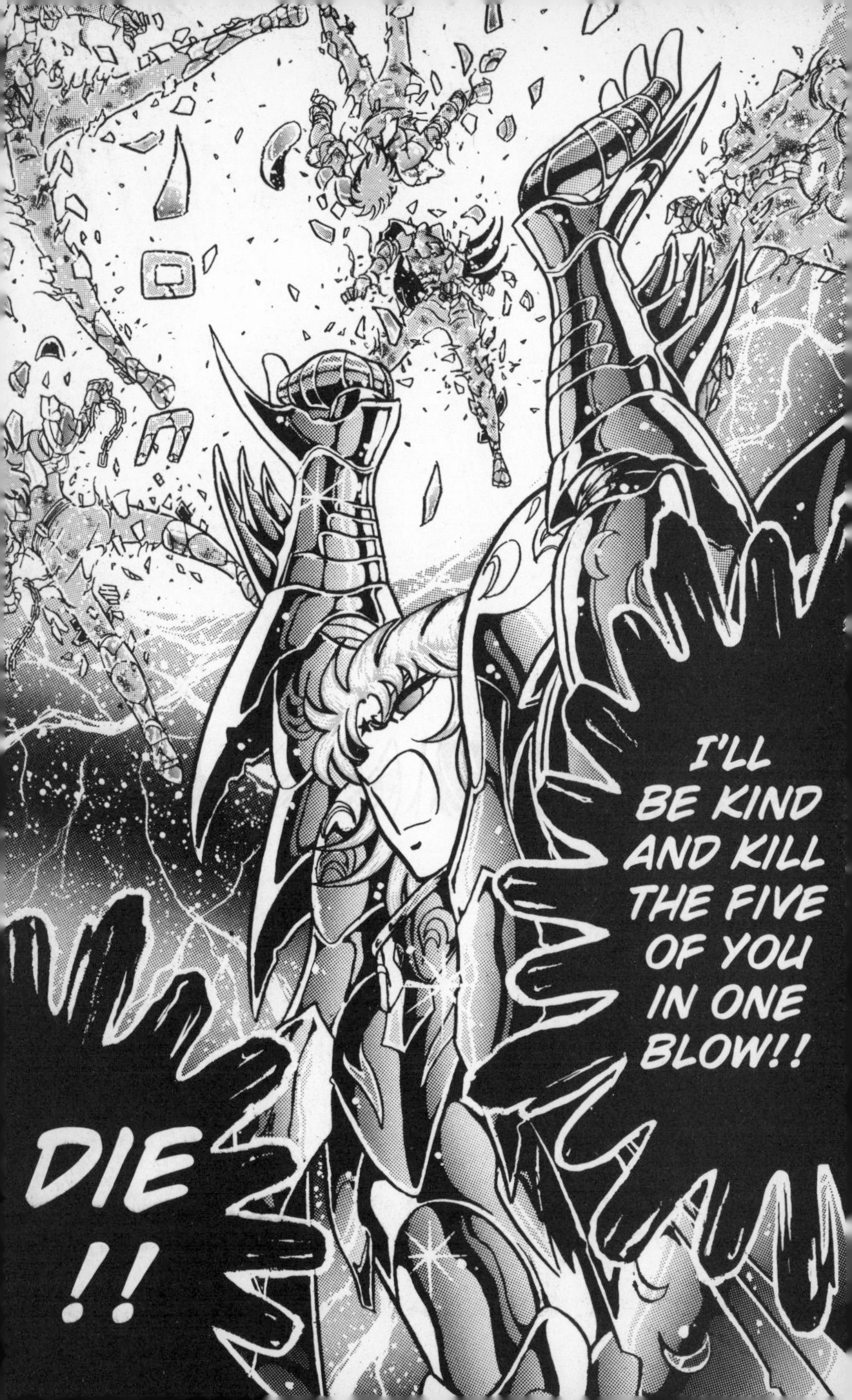
I'LL BE KIND AND KILL THE FIVE OF YOU IN ONE BLOW!!
DIE!!

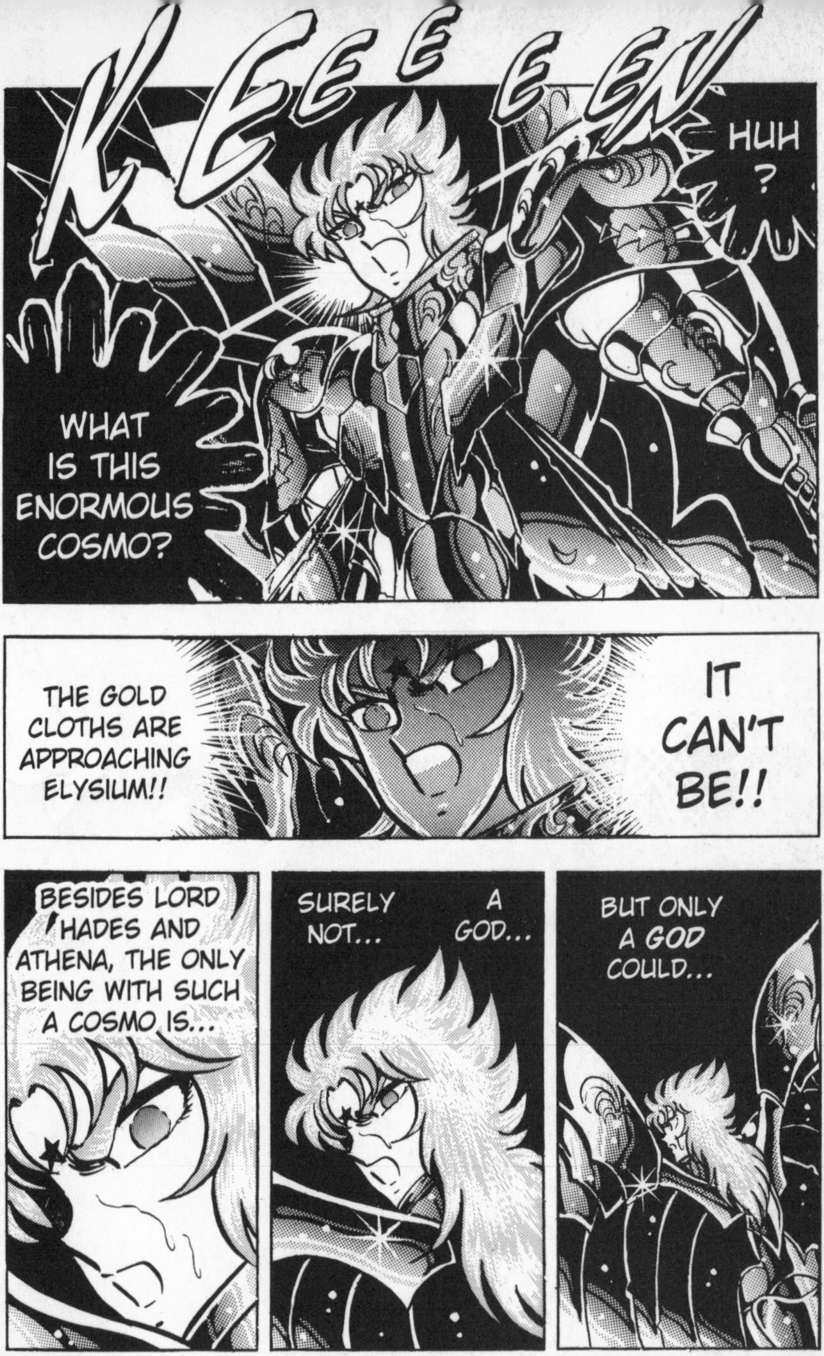
KCEEEEEN
HUH ?
WHAT IS THIS ENORMOUS COSMO?
IT CAN'T BE!!
THE GOLD CLOTHS ARE APPROACHING ELYSIUM!!
BUT ONLY A GOD COULD...
A GOD...
SURELY NOT...
BESIDES LORD HADES AND ATHENA, THE ONLY BEING WITH SUCH A COSMO IS...

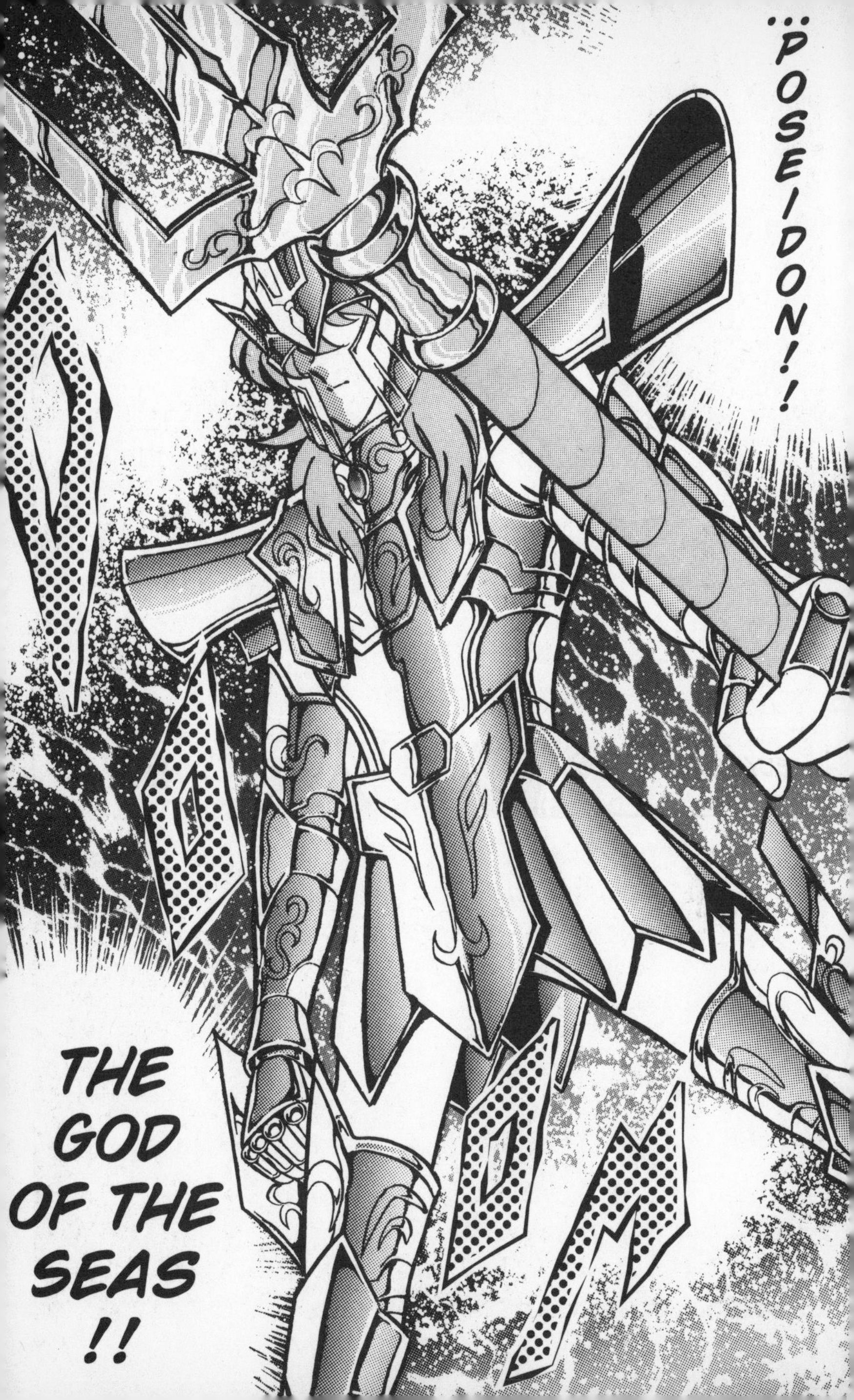
...POSEIDON!!
THE GOD OF THE SEAS!!

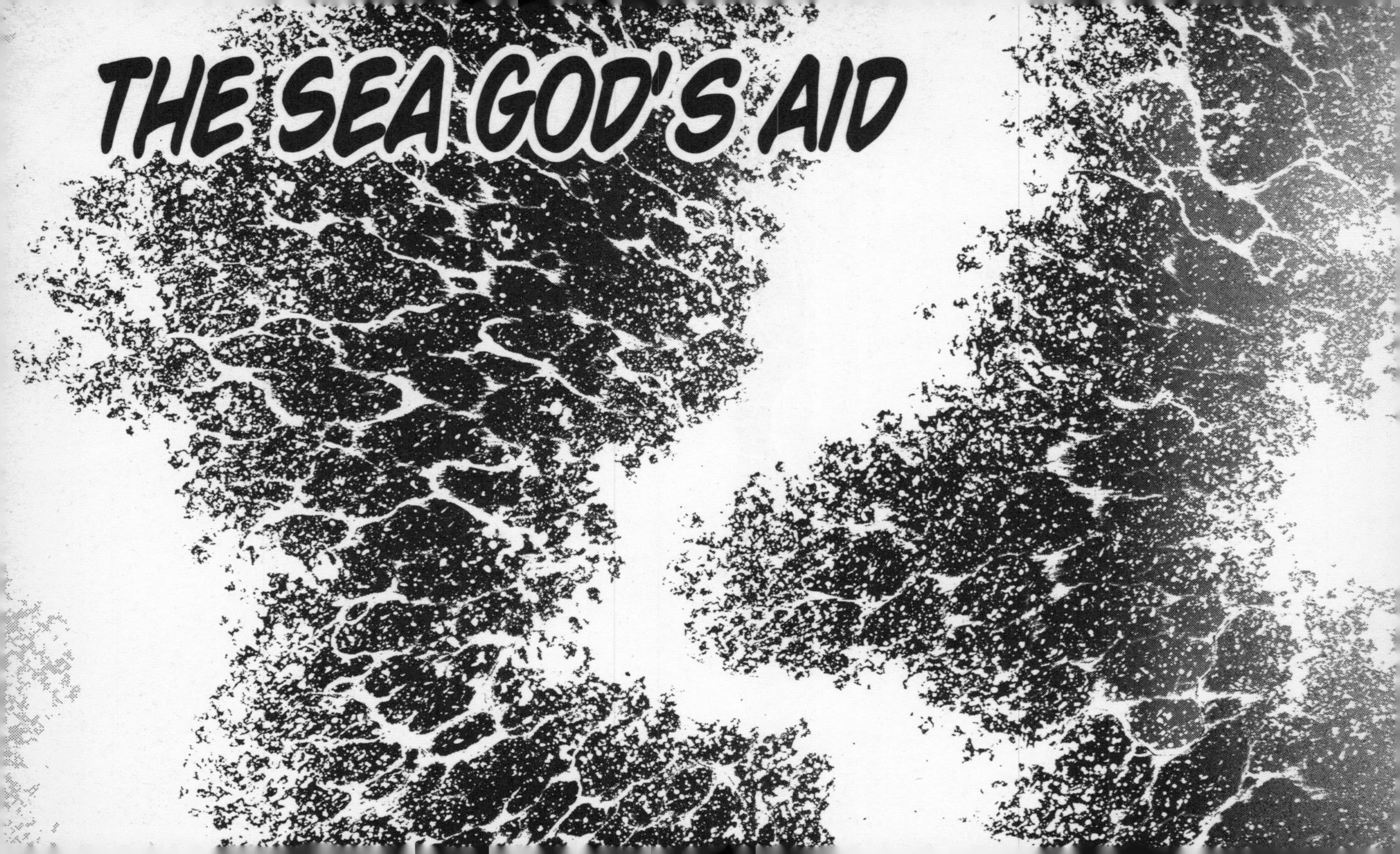
THE SEA GOD'S AID

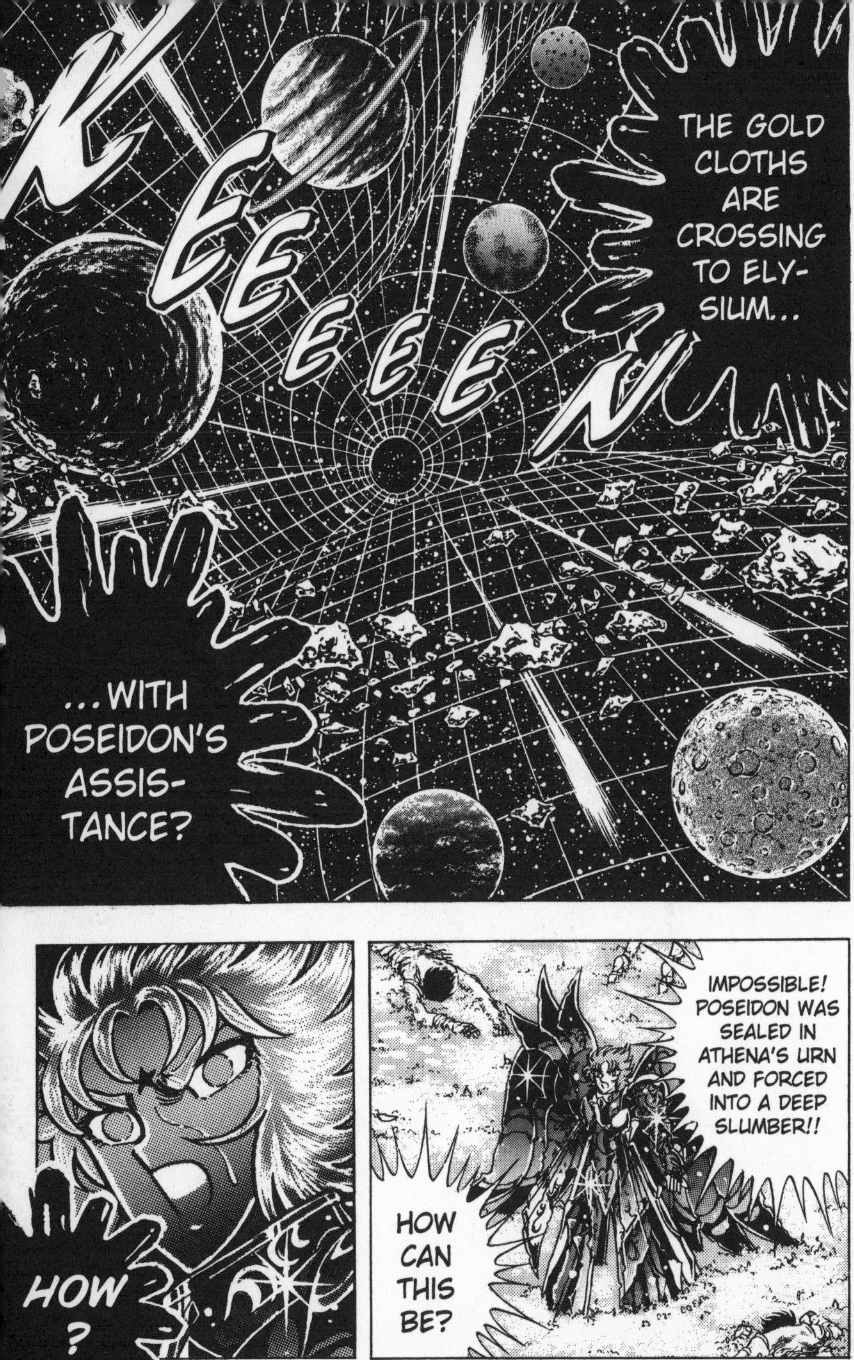
THE GOLD CLOTHS ARE CROSSING TO ELY-SIUM...
KEEEEEN
...WITH POSEIDON'S ASSIS-TANCE?
IMPOSSIBLE! POSEIDON WAS SEALED IN ATHENA'S URN AND FORCED INTO A DEEP SLUMBER!!
HOW CAN THIS BE?
HOW?

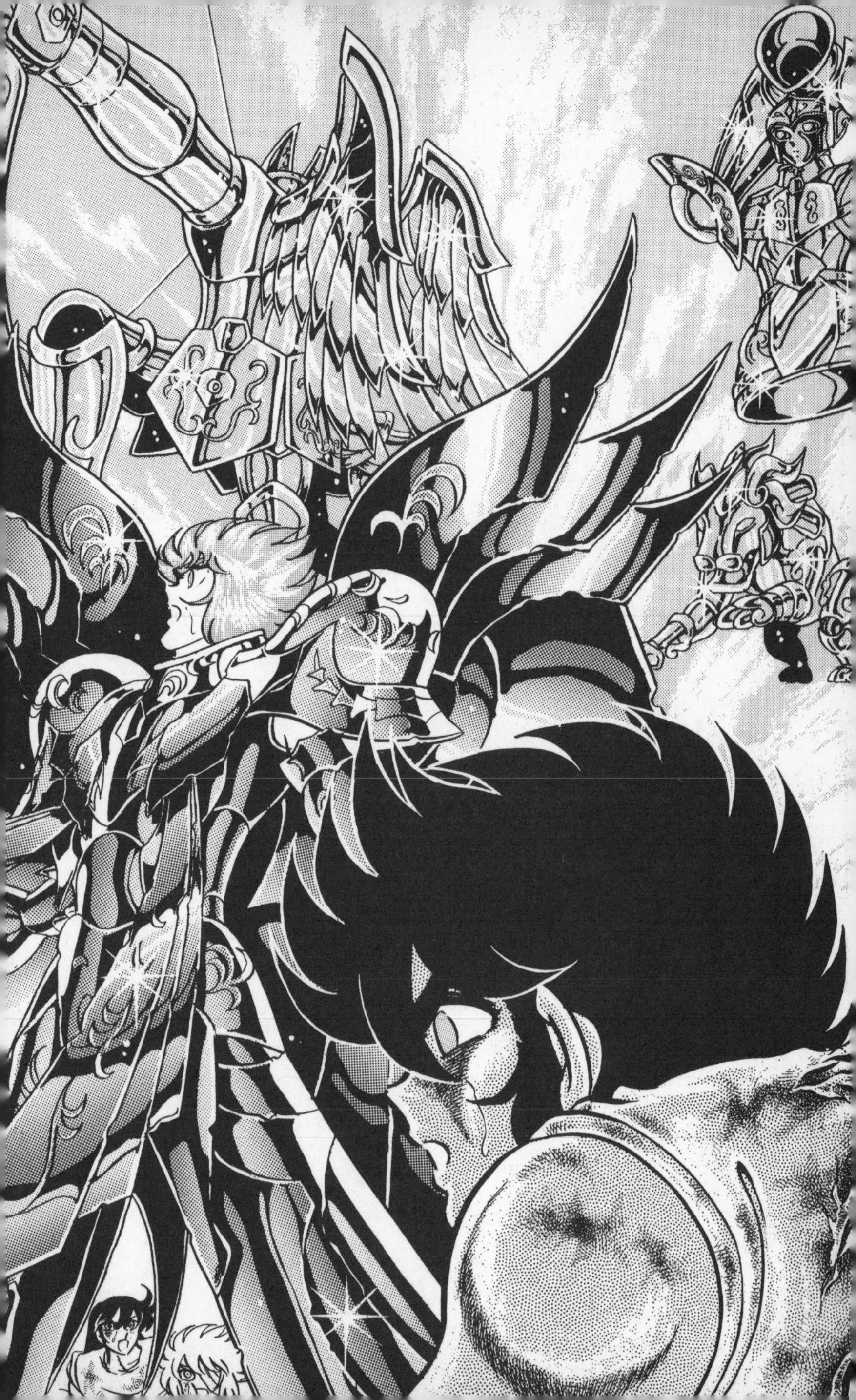

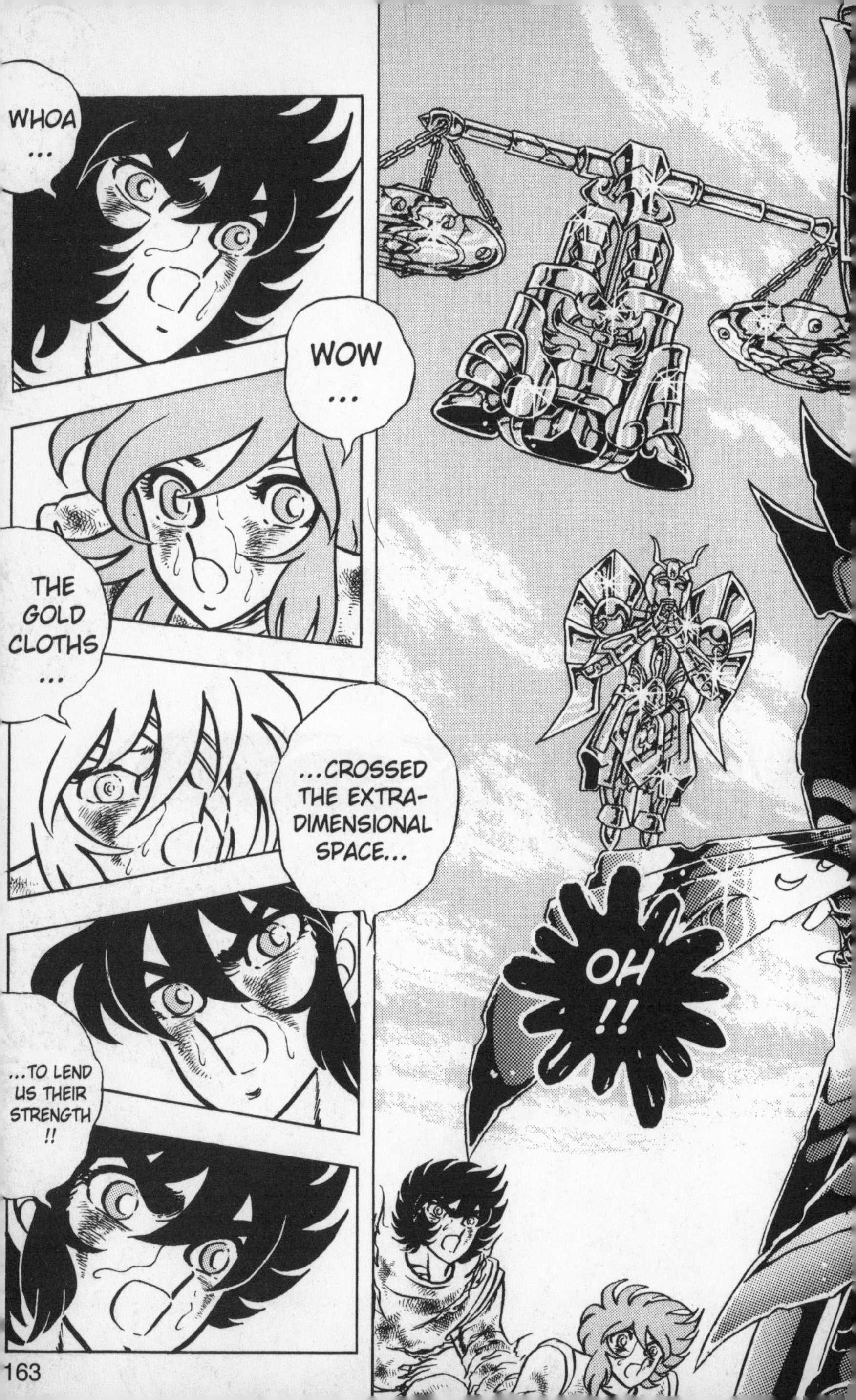
OH!!
WHOA...
WOW...
THE GOLD CLOTHS...
...CROSSED THE EXTRA-DIMENSIONAL SPACE...
...TO LEND US THEIR STRENGTH!!

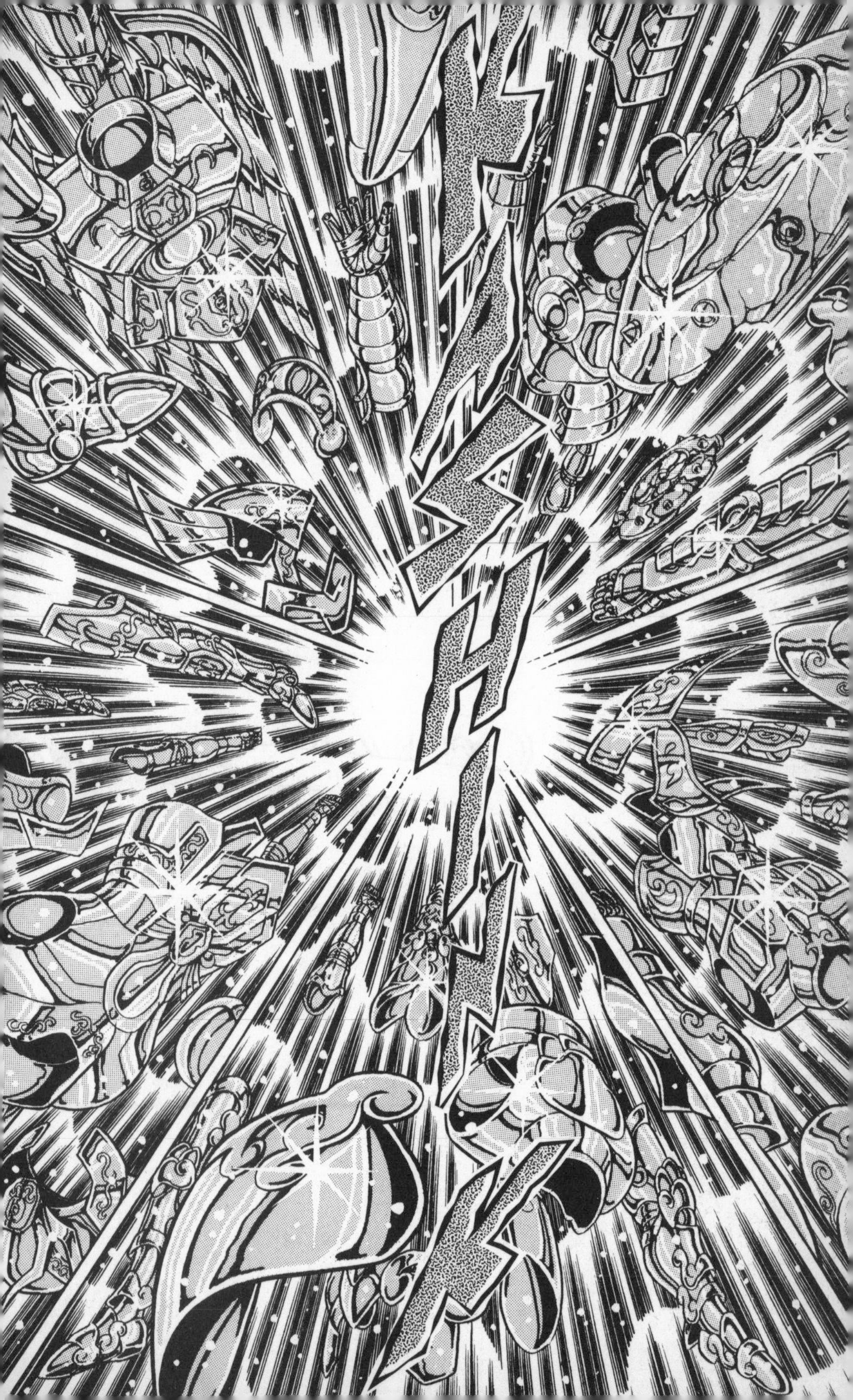

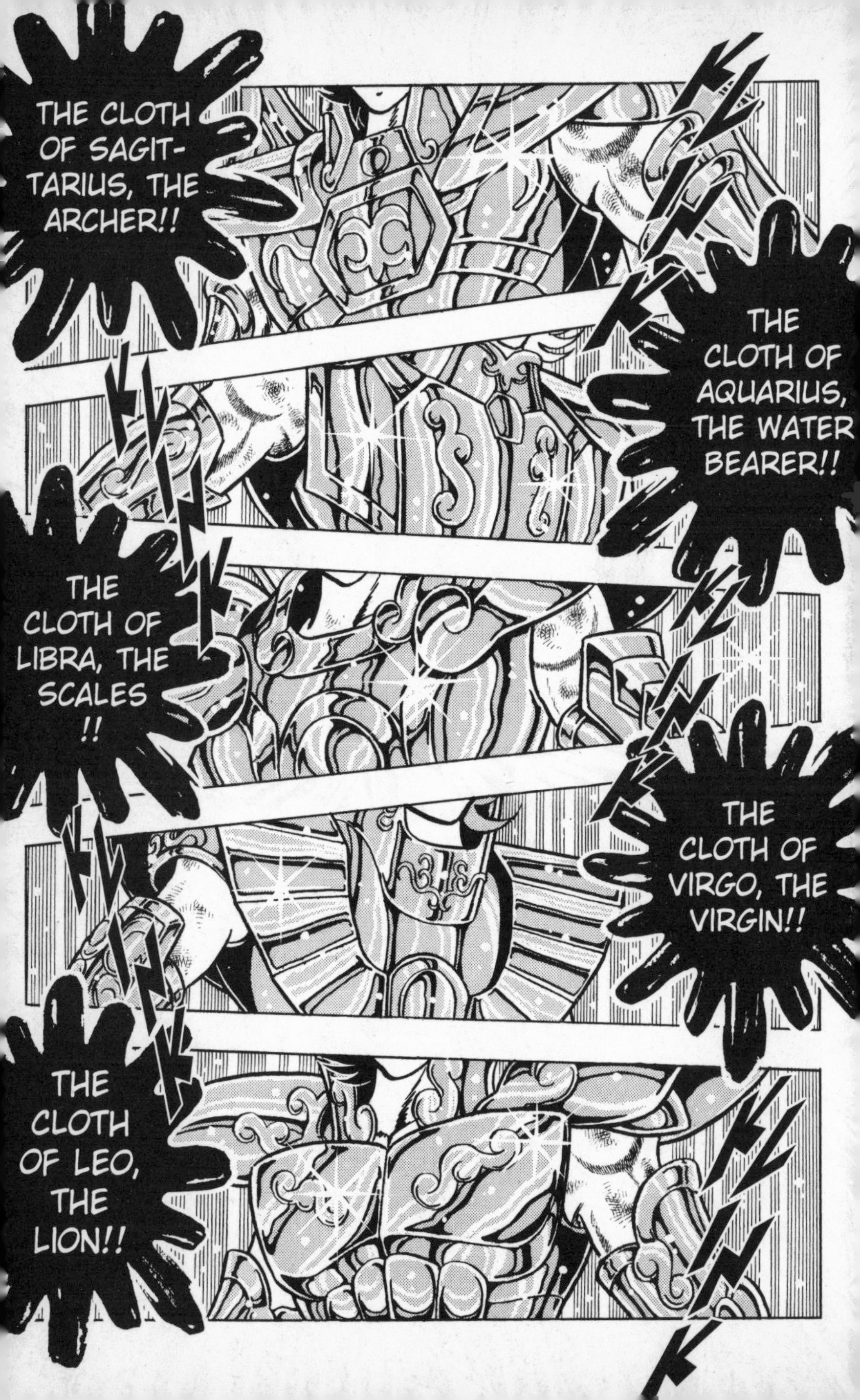
THE CLOTH OF SAGIT-TARIUS, THE ARCHER!!
THE CLOTH OF AQUARIUS, THE WATER BEARER!!
THE CLOTH OF LIBRA, THE SCALES !!
THE CLOTH OF VIRGO, THE VIRGIN!!
THE CLOTH OF LEO, THE LION!!

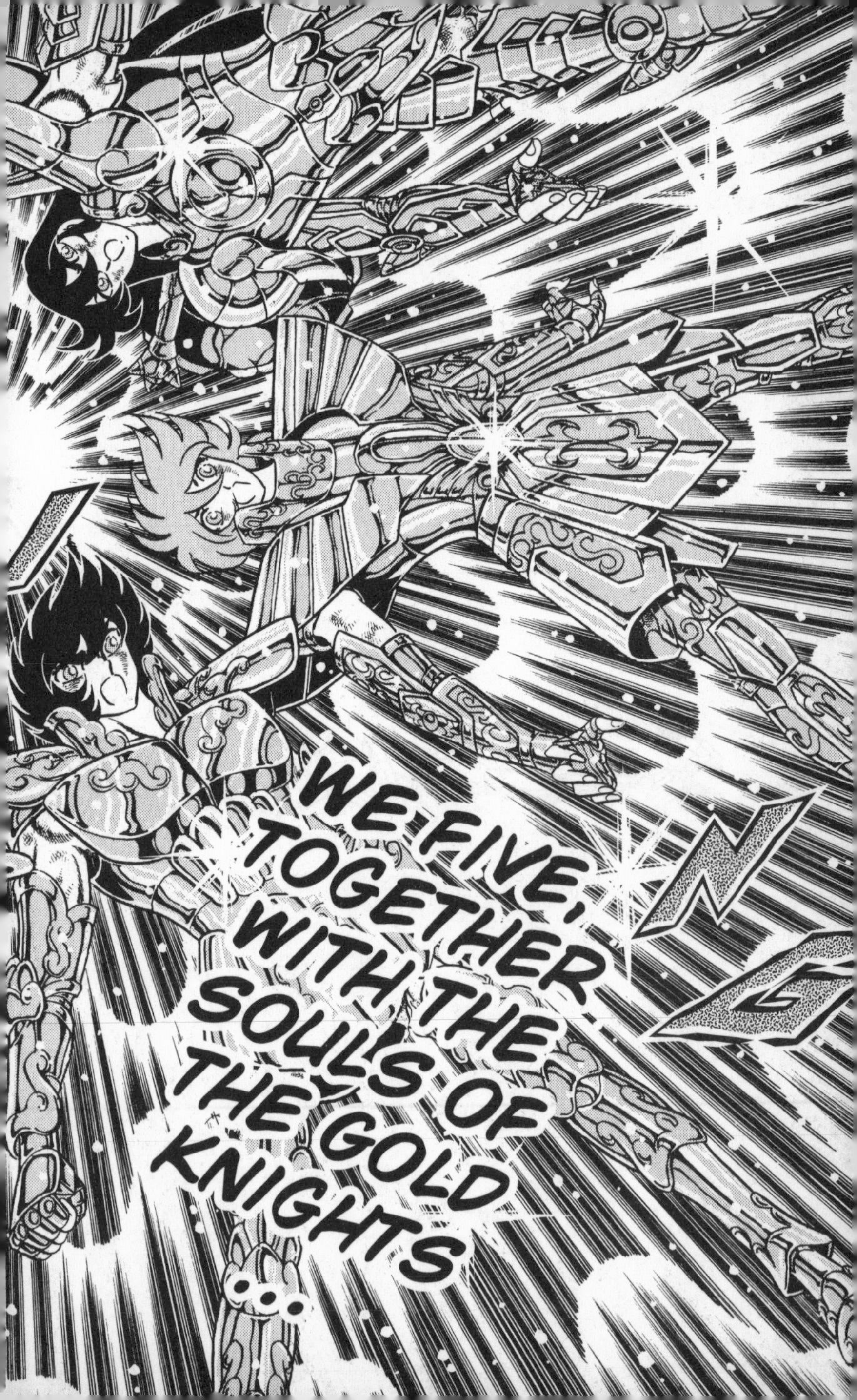
WE FIVE, TOGETHER WITH THE SOULS OF THE GOLD KNIGHTS...

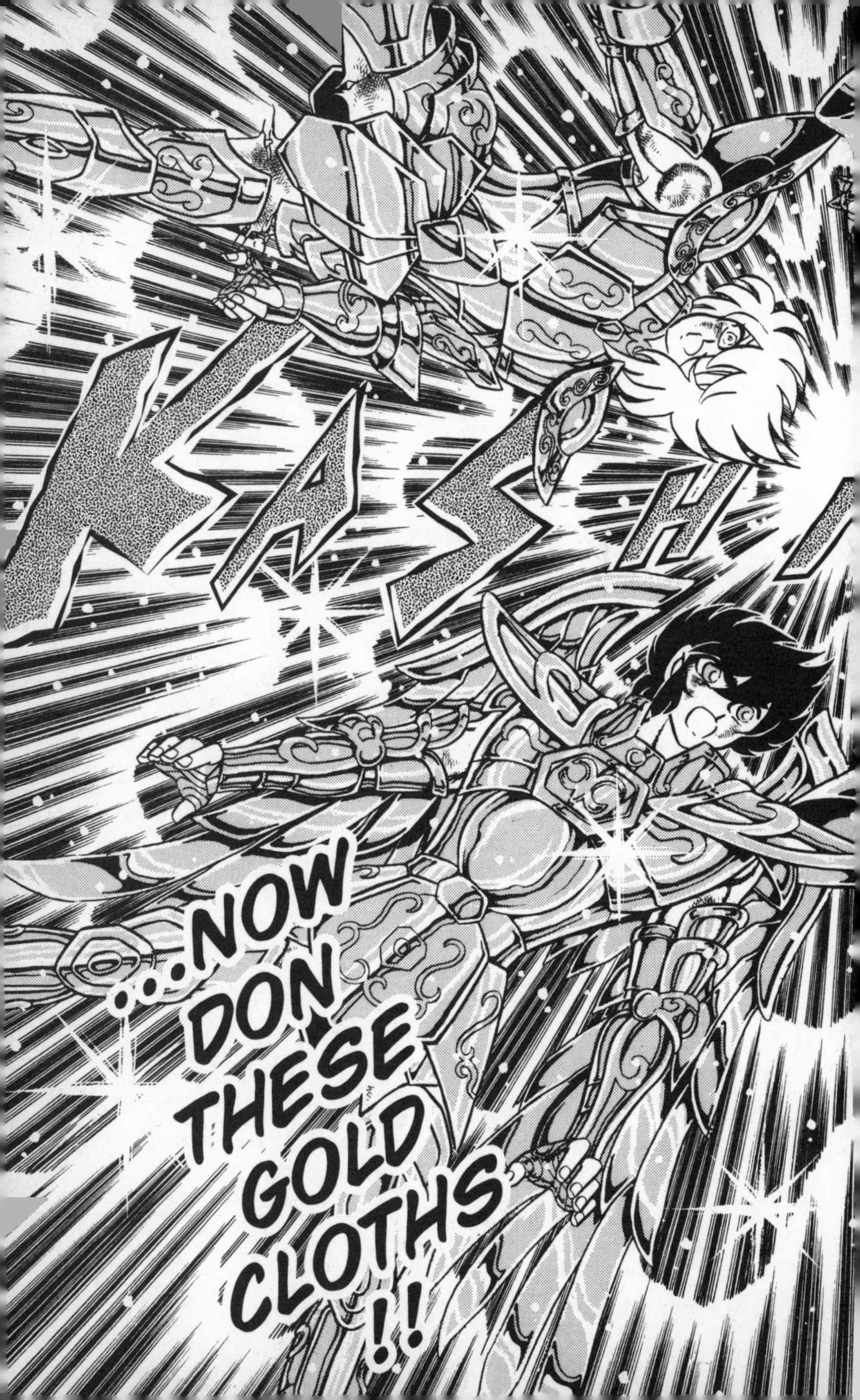
KASHH
...NOW DON THESE GOLD CLOTHS!!

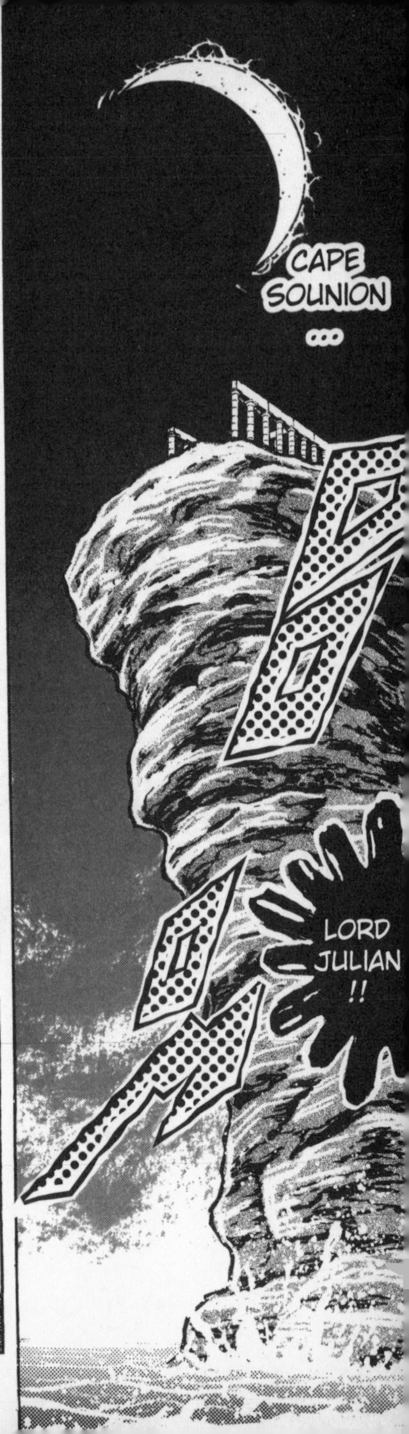
CAPE SOUNION ...
LORD JULIAN !!
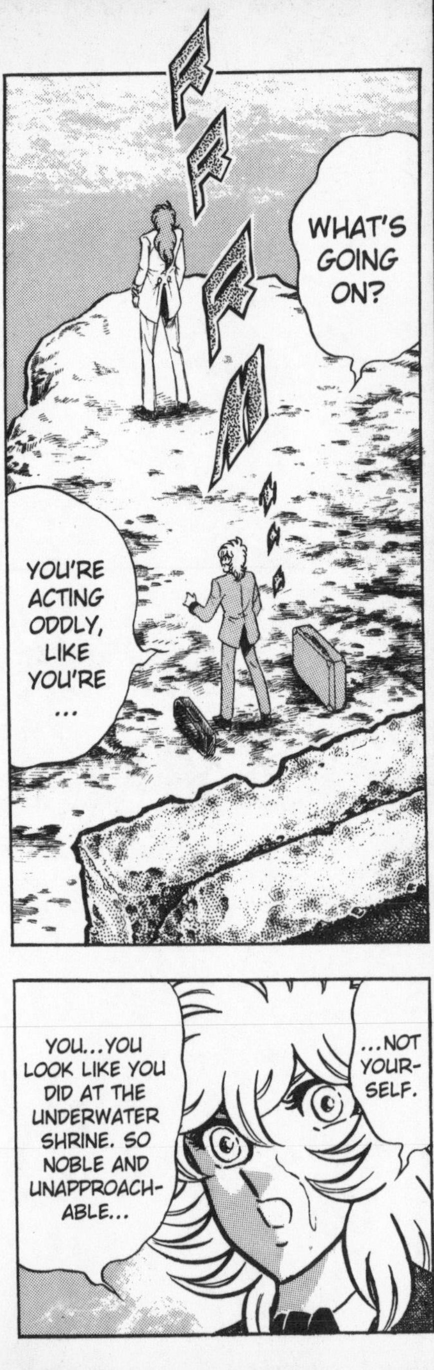
WHAT'S GOING ON?
YOU'RE ACTING ODDLY, LIKE YOU'RE ...
...NOT YOURSELF.
YOU...YOU LOOK LIKE YOU DID AT THE UNDERWATER SHRINE. SO NOBLE AND UNAPPROACHABLE...

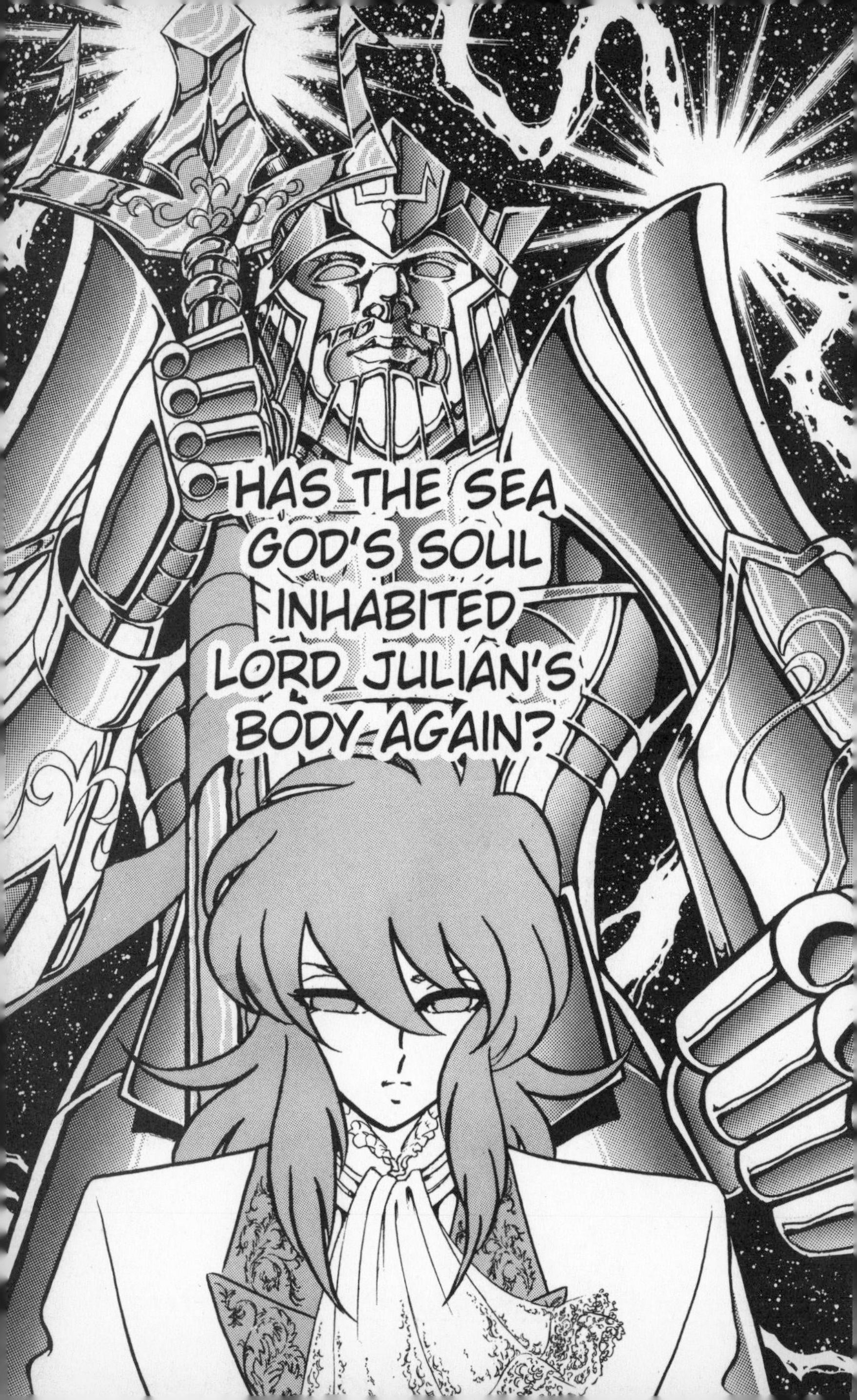
HAS THE SEA GOD'S SOUL INHABITED LORD JULIAN'S BODY AGAIN?

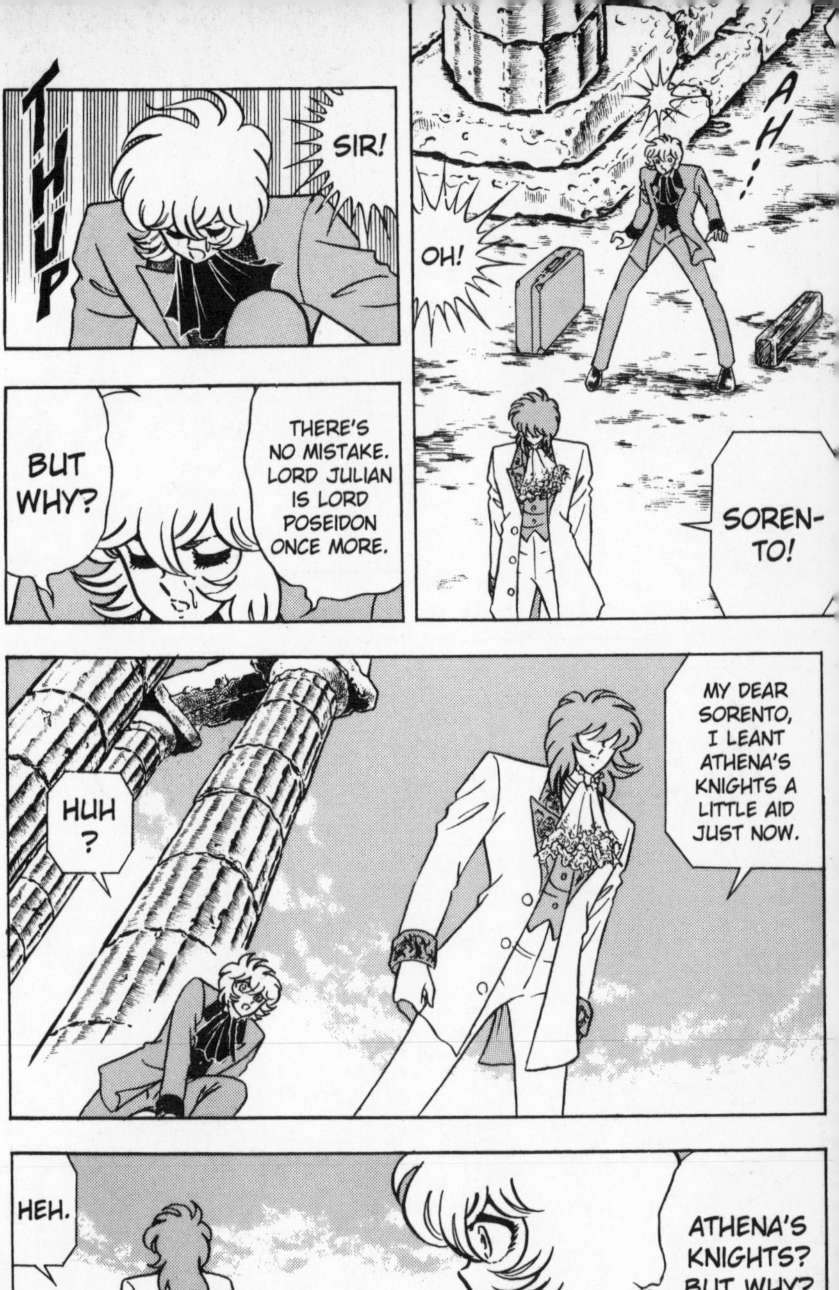
AH!!
OH!
SOREN-TO!
THUP
SIR!
THERE'S NO MISTAKE. LORD JULIAN IS LORD POSEIDON ONCE MORE.
BUT WHY?
MY DEAR SORENTO, I LEANT ATHENA'S KNIGHTS A LITTLE AID JUST NOW.
HUH?
ATHENA'S KNIGHTS? BUT WHY?
HEH.

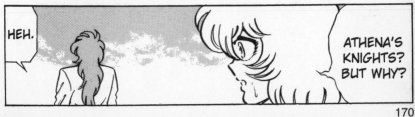

READ THIS WAY

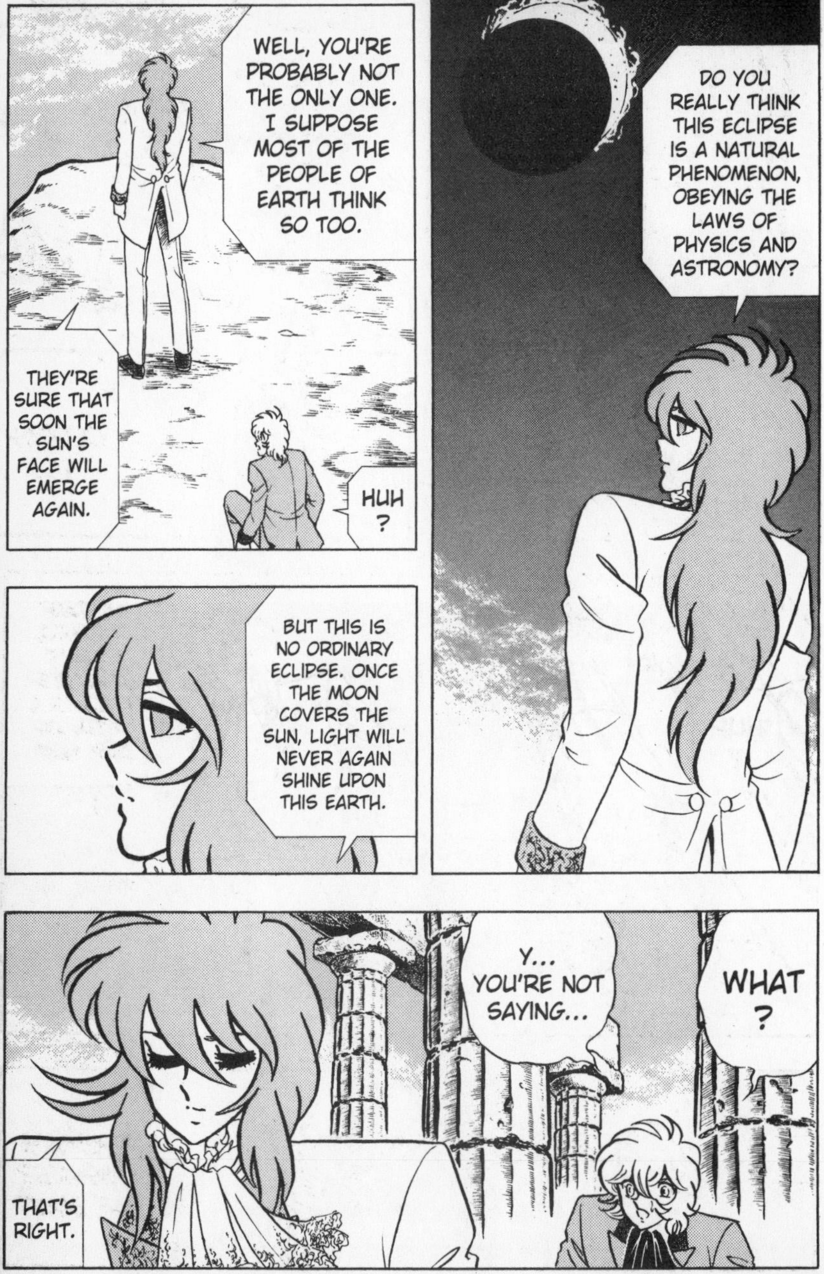
DO YOU REALLY THINK THIS ECLIPSE IS A NATURAL PHENOMENON, OBEYING THE LAWS OF PHYSICS AND ASTRONOMY?
WELL, YOU'RE PROBABLY NOT THE ONLY ONE. I SUPPOSE MOST OF THE PEOPLE OF EARTH THINK SO TOO.
THEY'RE SURE THAT SOON THE SUN'S FACE WILL EMERGE AGAIN.
HUH?
BUT THIS IS NO ORDINARY ECLIPSE. ONCE THE MOON COVERS THE SUN, LIGHT WILL NEVER AGAIN SHINE UPON THIS EARTH.
WHAT?
Y... YOU'RE NOT SAYING...
THAT'S RIGHT.

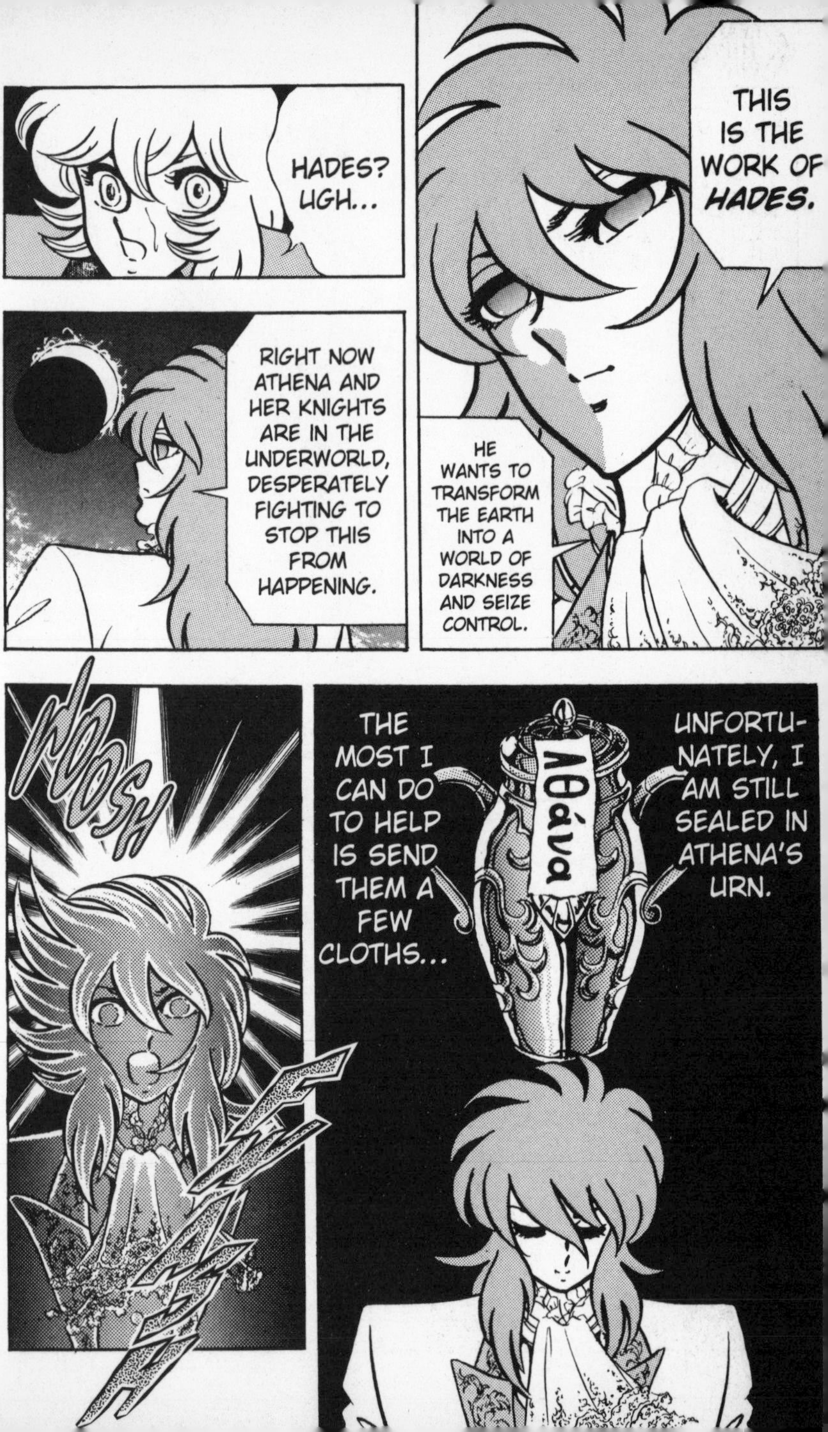
THIS IS THE WORK OF HADES.
HE WANTS TO TRANSFORM THE EARTH INTO A WORLD OF DARKNESS AND SEIZE CONTROL.
HADES? UGH...
RIGHT NOW ATHENA AND HER KNIGHTS ARE IN THE UNDERWORLD, DESPERATELY FIGHTING TO STOP THIS FROM HAPPENING.
UNFORTU-NATELY, I AM STILL SEALED IN ATHENA'S URN.
Αθάνα
THE MOST I CAN DO TO HELP IS SEND THEM A FEW CLOTHS...
WOOSH

READ THIS WAY

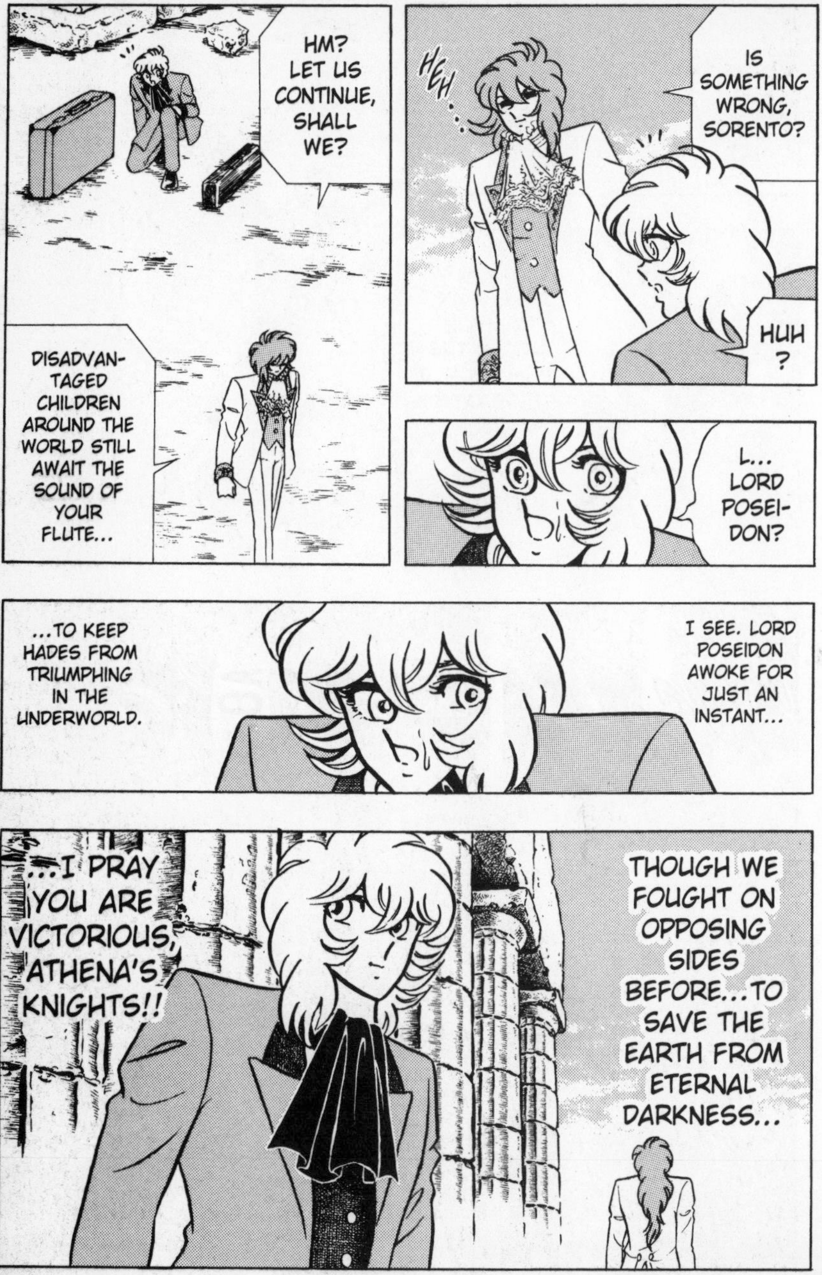

IS SOMETHING WRONG, SORENTO?
HEH...
HUH?
L... LORD POSEIDON?
HM? LET US CONTINUE, SHALL WE?
DISADVANTAGED CHILDREN AROUND THE WORLD STILL AWAIT THE SOUND OF YOUR FLUTE...
I SEE. LORD POSEIDON AWOKE FOR JUST AN INSTANT...
...TO KEEP HADES FROM TRIUMPHING IN THE UNDERWORLD.
THOUGH WE FOUGHT ON OPPOSING SIDES BEFORE...TO SAVE THE EARTH FROM ETERNAL DARKNESS...
...I PRAY YOU ARE VICTORIOUS, ATHENA'S KNIGHTS!!

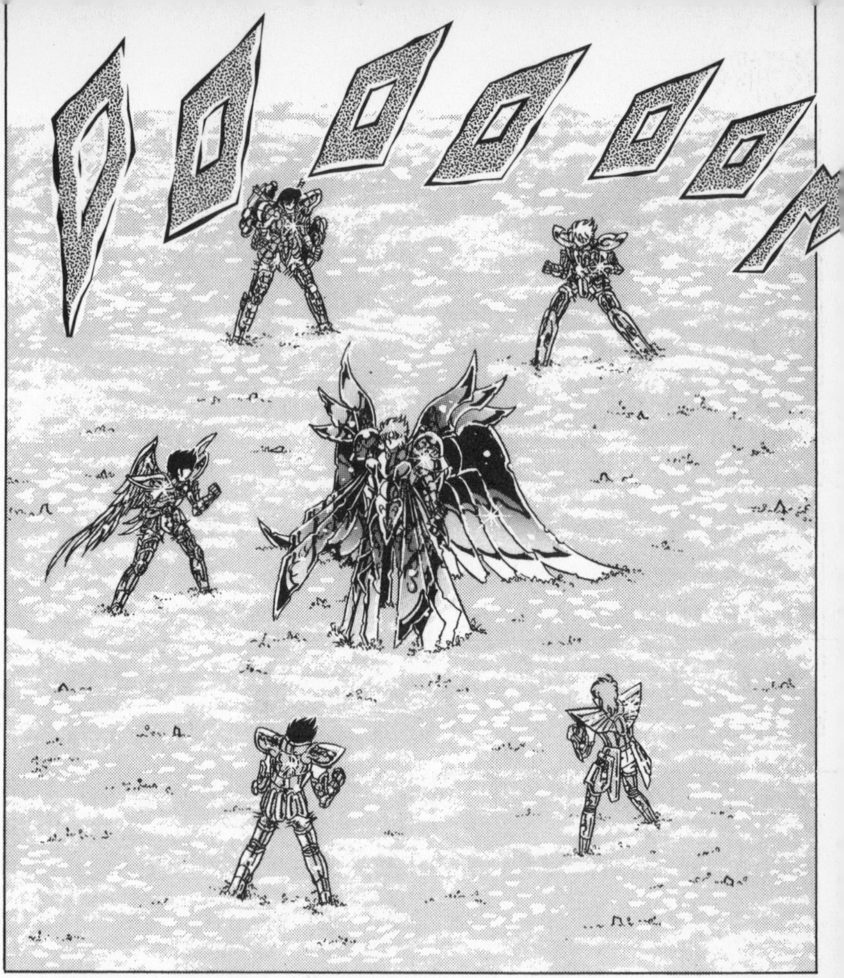
DOOOOOM
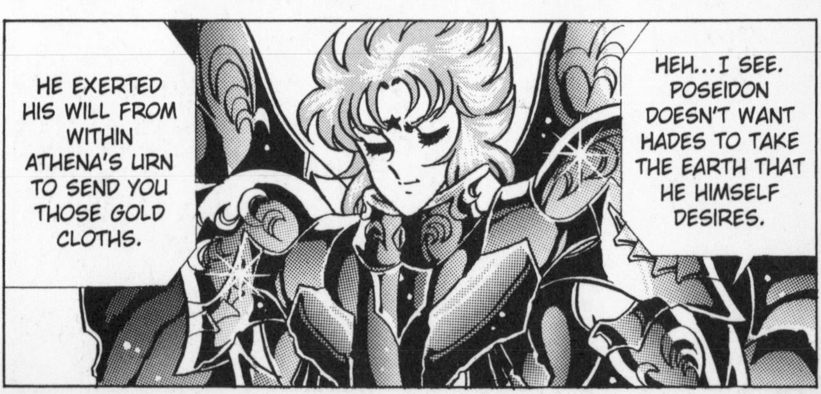
HEH...I SEE. POSEIDON DOESN'T WANT HADES TO TAKE THE EARTH THAT HE HIMSELF DESIRES.
HE EXERTED HIS WILL FROM WITHIN ATHENA'S URN TO SEND YOU THOSE GOLD CLOTHS.

READ THIS WAY

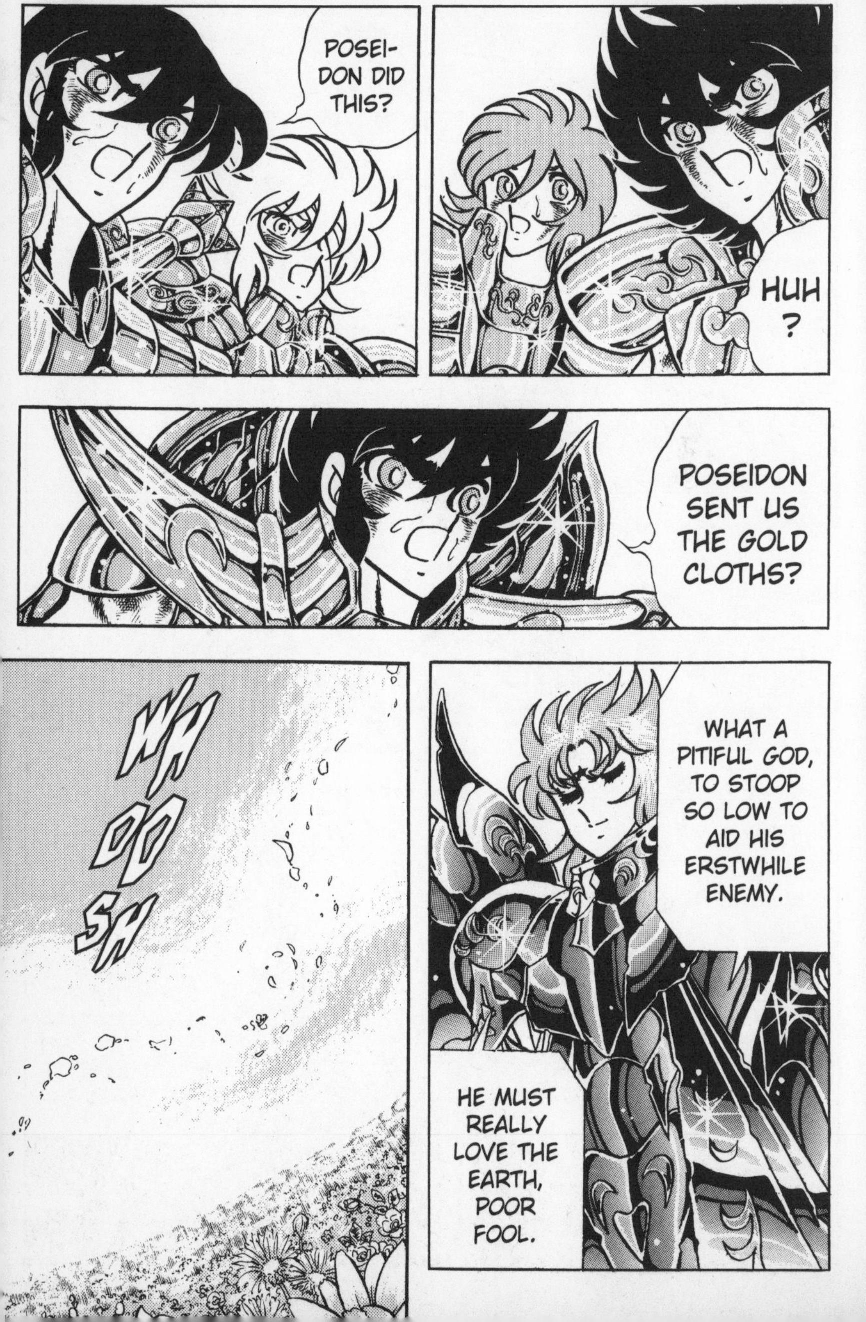
HUH ?
POSEI-DON DID THIS?
POSEIDON SENT US THE GOLD CLOTHS?
WHAT A PITIFUL GOD, TO STOOP SO LOW TO AID HIS ERSTWHILE ENEMY.
HE MUST REALLY LOVE THE EARTH, POOR FOOL.
WHOOSH

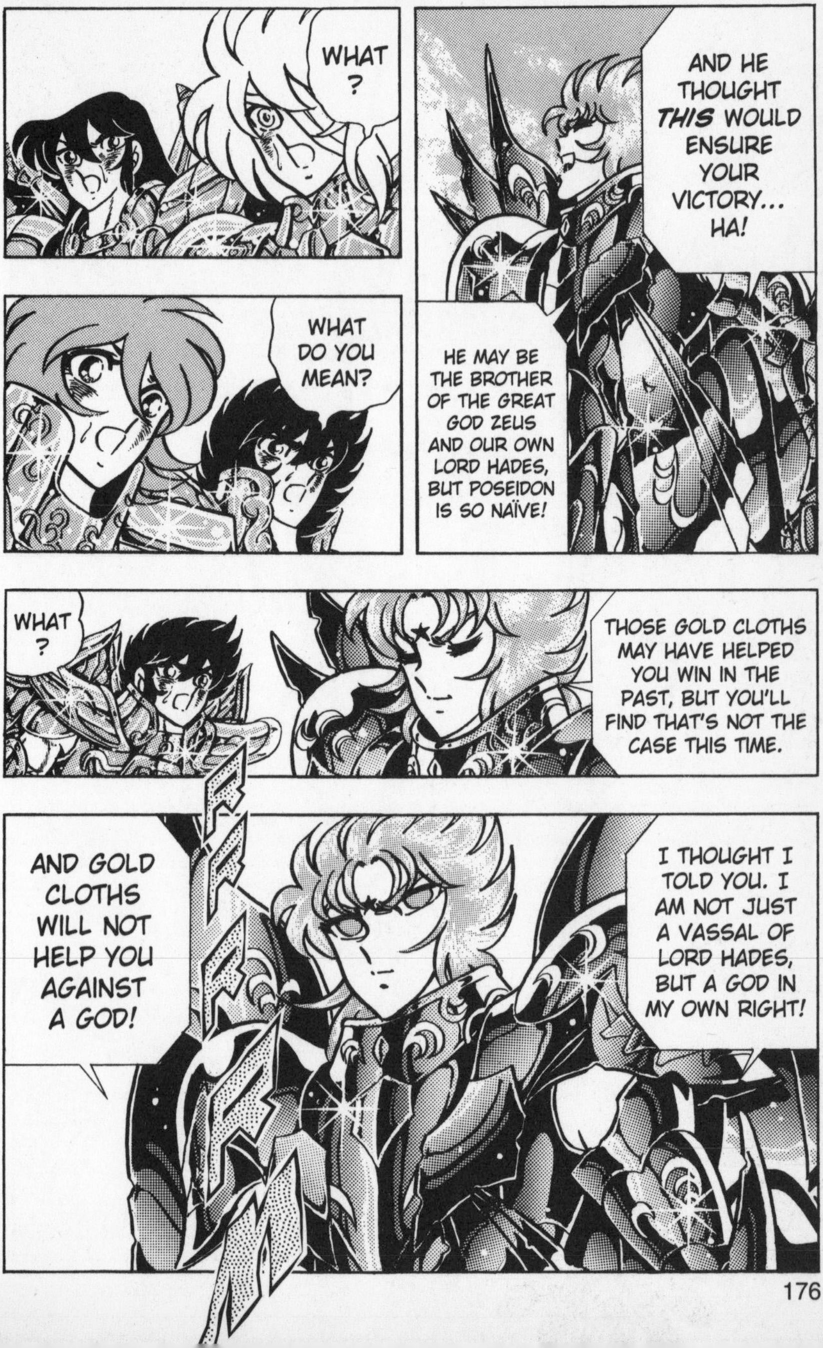
AND HE THOUGHT *THIS* WOULD ENSURE YOUR VICTORY... HA!
HE MAY BE THE BROTHER OF THE GREAT GOD ZEUS AND OUR OWN LORD HADES, BUT POSEIDON IS SO NAÏVE!
WHAT ?
WHAT DO YOU MEAN?
THOSE GOLD CLOTHS MAY HAVE HELPED YOU WIN IN THE PAST, BUT YOU'LL FIND THAT'S NOT THE CASE THIS TIME.
WHAT ?
I THOUGHT I TOLD YOU. I AM NOT JUST A VASSAL OF LORD HADES, BUT A GOD IN MY OWN RIGHT!
AND GOLD CLOTHS WILL NOT HELP YOU AGAINST A GOD!

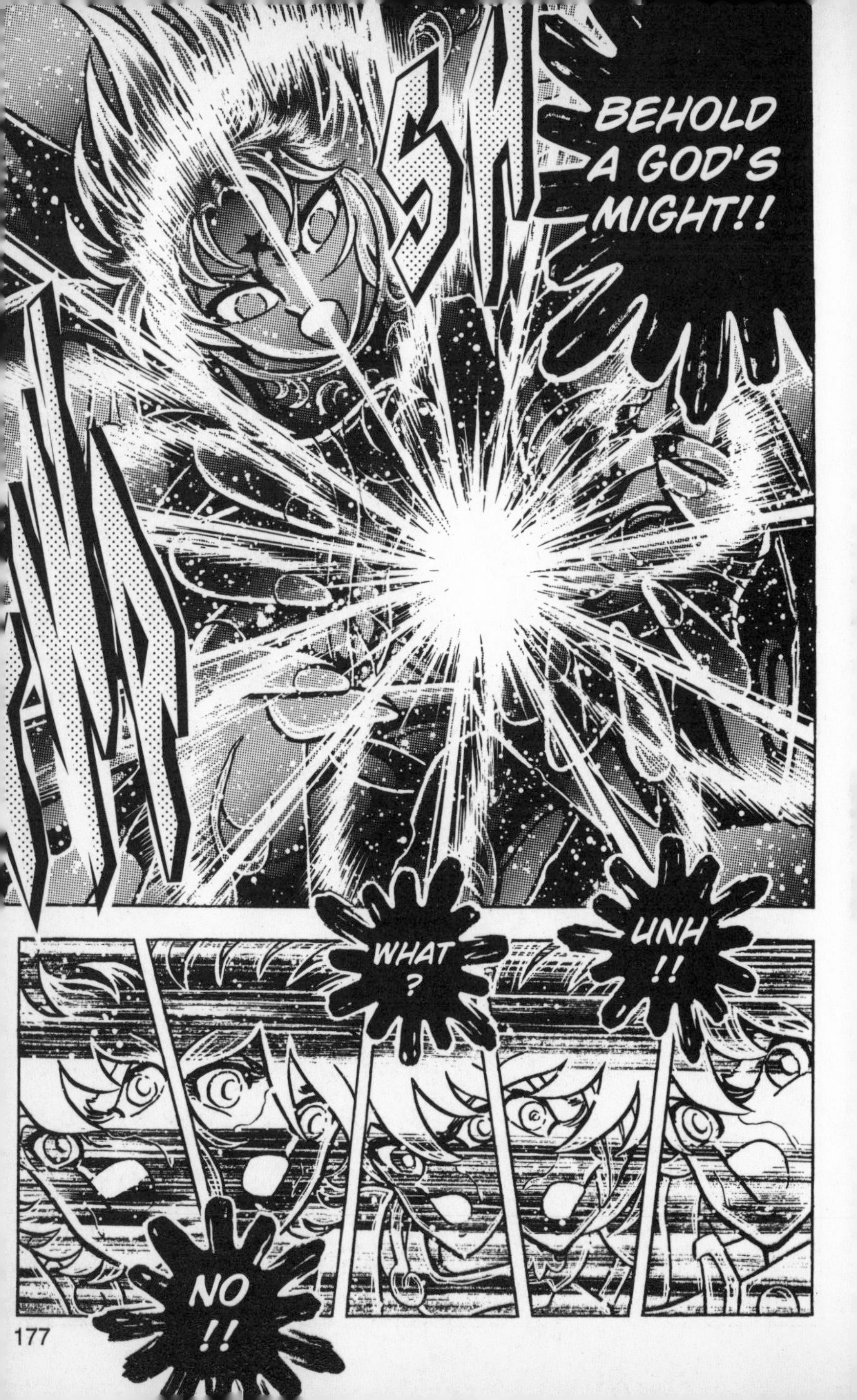
BEHOLD A GOD'S MIGHT!!
UNH!!
WHAT?
NO!!

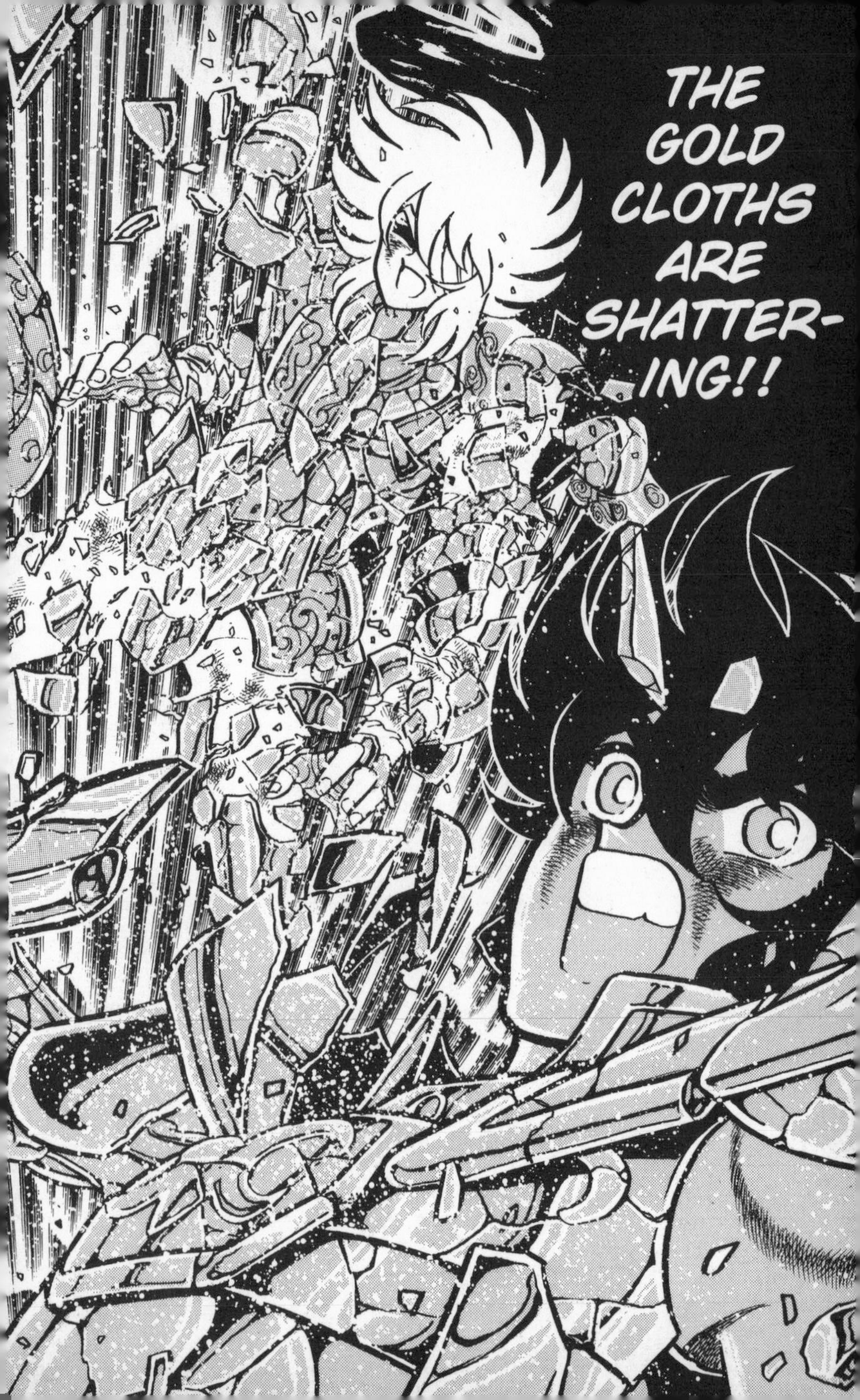
THE GOLD CLOTHS ARE SHATTER-ING!!

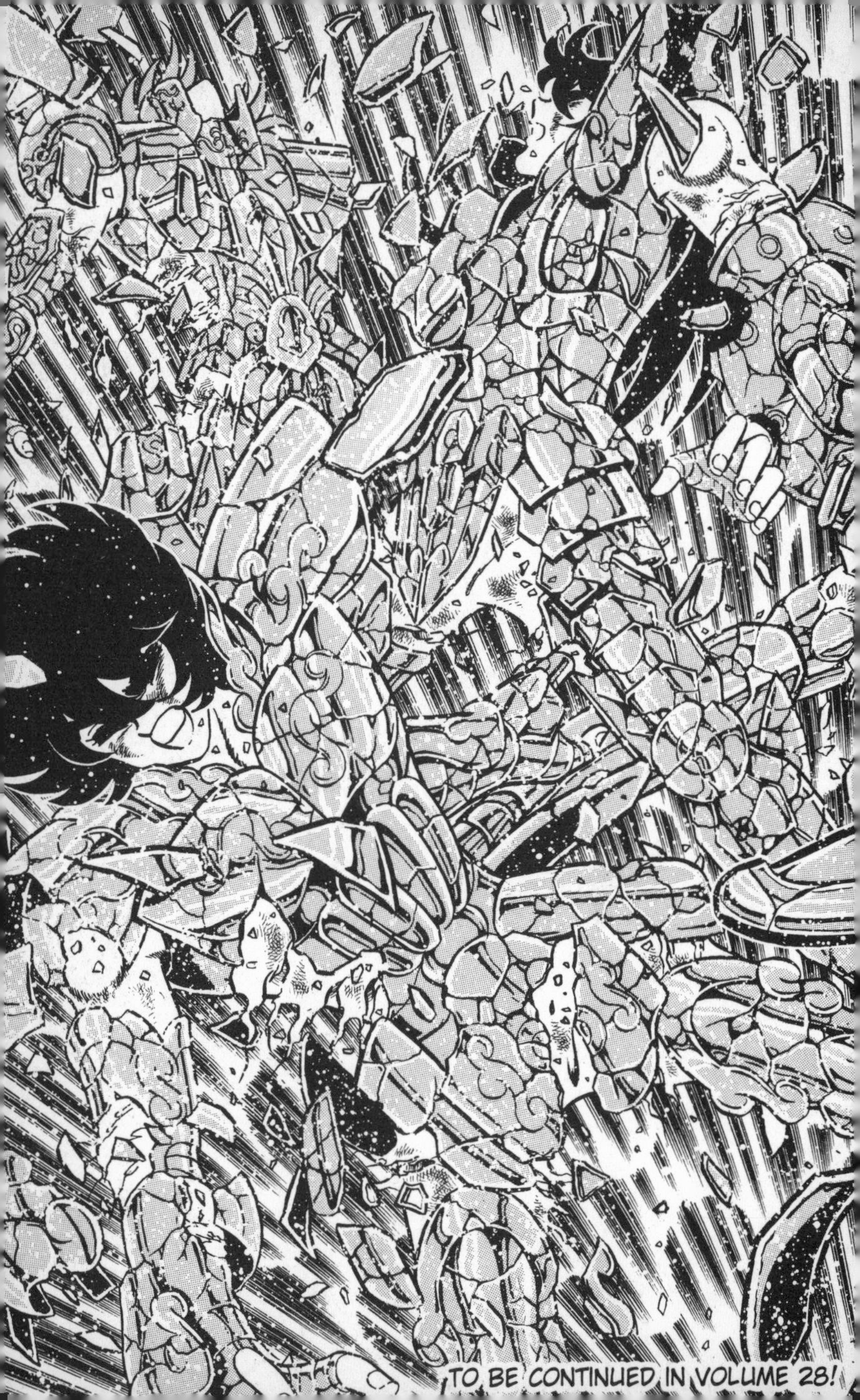
TO BE CONTINUED IN VOLUME 28!

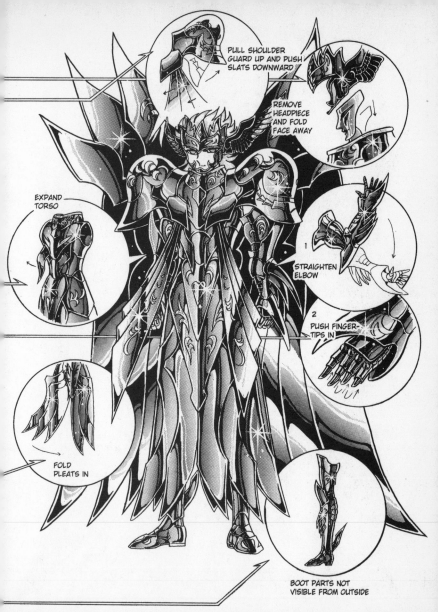

PULL SHOULDER
GUARD UP AND PUSH
SLATS DOWNWARD

REMOVE
HEADPIECE
AND FOLD
FACE AWAY

EXPAND
TORSO

1
STRAIGHTEN
ELBOW

2
PUSH FINGER-
TIPS IN

FOLD
PLEATS IN

BOOT PARTS NOT
VISIBLE FROM OUTSIDE

THE GOD WHO PRESIDES OVER DEATH
THANATOS SURPLICE

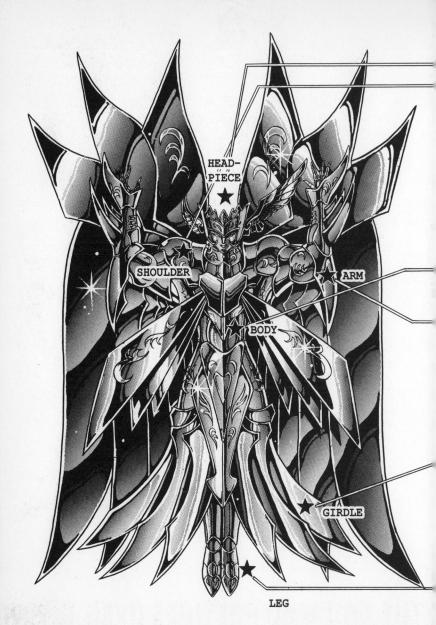

HEAD-
PIECE
★

SHOULDER ★

ARM ★

BODY ★

GIRDLE ★

LEG ★

SURPLICE BREAKDOWN AND FITTING CHART 21

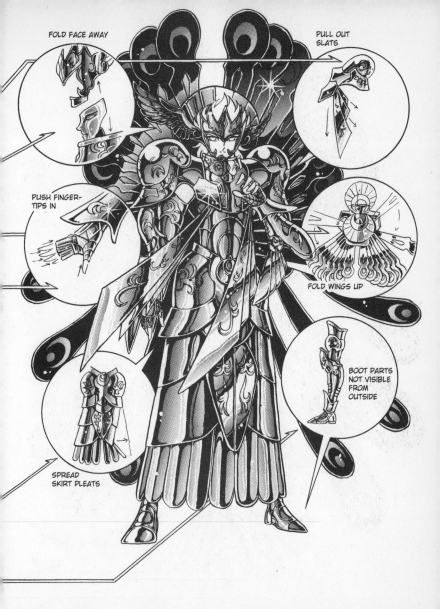

FOLD FACE AWAY

PULL OUT SLATS

PUSH FINGER-TIPS IN

FOLD WINGS UP

BOOT PARTS NOT VISIBLE FROM OUTSIDE

SPREAD SKIRT PLEATS

THE GOD WHO PRESIDES OVER SLEEP
HYPNOS SURPLICE

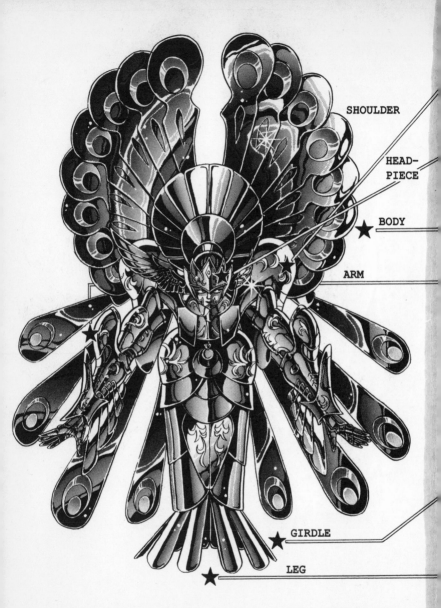

SHOULDER

HEAD-
PIECE

BODY

ARM

GIRDLE

LEG

SURPLICE BREAKDOWN AND FITTING CHART 22

COMING NEXT
VOLUME:

Their epic struggle at last
at an end, the Bronze